LAST-DAYS
SURVIVAL
GUIDE

A SCRIPTURAL HANDBOOK TO PREPARE YOU
FOR THESE PERILOUS TIMES

RICK RENNER

LAST-DAYS
SURVIVAL
GUIDE

A SCRIPTURAL HANDBOOK TO PREPARE YOU
FOR THESE PERILOUS TIMES

Last-Days Survival Guide: A Scriptural Handbook To Prepare You for These Perilous Times

ISBN: 978-1-6803-1410-6
eBook: 978-1-6803-1416-8

Copyright © 2020 by Rick Renner

8316 E. 73rd St.
Tulsa, OK 74133

Published by Harrison House
Shippensburg, PA 17257-2914
www.harrisonhouse.com

1 2 3 4 5 / 24 23 22 21 20

Editorial Consultants: Cynthia D. Hansen and Rebecca L. Gilbert
Text Design: Lisa Simpson, www.SimpsonProductions.net

ENDORSEMENTS

If a Christian were to read only one book other than the Bible during the remainder of his lifetime, this should be the one! Simply put — *Last-Days Survival Guide* by Rick Renner mirrors the Scriptures, giving timely instructions on how to stay on track during the last days. Using biblical principles, heavenly wisdom, and spiritual insight, Rick summons the Church to truth, discernment, and Kingdom living as he sounds the clarion call during perilous times.

Marcus D. Lamb
Founder and President
Daystar Television Network

What a marvelous opportunity it is for me to write an endorsement for Rick Renner's book *Last-Days Survival Guide*. His message in this timely book is definitely a "must" for every Christian, especially now. Each chapter will thrill you as you open your spiritual ears to hear what the Spirit is speaking to you and open your spiritual eyes to see what He wants you to see. There are choice morsels of revelation in each chapter that will absolutely thrill you as you see God's love being manifested to us, showing us the truth about the end times.

Be sure you take advantage of all the wonderful action steps that are written in this book to help you evaluate where you are spiritually at this time. Make the appropriate changes, and share this book with others who are in fear of the end times. Above all, enjoy the wonderful hope that is shared in this survival guide! Use it for an "over the top" Bible study, and know that God is on your side!

Marilyn Hickey
International Bible Teacher
Marilyn Hickey Ministries
Denver, Colorado

I don't know of a better teacher than Rick Renner to help you navigate the treacherous end-time storms based on the deep Greek meaning behind each word of the end-time prophecies in Scripture. I highly recommend Rick's book *Last-Days Survival Guide*.

Sid Roth, Host
It's Supernatural! Television Program

Rick Renner is a gift to the Body of Christ. His books have inspired many over the years — and he has done it again. His newest book is not just an important book that is "on time." Its contents are prophetically empowering to effect change in the heart of the believer — and in the Body of Christ — in order to rise to the challenges of this very late hour.

This book is a must-read to bring sober-minded perspective by the power of the Spirit concerning a last-days stormy sea. And it will equip you to powerfully navigate these end-time waters. You don't have to be storm-tossed, weak, or confused. You were born for this time.

Tag — you're it! Read *Last-Days Survival Guide*, and embrace the season!

Mike Bickle
International House of Prayer of Kansas City

We are living in challenging times — so challenging that many even in the Church are being ensnared by the deceptions of the day. Jesus made it clear that human behavior in the last days would become extremely volatile and sinful and that it would be commonplace for people to fall prey to the schemes of darkness. But falling into such evil doesn't happen suddenly and knowingly. It happens *slowly* and *unknowingly*. Last-days deception is about luring people into certain mindsets and ideals that are devoid of truth while they don't realize it's happening.

Author Rick Renner, one of the most prolific teachers and Bible scholars of our time, has done a masterful job with this writing. *Last-Days Survival Guide* is a must-read that will arm every believer with the necessary tools and strategies for the times in which we live. Let this book help you avoid becoming another "last-days statistic." Instead, become empowered to rise above as a last-days survivor!

Hank Kunneman
Pastor-Prophet, Conference Speaker, Author, Publisher, Broadcaster
Lord of Hosts Church and One Voice Ministries
Omaha, Nebraska

Rick Renner is one of my favorite programmers on GOD TV. He has an amazing anointing on his life to impart scriptural understanding and insight regarding what God is saying and doing in this hour. His teachings have touched hundreds of thousands of people around the world, including my own. His in-depth explanation of the Scriptures has been a daily resource for me personally.

Rick's book *Last-Days Survival Guide* is a common-sense, scriptural handbook to guide us through these prophetic end times in which we are living. This book is timely; it's urgent; and it's *now.*

Rick's message is loud and clear: Perilous times are here, and you don't have to be caught unaware or off-guard. We are the generation chosen for this hour, and it is our destiny to close out this age! And Rick doesn't just identify the problems; he also gives sound answers for thriving in these perilous last days. So stop everything you are doing, and read this *Last-Days Survival Guide* now! Your family's life could very well depend on it.

Ward Simpson
President and CEO of GOD TV

We have been in the last days since Jesus died and rose again, but as we approach the last of the last days, things here on earth will intensify in every way. Will we be ready? Will we be equipped?

In this very readable and practical book, rather than setting dates or preaching a theology of escapism, Rick Renner shows us how, through the Word, we can be fully equipped to remain victorious. In the Lord, we have everything we need to thrive in the midst of chaos and collapse. Read this survival guide, and learn how to be a last-days overcomer!

Dr. Michael L. Brown
Host of the *Line of Fire* Radio Broadcast
Author of *Jezebel's War With America*

DEDICATION

I dedicate this book to Dr. Roger Harmon, a precious man whose teachings gave me a love for studying the end times when I was a younger man. Dr. Harmon is now in Heaven with his wonderful wife Rose-Ann. Nonetheless, his influence continues to impact me as I study and teach the Bible. It was Dr. Harmon who helped me see that the Scriptures clearly forewarn us about events that will transpire as we approach the last days of the Church Age, and how they instruct us to prepare for them.

As I sat in Dr. Harmon's Bible study many years ago and listened, he opened the Scriptures to us about the last days as I had never heard it before. I was captivated by the way he showed us how up-to-date, timely, and relevant the Bible is at all times and how it speaks directly and precisely to us about the very times in which we are living.

So as an expression of my gratitude for this godly man's influence on my thinking about this last-days season we're living in, I wish to dedicate *Last-Days Survival Guide* to Dr. Roger Harmon.

CONTENTS

ACKNOWLEDGMENTS

I am thankful for the minds, eyes, and hands that have gone over this manuscript with me. James 3:1 says those who teach will be held to a higher standard pertaining to the spiritual fare they offer the Body of Christ and the extent to which they apply what they teach to their own lives. For this reason, I take the act of teaching and writing very seriously. In fact, I take it so seriously that everything I teach and write is submitted to scrutinizing eyes and minds that help assure me that I am consistently providing teaching that people can trust.

I wrote this material after many years of study on the subject; nonetheless, when it was time to put this teaching to paper, I deliberately passed on its contents for review to editors, co-workers, and fellow Bible teachers so that the eyes of others could help ensure its accuracy. I wish to especially thank Cindy Hansen for her editorial work on this book and my senior editor, Becky Gilbert, for her final editorial touch. I am profoundly thankful for each member's comments, contributions, and suggestions. This marvelous team has worked alongside me for many years, and I count you all a precious part of this serious process. A big thanks also to Maxim Myasnikov, my long-time Moscow assistant, who verified the accuracy of my Greek word studies in this book.

In addition, I want to express my gratitude to my wife Denise for hovering over every word with me, and to Paul Renner and Joel Renner for also carefully reading every word on each page before this book was approved to be printed.

Because of the nature of this book, I asked my attorney Dan Beirute to read large sections of it as well. I am grateful to Dan for his legal, professional insights, along with his common-sense approach to the Bible. I also want to express my gratitude to my publisher, Don Nori, along with Brad Herman and the excellent team at Harrison House Publishers. I am thankful for your partnership in the Gospel as we each do our part to present every man perfect in Christ Jesus both near and far (*see* Colossians 1:28). Together we are fulfilling the mandate to proclaim the truth and the power of the Gospel with excellence and to challenge Christians to live victoriously, grow spiritually, and know God intimately.

PREFACE

One may ask, "Rick, why did you write this particular book at this specific time?"

To be honest, even though this book is only now reaching your hands, I have been planning to write it for many years. It was percolating in my spirit for a long time, and I began the process of putting words to paper a few years ago. Then in the fall of 2019, I actively began to focus on developing this material. With recent events that have shaken the world, I can see *why* the Holy Spirit compelled me to do that in order to get this manuscript published as soon as possible. Because of these worldwide, life-altering events, nearly everyone has been awakened to the fact that we are truly living in perilous times.

More than ever before, we need a common-sense, scriptural handbook to guide us through the prophetic times in which we are living. Truthfully, the Bible is the ultimate Handbook we all need, but many people don't know how to read or understand the prophetic warnings in Scripture or know how to apply them practically to their lives.

So in this book, I have delved deeply into the Holy Spirit's last-days warnings that are written in Second Timothy 3. In that chapter, the Holy Spirit forecasts precisely what will happen in society at the very end of the age. Those prophecies were not written to *scare* us; they were written to *prepare* us so we would be protected from a plethora of ways that evil will assault society in these closing days of the Church Age. You and I are chosen by God to live in this hour, so these verses are especially important to us.

This book is jam-packed with insights and even statistics to demonstrate how accurate and timely the Holy Spirit's warnings are for us. It also provides numerous examples of scriptures from my still-developing *Renner's Interpretive Version* (*RIV*) of the New Testament.

I urge you to read each chapter to its conclusion, because every word in this book has been carefully crafted to help you see what the Holy Spirit is saying and know how to move forward with a faith-filled response. Furthermore, each chapter concludes with seven action steps designed to help you evaluate what you have read in light of your own walk with God and understand how to apply these truths to every area of your life in the days to come.

Perhaps you know already that I have written several other books related to events that will occur in the last days. Besides the *Seven Letters to the Seven Churches* series (*A Light in Darkness* and *No Room for Compromise*), two other books in this category are *Signs You'll See Just Before Jesus Comes* and *How To Keep Your Head on Straight in a World Gone Crazy.* I am amazed at the accuracy with which the Holy Spirit enabled me to write these books. If you haven't read them — especially *Just Before Jesus Comes* and *How To Keep Your Head on Straight* — I urge you to get them as quickly as possible because the insights contained in the pages of these books will greatly aid you in knowing how to interpret what is happening all around you today.

Last-Days Survival Guide specifically addresses the issues that you, your family, your friends, your church, and your society are confronted with every day, simply because you were born into this end-time generation. However, this book doesn't just identify the problems; it provides you with sound answers about how you should respond to the events all around you in order to live safeguarded from the ills that will dominate society in the last of the last days.

So now — it's time for you to get started reading *Last-Days Survival Guide*. I advise you to get a pen or pencil so you can underline and write notes in the margins of this book and at the end of each chapter. I believe you will find this book to be filled with revelation and practical insights to help you know how to successfully navigate the challenging *and exciting* days to come!

— *Rick Renner*
Moscow, Russia
March 2020

FOREWORD

This carefully crafted, researched, and easy-to-understand book is destined to become an essential resource for all believers of various denominations and non-denominational backgrounds. It is *not* just another book on "the last days."

First, Rick Renner is a scholar when it comes to the Koine Greek language, the original language of the New Testament. Rick is a master at taking the words of an entire paragraph and breaking them down into their original meaning inside their contextual, historical settings. This allows for the reader to learn the original intent of a verse and sheds an amazing light that is often not found, for example, in reading the Word in English with a Western mindset. This book is a treasure chest of word studies that will awaken the spirit of any believer hungry for the truth.

Second, Rick understands the historical setting of these passages and how they were understood by the early Christians. He is writing concerning the last days, the times in which we live, which makes this a "right now" message.

Third — and this is important — throughout various chapters, Rick skillfully gives you methods and instructions on how to apply what you are learning in a practical way. He lists the most important things you must do to make it through the perilous times ahead. Discover how to protect yourself and your family as you are guided through the times by having faith in the Word of God.

It is with great joy and excitement that I recommend this book to you, *Last-Days Survival Guide.*

Perry Stone Jr.
Founder of VOE, OCI, and ISOW

❧

This know also, that in the last days
perilous times shall come.

— 2 Timothy 3:1

❧

You emphatically and categorically need to know
with unquestionable certainty that in the very end of days —
when time has sailed to its last port and
no more time remains for the journey —
that last season will stand in the midst
of uncontrollable, unpredictable,
hurtful, treacherous, and menacing times
that will be emotionally difficult for people to bear.

— 2 Timothy 3:1 (*RIV*)

1

'TAG – WE'RE IT!'

When I was a boy growing up, my friends in the neighborhood would occasionally congregate in our large backyard to play tag. If you grew up playing that game, I'm sure you remember how it is played.

The game of tag begins when someone in the group starts to chase others in an effort to touch or tag them. I remember the glee each of us felt when we were "it," and we finally touched another player and yelled, *"Tag, you're it!"* In that moment, the person tagged became "it" for the next round of the game.

My friends and I would play tag for *hours*. We didn't quit until every kid had been tagged — and when that happened, it was our signal that the game was done!

As a boy, I really liked to play tag for several reasons. It was a group game; it was fast; and it required us to strategize about how we would dodge and outrun the person designated "it" to avoid getting tagged. A rambunctious game of tag caused my heart to pump with excitement as I dashed here and there to stay out of reach.

I also liked the game of tag because if anyone had to sit out for a round, he or she could then jump back in the game to begin playing again. What I *didn't* like so much were the times *I* was the one who got tagged. However, in the game of tag, everyone eventually got tagged before the game was over. Whether we liked it or not, at some point each of us was going to be "it" for a round of the game.

The reason I tell you about this simple childhood game is that it reminds me of the significance of this strategic time we are living in right now. For the last 2,000 years, the Church has been living in the midst of a time frame that is technically called "the last days."

However, now we have come to the very last of the last days — a time frame unlike any other that has preceded us in history. And God has chosen you and me to be part of the generation born at the very end of this age. You and I are "tagged" to live in this last round of the prophetic game. In a very real sense, God is saying to us, *"Tag, you're it!"*

Others in Church history were "tagged" by God to be "it" in their generation, for their own time. I could make a long list of such men and women who helped change the course of history to His glory during their time on earth. But now it is time for us to play *our* part as we serve Jesus in the wrap-up of this prophetic season. For you and me to come out winners as God has destined us to do, we'll need to learn how to move quickly and hear accurately as the Holy Spirit gives us strategies to dodge the enemy's attacks and combat the evil influences that are trying to affect so many in society right now.

The fact remains that we are living in the last round of this end-times age. That means we must know what God has specifically stated about events in society in the last days — and we must receive divine guidance to maneuver accurately in the midst of the attacks the enemy is waging against every stratum of society.

◆

**We are living in the last round of this end-times age.
That means we must know what God has specifically stated about events
in society in the last days — and we must receive divine guidance
to maneuver accurately in the midst of the attacks the enemy
is waging against every stratum of society.**

◆

One evening of watching the news is all that's needed to confirm to yourself that an all-out assault is being waged against the human race and against godliness. Society today is filled with violence, decadence, financial crises, political feuding beyond anything we ever imagined possible, and heightened tensions among the world's political leaders. Natural disasters occur with increasing regularity all over the earth.

These combined and cumulative events seem so overwhelming that it can feel like our very well-being is under continual threat. If it were not for the peace of God that rules our hearts and minds, we could easily be thrown into a state of panic, shaken by all of these disturbing developments. (*See* my book *Signs You'll See Just Before Jesus Comes* to learn of all the events Jesus predicted in Matthew 24 that we will see in the world prior to His next coming.)

Many of us remember growing up in a very different world, where life was slower and kinder — and so safe that we didn't even lock the doors to our houses. We didn't fear our neighbors, and we never had a single thought about terrorist activity. Does that description resemble the childhood you remember decades ago?

But the world has changed dramatically in the course of our lifetimes and has become a far different place than the one we grew up in years ago. What happened to the world we once knew? How is it possible that so many things could change so fast and so dramatically? Who of us in our growing-up years would have ever imagined that we'd see the day when so much nonsensical thinking would dominate society?

◆

What happened to the world we once knew?
How is it possible that so many things could change
so fast and so dramatically?

◆

My parents, along with our local church, reared me to believe the Bible, so we knew that we were most likely living in the last days. But now years have flown by, and the reality of these last days has hit with explosive force! It's no longer imaginary; it is *upon* us. *Whew!* We didn't know that life could change with such speed!

But change it did, and the slower, kinder, safer world we grew up in is nearly gone. With every new day, it seems like society is being inundated with new, once-unthinkable absurdities that have left many people bewildered and perplexed.

Whether we like it or not, times have changed — *very rapidly*. During our childhoods, it would have been hard to envision that things could change so much in relatively so little time.

But God knew these times were approaching, and approximately 2,000 years ago, His Spirit spoke very clearly to alert us — we who live in the last days — that such times would come. He wanted *this* generation to know that "perilous times" would emerge in society at the very end of the last days.

WHERE WE ARE IN TIME — GOD REALLY WANTS US TO KNOW

In this chapter, it is my intention to focus on Second Timothy 3:1. I want to dissect and examine it piece by piece to help you grasp exactly what the Holy Spirit is communicating to us in this powerful scripture.

As the apostle Paul wrote his second letter to Timothy, he said this in the opening verse of chapter 3: "This know also, that in the last days perilous times shall come." But let's begin by looking closely at the first part of the verse, where the Holy Spirit says, *"This know also…."*

The word "know" is a translation of the Greek word *ginosko*, which in this verse means *to know something definitely, emphatically, and with absolute certainty*. But it is also important to know that the tense used here depicts *something so urgent that it MUST be known, MUST be recognized, and MUST be acknowledged*.

In other words, what the Holy Spirit is saying in this verse — and in the passage that follows — should not be considered optional information for us to retain or not to retain at our discretion. The Greek tense makes the message of this verse *strong*. It is almost as if the Holy Spirit is raising His voice to get our attention. He is reaching out from the pages of Scripture to grab us, shake us, and cause us to sit up straight, hold our heads high, and open our eyes and ears so we truly grasp what He is about to communicate.

In this verse, the Holy Spirit speaks *loudly*, *authoritatively*, and *emphatically* because He wants us to fully grasp what He is about to say. His urgent desire is that we will be prepared and not taken off-guard when last-days events begin to take place with increasing, rapid-fire frequency.

What was coming in the future — in the very time in which you and I are currently living — was so ominous that the Holy Spirit *really* wanted to warn us in advance that perilous times were coming. His purpose was not to *scare* us, but to *prepare* us so we would be informed and spiritually equipped to navigate a last-days tempestuous storm. If we'll listen to what the Holy Spirit says in this verse and in the verses to follow, we'll be able to prepare ourselves — as well as our loved ones and friends — to sail victoriously through these stormy waters. And we'll not be overcome by the evil that Scripture says would inevitably emerge and become widespread in society as the age approaches its end.

Friend, God has "tagged" you and me to live in this time! And since He has chosen us for this late round of the game, we can be assured that He has also supplied us with everything we need to live in this season victoriously. If we'll pay attention to what the Holy Spirit has said in Second Timothy 3 and receive divine strategies from Him, we'll be able to:

- Shine as lights in a world growing ever darker.

- Build a hedge of protection around our families.

- Teach our children and grandchildren the Word of God so that while they live *in* this world, they will not be *of* this world or be negatively impacted by it.

- Stay unaffected by the changing moral landscape in society around us.

- Be protected and safeguarded by Scripture that has been stored in our hearts.

**God has "tagged" you and me to live in this time!
And since He has chosen us for this late round of the game,
we can be assured that He has also supplied us with everything
we need to live in this season victoriously.**

In Second Timothy 3:1, the Holy Spirit pointed His prophetic finger 2,000 years into the future to prophesy that perilous times would come in the last days. In this pivotal verse and the passage that follows, the Holy Spirit lucidly forecasted that certain characteristics would emerge in society at the very end of the age. In no uncertain terms, the Holy Spirit said that perilous times *would* come and that these disastrous developments would become prominent and commonplace in a world gone crazy.

The Holy Spirit was warning those of us destined to live at the end of the age about these things so that we'd be prepared to not be taken off-guard. But I want to stress again that the Holy Spirit didn't give us this prophetic insight to *scare* us; rather, He gave it to *prepare* us so we could avoid these detrimental end-time manifestations and live as victorious believers until Jesus comes again! Because the Holy Spirit has forewarned us of what is to come, we will know what to do to reinforce our lives so we can live victoriously as we await the glorious moment when Christ returns for His Church.

**The Holy Spirit didn't give us this prophetic insight
to *scare* us; rather, He gave it to *prepare* us
so we could avoid these detrimental end-time manifestations
and live as victorious believers until Jesus comes again!**

WHAT DOES THE WORD 'LAST' REALLY MEAN?

Under the inspiration of the Holy Spirit, the apostle Paul prophetically wrote, "This *know...*" (2 Timothy 3:1). As noted earlier, the word "know" in this verse describes *something that is definite, emphatic, and absolutely certain.*

But Paul went on to add, "This know *also*...." It's easy to read over that word "also" and go on without paying any attention to it. But in the Greek text, the word for "also" is very important. It is the little Greek word *de,* which means *indeed.* The use of this word adds the sense of *something that is emphatic* and makes this verse a *categorical* statement. By adding this little Greek word, the Holy Spirit is literally saying to you and me, "*You emphatically and categorically need to know with unquestionable certainty....*"

This unequivocally tells us that what the Holy Spirit is about to forecast is not something that may or may not come to pass. This verse clearly forecasts events that will *definitely* occur in the very end of the last days. God's intention in giving this scripture was not only to speak to readers living in the First Century when this verse was written, but also to especially inform *us* — those who would be alive at the very end of the age when these events would take place.

In Second Timothy 3:1, Paul wrote, "This know also, that in the last days perilous times shall come." Because Paul used the word "know," which is a translation of the Greek word *ginosko,* and the word "also," which is a translation of the little word *de,* he emphatically meant to convey the Holy Spirit's message here in the clearest and strongest of terms. It literally means, "*You emphatically and categorically need to know with unquestionable certainty....*"

But then the Holy Spirit dives deeper into His message and becomes more specific by adding that "...in the *last days* perilous times shall come" (2 Timothy 3:1).

What do the words "last days" really mean? The Greek word for "last" used in this verse is translated from the Greek word *eschatos,* a word that commonly depicts something that is *final.* It is the Greek word from which we derive the word "eschatology," the theological study of *end times* or the study of *last things.* This Greek word *eschatos* points to the *very last* or the *ultimate end* of a thing. It was used by ancient Greeks to describe the point that was *furthest away*.

In fact, the ancient world used the word *eschatos* as a seafaring word to describe *the last port of call for a ship*. Although a ship in transit stops at many ports en route to its final destination, the word *eschatos* was used to depict the very last port. This last stopping-off point signified that it was the end of the road and the journey was finished. Thus, the word *eschatos* indicated, *"This is the end, and you can go no further."*

Let me give you a few examples of *eschatos* to demonstrate the *finality* associated with this word. This word *eschatos* could be used to describe *the very last month* of a 12-month calendar. It could also refer to *the very last week* in a month or *the very final day* in a week. In other words, this Greek word *eschatos* points to *the very ultimate end* of whatever is being discussed.

In the discussion of the last days before the return of Jesus Christ, the word *eschatos* points to the very ultimate end of the last days. For this reason, Paul used it in this verse to point to the *very last* of a long last-days season. We could call it *the last of the last days*.

To be technically correct, I must point out that "the last days" started about 2,000 years ago on the Day of Pentecost when the Holy Spirit was poured out. In Acts 2:17, Peter responded to the outpouring of the Spirit by quoting Joel 2:28 in which the prophet Joel prophesied about the supernatural happenings in the last days. Peter said, "And it shall come to pass in the last days, saith God, I will pour out of my Spirit upon all flesh…" (Acts 2:17).

So when the Holy Spirit was poured out on the Day of Pentecost, it triggered a prophetic time frame called "the last days" that we've been living in for nearly 2,000 years. But in Second Timothy 3:1, the word *eschatos* points to the *very end* of that prophetic season — to the days you and I are living in right now at the *very ultimate end* of the age.

THE 'LAST PORT' IN THE JOURNEY

Make no mistake — the Greek word *eschatos* ("last days") in this verse means the *very ultimate* end or the *very end* of time, and it points to the *conclusion* of the age. The Holy Spirit is literally saying, "*...In the very end of days — when time has sailed to its last port and no more time remains for the journey...."*

This gives us a specific point of reference for the time frame we are about to study in this chapter from Second Timothy 3, which is solely concerned with events that will occur at the *very ultimate end* of this age. The events Paul described in this Bible chapter will hastily transpire in the very concluding days of the age. To this end-time generation, it will feel as if time has suddenly accelerated and end-time developments are quickly coming to pass at a speed that is *shocking* to the natural mind.

Does that sound like our times? If you say yes, I remind you that the Holy Spirit is saying, *"Tag, you're it!"* for this exciting wrap-up of the ages!

To this end-time generation, it will feel as if time has suddenly accelerated and end-time developments are quickly coming to pass at a speed that is shocking to the natural mind.

Second Timothy 3:1 could therefore be correctly translated, *"You emphatically and categorically need to know with unquestionable certainty that in the very end of days — when time has sailed to its last port and no more time remains for the journey...."*

Then the Holy Spirit begins to expound on what will happen in that concluding time frame called the last of the last days. He vigorously states that "perilous times shall come" to be experienced by people who live in that prophetic season. But before we look at the words "perilous times," we must first study the words "shall come," for they are very important in this text.

The words "shall come" are a translation of the Greek word *enistemi*, which is a compound of the words *en* and *histemi*. The word *en* means *in*, and the word *histemi* means *to stand*. But when these are compounded into a single word, the new word means *to stand in, to stand in the middle of, to be surrounded by, to be encumbered by*, or *to stand in the midst of* whatever is being discussed with the feeling that *it cannot be avoided* or that *one cannot escape from it*. It depicts someone who is so encompassed by whatever surrounds him or her that there is no way out of it.

By using this key word *enistemi*, the Holy Spirit prophetically declares that those who live in this last season will feel as if they are positioned in the very midst of — surrounded and encumbered on every side by — inescapable developments. To the people who are part of this end-time generation, it will feel like they are being assaulted by "perilous times" from every direction. In other words, there will be no escaping this period of time.

But remember — God "tagged" you and me to live in this strategic season at the close of the age! That means we can rest assured that His Spirit will enable us to dodge each of the enemy's attacks. He will also empower us to help others find freedom and liberty from the darkness that is presently encroaching on society across the entire planet.

As Paul wrote the words of Second Timothy 3:1, it is as though he supernaturally peered through a prophetic window that allowed him to see 2,000 years into the future — *to the very time in which we are living and the times directly before us*. By the inspiration of the Holy Spirit, Paul revealed what he had seen as he painstakingly and vividly wrote about the sweeping changes that would emerge and become commonplace in society and culture at the very end of this age.

It is as though he supernaturally peered through a prophetic window that allowed him to see 2,000 years into the future — *to the very time in which we are living and the times directly before us.*

Second Timothy 3:1 is *crucial* to what you are about to read in the rest of this book, so I want to make sure you truly grasp what the Holy Spirit has communicated in this verse. By alerting us to what will occur in the last of the last days, God is lovingly preparing us for what is coming. He desires that we would not be taken captive by a spirit of fear. He wants each of us to retain a sound mind that can wisely discern how to deal with the issues that will confront us.

But we must not hide from the world. Instead, we need to build a spiritual wall of protection around us so we can live in this world *victoriously* and not be brought down by it. Christ has called us to rise up as mighty, Spirit-filled victors! We are called to shine His light in the darkness, to rescue the perishing, and to do all we can to save those who are spiritually dying.

And regardless of the moral dilemmas that confront us in these times, you and I must *never* forget that we are called to be "more than conquerors" through the power of Him who loves us (*see* Romans 8:37). With the strengthening help of the Holy Spirit, we can overcome all things through Christ who empowers us — even the most intense battles in this prophetic season (*see* Philippians 4:13).

KEEP YOUR HEAD ON STRAIGHT
ABOUT THE LAST DAYS

It is vital that each of us and our family members know how to build a wall of protection around us as we approach the conclusion of this age. With that in mind, I want to give you seven simple steps to help protect you and your loved ones from what will become rampant in society and culture at the conclusion of the last days.

This first verse in Second Timothy 3 plainly lets us know that what the Holy Spirit is about to describe are events that will *definitely* come to pass with *absolute certainty*. The apostle Paul by the Spirit of God warned us of it in advance so that we would be prepared to withstand the onslaught of evil that will diffuse itself throughout society and culture in the very last of a last-days generation. Again, I remind you that the Greek tense used indicates that what the Holy Spirit was about to say through Paul is so urgent for those of us living in the last times that He considered it something that simply had to be *known*, *recognized*, and *acknowledged*.

As you will see, the apostle Paul forecasted severe, abrupt societal and cultural changes that will develop in the very end of the last period of the age. You will recognize that all of these changes are in evidence even now —- at this very moment — because we are already living in the final stages of the last of the last days. This means we are approaching the last port, the last stopping-off point, the end of the journey — and very little time remains.

The Holy Spirit wants *you* to know this information so you will be prepared and not taken off-guard as these events become commonplace. If you are informed and fortified by the truth of God's Word, you won't be shocked or shaken when these events begin to occur in a greater measure. Furthermore, the Holy Spirit does not want you — or *any* of God's children — to fall into the destructive behaviors and symptoms that will be associated with a morally sickened last-days generation.

———◆———

**You will recognize that all of these changes
are in evidence even now. This means we are approaching the last port,
the last stopping-off point, the end of the journey —
and very little time remains.**

———◆———

Because we are the ones living in this end-time generation to which the Holy Spirit is referring, it should be obvious to us that many of the things the apostle Paul wrote about are already happening. But Paul didn't write about these end-time events only in Second Timothy; he also referred to them in Second Thessalonians 2:1,2.

Before we continue in Second Timothy 3 to see what Paul specifically prophesied regarding the last days, I believe we must first undergird ourselves with the truth he wrote to the Thessalonian believers about this subject. These passages of Scripture are vital in helping us keep our heads on straight as we walk through the tumultuous developments that God says *will* occur as mankind approaches "the last port" of this journey called the Church Age.

Apparently, some believers in Thessalonica were disturbed by what they had learned of the events surrounding the coming of Jesus. It seems those believers were so panicked that the apostle Paul felt the need to write them to calm them down and curb their fears.

In Second Thessalonians 2:1 and 2, Paul wrote, "Now we beseech you, brethren, by the coming of our Lord Jesus Christ, and by our gathering together unto him, that ye be not soon shaken in mind, or be troubled, neither by spirit, nor by word, nor by letter as from us, as that the day of Christ is at hand."

Let's dig into these two verses to see what we can learn from them.

In verse 1, Paul began, "Now we beseech you...." This is very important, for the word "beseech" is a translation of the Greek word *erotao*, which conveys *the act of using one's position to make a strong request and to expect the listener to respond*. The word is used in other literature to depict *the act of making an earnest appeal* or *the act of sincerely and passionately entreating someone to do what is being requested*. This lets us know Paul was appealing to the Thessalonian believers from his heart, asking them to do exactly what he was requesting of them.

When Paul wrote about "the coming of our Lord Jesus Christ," the word "coming" comes from the Greek word *parousia*, which was sometimes used to denote the celebrated arrival of a royal sovereign. The phrase "our gathering together" comes from the Greek word *episunagoge*. This word is used in this context to point to that moment in the prophetic future when God will quickly *gather* or *collect* His people together to receive them to Himself at the conclusion of this present age.

Then in Second Thessalonians 2:2, Paul added, "That ye be not soon shaken in mind, or be troubled, neither by spirit, nor by word, nor by letter as from us, as that the day of Christ is at hand." It is clear from this verse that Christians in Thessalonica were shaken and troubled by the future events surrounding the very last of the last days. So Paul wrote to these believers to calm them down and assure them that being panicked is not the right response for any Christian who hears that the end of the age is close at hand.

Paul told them, "That ye be not soon shaken in mind, or be troubled...." The word "shaken" is the Greek word *saleuo*, and it means *to shake*, *to waver*, *to totter*, or *to be moved*. The tense points to events that cause *shock* or *alarm*.

The word "troubled" is from the Greek word *throeo*, and it indicates an *inward fright* that resulted from whatever news the Thessalonian believers heard that shocked them. The word *throeo* depicts something that causes one to be filled with *worry, anxiety,* or *fear*. However, this tense points to an *ongoing state of worry and inward anxiety* resulting from something that was disturbing these believers and disrupting their state of peace. It is as if there was no reprieve from these shocking, debilitating, and nerve-racking things they were hearing. The word *throeo* actually portrays a state of *jumpiness* or *nervousness,* as if they were living on the edge of their nerves.

Paul told these believers not to be shaken in "mind" — a word that comes from the Greek word *nous,* which describes *one's mind or intellect, will, and emotions* or *the ability to think, reason, and decide.* It is a fact that whoever or whatever controls a person's mind ultimately has the power to dictate the affairs and outcome of that person's life. Therefore, Paul was urging the Thessalonian congregation to be careful to whom they listened or what they opened their minds to when it came to last-days teachings. That same warning has applied to all Christians throughout the Church Age — especially to those of us who live in this end-time generation.

Whoever or whatever controls a person's mind ultimately has the power to dictate the affairs and outcome of that person's life.

Then in Second Thessalonians 2:2, Paul added, "That ye be not soon shaken in mind, or be troubled, neither *by spirit....*" This word "spirit" is a translation of the Greek word *pneuma,* which in this verse refers to *a spiritual experience* or *spiritual utterance* that is out of sync with the revealed Word of God. Some have even translated the word to mean *ecstatic utterances.* Paul was here referring to *strange utterances*, *weird revelations*, or *euphoric proclamations* that have no root in sound doctrine and eventually produce the negative effect of spiritually upsetting believers.

Paul continued writing, "That ye be not soon shaken in mind, or be troubled, neither by spirit, nor by word, nor by *letter* as from us...." The word "letter" is the Greek word *epistole*, which is where we get the word "epistle."

It seems Paul was aware that people with fraudulent motives were attempting to write their own epistles in the style of those Paul had written to the churches. He was aware that some of these imposters were even claiming that their epistles were written by Paul himself. Others admitted writing the letters but then falsely alleged that Paul had endorsed their epistles as written in his behalf. But whatever it was that these believers were reading or listening to, the counterfeit message was stirring up fear and alarm in their hearts.

Paul began Second Thessalonians 2:3 by saying, "Let no man *deceive* you by any means...." The word "deceive" is the Greek word *exapatao*, which means *to beguile*, *to cheat*, *to trick*, or *to mislead one to a false impression or a false conclusion*. Paul was literally telling the Thessalonian believers to use their minds and not believe everything they heard — to keep their heads on straight when it came to what and to whom they listened concerning the last days!

**In light of all we've just studied, the following is
Renner's Interpretive Version (*RIV*)
of Second Thessalonians 2:1-3:**

1. Brothers, listen carefully, for I am asking you in the strongest of terms to hear what I am about to say and to do exactly what I'm asking you to do. The appearance of the Lord Jesus Christ is very near. The moment we have all longed and waited for is almost

upon us! I'm talking about that moment when Jesus will finally gather us together for Himself.

2. Some things will be happening right before His coming that could shake you up quite a bit. I'm referring to events that will be so dramatic that they could really leave your head spinning — occurrences of such a serious nature that many people will feel alarmed, panicked, intimidated, and even unnerved! Naturally speaking, these events could nearly put you over the brink emotionally and make you feel apprehensive and insecure about life. I wish I could tell you these incidents were going to be just a one-shot deal, but when they finally get rolling, they're going to keep coming and coming, one after another.

That's why you have to determine not to be shaken or moved by anything you see or hear. You need to get a grip on your mind and refuse to allow yourselves to be traumatized by these events. If you let these things get to you, it won't be too long until you're a nervous wreck! You have to decide beforehand that you are not going to give in and allow fright to penetrate your mind and emotions until it runs your whole life.

I also want to tell you not to be too surprised if people start making weird spiritual proclamations and off-the-wall utterances during the time just before the Lord comes. All kinds of strange things are going to happen during those days! It's going to get so bizarre that you might even receive a letter from some person who claims that the day of the Lord has already come! Who knows — he might even attach my name to it, alleging to have my endorsement, or he might even send it as if it were written and sent from us!

3. In light of these things, I urge you to refuse to allow anyone to take advantage of you....

What we are about to study in the rest of this book are prophetic utterances concerning developments that will emerge at the end of the age. The purpose of this book is not to make you feel alarmed, panicked, intimidated, or unnerved. I am *not* on a mission to put your nerves on edge or to make you feel apprehensive and insecure about life!

However, we need to keep our heads on straight about the state of this world in this day we're living in. We must not bury our heads in the sand and ignore what the Holy Spirit clearly wants us to understand.

The radical changes in society that we are experiencing are just the tip of the iceberg — just the beginning of a worldwide mutiny that Paul prophesied about so long ago. According to the prophetic teaching of Scripture, societal and cultural changes will worsen as time passes.

The last-days spirit of iniquity is at work — and a steadily growing mutiny against God and His Word is rapidly spreading across the planet. A dark spiritual force is in full swing against the holiness of God and the voice of Scripture.

---◆---

**We must not bury our heads in the sand
and ignore what the Holy Spirit
clearly wants us to understand.**

---◆---

Can you see how the "mystery of iniquity" is spreading and infiltrating the world with greater and greater moral decay? Does this accurately describe what is happening in the culture of your time?

LIVING IN THIS PHASE OF HISTORY

People who are spiritually sensitive know that we have entered a final phase in this prophetic season. They understand the times in which they live and may feel disturbed by the destructive changes in behaviors and lifestyles they see happening in society, even among many who profess to be Christians.

But God spoke through the apostle Paul long ago to enlighten the eyes of those who profess Christ and to help His people understand what the world environment would be like in the concluding moments of the age. This knowledge is intended to help believers recognize the time in which they live and live soberly, with eternity in view. God wanted His people to be alert and awakened to this reality — *especially* the generations actually living in that time!

The time is short. That has often been said over the course of time, but it has never been more true than in this present hour. For this reason, we must use the time that remains wisely and shine the light of the Gospel into the hearts of those whom Satan has blinded (*see* 2 Corinthians 4:4).

◆

**The time is short.
That has often been said over the course of time,
but it has never been more true
than in this present hour.**

◆

Do you have friends or family who are unsaved and blinded to the Gospel or who have wandered from the truth? Now more than ever before, it's time to fervently pray for God to open their spiritual eyes so they can see the truth for themselves and be transformed by the power of Jesus Christ.

The floodgates of evil are swinging open wide as society races toward a cataclysmic collision with crises of a magnitude never before seen. Societal attitudes and moral standards have shifted and plummeted to depths that are almost unimaginable. As I wrote in *Signs You'll See Just Before Jesus Comes*, Scripture clearly teaches that natural catastrophes of unusual proportions will be witnessed in the last of the last days. Of equal concern will be the changing spiritual climate in which accommodation of the world system will become the norm — and the world will become increasingly hostile toward and intolerant of those who stand for moral absolutes.

The Bible prophesied that the last of the last days would be characterized as "perilous times." Few would doubt that this describes the age in which we live. *But remember, you and I are ordained by God to live in this time.*

We may not want to hear that the end is quickly drawing near, but the truth is, *someone's* generation has to be the last days.

"TAG — we're it!"

**We may not want to hear that the end
is quickly drawing near,
but the truth is, *someone's* generation
has to be the last days.**

CHAPTER 1

LAST-DAYS SURVIVAL GUIDE ACTION STEPS

TO BUILD A WALL OF PROTECTION AROUND YOUR LIFE

In the following paragraphs, I want to suggest action steps you can take to help build a wall of protection around your life so you are *protected* in this last-days environment. If these action steps are not already established habits in your walk with God, you should begin to implement them immediately to help you stay spiritually garrisoned even in the most troublesome of times.

These action steps are simple, but when acted on consistently, they will produce great power and spare us from all types of troubles that otherwise would invade our lives. Especially in these last days when evil abounds, it is essential that we make these simple elements a rock-solid wall of protection around our lives.

Of course, there are many more beneficial steps you should take to protect your heart and soul. However, these easy steps are a very good starting place to reinforce the spiritual wall of protection you must establish about your life and the lives of your family members in these last of the last days.

1. Pray every morning.

Start your day every morning with prayer as part of a plan to build a wall of protection around your life. In Psalm 5:3, David wrote of his commitment to spend time with God every morning. He said, "My voice shalt thou hear in the morning, O Lord; in the morning will I direct my prayer unto thee, and will look up."

Notice that the last part of that verse says, "...and will look up." David was surrounded with enemies both inside and outside his home, and he was tempted to struggle emotionally. He knew he needed to start every morning by "looking up," or things would escalate that could take him down.

Likewise, you need to start every day with the Lord "looking up" — or life will quickly take *you* down. If you ignore this spiritual principle, you'll end up troubled, nervous, and worried — and you will lack spiritual power in your life. On the other hand, if you do this, you'll remain in a state of abiding peace, able to walk through each day in confidence. You'll know you've done what is right, and you'll experience power to overcome the daily problems you face in life.

You can actually learn to live in a *continual* state of fellowshipping with the Lord in prayer. Ephesians 6:18 says, "Praying *always*...." You may say, "Is that really possible?" Yes, it is, but you must learn to do it. Becoming intentional about beginning each day with prayer confirms that you are serious about your commitment to God. It opens your heart to receive from Him, and it sets the tone for your day as you expect God's guiding presence and His goodness to manifest in your life.

As you set your heart to begin each day in prayer — and to stay in a prayerful frame of mind the entire day — you'll find yourself becoming more spiritually attuned to the things around you. A prayerful mindset will heighten and *sustain* your spiritual sensitivity — which is exactly what you need in these last days.

2. Read the Bible every day.

Make a commitment to read the Bible every day as part of a plan to build a wall of protection around your life. In Psalm 119:105, the psalmist wrote: "Thy word is a lamp unto my feet, and a light unto my path." You must determine that the Word of God will be the guiding light that leads you down every path and in every decision you make in life.

God told Joshua in Joshua 1:7: "...Turn not from it to the right hand or to the left, that thou mayest prosper whithersoever thou goest." According to this verse, a great part of your daily victory depends on you faithfully sticking with the Word of God and not allowing other voices or other ideas to sidetrack you along the way. By taking time to read the Bible and allowing its words to enter into your heart and mind, you give God the ability to do a supernatural work in your heart and to keep your soul free from the enemy's entrapments.

If you don't know where to start reading, find a Bible-reading plan to help keep you on track as a type of personal accountability. The Bible will feed you, help you, ensure that you stay on course, and keep your heart soft before the Lord.

I urge you to make God's Word the highest priority of your life. Put it before your eyes every morning. Let it fill your eyes, flood your mind, touch your emotions, and become your guide. Your life will be strengthened and changed if you will do this.

Hebrews 4:12 reveals the transforming power of God's Word: "For the word of God is quick, and powerful, and sharper than any twoedged sword, piercing even to the dividing asunder of soul and spirit, and of the joints and marrow, and is a discerner of the thoughts and intents of the heart." In these last days, it is vital for you to have the Bible in your heart and at your disposal to successfully defeat the demonic forces that will continually try to accost your mind.

3. Quickly confess sin and receive the cleansing of Jesus' blood.

Learn to quickly confess sin and receive the cleansing blood of Jesus as part of your strategic plan to build a wall of protection around your life. We all commit sin, some unintentional and, at times, some even intentional. Regardless, as soon as you realize that you've done something or meditated on something inappropriate, you must quickly act on First John 1:9, which says, "If we confess our sins, He is faithful and just to forgive us of our sins, and to cleanse us from all unrighteousness."

Proverbs 28:13 states it clearly: "He that covereth his sins shall not prosper: but whoso confesseth and forsaketh them shall have mercy." When we ignore or try to hide sin, it negatively clogs our spiritual lives and makes us susceptible to the attacks of the enemy. But by quickly confessing sin and submitting to the cleansing power of Jesus' blood, it keeps us free of self-condemnation and attack and keeps our hearts pliable.

Don't let your heart become hard by allowing unconfessed sin to build in your soul. *Quickly* confess sin and submit it to the cleansing power of Jesus' blood. As you do, you'll immediately receive forgiveness and mercy as the blood of Jesus cleanses you from any act or thought that has grieved the Spirit of God. This is how you stay spiritually free and help your soul stay free in these last days.

4. Put on the whole armor of God.

Ephesians 6:11 says, "Put on the *whole armor* of God, that ye may be able to stand against the wiles of the devil." God has provided mighty spiritual weapons for you with which you are to continually arm yourself. Each element of this spiritual armor — the loinbelt of truth, the breastplate of righteousness, the shoes of peace, the shield of faith, the helmet of salvation, the sword of the Spirit, and the lance of prayer and supplication — is a vital, effective, and powerful weapon for you to use every day against the devil's assaults against you.

So put on the whole armor of God as part of a plan to build a wall of protection around your life. The devil will try to wage attacks against you, but you have at your disposal this full array of spiritual weapons — ready for you to wield and to win the victory every time.

Especially in these last days as spiritual conflicts become more and more intense, you need this God-given spiritual weaponry to enable you to successfully withstand every attack and drive the enemy out of your space. With these "weapons of your warfare" in place (*see* 2 Corinthians 10:3-5), you are more than able to defeat any foe or demonic stronghold that would challenge your faith!

(To know more about spiritual weapons, I advise you to read my book *Dressed To Kill*. This book is entirely devoted to the subject of spiritual warfare, including how to use your spiritual weaponry to stay free from every attack of the enemy waged against you.)

5. Make a covenant with your eyes.

Very often, evil finds access into your mind and imagination through your eyes. So make a covenant with your eyes as part of your deliberate plan to build a wall of protection around your life. Psalm 101:3 says, "I will set no wicked thing before mine eyes...."

Matthew 6:22 (*NLT*) says, "Your eye is like a lamp that provides light for your body. When your eye is healthy, your whole body is filled with light." If your eyes are focused on what is healthy, it will bring good things into your mind. However, if your eyes are focused on what is unhealthy or foul, those vile things that gained entrance through what you allowed your eyes to see will enter into your mind and affect you negatively.

An ancient saying tells us, "The eye is the window to the soul." Although this saying is not found in the Bible, it is true that your eyes are the gateway to your mind and imagination and to what positively or negatively affects your thinking.

We are living in the last days, and that, for one thing, means we are living in an environment where wicked things — especially sexually lewd things — are constantly on display before our eyes. If you don't stop those images from entering your mind, you give the devil a tool to use against you. It is therefore essential that you make a covenant with your eyes, determining that you will *not* give permission for any wicked thing to be displayed in your sight.

6. Maintain a strong relationship with those to whom you are spiritually accountable.

You need to keep your relationship strong with those to whom you are spiritually accountable. This is a vital part of your plan to build a wall of protection around your life. Proverbs 11:14 says, "Where no counsel is, the people fall: but in the multitude of counsellors there is safety." Proverbs 24:6 *also* says, "…In multitude of counsellors there is safety." According to these verses, a person who has godly counselors in his or her life is a wise person.

The fact is, everyone needs someone to whom he is spiritually accountable and to whom he can turn for counsel in time of need. That person could be your pastor. It could also be someone who is further along in spiritual maturity than you, whose counsel you respect, and who is trusted, confidential, and mature.

In Psalm 54:4, David said, "Behold, God is mine helper: and the Lord is with them that uphold my soul." Whom do you have in your life who strengthens you in your soul — helping you think right about the situations you're facing and align your emotions with God's Word? You need people in your life like that.

There are times we all need someone to speak into our lives who will watch out for our souls. We need these trustworthy individuals who will pray with us, speak the Word to us, be honest and forthright with us, and hold us accountable. This is a healthy ingredient of our lives in God — especially in these last days when the enemy will do all he can to wage warfare against our soul.

By having such people in your life — those with whom you can talk and confide — you are provided a safety net to help you in times of need and to keep you strong. As David said, you need those who "strengthen your soul" during these last days when many will be tempted to fall into various temptations.

7. Regularly attend a church that teaches from the Bible.

You need to regularly attend a church where you will be encouraged from the Bible and strengthened in the presence of the Holy Spirit as you worship God with other believers. This is another essential part of a plan to build a wall of protection around your life.

Psalm 119:28 marvelously depicts the powerful effect of God's Word to divinely energize a person who otherwise would feel physically or emotionally weak. In fact, when the psalmist was confronted with his own humanity, he knew that the Word was the ingredient that would strengthen him to rise above it. That is why he said, "...*Strengthen* thou me according unto *thy word*."

The importance of finding a local body where you can receive a steady, healthy diet of God's Word cannot be underestimated in your life. In fact, the amount of spiritual fire you have burning at your core is directly related to how much of God's Word is planted in your heart — and where you regularly attend church is a vital factor in that equation.

Within the covers of the Bible are all the answers for every problem you will ever face. The Bible can bring new life to your heart, establish order in your mind, and refresh your soul when unruly emotions or tormenting thoughts threaten to disturb your peace. It is essential that you allow God to lead you to a company of other believers where you can receive a strong foundation of God's Word and commit to living out its truths within the spiritual family where He has placed you.

When you hear the Scriptures expounded by the anointing of the Holy Spirit and take it by faith into your heart, its supernatural power is *unleashed.* And when that happens, every part of your being — your heart, will, thoughts, emotions, and memories — are all touched by God's power.

Satan knows the life-transforming power that is locked inside the Bible. That's why he fights so hard to get believers and churches to back away from it, trying to convince them to water down, modify, or even eliminate the Bible from its critical role in the life of every local body. (I discuss this demonic attack in-depth in my book *How To Keep Your Head on Straight in a World Gone Crazy.* I urge you to obtain that book and read it.)

So I want to ask you — are you attending a church where the emphasis is on a solid foundation of Bible truth? In a world where deception is proliferating and growing darker all the time, this issue is more important than ever. You must fortify yourself and your family by sitting under preaching and teaching of the Word that encourages you, confronts you, and helps you conform to the likeness of Jesus Christ.

If you are currently attending a church where the Word of God is *not* taught in power, or where a weakened and watered-down version of the Bible is preached, I urge you to begin looking for a pastor who will feed you the Bible in a way that leads to personal transformation. In these last of the last days, you must have the spiritual strength and vital support found in a church that is led by a pastor and filled with believers committed to biblical truth.

2

WHY GOD CALLS THE LAST DAYS 'PERILOUS TIMES'

God speaks to His people well in advance to warn them of what they need to know about the future. That is exactly what we find in Second Timothy 3. In this powerful passage of Scripture, Paul prophetically forecasted events that would occur when time had sailed as far as it could go and the end of the age had reached its culmination. Verse 1 begins, "This know also, that *perilous times* shall come...."

As we have already seen, even the words "shall come" in this verse are very important. These words are a translation of the Greek word *enistemi* — a compound of the words *en* and *histemi*.

In review, the word *en* means *in*, and the word *histemi* means *to stand*. When compounded into a single word, the new Greek word formed is *enistemi*, which means *to stand in; to stand in the middle of; to be surrounded by; to be encumbered by*; or *to stand in the very middle of whatever is being discussed, with a sense that it cannot be avoided*. This word *enistemi* depicts being completely encompassed about by something to the extent that one feels as if there is no way out of it and no way to escape it.

Even though prayer *is* powerful when believers pray in faith — in fact, God's Word *commands* that we pray — prayer cannot keep this prophetic season of "perilous times" from happening in the last of the last days. It will be inescapable. Prayer *can*, however, help us live as overcomers in Christ in the midst of these times and provide deliverance and protection for those we love.

For those of us living in the close of the age, it will seem as if we are surrounded and encumbered on every side with events that are difficult, hazardous, and hurtful. But because it is an end-time season destined to transpire on God's prophetic clock, we can know that we have been chosen and anointed to sail through these challenging times in His victory!

The word "encumbered" is a good rendering of the word *enistemi*, translated "shall come" in Second Timothy 3:1. It describes precisely what the Holy Spirit forecasted in this verse about events that would overtake the generation living at the very end of the age. It also reminds me of the words Jesus spoke to His disciples regarding end-time events.

**Because it is an end-time season destined to transpire
on God's prophetic clock, we can know that
we have been chosen and anointed to sail through
these challenging times in His victory!**

I discussed this last-days discourse between Jesus and His disciples in my book *Signs You'll See Just Before Jesus Comes*. I wrote:

> **In Matthew 24:4-7, Jesus catalogued a list of signs that would
> confirm the end of the age and His return was at hand. These signs
> are occurrences Jesus said would happen with greater frequency**

and intensity as we approach nearer and nearer to the wrap-up of the last days.

Then in Matthew 24:8, Jesus stated that all of these types of events would signify *the beginning of sorrows*. What did Jesus mean by using this word "sorrows" to describe this final slot of time?

The word "sorrows" in Matthew 24:8 is translated from the very same Greek word that is used to describe the contractions a pregnant woman experiences as the time of her delivery draws near. Although there are exceptions, it is generally true that in the beginning stages of labor, a woman's contractions are spaced sporadically apart. Those early labor pains unpredictably come and go with irregularity. But as she comes closer to her moment of delivery, those contractions occur more frequently and with greater regularity and intensity as her body prepares for the task of bringing a baby into the world.

Jesus used this phrase "the beginning of sorrows" to tell us that as this period entered its last phases, the signs He was about to enumerate would occur irregularly at first. But by using the word "sorrows" — the very Greek word for a woman in travail — Christ was telling us that when the moment of His return and the conclusion of the age is *right upon us*, these signs will occur with greater regularity and intensity, almost like a woman in the pains of childbirth. Finally, when it seems the pace and pain of these events can grow no worse, this period will end, Christ will come, and a new prophetic time period will be birthed.

According to Jesus, these last-days "contractions" will begin slowly at first, just like the early stages of labor for a pregnant woman. Then these events will occur closer and closer together — like *birth pains* — until they will seem like they're happening rapid-fire, one after another.... These "sorrows" will be felt in the earth's atmosphere, in the physical structure of the earth, in politics, in world events, and in society at large, especially as this age wraps up in its final moments.

Jesus stated that no one but the Father knows the exact day or hour when Christ will return (*see* Matthew 24:36). But Jesus said it's possible for us to know when we're *approaching* the outer boundaries of the age by looking at the *signs* (*see* Matthew 24:4-7). There are many such indicators to alert us that we have already entered the territory of the closing of this period in history. And we will see many more signs or events that will occur in the years, months, and even days leading up to Christ's return for His Church.

One of the ministries of the Holy Spirit is to show us things to come so we'll know what to expect as we move forward in time (*see* John 16:13). Armed with knowledge, we can protect ourselves, our families, and our loved ones from the destructive trends that will be associated with the closing days. And we can resolve to stand strong and do the will of God, shining as lights in the darkness that will certainly increase just before Jesus returns....

Most of us already sense the shifting and changing that is occurring in the world today — and that unsettling impression is producing a heightened sense of urgency concerning the time in which we live. Most committed Christians who know and believe the Bible are certain about where the signs are leading us. Many are seeking God with unprecedented fervor for His intervention in the affairs of man — for His purposes to be wrought in this generation and His plans to be consummated on the earth.

Just as the disciples wanted to know when the age was going to close, believers today want to know what the signs are that will pinpoint this culmination and the Lord's imminent return. There's no question that Jesus *will* return, and we have never been closer to that moment than we are right now!

The Holy Spirit wants us to know about the signs on the prophetic road that we'll see as we enter this new territory of the wrap-up of the age. He wants us to know the signs to *prepare* us for the times ahead. [1]

The fact that you're reading *Last-Days Survival Guide* right now is evidence to me that you're among the serious believers who want to know what the future holds. This book answers one aspect of that question, focusing on what the Holy Spirit prophesied would take place in society itself — across the board — as we come to the end of this age. But if you haven't read my *Signs* book I just quoted from, I urge you to get a copy, because it covers many types of signs we'll see just before Jesus comes that are not covered in this book.

Using this Greek word *enistemi* ("shall come"), the Holy Spirit prophetically declares that those who live in this last season will feel as if they are completely surrounded and encumbered on every side by dark and inescapable developments. It will seem like they are being assaulted from every direction by the backlash of these "perilous times," with no possibility of escape. Yet those who have listened to the Holy Spirit, fortifying and equipping themselves for the days ahead, will live *victoriously* and *unaffected* by the disturbing developments that seem to surround them on every side.

Consider that moment when the angel of death passed through the land of Egypt prior to the Israelites' exodus from Egypt (*see* Exodus chapters 11 and 12). God warned His people in advance — as He always does — of the difficult times that were coming. He told them clearly what actions they needed to take in order to avoid being negatively impacted by the judgment that was to come upon the land of Egypt. They were to smear the blood of a lamb upon the door lintel and side posts of their homes so the death angel would see the blood and "pass over." As the Israelites obeyed, they would be

---

[1] Rick Renner, *Signs You'll See Just Before Jesus Comes* (Tulsa, OK: Harrison House, 2018), pp. 23-24,26.

unaffected by the judgment that would fall upon all in Egypt who were not under the covering of the blood of the lamb.

When death visited Egypt that night, it infiltrated every Egyptian home, from the greatest to the least, and took the firstborn of each family. Egypt was so surrounded by death that even the firstborn of all the animals died that night. Yet not a single firstborn child among the people of God was touched, because they had heard what He said and heeded His instructions.

By telling Israel what was about to happen, God was not trying to *scare* His people, but to *prepare* them. His desire was to *protect* them and to tell them what to do so they would not be negatively affected in that critical hour. Because God told the Israelites in advance what was coming — and because they heard, acknowledged, embraced, and followed His explicit instructions — every one of them lived through that perilous night when death came to visit a nation.

If the children of Israel had chosen to ignore God's prophetic warning to them, they would have been affected in the same way the Egyptians were that night. But they seriously heeded God's merciful warning in advance, and they took action to prepare for what was coming. The Israelites' decision to both hear God and obey His instructions allowed them to live in the midst of destruction, yet remain unaffected and completely untouched by it.

◆

**Egypt was so surrounded by death
that even the firstborn of all the animals died that night.
Yet not a single firstborn child among the people of God was touched,
because they had heard what He said
and heeded His instructions.**

◆

Likewise, God is speaking to us in Second Timothy 3:1 as a way to prepare *us* regarding events that will occur in a last-days society. The voice of the Holy Spirit in this prophetic scripture is urgently calling out to anyone who has ears to hear — warning God's people in advance that perilous times are coming at the end of the age.

We can hear, heed, obey, and be protected — or we can ignore the Holy Spirit's tender, yet impassioned pleading. If we choose the latter, we will be affected along with the rest of society by the perilous times that will encumber the world as the time approaches for Jesus' return.

The words "last days" in this context unquestionably point to the very conclusion of the age — to that moment when we've reached the end of the prophetic road and we can travel no further in this period called the last days. But as believers, our response is *not* to hide from the evil that is prophesied to emerge on a scale unlike anything we've imagined. We who believe in the authority of the Bible and the power of the Holy Spirit must remain committed to the truth of Scripture and steadfastly advance to shine the light of God's Word in an end-times world that lies in darkness.

This is not a time for us to get into fear — it's a time to hear the Holy Spirit's voice. We must also fortify ourselves with the Word of God so that we, like the children of Israel, will live through this last-days period with no ill effect. It is time for us to use our heads, apply both spiritual and common sense to our lives, and responsibly build walls of protection around ourselves, our families, and our friends. Such spiritual walls can shield us and those we love from evil forces that are already prevalent in the world around us.

◆

**This is not a time for us to get into fear —
it's a time to hear the Holy Spirit's voice.**

◆

A LOST SOCIETY IN FIERCE TIMES

In Second Timothy 3:1, the Holy Spirit points toward a worldwide global future and prophesies that in the last of the last days, there will arise a unique period of time filled with risk and danger. He makes it very clear that these destructive characteristics will become prominent and commonplace in society.

In the chapters to come, we will focus on the specific characteristics that the Holy Spirit lists as societal and cultural characteristics in a last-days generation. We'll see how these scriptural predictions line up with the present environment — and how they are developing and increasing before our very eyes, even at this present moment.

But, first, we need to understand what the Greek word translated "perilous" means. What kind of "perilous" times actually await us?

When you understand the original meaning of the word "perilous" in the Greek text, I believe you'll see why it's so imperative that we commit our lives to God and seek His face diligently in this hour. You'll also better understand what you must do to protect yourself, your loved ones, and your friends, as well as how to reach out to those the devil wants to destroy and ravage in a wandering, last-days society.

The word "perilous" in Second Timothy 3:1 is translated from the Greek word *chalepos* — a word that is used only one other time in the New Testament. This Greek word describes *something filled with danger, risk, and hurt* or *something that is wounding.* It is the very word used in the literature of New Testament times to depict *wild, vicious animals that are unpredictable, uncontrollable, and dangerous.* It portrays *a deadly menace* or *anything that has the potential to be treacherous or hurtful.*

This Greek word *chalepos* was also the word used to describe *words or actions that are emotionally difficult to bear*. It expresses the idea of any action, place, person, or thing that is *harsh, harmful, cruel, ruthless, cutting,* or *wounding*. Significantly, this word *chalepos* was also the word used to describe a geographical region filled with so much *risk* and *danger* that it needed to be avoided at all costs. To knowingly go into a territory that was *chalepos* was an action that would put one's life at risk of suffering something *harsh, harmful, cruel, ruthless, cutting,* or *wounding*.

In ancient Greek secular texts, the word *chalepos* carried the entire range of all those meanings — and this is therefore how Second Timothy 3:1 is translated in *Renner's Interpretive Version (RIV)*.

**Taking all the varied meanings
in these first two chapters into consideration,
the *RIV* of Second Timothy 3:1 is as follows:**

You emphatically and categorically need to know with unquestionable certainty that in the very end of days — when time has sailed to its last port and no more time remains for the journey — that last season will stand in the midst of uncontrollable, unpredictable, hurtful, treacherous, menacing times that will be emotionally difficult for people to bear.

However, to get a sense of this word *chalepos* as it is used in Second Timothy 3:1, we need to go to Matthew 8:28, the only other instance where it appears in the New Testament. When you see how *chalepos* is used in that verse, I believe you will begin to get a "feel" for the reason the Holy Spirit used this particular word to describe the societal and cultural developments that will emerge in the very last of the last days.

In Matthew 8:28, we are told, "And when he [Jesus] was come to the other side into the country of the Gergesenes, there met him two possessed with devils, coming out of the tombs, *exceeding fierce,* so that no man might pass by that way."

In this verse, Matthew related the story of two demonized men who lived in the country of the Gadarenes. In the gospels of Mark and Luke, they only reported one demoniac man in this same account, but Matthew's gospel clearly says there were two demoniacs. Matthew's account gives a broader picture of the story, while the gospels of Mark and Luke focus on the one who was the most demonized of the two. But Matthew's account uses the words "exceedingly fierce" to describe these men and the fear they imposed on the people of that region.

These words "exceeding fierce" are translated from the word *chalepos* — the same Greek word translated "perilous" in Second Timothy 3:1. This emphatically means these demoniacs presented *danger, risk, hurt, hazard,* and potential *wounding* to people who passed through the territory where they dwelled. The behavior of these demoniacs was like *wild, vicious, and uncontrollable animals.* They were *unpredictable* and *dangerous.* In fact, they were potentially *treacherous* and *hurtful* to anyone who tried to pass by that way. As a result of their well-known, dangerous behaviors, people found this situation *emotionally hard to bear.* Make no mistake about it, the Greek word *chalepos* means these demoniacs were *harsh, harmful, cruel, ruthless, cutting,* and *wounding.*

This is why Matthew 8:28 goes on to say, "…There met him [Jesus] two possessed with devils, coming out of the tombs, exceeding fierce, *so that no man might pass by that way.*"

The word "way" is a translation of the Greek word *hodos,* which means *a road.* This perfectly matches the history and geography of the country of the Gadarenes during the First Century, where a road ran along the entire eastern side of the Sea of Galilee. Just beyond the far side of the road was a cliff with caves and tombs, and this was where the demoniacs dwelled. Even today in that location are the ruins of a Fifth Century church built on this site to commemorate the biblical event that occurred there.

But before Jesus liberated the demoniacs, they'd made a habit of charging out of the caves and tombs to terrify people who tried to pass by on the seaside road that ran along the east seashore near their dwelling. These men presented a real danger. They were *vicious, ferocious, fierce, unruly, uncontrollable, unpredictable, harsh, harmful, cruel, ruthless, cutting,* and *wounding.* All of this gave rise to a local situation that was *emotionally hard to bear* for the people who lived in the region and had to deal with these men — as well as for all the travelers who needed to pass through that area by way of the seaside road.

Matthew informed us that people in that region tried to avoid this area and to keep a distance between themselves and those demoniacs. The local population was aware that if they ventured into the territory where the demoniacs lived, they were walking into a hazardous situation. As a result, people tried to steer clear of that "perilous" region where these "exceeding fierce" and demonized men lived.

This is why the words "exceeding fierce" in Matthew 8:28 are translated from the Greek word *chalepos* — the same word the Holy Spirit uses in Second Timothy 3:1 when He forewarns that perilous times will come in the very last of the last days. This unmistakably means that the Holy Spirit is forecasting that the close of the age will be "exceeding fierce" — *vicious, ferocious, fierce, unruly, uncontrollable, unpredictable, harsh, harmful, cruel, ruthless, cutting,* and *wounding* — and that it will be a time that people will find to be *emotionally hard to bear.*

But remember — *nothing* takes God by surprise. And the events that are going to happen — and that are happening around us today — are no exception. God knew 2,000 years ago that this wrap-up of the age would be filled with peril, and that is why the Holy Spirit used this word *chalepos* to tell us well in advance that these things would occur. These prophetic words were given so we wouldn't be taken off-guard. God's desire is that we are alerted to take action in order to become established, strengthened, steadied, and protected even in the midst of these last-days events as they begin to take place.

WE ARE CALLED TO TRIUMPH IN JESUS CHRIST

In Second Corinthians 2:14, Paul wrote to believers who were encumbered with societal ills and problems that were assailing them in their generation. Because of the outside pressures that were besetting the Corinthian congregation from every side, Paul wrote to remind them that they were victorious in Christ despite the difficulties they were encountering. He told them, "Now thanks be unto God, which *always* causeth us to *triumph* in Christ…."

The word "always" is important in this verse. Paul used it to underscore the fact that we *always* have victory in Christ, regardless of what is trying to assault us from without. The word "always" is a translation of the word *pantote*, a word that emphatically means *at all times*, *in every place*, and *in every way*. Paul's use of this word leaves no room for misunderstanding — it means we are *at all times*, *in every place*, and *in every way* triumphant in Christ!

But pay attention to that word "triumph" in this verse. It is a translation of the Greek *thriambeuo* — a very special word that was used *only* to depict a *triumphal parade* designed to honor and celebrate a military commander who victoriously returned home from battle.

This was the custom in ancient Rome. When news reached the city that an enemy had been defeated, the planning for the return of their victorious commander and his army commenced. And when the gates of the city finally opened to welcome the victors home, a grand celebration began that was called a *triumphal parade*.

Triumphal parades were carried out at great expense to commemorate these exceptional victories won by notable individuals. To be honored in this way was the single greatest military honor that could be given in the Roman Empire.

Such landmark parades were extravagant, elaborate celebrations intended to be recorded as historical events. Because triumphal parades occurred very rarely, no one was in a hurry to see such a special occasion concluded when they did take place. This is one reason why historical records show that some triumphal parades lasted for days!

When the parade commenced, the larger population of Rome gathered along the route of the procession to fix their eyes on the defeated foe — the leader of the enemy forces who had been taken captive. This defeated commander would be bound in heavy chains and made a spectacle for the onlookers to mock and disdain. Back behind the now-defunct commander trudged his allied leaders, also chained and made objects of mockery and ridicule before the masses of onlookers. Next came the enemy soldiers who had been taken captive and were headed to prison or to execution.

Behind all the defeated captives followed oxcarts that overflowed with weapons, armor, gold, silver, statues, monuments, and other treasures confiscated *by force* from the enemy's territory. Next in the parade came the city's regally dressed senators, magistrates, and other high-ranking officials, marching in the parade to demonstrate honor to the returning commander.

Finally, the commander being honored joined the procession as the climax of this momentous event. Riding in an ornate chariot that was pulled by a team of four majestically adorned horses, the triumphant leader stood in the chariot, draped in sumptuous purple garments embroidered with gold and with a laurel crown on his head. The chariot moved slowly to give spectators along the route the opportunity to see him as he rode toward the grand finale.

The celebrated victor majestically rode along the parade route as throngs of people threw flowers and jubilantly shouted relentless exultation.

All of that was a part of a *triumphal parade* — and everything you have read in the previous paragraphs is included in the word "triumph" that Paul used in Second Corinthians 2:14 to depict the victory that belongs to you and me in Jesus Christ.

This means that in Christ, *we are mighty champions*. God sends us to invade the enemy's territory to plunder him! And regardless of what type of season you and I are living in right now, Christ's power enables us to overcome every obstacle, barrier, and difficulty and to victoriously share in Christ's triumph over the enemy. That is what Paul meant when he said, "Now thanks be unto God, which *always* causeth us to *triumph* in Christ...."

I believe this is important for us to keep in mind as we study what the Holy Spirit prophesied about the "perilous times" that will occur in the last days. We are not *victims* — we are *victors*! It is vital to never forget that Christ has given us a position of *victory*. And if we will reinforce ourselves with the Word of God, avail ourselves to the power of the Holy Spirit, use the weapons of warfare given to us, and learn to lean on others who are in the fight with us — we can live as *triumphant victors*, even in these last days!

As we study what the Holy Spirit prophesied about the "perilous times" that will occur in the last days, it is vital to never forget that Christ has given us a position of *victory*.

But God loves us so much that He wants to let us know key developments that are to transpire in the future so we can protect ourselves and our loved ones from the harmful effects and influences that will try to engulf a last-days generation. By telling us these things in advance, God in His love is awakening us to what is coming so we will do what is necessary to maintain victorious living in the midst of the unprecedented challenges of this end-time season.

Before Jesus left the earth, He said that one of the ministries of the Holy Spirit would be to show us things to come (*see* John 16:13). In Second Timothy 3:1, that is precisely what the Holy Spirit does when He speaks in an emphatic and categorical tone about what is coming at the end of this age.

As we saw earlier, Second Timothy 3:1 could be interpreted to mean, *"You emphatically and categorically need to know with unquestionable certainty that in the very end of days — when time has sailed to its last port and no more time remains for the journey — that last season will stand in the midst of uncontrollable, unpredictable, hurtful, treacherous, menacing times that will be emotionally difficult for people to bear."*

I think of how God prepared Esther in the Old Testament to step into her role at just the right time in history. So we, too, were born and destined to live in this age "for such a time as this" (*see* Esther 4:14). *Jesus is coming back soon for His Church!* And the *last* days of the Body of Christ on this earth will be her *best* days as she is equipped by God to bring the light of Christ to those who are in darkness and to deliver those who are bound. God is faithful who promised it!

———————◆———————

**The *last* days of the Body of Christ on this earth
will be her *best* days as she is equipped by God
to bring the light of Christ to those who are in darkness
and to deliver those who are bound.
God is faithful who promised it!**

———————◆———————

HOW SHOULD WE RESPOND TO THE HOLY SPIRIT'S WARNING?

How should we respond to events that the Holy Spirit prophesied would come at the end of the age? Should we stay in our homes, close the blinds, and hide from the world? Should we become reclusive and disappear from society? What should be our proper response to a world that seems to be sinking all around us? Does God have an expectation of us in this last hour?

First — *we must refuse to allow fear to grip our hearts.*

We are honored to live in this season that prophets foretold so long ago. Rather than run and hide, we must follow Jesus' example when He came into the region of the Gadarenes where the demoniacs lived. That region was filled with *chalepos* — risk, danger, and peril — but Jesus stepped into that moment to exercise His authority and to cast the demons out of those men, thus freeing an entire population from the fear that had paralyzed them for so long.

Jesus is our Example. What terrified others called Him to *action*. The same should be true of us today.

Others would have turned around, gotten back into their boat, and sailed away to get out of the area. But Jesus was called to that place at that time to bring deliverance to the demoniacs in the country of the Gadarenes. Had He run away from that divine assignment, He would have missed the opportunity to set an entire region free. As "perilous" and "exceedingly fierce" as those demoniacs were, Jesus pressed forward in the power of the Spirit and with the weapons of God, and He transformed that dire situation with the glory of God!

Likewise, in these last days, we need to hear God's Spirit beckoning us to step forward with the authority of Jesus Christ to bring deliverance, freedom, and peace to people and places where the devil has tried to bring chaos, hazard, and hurt. People need us, and that makes this our greatest hour!

Jesus is our Example.
What terrified others called Him to *action*.
The same should be true of us today.

It is certainly true that not everyone desires freedom. But there are multitudes of hurting, confused people who are wounded by the chaos of the hour in which we live — and they are crying out for someone like you and me to bring them the answers to the destruction that is wreaking havoc in their lives.

It's time for us to do what Jesus did. *We must fearlessly press forward, advance against the enemy's strategies, and allow the power of God to flow through us to cause God's purposes to prevail in every situation!*

THIS IS OUR TIME TO RISE AND SHINE!

In Isaiah 60:1 and 2, the prophet Isaiah also prophesied of this age. He said, "Arise, shine; for thy light is come, and the glory of the Lord is risen upon thee. For, behold, the darkness shall cover the earth, and gross darkness the people: but the Lord shall arise upon thee, and his glory shall be seen upon thee."

Although this prophecy first referred to Israel arising to a place of prominence, it has a dual meaning, speaking of the Church's assignment to "arise" and "shine" during a future dark season that will attempt to cover the earth in the end of the age. This means that when this season of "gross darkness" arrives, Christians will be needed more than ever before.

God has called, chosen, and anointed us to live for Jesus in these times, so we must lay hold of God's promises and rise up in this hour to let our light shine. *We must wake up and realize that we are the generation called to close out the age. We were chosen for this hour — it is our destiny!*

If you've been tempted to feel hopeless about the changes occurring in society all around you in this age, it's time for you to tell that hopelessness to *leave* in Jesus' name. Instead of allowing hopelessness to dominate your thinking, it's time to embrace the challenge and ask God to help you bring delivering power and freedom to those who are confused and gripped with confusion in our times. People are looking for hope — *and you have hope to give them!*

**We must wake up and realize
that we are the generation called to close out the age.
We were chosen for this hour — it is our destiny!**

Instead of retreating in fear, it's your responsibility as a believer to step forward and face the challenge, just as Jesus did when He encountered the demon-possessed men of the Gadarenes. *What terrified others and made them retreat in fear is what beckoned Jesus to action.*

In this hour, we must *not* retreat. Rather, we must charge forward into the darkness in the power of the Spirit and, with faith-filled hearts, set people free. The situation that exists in the world today is our opportunity to let the power and glory of God manifest through us!

Although the world sinks deeper in darkness, this is our hour to let the glory of God shine through us! So instead of yielding to fear, we must command it to *stand down* and leave us in Jesus' name — acknowledging that fear itself is evil (*see* 2 Timothy 1:7) and that it has been *defeated* by Jesus Christ. Then we must embrace the opportunities we encounter to bring deliverance and freedom to people who are gripped with the spirit of fear in this last-days age.

What terrified others and made them retreat in fear is what beckoned Jesus to action.

Think of it — God says you are "always" in a "triumphant" position in Christ Jesus! You are not a victim — you are a *victor*. He has gifted you, empowered you, and deemed you well able to fulfill His purposes for your life in the midst of the last days! So embrace the honor, and determine to be everything He needs you to be in these final hours of this age.

CHAPTER 2

LAST-DAYS SURVIVAL GUIDE ACTION STEPS

TO BECOME A PERSON GOD WILL USE TO TOUCH PEOPLE IN NEED

Living in the last of the last days is a guarantee that you will meet people with serious needs. These end times you live in are going to become increasingly filled with hurt and pain — with people who are crying out for the answers you carry because you have the Holy Spirit residing within. At any time, you can tap into His divine power to help family members, friends, and individuals you encounter who are under assault. There are people all around you who need God's healing touch, and you can give it to them.

If you'll act on the following seven simple steps and make them a consistent part of your life, they will help you become more spiritually sensitive to recognize those whom God has put in your path to help. Practicing these steps as a way of life will help you get your mind off yourself and become more focused on the needs of others. All of these steps are a vital part of your becoming a vessel of deliverance, healing, and power whom God is well able to use to help struggling people become strong and get on their feet again.

These points are simple, but if you will practice them, you will position yourself for God's power to flow through you to others. There are so many needy people in our time, and God wants your voice to become His voice to those who are crying out for answers. Your hands can become His hands to bring deliverance and healing to those who need a divine touch. Your feet can become His feet to bring answers to those in darkness whom Satan has tried to keep blinded to the truth.

For you to become a highly effective instrument in God's hands to bring His love to hurting humanity, I suggest the following simple, life-transforming action steps.

1. Get your eyes off yourself.

You will become a person God can use to help people in need only when you get your eyes off yourself and start focusing on those around you. Philippians 2:4 says, "Look not every man on his own things, but every man also on the things of others."

Perhaps you are dealing with certain issues that seem like mountains in your life — but always remember, there are people around you who are facing much more difficult challenges than you are right now. A trick of the devil is to get you so self-focused that you are swallowed up in your own needs and fail to see the needs of those around you. God wants you to shift your focus to others so you can enter the territory that the devil has gained in people's lives to set them free and help them take back what he has stolen.

As you surrender to the Holy Spirit, He will empower you to bring help to those around you, and He will also meet *your* needs. Galatians 6:7 says, "Be not deceived; God is not mocked: for whatsoever a man soweth, that shall he also reap."

Never forget that the law of sowing and reaping is true. It will go into effect for you when you begin to focus your attention on others. As you meet their needs, God will see to it that your own needs are met as well.

So I encourage you to ask yourself these questions:

- *Who are the people in my life who need my voice to bring an encouraging word to them?*

- *Who are those individuals who need my hands to impart a healing touch to them?*

- *Who are the ones who need my feet to bring them strength and support?*

In these last of the last days, you are going to meet many people who need answers and help that only God can give, and He most often uses His people who have become yielded instruments in His hand. You are called to be one of those instruments. However, to be effective in that divine role, you must shift your focus off yourself, open your eyes, and allow the Holy Spirit to show you the needs of others whom He will send across your path.

2. Evaluate the spiritual environment around you.

You must learn to evaluate the needs of others — their spiritual needs and their level of spiritual receptivity — if God is going to use you to help people. Jesus referred to this type of sensitivity with a very unusual example in Matthew 10:16. He said, "…Be ye therefore wise as serpents…."

The word "wise" in this verse is from a Greek word that means to be *prudent, careful, cunning, discerning, thoughtful, intelligent,* or *sensible.* It is a perfect word for Jesus' illustration of snakes that He used to instruct us on how to be His representative on this earth, for snakes are *careful, discerning, intelligent,* and *prudent* in how they act.

For example, when a snake moves into new territory, it lies low, stays quiet, blends into the environment, and evaluates the situation to see opportunities in the area. That is a wise strategy to adopt when God is asking you to touch someone's life who is new to you.

- Move carefully as you begin to step out to obey the Lord.

- Lay low, stay quiet, blend into the environment for a while, and evaluate that person's spiritual needs and spiritual condition before you act.

- Allow the Holy Spirit to give you insight and wisdom on what He is asking you to do to help that person. Then when you sense a green light from Him and you have a sense of what your part is in reaching out to that person, seize the opportunity to reach out.

- Don't ignore the Holy Spirit's prompting when it *is* time to act. Become the source of help that individual needs at that moment. If you wait too long, the opportunity may pass because you didn't act in God's timing.

In the closing days of this age, you'll find yourself in all kinds of spiritual environments and will meet people with all different types of spiritual needs. So apply yourself to learning to discern the Holy Spirit's leading in your spirit. Allow Him to develop spiritual discernment in you so you'll know when and how to administer help at the right time and in the right way.

3. Get rid of judgmental attitudes toward people.

You must free your heart of *judgmental attitudes* if you are to be a person God can use to help people who are in need. Having sound and reasonable *judgment* is not the same as being *judgmental*. Having sound *judgment* refers to being able to comprehend a situation clearly so you can arrive at an accurate conclusion about that situation. On the other hand, being *judgmental* refers to *maintaining a negative, nitpicking, disapproving, condemning, and hyper-critical attitude regarding a situation or a person in need.*

If you are going to be a person God uses to help others, you must be able to *judge* a situation without being *judgmental* about it.

In John 8:3-11, we read where Jesus was confronted with a woman who had been caught in the act of adultery and was being condemned by religious leaders. When Jesus saw the judgmental attitude of those religious leaders, He intervened in the situation to save her life. It's important to note that Jesus never condoned her behavior; He acknowledged it was wrong. But then He spoke words of liberation as He told her to go and sin no more. Jesus *judged* her situation but was not *judgmental* of her, as were the religious leaders.

Frequently Christians get confused about the difference between *making a sound judgment* and *being judgmental*. You must be able to come to a reasonable *judgment* about a person's situation in order to help that person. But if you are *judgmental* toward the one who needs your help, it will hinder the love of God from flowing through you to that person.

Especially in these last days when people's morals have become confused, it is important for you to be able to judge situations without being judgmental. So be diligent to rid yourself of judgmental attitudes so you can remain a clear channel that God is able to continually work through to bring help and deliverance to others.

Take Jesus as your Example. Do what He did when He was confronted with that woman caught in the act of adultery. Evaluate each person and situation; see that person's situation in light of God's Word; and then come to a conclusion *without* falling into the trap of being judgmental in your attitude. This will keep your heart free to be a channel through which the love of God flows, and you'll become a ready help to those in need.

4. Assume everyone needs encouragement.

You must develop the mentality that everyone you meet needs encouragement if you are going to be someone God uses to help people. You are surrounded every day by people who are struggling in their personal lives, in their minds and emotions, and in their relationships. They may not open up to you about it, but many people you know are deeply struggling even now as you read these words. They need your encouragement, even though they may not realize it themselves.

In this end-time hour we're living in, so many people have morally veered off track. So many people's lives are not built on a solid foundation. More than ever, people need the help and strength that Jesus Christ offers them. Very often, God will provide that strength and encouragement through His obedient children. And He wants to use *you*.

I advise you to play it smart and assume that everyone you know needs some type of encouragement.

In Romans 14:19, Paul exhorted us to get busy finding ways to "edify" other people. That word "edify" is a translation of the Greek word *oikodome*, which is a compound of the words *oikos* and *doma*. The word *oikos* describes *a house — fully built and complete*. The word *doma* pictures *the roof of a house*. When compounded, the new word *oikodome* pictures *a specific, well-thought-out plan to construct a well-built house from its foundation all the way to its roof.* In other words, this word depicts *the complete building process from start to finish.*

To build a house well all the way to its conclusion leaves no room for sloppy, last-minute planning. Careful consideration of every detail is required. Likewise, there is no room for careless thinking when it comes to edifying and encouraging others.

God knows exactly what is needed to encourage those whom He brings across your path. The Holy Spirit — who is the Chief Architect and Engineer — wants to show you how to edify those around you. So ask yourself:

- *Am I ready to receive His plan?*

- *Are my spiritual ears open to hear His plan?*

The Holy Spirit is ready to give you that plan — *if* you will listen and allow Him to work through you to encourage those who really need it. Romans 14:19 states clearly that this is the will of God. So get in agreement with Him about your assignment, and start learning today how to become a continual source of encouragement, ready to edify and encourage those in your life who need it — *and more people need it than you think*!

5. Surrender to the gifts of the Holy Spirit.

You must surrender to the gifts of the Holy Spirit that are resident within you if you are going to be a person God can use to effectively help people in need. In First Peter 4:10, we are told, "As *every man* hath received the gift...." According to that verse, every believer has received gifts from the Lord that empower him or her to minister to others (*see* Romans 12:6-8; 1 Corinthians 12:4-11; 1 Peter 4:10,11).

The words "every man" in this verse are translated from the Greek word *hekastos*, which is an all-inclusive word that literally means *every single person, no one excluded*. This means that every person who has been born of the Spirit and who declares that Jesus is Lord has been supernaturally graced or endowed from on High with divine gifts — and that includes *you*!

But the verse continues, "As every man hath *received* the gift...." The word "received" is from the Greek word *lambano*, and it means *to receive into one's possession* or *to take into one's own control and ownership*. It carries the idea of *taking hold of something, grasping onto something, or embracing something so tightly that it becomes your very own*. This means that God wants you *to accept and take ownership of spiritual gifts as your own*.

As a child of God, you've been richly endowed with gifts that have the power to make a powerful difference in someone else's life. But you must embrace those gifts and allow them to flow through you if they are going to benefit those near you who are in need. For you to become an effective instrument whom God can use to help people, it is imperative that you surrender to these remarkable gifts and allow them to flow through you by the power and leading of the Holy Spirit.

If you will yield to the Holy Spirit in this area, these spiritual gifts that lie resident within you will flow from you to bring His help to those in need right when it's needed. These gifts are intended to help people — so make the decision today to become skilled at yielding to the Holy Spirit's promptings and allowing His gifts to flow through you to those who are in need of a divine touch from Heaven.

6. Don't let fear stop you.

You have to say farewell to a spirit of fear if you are going to be a person God uses to help people in need. In Second Timothy 1:7, Paul said, "For God hath not given us the spirit of fear; but of power, and of love, and of a sound mind."

The word "fear" in this verse is translated from the Greek word *deilia*, which depicts a *cowardly* and *timid* person. If this is how you feel about yourself, it is time to rid yourself of that feeling once and for all! Second Timothy 1:7 clearly says that God did not give you a cowardly or timid spirit. You have the Holy Spirit dwelling inside you, and He will give you His supernatural gumption to do *whatever* God needs you to do!

For God to be able to use you to effectively help others, it is essential for you to tell cowardice and timidity farewell *forever*. If you don't, that timidity will stop you in your tracks when it's time to help someone, because you'll be too afraid to step out of your shell and do what is necessary. That timidity is a satanic trap to stop you from ever becoming a person God can use.

So boldly use the name of Jesus, and rebuke the spirit of fear in that great name! Take authority over intimidation, and tell it goodbye forever! Quit being robbed of resolve! For God to use you to touch those in need, you have to allow Him to develop an unshakable core of Holy Ghost boldness on the inside of you!

7. Remember that you are *always* on assignment.

You must remember that you are always on assignment if you're going to be a person God uses to help people who are in need. In First Peter 3:15, the apostle Peter wrote, "But sanctify the Lord God in your hearts: and *be ready always* to give an answer to every man that asketh you a reason of the hope that is in you with meekness and fear."

The words "be ready always" are a translation of the Greek words that mean *to be ready* or *to be prepared.* It is an attitude that is always *set to go, eager, prompt,* and *raring to get started.* It is a perpetual mindset of being *ready to take on a challenge* or *ready to take initiative of some sort.* Inherent in this command to *be ready* is the idea that *one must do everything in his power to equip himself for that moment when he is to be called to action.*

This perpetual mindset to "be ready always" is made even clearer by the use of a tiny Greek word in this verse that means *always, at all times, constantly,* or *perpetually.* Peter was urging us, *"...Be constantly and perpetually ready, set to go, and prompt to act...."*

Peter continued to say, "...Be ready always to give an *answer* to every man that asketh a reason of the hope that is in you...." The word "answer" in Greek means *to answer back, to reply, to respond, to explain,* or *to defend.* Peter unmistakably was telling you that as a Christian, you must *"...be constantly and perpetually ready, be set to go, and be prompt to answer every man who asks a reason for the hope that is in you...."*

Especially for those of us who are living in these last days when fewer people were raised in church and so many have so little knowledge of the

Bible, we should not be surprised if people ask us about our faith. In fact, we should anticipate that they *will* ask. This is why this verse urges us to be *prepared* and *ready* to answer. In other words, *we need to embrace the fact that we are always on assignment!*

This is a prerequisite if you want to be used by God to be His instrument of love and help in people's lives. You have to accept the fact that you are always on assignment — regardless of where you are or what you are doing.

So ask yourself:

- *Am I willing to be on perpetual assignment to help anyone in need whom the Holy Spirit asks me to help?*

If you can say with conviction, "Yes, I *will* accept this assignment," God will use you mightily in the lives of people who so desperately need the power of His love and presence that you carry.

3

WHY THIS WARNING
TO THE CHURCH?

I n the city of Pisa, Italy, stands the renowned Leaning Tower of Pisa. When architects began to construct it in 1172, they miscalculated the depth needed for its foundation. Because the foundation was defective, the tower started to noticeably lean as early as 1178. To remedy the problem, a decision was made to compensate for the tilt by building its upper floors with one side taller than the other. But with each subsequent floor, the tower leaned more off-centered and further off-balance. Millions of tourists from around the world have traveled to see the Tower of Pisa and have been reminded of what happens when anything is built on a flawed foundation.

In this chapter, I will show you from verses in Second Timothy 3 what happens when society is built on a flawed and faulty foundation. But before we proceed, let me remind you again that Second Timothy 3:1 (*RIV*) is interpreted as follows: *"You emphatically and categorically need to know with unquestionable certainty that in the very end of days — when time has sailed to its last port and no more time remains for the journey — that last season will stand in the midst of uncontrollable, unpredictable, hurtful, treacherous, menacing times that will be emotionally difficult for people to bear."*

The Holy Spirit gave this urgent warning to the Church so that those who would actually live in the very last of the last days would be mentally and spiritually alert and well-equipped to overcome whatever the devil tries to throw against them. The Holy Spirit's desire was also to position and empower God's people to help anyone victimized by the evil that would emerge in society at the very end of the age.

This is so important for us to grasp. For those of us who know Christ and are established in His Spirit and His Word, we are presented an ongoing, powerful opportunity to reach out to those shattered by the devastation that can result from living in the last of the last days.

In the chapters to come, you and I will study exactly what the Holy Spirit prophesied regarding society and culture and how events will unfold as we approach the end of the age. Rather than hide in fear, we must get *God's* perspective about what is going to happen and what we need to do to help people who have already been victimized.

Each one of us must take responsibility for building a spiritual wall of protection around ourselves, our family, and our loved ones that will guard us against the enemy's attacks. We must take steps to become instruments God can use to help those who are being devastated by the times. Our intimacy with Jesus and our personal knowledge of Him is what will make the difference and serve as our sustaining force in the days that lie ahead.

**Our intimacy with Jesus and our personal knowledge of Him
is what will make the difference and serve
as our sustaining force in the days that lie ahead.**

TAKING OUR PLACE AS VICTORS
AT THE END OF THE AGE

In recent years, our ministry team has noticed that the prayer requests that come into our office are much graver in nature than they were in the past. What used to be a serious prayer request is now relatively minor compared to the new level of dire problems people are asking us to pray for regarding their marriages, families, jobs, finances, and so on. The evil already working in the world has infiltrated homes and families — the core of society — and is attempting to penetrate every sphere of life.

Because we are in the world, we cannot avoid the times we live in or the challenges that are currently facing society. Hence, it is *essential* that we prepare ourselves spiritually to walk as overcomers in life. The Scriptures and the power of the Holy Spirit are more than enough to make us victorious even in these perilous times.

We are living in an end-time era that is brimming with all types of hazards and danger. Only those who live by the Word of God and the power of the Holy Spirit will escape the peril that will confront this last-days generation. This is the message we must boldly believe and herald!

This is also the reason you need to be attending a church that adheres to the uncompromised teaching of the Word of God that will strengthen your heart and mind, reinforce your beliefs, and transform your life. You also need friends who are committed to the Bible and to living their lives as authentic disciples of Jesus. More than ever before, it is essential that you practice a consistent walk with God of personal Bible study, local church attendance, and fellowship with committed believers in order to keep your head on straight and successfully navigate the age that is upon us.

All around us, the world is changing at a staggeringly rapid pace, and events long ago foretold in Scripture are unfolding before our eyes. In light of the increasing turmoil in the world, it could be tempting to succumb to feelings of uncertainty or anxiety regarding the future.

◆

**It is essential that you practice
a consistent walk with God of personal Bible study,
local church attendance, and fellowship with committed believers
in order to keep your head on straight
and successfully navigate the age that is upon us.**

◆

But we don't have to wonder what the future has in store because the Holy Spirit has laid it out for us very clearly in Scripture. Our task is to *know* those Scriptures and to hold fast to God's higher perspective as we take our place, positioned as victors in this hour — no matter *what* is going on around us! God's Word not only provides us with a clear picture of what we can expect in the coming years, but it also gives us every spiritual tool we need to face in these turbulent times. We are fully equipped to remain victorious!

WHY GOD GIVES US PROPHETIC SCRIPTURES

As we continue exploring further into Second Timothy 3, we will see that the Holy Spirit has enumerated for us the characteristics that will emerge at the very end of the age. These are intended to be "signposts" to let us know we have entered the final stage. If we see these characteristics occurring on a wide-scale basis, we should take it as a signal that we have "turned a page" and have entered the final chapter in this present age.

We may not be able to pinpoint the exact time of Jesus' coming — but thank God, by studying the Scriptures, we can identify where we are on God's timeline. Because He loves us, He spoke to us by His Spirit to enlighten our eyes and help us see what the world environment — and, specifically, society — will be like in the concluding moments of the last of the last days.

Having this knowledge helps us live soberly and with eternity in view. Because the time is short, we must use the time that remains wisely and shine the light of the Gospel into the lives of those whom Satan has blinded (*see* 2 Corinthians 4:4).

As a committed Christian, you have a responsibility to live with your eyes wide open to the events that are occurring around you. And if you have friends or family who are unsaved, backslidden, or blind to the truth, it is time for you to fervently pray for God to give them eyes to see and ears to hear!

———◆———

As a committed Christian, you have a responsibility to live with your eyes wide open to the events that are occurring around you.

———◆———

REACHING PEOPLE
WHO ARE BLIND TO THE TRUTH

I once watched a television interview with a very famous individual who is well known for his public opposition of biblical teaching. During the conversation, the interviewer asked this famously rich person for his opinion about the state of the world today. I was shocked to hear how he answered!

The man replied that the world in general had never been in better shape than it is in right now. As evidence to support his claim, he specifically mentioned the shift of morality away from traditional values, the widespread acceptance of same-sex marriage, and the emergence on the political and economic scene of a one-world system that he believed will turn the planet into an altogether better place. I was stunned at his answers. I wondered, *How can anyone be so blind to what is taking place in the world today?*

There does seem to be a very real form of blindness that causes a person not to see what is happening in this modern age. What really amazes me is that often the people who make these comments are actually intellectually brilliant! As I listened to this man speak, I wondered, *How can people be so smart and yet so blind to the truth?* But the Holy Spirit reminded me of Paul's words in Second Corinthians 4:4, where he wrote, "In whom the god of this world hath blinded the minds of them which believe not, lest the light of the glorious gospel of Christ, who is the image of God, should shine unto them." *According to Paul, some people really are blind to the truth!*

When Paul wrote that Satan has "blinded" the minds of unbelievers, he chose the Greek word *tuphloo* for the word "blinded." This is very important because the word *tuphloo* doesn't just depict a person who is unable to see; rather, it vividly portrays a person who has been *intentionally blinded* by someone else. Someone has deliberately removed that individual's eyes and permanently blinded him. This person hasn't just lost his sight; *he has no eyes to see.*

Paul continued by saying that Satan "...blinded the *minds* of them which believe not...." This word "minds" is the Greek word *noema*, which is a form of the word *nous*. The word *nous* simply means *mind*. However, as the word *noema*, it no longer refers to the physical mind, but rather denotes the *thoughts, reasoning, opinions, feelings, beliefs,* or *views* that a person holds. Thus, Paul's words in Second Corinthians 4:4 explicitly state that Satan has "gouged out" the spiritual eyes of skeptics and unbelievers to such a degree that *it has affected their ability to see things correctly.* Their *thoughts, reasonings, opinions, feelings, beliefs,* and *views* of what they experience and perceive are *obstructed, hindered,* and *impeded.* As a result, they are *blinded from a correct view* of the way things really are.

If you have any friends or relatives who are either unsaved or backslidden Christians and they seem "blind" to the truth, this verse may explain why they can't seem to see the true state of things. Pray for the Holy Spirit to open their spiritual eyes so they can see the truth. The fact is that we are living in the last of the last days, and the world around us is changing very quickly. Events that were long ago prophesied in Scripture are unfolding before our very eyes. We have turned a page and have entered into the final chapter of history as we know it.

Thank God that by studying the Scriptures, we can identify the time and exact age in which we live. With this knowledge before us, we can live soberly with eternity in view. Time is short, so we must wisely use the time that remains and shine the light of the Gospel into the lives of those whom Satan has blinded. The moment they believe, the Holy Spirit creates eyes for them to see. That is why it is so important that we don't stop preaching the Gospel — even if people act like they don't want to hear it.

As committed Christians, we must determine to live with our eyes wide open to the times we live in and to the events that are occurring around us. If we have friends or family who are unsaved and therefore blind to the truth, it is more urgent than ever that we fervently pray for God to give them eyes so they can see the truth that will save and deliver them.

◆

**Thank God that by studying the Scriptures,
we can identify the time and exact age in which we live.
With this knowledge before us,
we can live soberly with eternity in view.**

◆

Soon Jesus will come, and everything will change forever. Until then we have time to pray for those whom Satan has blinded. It isn't that they are naïve — they are *blind*. Satan has gouged out their spiritual eyes, blocked their view, and affected their minds. They have no eyes to see. Spiritual eyes are created for them to see only as the Gospel is preached and the Holy Spirit opens their hearts to receive its life-transforming truth.

Are you someone God wants to use so people's eyes will be opened to see the light of the Gospel? Maybe it's time for you to quit praying for others to fill that role and recognize that God is asking *you* to be the one to share Jesus with those who don't know Him and bring them to a saving knowledge of Christ. Keep your eyes open for opportunities to help the spiritually blind see, and the Lord will accommodate you with people who are hungry to listen and ready to open their hearts and receive new spiritual eyes.

Are you the one God wants to use to share the message of Jesus with the people you encounter? Are you the vessel He will use to minister a piercing word that causes their eyes to be opened to truth? Will you administer words of true hope that others can grasp in the midst of these turbulent times?

If you're praying for someone else to fulfill that holy responsibility, maybe you should just accept what your heart already knows: that God is asking *you* to share the Gospel with those who come across your path. But you don't have to do it on your own! He has thoroughly equipped and empowered you by His Spirit to be His witness to a lost world in these very last days of the age!

CHARACTERISTICS OF A SOCIETY WITH NO ANCHOR

Let's move on to see what Paul prophesied will be the *chief characteristic* of man's fallen nature in a world gone astray at the conclusion of the age. Pay careful attention to what you are about to read — for what the Holy Spirit mentions *first* is foundational to everything else that He will foretell regarding what will ensue during this time. As Paul wrote under the inspiration of the Holy Spirit, he enumerated 25 points that will tragically become mainstream characteristics in society as we draw closer to the very end of the age.

In my book *Signs You'll See Just Before Jesus Comes*, I discuss in-depth another distinctive last-days list: the signs that Jesus said we would see on a worldwide basis just before He returns for the Church. Jesus' explanation of these signs can be found in passages of three gospels: Matthew 24:4-14, Mark 13:5-13, and Luke 21:8-19.

According to these three accounts, the following list includes the events or conditions that Jesus prophesied would escalate in the last of the last days. Some of the signs He spoke of have been occurring to a certain degree throughout the ages. But Jesus forecasted that these particular signs would escalate in intensity and experience a worldwide increase as mankind approached the very end of the age. The following include the signs Jesus told God's people to watch for: deception, signs in the heavens, economic instability, great seismic activity, prosecution and imprisonment of Christians, warring political systems, famines, wars, pestilences, commotions, ethnic conflicts, emergence of false prophets, the love of many waxing cold, fearful sights, unknown diseases, and rumors of wars.

Years later, the apostle Paul would write a second epistle to his spiritual son, Timothy, under the inspiration of the Holy Spirit. In this second letter, Paul would enumerate 25 characteristics that would develop in society and that we who live in the last of the last days would witness. In other words, when all of these dark characteristics of society and culture are manifesting simultaneously, it should be taken as a big "welcome" sign that announces we're no longer journeying *toward* the last of the last days — we have finally *entered* them! We can know that one part of our journey is over and that we've finally crossed over into the territory of the very last days.

**When all of these dark characteristics of society and culture
are manifesting simultaneously, it should be taken
as a big "welcome" sign that announces we're no longer
journeying *toward* the last of the last days —
we have finally *entered* them!**

The following list found in Second Timothy 3:1-9,12, and 13 enumerates the characteristics of a lost society that has run amuck. These are the *signposts* the Holy Spirit has given to alert us that we have entered the last of the last days. As I read what Paul wrote by the inspiration of the Holy Spirit nearly 2,000 years ago, I am amazed at the accuracy of the Holy Spirit found in these verses:

This know also, that in the last days perilous times shall come. For men shall be lovers of their own selves, covetous, boasters, proud, blasphemers, disobedient to parents, unthankful, unholy, without natural affection, trucebreakers, false accusers, incontinent, fierce, despisers of those that are good, traitors, heady, highminded, lovers of pleasures more than lovers of God; having a form of godliness, but denying the power thereof: from such turn away.

For of this sort are they which creep into houses, and lead captive silly women laden with sins, led away with divers lusts, ever learning, and never able to come to the knowledge of the truth. Now as Jannes and Jambres withstood Moses, so do these also resist the truth: men of corrupt minds, reprobate concerning the faith. But they shall proceed no further: for their folly shall be manifest unto all *men*, as theirs also was.... Yea, and all that will live godly in Christ Jesus shall suffer persecution. But evil men and seducers shall wax worse and worse, deceiving, and being deceived.

As we take each characteristic one at a time and dig into the original Greek meanings, I believe you'll discover just how accurate the Holy Spirit truly is in these verses and how clearly the words He chose describe our present-day society that is edging ever closer to the conclusion of this age.

THE SUPREMACY OF SELF AT THE END OF THE AGE

In Second Timothy 3:2, Paul began with the *chief characteristic* that will mark an end-time, off-track society. Verse 2 says, "For men shall be lovers of their own selves...."

The phrase "lovers of their own selves" alerts us to the principal sign that will let us know we have entered the very last of the last days. This glaringly evident sign will be inordinate *self-love*. In this verse, the Holy Spirit depicts a society that is *self-focused*, *self-centered*, *self-absorbed*, and *self-consumed*.

Let's look more deeply at the words "lovers of their own selves." These words are a translation of the Greek word *philautos* — a strange compound of two Greek words that don't seem to fit together for reasons you will see. But in spite of the oddity of this word, this is precisely the word that the Holy Spirit chose to use to make this significant point about society at the very end of the age.

This word *philautos* is a compound of the Greek words *phileo* and *autos*. The word *phileo* means *to love* or *to be fond of*, and it denotes the *love, fondness, attraction*, or *romantic feelings* one has for *another*. This word describes *a deep and profound love that is directed toward someone else*. The second part of the word is *autos*, which is the Greek word for *oneself*.

But something strange and curious happens when *phileo* and *autos* are joined together. As a compound, they become *philautos* — a weird word that doesn't seem to make logical sense. As noted above, *phileo* denotes *love, fondness, attraction*, or *romantic feelings* that one has for *another*. It describes *a deep and profound love that is directed toward someone else.*

But when it is combined with *autos*, the meaning is dramatically altered to picture a deep and profound *love of self.* Rather than possessing *love, fondness, attraction*, or *infatuation* for *another*, those who fit the description portrayed by this aberrant word *philautos* are in love with *themselves.* In other words, they possess *an excessive self-fondness or self-attraction*, and they are *inordinately self-focused and self-infatuated.*

As used in this verse, this word projects an end-time society that has become smitten with itself — *self-absorbed, self-focused*, and *self-consumed.* Flowing out of this idolatrous worship of *self*, society will veer into a wide range of catastrophic miscalculations. Indeed, this trait of inordinate self-love will be the catalyst to cause all the other societal dangers Paul talks about to come spilling forth into every facet of the world.

MISDIRECTED LOVE

Paul began this last-days list with the word *philautos* to let us know that there will be a gross misdirection and misuse of *love* at the end of the age. The use of the words "lovers of their own selves" — the Greek word *philautos* — suggests that what is fundamentally wrong with these people is that their love is misdirected to self rather than to others as was intended. This misdirection puts *self* above all others — and when *self* is made the central focus of one's life, all else goes astray.

By saying, "For men shall be lovers of their own selves," the Holy Spirit foretells that people at the end of the age will be loyal to themselves above all else. Their chief loyalty will *not* be to God or to their nation, to their family, to their employer, to their employees, or to those whom they call friends. A self-consumed, end-time society will be populated with those who are chiefly loyal to *themselves* and whose lives are consequently and fundamentally lopsided, off-balance, and off-center.

◆

**This trait of inordinate self-love will be the catalyst
to cause all the other societal dangers
Paul talks about to come spilling forth
into every facet of the world.**

◆

I think of what I've observed in a major city of the former USSR. In that city stands a horrible architectural monstrosity. When the planners started to build it, they were in such a rush to complete the project that, like the Leaning Tower of Pisa, they inadvertently built the first floors off-balance. As the building rose higher and higher, it became evident that they had constructed a huge tower that was lopsided, off-balance, and off-center. The building was dangerously crooked because the foundation wasn't right.

Today that building has been standing empty in a prime location for decades because it is too dangerous to occupy. It is used as a massive, ugly "billboard," with gigantic advertisements painted on its tower, and it stands as a glaring reminder of what happens when a faulty foundation is laid before a building is ever erected.

In the same way, when *self* is the foundation of a person's life — or of society as a whole — it causes everything in that person's life or in that society to become off-balance and lopsided. Nothing that is built afterward will go quite right because the foundation is bad.

The words, "For men shall be lovers of their own selves" point to just such a flawed foundation that will come to exist in society in the last of the last days. These words in Second Timothy 3:2 carry the idea, "For men shall be *self-focused*, *self-centered*, and *self-absorbed*...." In this verse, we see that the Holy Spirit is depicting *self-consumed* individuals whose own wants and needs are the center of their lives above all else. Their first consideration is always and at all times their own *self*-interest.

**When *self* is the foundation of a person's life —
or of society as a whole — nothing that is built
afterward will go quite right because the foundation is bad.**

The message the Holy Spirit is giving us is plain: In the last days, society will be consumed with *love of self*. If this is the case, it means people will be *philautos* — their focus and love will be primarily directed toward themselves. This means in the last of the last days, society itself will be *narcissistic, self-consumed, off-balance*, and *faulty at the core*.

But Paul's words are plural — "lovers of their own selves" — which implies that this characteristic will be widespread and prominent in the last of the last days. This means that not only individuals, but also society itself will be built on a flawed foundation of self-love, thus eventually becoming lopsided. Since this list in Second Timothy 3 begins with this type of misdirected love, it is logical to deduce that everything else that follows will continue to build on this off-centered foundation, causing society to lean further and further off-balance as the conditions enumerated become more developed and pronounced.

If you question the preeminence of this modern fixation on *self*, try visiting a local bookstore and walk through the Christian/Psychology/Motivational sections of the store to see what titles line the shelves. You'll see that those sections are filled with books that encourage people to *love themselves* first and foremost.

Certainly, there is nothing wrong with loving ourselves. Jesus said we should love our neighbors — our fellow man — as we love ourselves (*see* Matthew 22:39). It is important to maintain a healthy love of self.

But in Second Timothy 3:2, the Holy Spirit is not referring to a healthy self-love. Rather, He is forecasting a *self-love* that is completely out of balance, similar to the plight of the Tower of Pisa and the horrendous tower in the former Soviet republic I referred to earlier. A person or a society who continues to build on such a flawed foundation will become more and more off-center and unbalanced until the situation becomes critical and potentially very dangerous to everything else around it.

That is what the Holy Spirit prophesied regarding an end-time society. The result of this "leaning syndrome" eventually results in *selfishness* on an epic scale. That leads us to the next point in this prophetic list given to us by the Spirit of God.

MISDIRECTED MONEY

Out of this misdirection of love, the other vices included in this passage of Scripture flow. For example, Paul next stated that society at the end of the age will be "covetous" (*see* 2 Timothy 3:2). This word "covetous" is the Greek word *philarguros* — another very odd word similar to the word *philautos* used to depict "lovers of their own selves."

It's odd because it is a compound of the words *phileo* and *arguros* — two words we also would not expect to find used together. As we saw earlier, the word *phileo* means *to love* or *to be fond of*, and it denotes the *love, fondness, attraction*, or *romantic feelings* one has for *another*. This word describes *a deep and profound love that is directed toward someone else*.

But the second part of this word is *arguros*, which is the Greek word for *silver* or *money* and could refer to *material possessions*. But something strange and curious also happens when *philos* and *arguros* are joined together. Compounded, these words become *philarguros* — a word that depicts *an inordinate love for money*; *an abnormal preoccupation with money*; or *a profound fixation on material possessions*.

In ancient Greece, this word commonly depicted individuals who had money, but they were so self-absorbed with their own wants that they refused to share their resources and wealth with others. Hence, the age-old ideas of *self-embellishment* and *greediness* are conveyed in this Greek word *philarguros*, the word translated "covetous" in Second Timothy 3:2. The word can also be said to depict *an insatiable desire to always have more and more*.

Ecclesiastes 5:10 says, "He that loveth silver shall not be satisfied with silver…." The reason this kind of person is never satisfied is that the covetous soul always wants more and will never be satisfied, regardless of how much he embellishes himself.

I must add here that I am completely convinced it is God's will to bless and prosper His people. However, we must never forget that the Bible warns us, "…If riches increase, set not your heart upon them" (Psalm 62:10).

Deuteronomy 8:18 tells us, "But thou shalt remember the Lord thy God: for it is he that giveth thee power to get wealth, that he may establish his covenant which He sware unto thy fathers, as it is this day." Establishing God's covenant on the earth should be a chief financial priority for a committed Christian! But if any believer has fallen into the trap of self-consumption — never satisfied and always wanting *more* — that believer needs to evaluate whether he or she has fallen prey to the spirit of the age.

We must guard ourselves from ever falling prey to this covetous tendency that will be entrenched in society at the end of the age. It is vital for us to determine that, first and foremost, we will dedicate our resources to God and stay ready to give into His work as He leads. Each of us is responsible to take part in advancing the preaching of the Gospel around the world, funding missionaries and organizations that are focused on taking the Good News to their neighbors and to the ends of the earth!

In Matthew 6:21, Jesus said, "For where your treasure is, there will your heart be also." In this verse, Jesus made it clear that where a person's treasure is — that is, the value that person places on his money and what he does with his money — is the great revealer that truthfully reveals where his heart is.

So if you want to know where *your* heart is, follow your money and you'll find out — because money really does tell the truth.

This may sound simplistic, but the words of Jesus are true. If I were able to follow the trail of your money — or if you were able to follow mine — we could each discover what the other loves and cherishes above all else.

In light of what Jesus said, what does your money trail reveal that you love and cherish above everything else? *What does your money say about you?*

If you want to know where *your* heart is, follow your money and you'll find out — because money really does tell the truth.

THE ALTAR OF SELF

In the ancient pagan world, when a person came to worship a god, he brought sacrificial offerings to demonstrate his devotion to that god. These were often extravagant offerings. But because a last-days society will be self-fixated and self-worshiping, that end-time generation will extravagantly sacrifice at the *altar of self* and will demonstrate that they adore and love *themselves* more than anything else.

Because the people the Holy Spirit describes in Second Timothy 3:2 are *philautos* — that is, in love with themselves — it logically follows that they will also be *philarguros*. In other words, they will be devoted to using their resources primarily for themselves and will know no limitations for self-aggrandizing and self-embellishment. They will be self-lovers who invest more in themselves than in anything else. They will be the center of their own world; hence, their resources — including money, giftings, and time — will be consecrated to meeting their own self-cravings.

With all this in mind, the *RIV* of the opening words of this verse is interpreted as follows: *"Men will be self-focused, self-centered, self-absorbed, self-consumed, and in love with themselves more than anyone else. As a result of this self-love, they will be driven to obtain more and more and more...."*

No condemnation is intended, for we have all veered off track into selfishness from time to time. We all make mistakes along the way with money and resources. But to help us stay on track spiritually, it is healthy to do a self-examination and allow the Holy Spirit to search our hearts to show us if *self* is too highly exalted in our lives.

We have discussed at length the first two characteristics — *lovers of self* and *lovers of money* — that Paul said would become epidemic as signs of a last-days society. Both of these are the result of a love that is misdirected and lopsided, focused on self rather than on God and others. The pervasive, poisonous influence of these characteristics will produce a faulty foundation that causes the entire structure of society to lean dangerously off-balance. And it will not remain a static situation — it will worsen. The Bible says society will lean further and further toward the brink of collapse as we draw closer and closer to the end of the age.

To help us stay on track spiritually, it is healthy to do a self-examination and allow the Holy Spirit to search our hearts to show us if *self* is too highly exalted in our lives.

Now let's continue in Second Timothy 3 to see how misdirected love negatively affects everything else in both the life of a person and in society as a whole. The Holy Spirit spoke emphatically that these developments *will* occur in the last of the last days. If we are living in those days — and I'm convinced that we are — we should be able to see these developments all around us.

Meanwhile, we must make sure that we ourselves do not fall prey to the self-focused, self-absorbed spirit of the age. God is urgently calling each of us to take action to guard ourselves so that selfishness and covetousness *never* find a place in our lives!

CHAPTER 3

LAST-DAYS SURVIVAL GUIDE ACTION STEPS

TO HELP DETERMINE WHETHER YOU ARE AFFECTED BY THE SELF-FOCUSED SPIRIT OF THE AGE

In Second Corinthians 13:5, Paul told us it's wise to "examine ourselves" from time to time to see if we are in the faith. This is especially true as we witness the alarming direction that society is headed in these last of the last days.

That word "examine" is the Greek word *peiradzo*, which actually refers to *an intense examination*. This could include a test by fire, a test based on questions, or a test that includes some type of *self-examination*. This last option is the most pain-free of the three, even if the questions you must ask yourself require answers that are uncomfortable to confront.

So today why don't you do a little self-examining and see how well you fare? Open your heart, be honest, and talk to yourself and to God about these questions. They are designed only to help you as you consider possible areas of your life in which you need to change.

All of the following questions require you to be honest with yourself in order to get to the real answer. God already knows all the answers, but *you* need to know them as well. After pondering each question, determine what steps you need to take in order to make any necessary course correction. And remember — the Holy Spirit is your ever-present Helper, Counselor, and Guide to assist you along the way!

1. "What do I give financially into the work of God's Kingdom?"

Since actions speak louder than words, take a look at your financial giving and see what it reveals about whom you love most.

Be honest as you ask yourself this revealing question:

- *Do I give the tithe on all my increase, as commanded by Scripture (see Malachi 3:8-12)? Or do I regularly make excuses for not giving and then use the money elsewhere for my own needs and personal pleasures?*

Remember, if you follow your money, you'll discover where your heart is (*see* Matthew 6:21).

In this last-days season when people will tend to be selfish, you can guard against this in your own life by periodically asking yourself:

- *If someone followed my money today, would it reveal that I love God or that I primarily invest only in my own interests?*

This is an awkward question, but it's one you need to ask yourself to make sure you haven't fallen victim to the spirit of this end-time age. God already knows the truth. He doesn't need your answer — but *you* need it so you can see what adjustments you need to make to stay free in this critical hour.

2. "What do my spending habits reveal about me?"

This question follows the first: Take a look at the money you spend on your hobbies, personal possessions, and other non-essentials; then compare it to the amount of money you invest in the Gospel.

After your evaluation of your finances, ask yourself:

- *What do my spending and giving habits reveal about my love for God and concern for others who need to hear the saving message of Jesus Christ?*

We can all mislead ourselves into thinking we are generous, but if God Himself gave His view of what your spending habits reveal about your priorities, what would He say about you? Would He say the Gospel is most important to you, or would He say your spending habits reveal that your driving motivation in life is simply pursuing comfort and pleasure?

This, too, is an awkward question, but it is a healthy question to ask yourself. God already knows the truth. But *you* need to know the truth so you can see if you have been affected in any way by the self-focused age in which we live.

3. "What do I do with my time?"

Because the Bible says people living in the last days will be prone to being self-consumed, you should honestly evaluate what you do with your time. Ask yourself:

- *Do I spend my time mainly on myself and my own interests, or do I use significant parts of my time to serve my church and others?*

- *Do I spend time with God as a top priority in my life? Or do I complain that I don't have time to pray or read the Bible, yet somehow I find time to watch television, go to the movies, and do other things I want to do?*

God is watching you. From what He observes about your use of your personal time, what would He say you love most?

I realize this is also an uncomfortable question to ask yourself. However, asking ourselves probing questions of this sort is very helpful, as long as we answer honestly, in evaluating whether or not the selfish spirit of the age has affected us. You don't want to be a victim of the enemy's agenda for this time, so I encourage you to answer truthfully and then listen for the Holy Spirit's wisdom on how to begin to make any necessary adjustments.

4. "What do I do to serve others?"

Words are easily spoken and often do not match reality. So it is important to ask yourself:

- *Do my words and life reveal that I am genuinely doing my best to be a blessing by serving other people?*

Christians know that they are called to serve others, and usually they even say they want to do it. But life itself shows the truth of the matter about this question. In this last-days environment, we need to honestly evaluate whether we are only self-interested or whether our actions reveal that we are interested enough in others to make a way to serve them even above our own interests.

It is amazing how many people say they want to be a blessing but never seem to be able to make time in their schedule to serve God in a practical way in a local church or in meeting the needs of others. Again, words are easily spoken, but actions prove a person's sincerity.

This is another awkward question, to be sure — but there is a fuller, richer walk with God on the other side of the answer! So evaluate your way of life, and decide whether God would say that your actions prove you are more devoted to your own needs and interests — or that your life demonstrates you are in love with His Church and are giving of yourself to serve others.

5. "When I pray, do I pray about myself only, or do I pray for the needs and dreams of others?"

The tendency to be self-focused and self-obsessed can even manifest in your prayer life. So ask yourself:

- *When God hears me pray, what does He hear?*

- *If God were to relate the things He hears me pray about, would He report that I am an unselfish person who is concerned about the needs and dreams of others? Or would He report that I am primarily concerned only about myself and my own needs?*

It's easy to focus on your own needs and desires, but how often do you focus your prayers on the concerns of others?

This is another uncomfortable but important question to ask yourself. Listen to yourself when you pray to see how self-focused you are in your prayer life. There is certainly nothing wrong about praying for your own needs and plans. But *especially* in this area of prayer — as in every area of your life — you must avoid at all costs being affected by the self-focused spirit of the age in these last times!

6. "What personal sacrifices do I make to serve the Lord?"

If God opened the books to reveal the sacrifices you have made for Him or others, would the record reveal that you care deeply for God and live in obedience to His commands? Or would it show that you are unwilling to inconvenience your life in any way or sacrifice any of your private plans?

It's important to stop and honestly assess your past record in this area. Ask yourself these questions:

- *How long has it been since I gave up something or changed my schedule to help someone else or to walk in obedience to God's plan?*

- *Can I honestly say that I am picking up my cross and dying to my own interests in order to serve others and to make a difference in someone else's life?*

Here we have another uncomfortable question, but it's one you need to ask because it is a very revealing question. If you never give up anything to serve the Lord or to serve others, God will find someone else to step in and take your place. But He wants to use *you*, so I encourage you to answer this question truthfully. It's crucial to determine if you need to make any adjustments in order to stay free of the self-focused spirit that is running rampant throughout society in this last-days hour.

7. "What am I sacrificing to be obedient to God?"

Finally, we come to the last important question.

Ask yourself:

- *Is there anything I am personally laying down in order to walk in obedience to God and His Word? Or would I have to honestly say that I don't sacrifice much for God or others?*

- *Am I willing to be inconvenienced to help someone else or to serve in the church — or am I unwilling to jeopardize my own comforts and pleasures?*

When people are self-focused and self-consumed, they often aren't willing to make any personal inconveniences to serve God or anyone else because they are all about themselves. Is that true of you, or can it be said that you are doing whatever is required to serve God as your highest aspiration in life?

The things you do for Jesus are the most important things you'll ever do. They are the things that last forever. Are you spending your life on temporal or eternal things? Since eternity is ever in front of you, I urge you to make sacrifices and investments now that will count for all of eternity.

All of these questions require a high level of honesty with yourself to get to the real answer. I remind you — God already knows all the answers, but *you* need to know the answers so you can ascertain whether or not you have been affected by the spirit of the age in these last days. After pondering each question, ask the Holy Spirit to help you determine what steps to take to make a necessary course correction. Never forget — you don't walk this path alone as you secure your footing for the critical days ahead!

4

BOASTFUL, PROUD, BLASPHEMOUS, AND DISOBEDIENT TO PARENTS

We have seen what the Holy Spirit prophesied through the apostle Paul — that perilous times would emerge in society at the end of the age. In the first three chapters, we have studied in-depth the exact words in the first two verses that were used in the original Greek text to depict happenings in the last days.

So far we have seen that the *RIV* of Second Timothy 3:1,2 reads as follows:

> **You emphatically and categorically need to know with unquestionable certainty that in the very end of days — when time has sailed to its last port and no more time remains for the journey — that last season will stand in the midst of uncontrollable, unpredictable, hurtful, treacherous, menacing times that will be emotionally difficult for people to bear. Men will be self-focused, self-centered, self-absorbed, self-consumed, and in love with themselves more than anyone else. As a result of this self-love, they will be driven to obtain more and more and more....**

After Paul finished prophesying that a *self-consumed* and *covetous* society would become widespread in the very last of the last days, he continued to prophetically forecast other disturbing developments that would emerge and be predominant in society at the end of the age. Paul went on to write that the end-time society would be influenced by vast numbers of people who are "…boasters, proud, blasphemers, disobedient to parents…" (2 Timothy 3:2). As we continue, we'll look successively at each of these words Paul listed.

END-TIME BOASTERS

In the *King James Version*, Second Timothy 3:2 says, "For men shall be lovers of their own selves, covetous, boasters, proud, blasphemers, disobedient to parents, unthankful, unholy.…" We've already covered "lovers of their own selves" and "covetous," so let's proceed now to the word "boasters."

The word "boasters" is a translation of the Greek word *alazon*. It carries a wide range of meanings, including that of *a braggart* or *one so committed to his own self-promotion and personal agenda that he is willing to exaggerate, overstate the facts, stretch the truth, embellish a story, and even lie if it will have a positive effect on his position or situation.*

Today we would call this an example of *situational ethics* — that is, the hurling away of fixed ethics or moral absolutes to embrace a "floating ethics" mode that is easily adapted to whatever one deems necessary. A good example of this would be politicians who change their ethics and policies to fit whatever the populace wants to hear them say. A person with this mindset will nearly do or say whatever is needed to further a personal agenda, even if it clashes with conscience, conviction, or *truth*.

Unfortunately, today this amoral philosophy is being proliferated in media, education, and in nearly every sphere of society. Evidence abounds revealing how far delusion and a widespread mutiny against God and His Word have already advanced in the world today. Today we are witnesses of a society that has gone morally adrift and is regretfully being led by "boasters." In other words, these leaders hold views that continually float, fluctuate, and shift. Their beliefs are affected by the ever-changing current of thought and by the most recently accepted norms, whatever they may be.

This way of thinking is being perpetuated in the education of children and young people in schools and universities. In addition, through the media and every other avenue possible, this world view is being aggressively pushed by "progressives" who believe they have the right to subject everyone else — including Christians — to their new moral code.

Those believers who stick with the Word of God and refuse to go the way of the world have already been awakened to the reality that they are on a collision course with a culture in decline. So-called "progressives" are hurling away fixed ethics and moral absolutes and are trying to move society to a "floating ethic" mode.

But there is a larger satanic plan at work that even these progressives are unaware of. It is a plan to lead society along the prophetic route to a day when the Antichrist will be revealed to the world.

Believers who stick with the Word of God and refuse to go the way of the world have already been awakened to the reality that they are on a collision course with a culture in decline.

It is impossible to overstate the influence that this attitude of "floating ethics" exerts as the world heads toward becoming "lawless." It's all about getting mankind primed and prepared for the ultimate manifestation of the Antichrist at the end of the age.

You will see in the following section that since the beginning of time, the devil has been looking for a way to unseat God's authority in the earth. Satan has been conspiring to enact a master plan — a hidden and long-laid agenda, plot, and conspiracy — intended to clandestinely lead the entire world into the lap of the Antichrist. This operation is so stealth that the population of the world will bite the bait without comprehending that it is being led astray.

A WORLDWIDE MUTINY AGAINST GOD AT THE END OF THE AGE

The apostle Paul said that a mutinous attitude against God and all things godly will emerge in the very last of the last days as a part of this demonic, stealth operation to seduce the world into a state of lawlessness. Paul wrote, "Let no man deceive you by any means: for that day shall not come, except there come a falling away first…" (2 Thessalonians 2:3).

This verse lets us know that the Christians who live in the end of the age will be witnesses to this abandoning of morals and truth as a worldwide mutiny arises against God and His Word, along with an all-out assault against morality and godliness on a broad scale. We are living in those days, which is why we see an abandoning of godliness in society today.

This verse is so important in understanding the climate of this end-time hour that we must delve deeply into it. The words "falling away" are translated from the Greek word *apostasia*, which depicts *a falling away* or *a widespread revolt*. The ancient writer Plutarch used the word *apostasia* to describe *a political revolt* against authority. Other documents written during the time of the Old Testament use this word to describe *a turning away* from the Lord. This word also occurs in the Septuagint version of Joshua 22:22, where it also describes *rebellion* against God.

Now in Second Thessalonians 2:3, Paul — a scholar who understood the meaning of this word *apostasia* — used it to forecast a *rebellion*, *mutiny*, or *insurgency* against God that would occur on a worldwide basis against God in the very end of the last days as the age comes to a final conclusion.

But Paul continued to say, "Let no man deceive you by any means: for that day shall not come, except there come a falling away first, and that man of sin be revealed, the son of perdition...."

Paul called the Antichrist "that man of sin." The word "sin" in this case is *anomia*, which is actually a form of the word *nomos*, which is the Greek word for *law*, used to depict *the standard of what is legally or morally correct*.

But when an *"a"* is attached to the front of this word, it becomes *anomia*. That *a* has a *canceling* effect. So rather than depict *law* or *a correct moral standard*, the word *anomia* holds the opposite meaning — that is, *without law* or *lawless* — and it pictures *people who possess no fixed moral standards*. It depicts *those who live void of standards, without law, or in a state of lawlessness*. It is used prophetically to depict a last-days society that will throw out all previously agreed-upon moral standards and depart from God's well-established laws at the very end of the age.

The Bible tells us that as part of a last-days scheme, society will construct a new world order that has few, if any, hard and fast rules of what is morally right and wrong. In essence, this will be *a lawless world* — that is, a world free from the "outdated" voice of the Bible. Society will attempt to disconnect from most moral standards that were once held to be the common rule and view of society.

That is what *lawlessness* means. That is the atmosphere in which these end-time *boasters* will proliferate. (In the pages that follow, we'll read more regarding these boasters and how they help set up this free-floating state of lawlessness in society as a whole.)

Because Paul used the word "sin" — the Greek word *anomia* — in connection with the Antichrist, we know that this individual will be *void of standards* and *without law*. He will throw out all previously agreed-upon moral standards and rise as an aggressive proponent of departing from God's well-established laws. He will not be just a person with a lawless attitude; he will be *the* man of lawlessness — the epitome of one who has fully discarded God's well-established laws to become Satan's perfect candidate to lead a mutinous world that has likewise rejected the voice of God and of Scripture as its internal compass.

The current trend toward lawlessness — that is, the construction of a new world order with morals contrary to those stated in God's Word — will eventually produce a collective mindset in society that no longer feels the pain or conviction of sin and is numb to its consequences. And according to Paul, that mutinous society will be primed and prepared for the Antichrist to be "revealed" at that time.

The word "revealed" referring to the man of sin in Second Thessalonians 2:3 is the Greek word *apokalupsis,* a compound of *apo* and *kalupsis.* The word *apo* means *away,* and the word *kalupsis* refers to *something that is veiled, covered, concealed, or hidden.* But when these words are compounded into a*pokalupsis,* the new word depicts *a veil that has been removed, exposing what was behind the veil and concealed or hidden from view.* It is clear that Paul used this word to inform us that a day is coming when the Antichrist — who until this time has been concealed and hidden from public view — will suddenly appear and step onto the world stage for all to see.

——◆——

**The current trend toward lawlessness — that is,
the construction of a new world order with morals
contrary to those stated in God's Word — will eventually produce
a collective mindset in society that no longer feels the pain
or conviction of sin and is numb to its consequences.**

——◆——

Paul also called the Antichrist the "son of perdition." The word "perdition" is a translation of the Greek word *apoleia*, and it speaks of something *doomed*, *rotten*, *ruinous*, or *decaying*. Although the Antichrist will claim to lead the world into a more progressive future, what he will bring to the world is *doom*, *destruction*, *rot*, *ruin*, and *decay*. There will be absolutely no redeeming values in anything produced by his rule.

It is also important to note that the Greek text uses a definite article before this individual's name, and this signals that he will be in a category like none other before him. This is not simply an evil person; this is *the* son of doom and destruction.

When we take all of these original word meanings into consideration, the *RIV* of Second Thessalonians 2:3 reads as follows:

> **In light of these things, I urge you to refuse to allow anyone to take advantage of you. You ought to know by now that this day cannot come until first a worldwide insurgency, rebellion, riot, and mutiny against God has developed in society. Once that occurs, the world will then be primed, prepared, and ready to embrace the Man of Lawlessness, the one who hates law and has rebellion running in his blood. This is the long-awaited and predicted Son of Doom and Destruction, the one who brings rot**

and ruin to everything he touches. When the time is just right, he will finally come out of hiding and go public!

Then in verse 4, Paul described the Antichrist as one "…who *opposeth* and exalteth himself above all that is called God, or that is worshipped; so that he as God sitteth in the temple of God, shewing [declaring] himself that he is God."

The word "opposeth" is translated from the Greek word *antikeimai*. It is a compound of *anti* and *keimai*. The word *anti* means *against*, and *keimai* means *to set* or *to lay in place*. When the two words are compounded, the new word depicts *an entrenched position against everything established*. The tense paints the picture of a *continual, unending, and perpetual resistance*, revealing that rebellion is *ingrained* in this individual. He is *antichrist* — from the prefix *anti* and the word *Christ*. The prefix *anti*, which means *against*, in itself alerts us that this evil person will have a deeply rooted rebellion ingrained in his disposition that sets him *against* Christ and *against* everything that Christ represents.

If you add the name *antichrist* to the Greek word *antikeimai* — the Greek word translated "opposeth" in Second Thessalonians 2:4 — it categorically tells us that the Antichrist will be *brazenly against* every previous godly way of thinking. He will lead a lawless world in an effort to bulldoze former dogmas and established codes of morality out of the way. His goal will be to construct a new world order — one that is utterly free of God's influence.

Furthermore, the Antichrist will be one who "exalteth" himself. The word "exalteth" is translated from the Greek word *huperaino* and means *highly exalted*. Thus, when the Antichrist finally appears on the world stage, he will quickly begin to exalt himself in the eyes of the world — to such an extent that he will even sit in the "temple" (v. 4).

The word "temple" is from the Greek word *naos*, the word used to depict to the innermost part of the temple in Jerusalem. It may also refer to the Holy of Holies in a future, rebuilt temple. Consequently, some scholars assert that a day will come when the Antichrist will enter a rebuilt temple in Jerusalem, go into the Holy of Holies, and decree himself to be God.

Paul wrote that the Antichrist will "shew" himself as God. The word "shew" is the Greek word *apodeiknumi*, which means to *vividly portray*, *to point out*, *to illustrate*, *to show off*, or *to make a vivid presentation*. In some way, the Antichrist will declare himself as God and will use all possible means to demonstrate his power to "shew" himself as God — including signs and lying wonders (*see* 2 Thessalonians 2:9).

**Taking all of these amazing Greek words into consideration
as they are used in Second Thessalonians 2:4,
we come to the *RIV* of this verse:**

Do you understand who I am talking about? I'm describing that person who will be so against God and everything connected with the worship of God that, if you can imagine it, he will even try to put himself on a pedestal above God Himself — sitting in God's rightful place in the temple and publicly proclaiming himself to be God!

WHAT IS STOPPING ALL OF THIS FROM HAPPENING RIGHT NOW?

Paul stated that the only reason Satan has not already brought this end-time evil leader on to the world stage is the active restraining force that has hitherto stopped this diabolical move. In Second Thessalonians 2:6, Paul wrote, "And now ye know what *withholdeth* that he might be revealed in his time." There is a force that "withholdeth" this personification of evil from being manifested.

This word "withholdeth" is a translation of the Greek word *katecho,* which is a compound of *kata* and *echo.* The word *kata* gives the ideas of *domination* or *suppression.* The word *echo* means *to hold* or *to embrace.* But when these two words are compounded into *katecho* — which in this verse is translated "withholdeth" — it means to *hold down* or *to suppress something.* It depicts a *restraining force* that puts forth its energy to *hold down* this evil and to *suppress* it from rising to a place of prominence.

So again, this means that the sole reason the Antichrist and his accompanying evil has not already been fully unleashed into the world is that there is *a restraining force holding back* the manifestation of this satanic agenda. Paul stated that this restraining force works to *stall,* *delay,* and *postpone* this end-time evil. The apostle also wrote that one day the restrainer will be removed — and in that moment, evil will be unleashed with full force into the world.

As we saw earlier, the word "revealed" comes from the Greek word *apokalupsis* and pictures *a veil that has been suddenly removed, exposing what was behind the veil that was concealed or hidden from view.* Thus, a day is coming at the conclusion of the age when the restraining force will be taken out of the way. When that removal occurs, this evil leader and the wickedness that accompanies him will make an entrance onto the world stage.

◆

**The sole reason the Antichrist and his accompanying evil
has not already been fully unleashed into the world
is that there is a restraining force holding back
the manifestation of this satanic agenda.**

◆

The Bible says the revealing of the Antichrist will happen in his "time," which is from the Greek word *kairos.* This emphatically tells us that there is a prophetic, appointed moment when the restraining force will be removed and the manifestation of the Antichrist will quickly occur. The veil that has concealed his identity will be removed, and he will step out from behind the curtain to be seen by all.

———◆———

There is a prophetic, appointed moment when the restraining force will be removed and the manifestation of the Antichrist will quickly occur. The veil that has concealed his identity will be removed, and he will step out from behind the curtain to be seen by all.

———◆———

In light of these remarkable Greek words in Second Thessalonians 2:6, the *RIV* of this verse reads as follows:

Now in light of everything I've told you before, you ought to be well aware by now that there is a supernatural force at work preventing the materialization of this person and the disclosure of his identity. This restraining force I'm referring to is so strong that it is currently putting on the brakes and holding back the unveiling of this wicked person, stalling and postponing his manifestation. But when the right moment comes, this evil one will no longer be withheld, and he will emerge onto the world scene! The screen that has been hiding his true identity and guarding him from world view will suddenly be pulled back and evaporate — and he will step out on center stage to let everyone know who he is.

Then Paul added, "For the mystery of iniquity doth already work: only he who now letteth will let, until he be taken out of the way" (2 Thessalonians 2:7).

What is the "mystery of iniquity?" The word "mystery" is the Greek word *musterion*. It communicates the idea of *a higher knowledge that is known only by a limited number of individuals* or *a knowledge that is not available to the general public but only to those who have been specially initiated and invested with insight*. It is *a plan, thought, or arrangement that is held in the hands of a few*. In this case, the word implies a secret plan or some type of secret arrangement known to spiritual powers but held so confidentially that they are able to execute the plan without anyone catching on to what they are doing.

Once again, the word "iniquity" comes from the Greek word *anomia* — depicting a people or a world that is *without law* or *lawless*. It pictures *people who possess no fixed moral standards* living in a *lawless world*, free from the "outdated" voice of the Bible.

The use of "iniquity" (*anomia*) in the same phrase as "mystery" (*musterion*) tells us that the current state of affairs in our time is the result of a secret plan set in motion long ago. Current society did not accidentally arrive at its present sad state of affairs. Its downward trend has been strategically orchestrated step by step, year by year, and century by century by a devious satanic plan designed to prepare the way for the man of lawlessness.

The word "already" in this verse affirms this is a plan that has been working for a long time. The word "work" is translated from the Greek word *energeo*. As used here, it describes a secret plan that has been supernaturally *energized* to keep things moving toward the fulfillment of its demonic agenda over the ages, like a force propelling something toward its conclusion.

Certainly it's true that believers of *every* generation have had to deal with issues of moral degradation and societal ills in the world around them. But in these last of the last days, it seems as if *all* restraints have been thrown off and society is galloping along on a collision course with disaster. And the closer we get to the end, the deeper this lost world will sink into deception and depravity.

—◆—

**Current society did not accidentally arrive
at its present sad state of affairs. Its downward trend
has been strategically orchestrated step by step, year by year,
and century by century by a devious satanic plan designed
to prepare the way for the Man of Lawlessness.**

—◆—

Rather than fear or run looking for a place to hide, we must press into Christ and clothe ourselves with the power of the Holy Spirit so we can make a mark for eternity in as many lives as possible before this current age ends. *The opportunity before us is remarkable and unprecedented.*

But we must also stay alert to the fact that we are living in the last minutes of the age when the devil is attempting to groom and modify society as a whole so that it will receive the man of lawlessness. The world is largely unaware of how it's being used to fulfill a satanic agenda. Regardless, a massive undertaking is being executed to lead the world into a state of epic lawlessness so it will more readily embrace this Satan-inspired individual. Everything is being primed and prepared at this very moment for that time.

In the midst of this profound process of a worldwide shift, we will witness things changing around us more and more. Evil spiritual forces will seek to set an entire spectrum of destructive fires, designed to consume as many lives as possible. But as Paul stated, until it is time for the Antichrist to be revealed, a *restraining force* will be present in the earth to stall the manifestation of this evil one.

Paul used the word "let" in Second Thessalonians 2:7 to describe this restraining force: "…Only he who now *letteth* will *let*, until he be taken out of the way." This old English word is translated from the Greek word *kathecho* — the same

Greek word translated "withholdeth" in verse 6 to picture the *restraining force* that is stalling and postponing this end-time evil leader and the unprecedented wickedness that will accompany him.

◆

**Rather than fear or run looking for a place to hide,
we must press into Christ and clothe ourselves with
the power of the Holy Spirit so we can make a mark for eternity
in as many lives as possible before this current age ends.
The opportunity before us is remarkable and unprecedented.**

◆

Paul stated that not only has the restrainer been restraining in the past, but also "will let" — in other words, *will be* a restraining force — in the future. That function will continue until this round of the end-time game reaches a conclusion. In fact, Paul wrote that the restrainer will keep restraining until the moment comes when that force will be "taken out of the way."

At that split moment in time, the restrainer will suddenly be removed. In that moment, evil forces that have long been suppressed will be abruptly energized, and the devil's wicked plans, purposes, and desires will break free of all restraint. (We will look at just what — or who — this "restrainer" is in the pages that follow.)

**As we combine the meaning
of all these original Greek words in Second Thessalonians 2:7,
the *RIV* of this verse reads as follows:**

**These events have been covertly in the making for a long time, but
the world doesn't realize that a secret plan is being executed right
under their own noses. The only thing that has kept this plan from**

already being consummated is the supernatural force that has been holding it all back until now. But one day this force will be removed from the picture — and when that happens, these events will quickly transpire. The removal of this restraining force will signal the moment when the Lawless One will finally make his grand appearance to the world....

THE ROLE OF FREE-FLOATING ETHICS IN THE DEVIL'S PLAN OF SEDUCTION

What I described in the previous section both biblically and prophetically pinpoints where the world is headed. But let's go back to Second Timothy 3:2 now. Paul wrote that "boasters" will play a role in this satanic end-time scheme.

Again, that word "boasters" is a translation of the Greek word *alazon*. As mentioned earlier, that word means a *braggart* or *one so committed to his own self-promotion and personal agenda that he is willing to exaggerate, overstate the facts, stretch the truth, embellish a story, and even lie if it will have a positive effect on his position or situation.* The "boasters" the Holy Spirit portrays will play a big role in how the devil will pull off all of this and bring end-time lawlessness and nonsense into the mainstream of society.

You see, as fixed ethics, or moral absolutes, are hurled away and society is shifted to a "floating ethics" mode, everything once believed to be morally correct begins to be erased. In its place, a "progressive mindset" is promoted that purports to be an upgraded way of thinking, yet in reality has disastrous consequences.

If you're skeptical about the prevalence of "floating ethics and morals" in modern society, simply ask the youth and young adults in your life what is being promoted in their schools and on university campuses. Ask college students about their classes. They will tell you that although tolerance and free thinking should be encouraged in universities, most professors are actually *in*tolerant and disdain those who stick with more traditional ways of thinking. Tolerance is usually only extended to those who embrace the new morality, with widespread intolerance of those who adhere to biblical morality and traditional Christian beliefs.

Unless your children or grandchildren are being home-schooled or educated in a Christian school, I think you already, by *experience*, know this to be the truth. Sadly, this state of "floating ethics" is even finding its way into mainstream churches. (I urge you to read my book *How To Keep Your Head on Straight in a World Gone Crazy* to understand how to avoid being seduced into the deception trying to invade the contemporary Church today.)

I will add one more point about "boasters" before we proceed further into Paul's list in Second Timothy 3 of a wandering end-time society. The only other place the word "boasters" — the Greek word *alazon* — is found in the New Testament is in Romans 1:30, where Paul described a lawless world. Romans 1:29-31 depicts a godless society as follows: "Being filled with all unrighteousness, fornication, wickedness, covetousness, maliciousness; full of envy, murder, debate, deceit, malignity; whisperers, backbiters, haters of God, despiteful, proud, *boasters*, inventors of evil things, disobedient to parents, without understanding, covenantbreakers, without natural affection, implacable, unmerciful."

In these verses, I italicized the word "boasters" for emphasis. In Romans 1, it is positioned right in the middle of a horrendous list of godless behaviors exhibited by a world that has thrown fixed moral absolutes to the wind.

This situation with "floating ethics" is so common that it doesn't even shock us anymore when politicians, for example, change their political platforms regarding their stance on moral issues or when major corporations change their policies to fit an ever-changing moral environment. Many applaud such a move as forward progress.

But, in truth, this constant changing of moral standards and the easy mod-ification of what people believe or stand for could be included in this word "boasters." The word "boasters" (*alazon*) includes all the "situational ethics" meanings we have discussed, including flip-flopping on issues of morality, drastically altering one's belief system, and vacillating on issues of right and wrong. All of these will be signs of "boasters" in the very last days of this age.

This is an unstable and unreliable path that floats on changing trends rather than on faith that is fixed in absolute truth. Those of us who stick with what we have always believed may be accused of being narrow-minded simply because we adhere to a fixed standard from which we will not budge. Consequently, some may harbor ill feelings about our strong stance and think us to be *antisocial, contrary, noncompliant, intolerant, narrow-minded, noncon-formist, inflexible, obstinate,* and *uncompromising.*

If you feel hostility from those who don't agree with your unwavering stance of faith and conviction, don't let it disturb you too deeply. It just goes with living in perilous times. Rest assured that the Holy Spirit will reinforce and equip you to become a lighthouse that attracts people who have been devastated by the destructive progressive thinking of this age. There are multi-tudes who are seeking answers that only the Word of God can provide about how to recover from the ravages of the age. As you continue to stand strong on God's immutable truth, you will be in a position to help those who come across your path.

'PROUD' — AN ATTITUDE OF SUPERIORITY AS A MARK OF A LAST-DAYS CULTURE

Paul went on to tell us that an anti-God, anti-Bible end-time society will also display a "we know better than you" attitude toward those who adhere to biblical truth as their standard. Does this sound anything like the attitudes of "progressives" who are attempting to erase the moral slate and reset a new moral agenda for the rest of the population?

This is why Paul next listed the word "proud" in his list of characteristics that will emerge in society at the end of the age. In Second Timothy 3:2, he wrote, "For men shall be lovers of their own selves, covetous, boasters, *proud....*"

The word "proud" is a translation of the Greek word *huperephanos* — which is a compound of the words *huper* and *phanos.* The word *huper* means *above* or depicts something that is *superior.* The word *phanos* means *to be manifested.* But when these two words are compounded, the new word portrays a person who sees himself as *above* the rest of the crowd. This represents *an arrogant, haughty, impudent, snooty, high-and-mighty, insolent attitude,* possessed by people who believe they are intellectually advantaged and therefore possess the right to set the agenda for everyone else.

What an accurate description of those who would like to force their liberal agenda on the rest of us! This Greek word *huperephanos* — translated in the *King James Version* as "proud" — is especially seen in the media, the political world, and the courts, in which many "snootily" vaunt themselves as the vanguards of society. These leaders see themselves as a more sophisticated set of people than the rest of us, touting themselves as the rightful agenda-setters for society, culture, and the world.

The visible roles of leadership that were once allocated to pastors and church leaders has been transferred to those in the mass media or to those who "have the ear" of the general public. Through legislation and laws that are enacted — often without our knowledge — this group forces its way forward to set the agenda for the rest of us. The role of pastors and church leaders — those who once set the moral tone for the nation — has become mocked and disdained, while new agenda-setters have tried vigorously to set aside spiritual leaders as irrelevant. At the same time, this "superior lot" arrogantly promote themselves as champions of enlightened thought and the new moral code for the world.

Of course, this is not true of all judges, politicians, and media personalities, so I don't want to sound like I am categorizing them all as such. But to a great and very disproportionate extent, those who have access to the airwaves are the ones who are trying to set the new agenda. Forgive me for being so blunt, but it seems that visibility in front of the world has gone to the heads of these liberal influencers. As a result, they are abusing their trusted positions to force their own liberal and progressive views and agendas on the rest of us. From their public platforms in the media and in Hollywood, their podiums in the courtrooms, and their lecterns of university classrooms, they haughtily mock, sneer, disdain, disparage, and scorn people they deem relics of the past who stay true to their biblical convictions.

These agenda-setters see anyone who holds fast to past moral codes and beliefs as a hindrance to the new world they want to create. And in truth, that is the case! We who refuse to budge from our Bible-based convictions are part of the restraining force Paul referred to in Second Thessalonians 2:6,7. As we hold to our stance of faith and shine the light of the Bible into a darkened world, we are forestalling the onslaught of evil that will eventually be released into society in full force.

But before we proceed to the next word that Paul listed in Second Timothy 3:2, let's see how all the words we have studied so far could be interpreted.

The *RIV* of Second Timothy 3:2
up to this point in the text reads as follows:

Men will be self-focused, self-centered, self-absorbed, self-consumed, and in love with themselves more than anyone else. As a result of this self-love, they will be driven to obtain more and more

and more. These boasters are so committed to their own agenda that they are willing to exaggerate, overstate the facts, stretch the truth, embellish a story, and even lie if it will get them the position, advantage, or goal they desire. They are arrogant, haughty, impudent, snooty, and insolent....

THE ROLE OF BLASPHEMY
IN THE LAST OF THE LAST DAYS

Paul continued to say, "For men shall be lovers of their own selves, covetous, boasters, proud, *blasphemers*...."

Each of Paul's points in this passage are built on subsequent points. So when he listed "blasphemy" next, we can conclude that it is connected to "boasters" and "proud," which he used to depict arrogant intellectuals who deem themselves a cut above the rest of society and believe they have the right to set the agenda for everyone else. Although blasphemy in general will be widespread, it seems Paul was implying that especially *this* group will become blasphemers.

The word "blasphemers" is translated from the Greek word *blasphemeo*, a form of the word *blasphemos*, which means *to slander, to accuse, to speak against*, or *to speak derogatory words for the purpose of injuring or harming another's reputation*. It signifies *profane, foul, unclean language*. It can refer to *blaspheming the divine*, but the broader meaning includes any type of *debasing, derogatory, insulting, nasty, shameful, ugly speech or behavior intended to humiliate someone*.

It must also be noted that the word *blasphemeo* was used in ancient literature to depict those who use *foul language*, including "curse words," as a regular part of their conversation. But it can depict blasphemous *behavior* in general — a point that is important, for not all blasphemy is *spoken*. Some demonstrations of this word are behavioral or in graphic form, yet they are nonetheless blasphemous.

When people hear the word "blasphemy," they generally think of something spoken that is blasphemous about God. Certainly this word can refer to this meaning. But overall, the word "blasphemy" used in Second Timothy 3:2 depicts people who will go unhinged in the closing days of the age in their use of *debasing, derogatory, insulting, nasty, shameful, ugly speech or behavior to humiliate others.* Because this word *blasphemeo* is used in its plural form, it signifies *widespread blasphemy* in the last of the last days.

This broader definition of the Greek word *blasphemeo*, translated "blasphemy," perfectly depicts what I recently viewed in political hearings on television. I was shocked at the blasphemous words and behaviors spoken by politicians — ugly words and repulsive behaviors broadcasted right onto TV screens, computers, and mobile devices to invade our private lives.

Has there ever been a time in our age when political parties and various warring ideologies have been more uncivil? *Shocking* is the only word I can think of to describe the embarrassing public behavior of politicians that displays such a sharp descent from respectful disagreement to an ugly mess of intolerance and mudslinging. To make it much worse, a widespread weaponizing of the media is being used to perpetuate this indecent assault. This is the type of *debasing, derogatory, insulting, nasty, shameful, ugly speech or behavior designed to humiliate* that is conveyed in the word "blasphemy" in Second Timothy 3:2.

Historically, profanity was considered blasphemous and punishable. I'm talking about language that is called a variety of names, such as cursing, swearing, cussing, and using expletives. But that has all changed in today's toxic environment.

An online website that is tasked to study political officials has tallied up how many times politicians publicly use obscene language. The statistics show that obscene words used by politicians publicly have hit an all-time high, up more than 100 percent in recent years, and that the use of profane expletives by politicians on their social-media platforms is off the charts.[2]

Let's not forget the biblical principle that whatever is on the head of a nation will eventually come on the nation (*see* Psalm 133). If those who are leaders of nations have mouths filled with expletives, why would it surprise us that profanity has come upon these nations to infiltrate nearly every sphere of life?

In fact, blasphemous language has become such a regular component of speech in our time that even taboo words — once considered vulgar and extremely offensive — have found their way into mainstream conversation. Historically such language was considered to be impolite and rude. But we have devolved so terribly, and the use of foul language is so prevalent on television, that computer programs are now available to install on your television to "bleep" the profanity before it is broadcast into our homes and our ears. Someone who uses this "bleeping" program testified that when the "bleep" is activated on his television set, there are sometimes so many words "bleeped" that he cannot make sense of the conversation he is hearing!

Neurologists and psychologists who study patients with Alzheimer's and degenerative dementia have noted that when the mind is in a state of degeneration, despite the loss of many language skills, patients still often retain the ability to swear and use profanity. That means profanity and swearing can thrive in a degenerating mind.

Another scientific study revealed that the use of profanity generally produces profane behaviors. This tells us that when the bar is lowered regarding

---

[2] "Potty-Mouthed Politicians," November 30, 2018, GovtPredict.com, https://www.govpredict.com/blog/potty-mouthed -politicians/.

what comes out of the mouth, the bar is also lowered concerning people's behavior or other actions. It is also interesting to note that there is scientifically proven correlation between profanity and dishonesty.

Some may argue that governmental censors prohibit obscene, indecent, or profane language. But so much of what was once considered obscene, indecent, or profane is no longer included in the profanity category. The bar has been lowered to such an extent that what was once shocking to people no longer produces the same shock effect because they have become desensitized. Society has descended into such a moral abyss that blasphemous language in private life and in public forums goes nearly unnoticed.

I feel no judgment, but it saddens me to know that people have become so uncultured that they think this is acceptable. As my wife and I dine out for an evening together and we hear foul language being spoken at a nearby table, it grieves us. When I await a flight at the airport, I am frequently stunned by foul language used by people sitting near us. I wonder, *How can anyone think it is normal to subject everyone around them to this language?* But this verbal sewage is what the Holy Spirit prophesied would become commonplace at the end of the age in Second Timothy 3:2.

Most reading this book would agree that blasphemous language is *excessive* in modern movies and in television programs. But how about the foul language that has found a home in the mouths of news anchors and news commentators who employ rude, crude words, even though it is unnecessary and insults the ears of their viewers and listeners? This epidemic of profanity is in comedy, satire, talk shows, news, movies, literature, and musical lyrics.

But the problem is not limited to blasphemous language; it extends to blasphemous behaviors. Without making a long list of immoral behaviors, let me simply state that what was once immoral — that is, behaviors and lifestyles not condoned by the Bible — is now paraded before us on television, in Hollywood, in the press, and in the courts. What God judged Sodom and Gomorrah for is now brazenly applauded and celebrated by eminent professors, celebrities, educators, media, and the courts and is being propagandized to a younger generation. This falls into the category of "blasphemers."

Not long ago I saw a news program about transvestites who are now invited to read fun stories to children in public libraries. Men dressed as women, with outrageous outfits, hairstyles, cosmetics, and false breasts were shown seated in front of children — reading stories to and entertaining the young impressionable listeners. The liberal plan is to desensitize children to the shocking image in front of them by providing a fun time with a man dressed as a woman. The message conveyed to the children by the experience is clear: There is nothing wrong with a man wanting to be a woman.

I feel compassion for anyone who is trapped in deception, and I believe we have the message to bring people freedom. So please don't misread me as being judgmental. But we need to realize that this is an assault against impressionable minds. Such behavior was considered blasphemous not so long ago — a perverse, deviant behavior that was even viewed as a psychological illness by many in the medical profession. But now the taboo has been eliminated, and hell is parading its confused and twisted behaviors with no shame. Taking this even further is the assault on gender and the blasphemous belief that gender is not a sacred gift, but rather something that can be changed by elective surgery. (For more on this, read pages 22-36 in *How To Keep Your Head on Straight in a World Gone Crazy*.)

But before I conclude this point, please let me take this one step further. Because the word "blasphemy" points to a culture of disrespect, I want to remind you that in a time not so long ago, when we were younger, our parents taught us to speak respectfully to elders. We were taught to say "yes, sir" or "yes, ma'am" when addressing elders or those who were in authority. But society has so thoroughly tossed respectful speech to the wind that even basic elements of respect in language are disappearing from the vocabulary of children. Society claims to be sophisticated and progressive, but evidence shows that language is being debased and emptied of long-valued terms of courtesy, manners, and basic respect. This is so pandemic that when a child says "yes, sir" or "yes, ma'am," it stands out because manners and verbal respect are so out of sync with the majority of younger people today.

THE MOUTH IS THE GREAT REVEALER

But in Second Timothy 3:2, the Holy Spirit clearly warned us that increased "blasphemy" would evolve in a last-days society — a prophecy regarding an end-time culture of dishonor and disrespect. But this issue of blasphemy does not just involve a person's mouth or actions. Blasphemous behaviors and language are *symptoms* of a deeper problem. In Matthew 12:34, Jesus said, "...Out of the abundance of the *heart* the mouth speaketh."

This means the *mouth* is the *great revealer*. If a person's mouth is filled with foul language, one can surmise what lies at that person's core. Jesus clearly taught that the *mouth* is the *outlet* for what is inside a person.

You see, there simply is no spiritual "law of gravity" powerful enough to permanently hold down and confine what is at the core of a person's being. What is on the inside eventually comes out. And what lies at the core of an individual will ultimately come out of his mouth because *the mouth is the great revealer of what is at a person's core.*

So the problem with blasphemous language is deeper than bad language itself. As the last days progress and society becomes more spiritually darkened, the mouth will pour forth the spiritual darkness that lies within.

Language is spiritual because it flows from a person's inner being. Therefore, considering the spiritual nature of language and how it reveals the contents at the core of a person or of a society, we can safely predict an inevitable outcome as the heart of society becomes darker and the conclusion of the age draws near. It is a certainty that *debasing, derogatory, insulting, nasty, shameful,* and *ugly* speech will become more and more pervasive as a revealer of what is transpiring throughout society from the inside out.

There simply is no spiritual "law of gravity" powerful enough to permanently hold down and confine what is at the core of a person's being. What lies at the core of an individual will ultimately come out of his mouth because *the mouth is the greater revealer of what is at a person's core.*

The use of this kind of language was once considered inappropriate, but today it is heard regularly coming out of people's mouths. This should be no surprise, for the Holy Spirit prophesied that blasphemy would become commonplace as we approached the end of the age.

Given the state of this last-days society, I offer this counsel to you if you are serious about your spiritual life: Be very careful about what you allow into your eyes and ears. Remember that Lot was negatively affected by "seeing and hearing" blasphemous activities in Sodom (*see* 2 Peter 2:8).

Even current statistics prove that if a person watches enough filth on television, his sensitivity to it will become numbed. If a person watches enough pornography, in time that person will lose his sensitivity to the wrongness of this behavior and become *numb* to it. What we watch and hear determines what we eventually become.

Lot watched and heard so much wickedness in the activities that transpired around him on a regular basis that he became numb and hardened to the evil of it. In fact, he became so calloused in his heart to the wrong he continually witnessed that he was able to live in the midst of it for an extended period of time. The Bible says that by persistently hearing and seeing wrong images, he eventually "*vexed* his righteous soul."

This word "vexed" is a translation of the Greek word *basanidzo*, which is the Greek word for *torture*. The word *basanidzo* tells us that at least at first — before Lot became numbed to his environment — seeing and hearing those sinful activities internally tore him to pieces. By willfully living in that dark and sinful environment, where he should not have lived, and by accommodating what he knew to be wrong, Lot subjected his mind and soul to unrelenting torment — eventually reaching the point of inner *torture*.

I remember hearing the old rhyme when I was a child that said, "Oh, be careful, little eyes, what you see.… Oh, be careful, little ears, what you hear.… Oh, be careful, little tongue, what you say.… Oh, be careful, little hands, what you do.… Oh, be careful, little feet, where you go.…" In this last-days society, people have become irresponsible about what they look at, listen to, say, touch, and do.

But let's take this rhyme to heart and determine to use caution so that we do not *also* become victims to the spirit of the age. Blasphemous words and behaviors are *not* acceptable in God's sight and should not be practiced by us. Words and behaviors have consequences, so let's not minimize this behavior. Let's make sure our eyes, ears, hands, and feet are looking at, listening to, touching, and headed in places that God's Spirit would condone!

**If we add the Greek word *blasphemos*
to the previous words listed in Second Timothy 3:2,
the *RIV* of this verse would read as follows:**

**Men will be self-focused, self-centered, self-absorbed, self-consumed,
and in love with themselves more than anyone else. As a result of this**

self-love, they will be driven to obtain more and more and more. These boasters are so committed to their own agenda that they are willing to exaggerate, overstate the facts, stretch the truth, embellish a story, and even lie if it will get them the position, advantage, or goal they desire. They are arrogant, haughty, impudent, snooty, and insolent. They disdain, mock, slander, and speak ill of anyone who stands in the way of their ideology and freely use foul language....

DISOBEDIENT TO PARENTS —
DISRESPECT FOR AUTHORITY
IN THE LAST OF THE LAST DAYS

But Paul continued in Second Timothy 3:2 to give us the next characteristic that will be evident in a last-days generation gone astray. He wrote, "For men shall be lovers of their own selves, covetous, boasters, proud, blasphemers, *disobedient to parents....*" In a last-days society where situational ethics reign, fixed moral absolutes are thrown to the wind, and foul language and blasphemous behaviors become commonplace, there will also emerge an epidemic of children who are "disobedient to parents."

The word "disobedient" is a translation of the Greek word *apeithes*, which is formed from the verb *peitho*, a word which means *to persuade* or *to convince*. But when an *a* is attached to the front of *peitho*, it is transformed into *apeithos*. That little *a* at the front of the word has a canceling effect. Rather than being persuadable or convincible, it means *unpersuadable, uncontrollable,* or *inconvincible*. It means *no longer able to persuade, control, lead, or exercise authority over*. It depicts *a loss of control* or *a lack of ability to persuade, to lead, or to influence*. The word "parents" is the plural form of the Greek word *goneus*, a word that means *a begetter* or *a parent*, and it is used to picture *biological parents* and *those who are also entrusted with the responsibilities of raising a child to adulthood*.

The phrase "disobedient to parents" prophetically forecasts an unusual period at the end of the last days when children — whose parents have been given the God-given responsibility to raise them to adulthood — will become *unpersuadable, uncontrollable, inconvincible,* or *unable to be led*. The Holy Spirit says parenthood will come under assault as parents begin to feel the loss of ability *to persuade, control, lead,* or *exercise authority over* their own children.

This means a day is coming — and in large part, is already here — when children will no longer submit to or follow the leadership of their parents. They will deny their parents' right to lead them, often disrespectfully. They will even assert their own right to make decisions for themselves without parental influence or intervention — including decisions that in many cases will be life-altering or detrimental to their long-term well-being.

In other words, Paul was saying that a day would come when children in many homes would no longer submit to or follow the orders and leadership of their father and mother. Certainly there are cases when parents have lost their parental rights as a result of their own wrong lifestyle choices. This type of situation may certainly increase in the last days due to a rise in selfish, self-focused living. But the Holy Spirit is speaking of a more all-encompassing phenomenon that will occur in homes throughout society in the last of the last days.

The Bible prophesies in this verse that parental authority in the home will be compromised at the end of the age. Regardless of why it will occur, many parents will find themselves attempting to *negotiate* with their children rather than leading them as God expects them to do.

In the beginning of this book, we saw that the foremost characteristic of a last-days generation will be "lovers of their own selves." I stated that when society is self-focused and self-absorbed, people become self-centered and selfish. This includes children who have been indoctrinated in school and by liberal propaganda that they are in charge of their own lives and destinies, have their own rights, and should not allow their parents to enforce rules or tenets of faith on them that they don't find agreeable.

Parental authority in the home will be compromised at the end of the age. Regardless of why it will occur, many parents will find themselves attempting to *negotiate* with their children rather than leading them as God expects them to do.

If you speak to any family counselor, he or she will affirm that the problem of eroding parental influence is widespread, even in Christian homes. And if this is true in Christian homes, how much more in a lost world that has no biblical foundation? In this verse, the Holy Spirit forewarns us: This issue of lost parental influence *will* be on the rise as we come closer to the very last of the last days.

Already today some parents are hesitant to discipline their own children, lest the children press charges against them and get them arrested for child abuse. And certainly many children have been rightfully protected in cases of real abuse. But the fact is, laws are being enacted that put children in a superior position over parents in the eyes of the legal system. This weakens the leadership of parents to teach, discipline, and lead their own children. Already many children have used these laws to sue their parents. Just as Paul prophesied, the day has come when parents are under pressure to surrender their God-given parental authority to lead and influence their own children.

Law states that children are entitled to a safe environment, good nutrition, health care, and education. Although parents have the right to raise their children as they see fit, they are responsible for their safety. If the state does not agree with the way the parents are carrying out that responsibility to keep the child safe, the child can be forcibly removed from the home and the parent can legally lose parental rights. This is right and good — *until* the situation is interpreted by legal authorities who are virulently progressive and liberal in their view. Take, for instance, the cases where children sued their parents for trying to force their faith upon them, and the court stood by the children.

I wish the following story was an exception, but this kind of situation is occurring with greater regularity. I personally know parents who had their daughter removed from their home for several years because a schoolteacher was alarmed by the respectful attitude the child demonstrated toward everyone in authority.

Their daughter's respectful attitude to anyone in authority was so vastly different compared to the attitudes of other children that the teacher surmised that the daughter was being abused by her parents at home! The teacher reasoned that the only explanation for that level of respect toward authority figures *had* to be due to fear.

A complaint was privately filed with child services of alleged child abuse — and as a result, godly parents lost their daughter *because she was taught to be respectful*! She was actually removed from the home and the parents' rights were forfeited until the courts were convinced the allegations about them were false. For the entire legal process that took more than two years, these parents had *no* access to their daughter.

It is good to help children who are abused, but this is not what the Holy Spirit was referring to in Second Timothy 3:2. This situation of children turning away from parents' leadership is so painfully real already that if you interview school teachers who have taught in public school for decades, they frequently will testify that they have witnessed the trend — a gradual transfer of parental authority to the children themselves.

It may seem bizarre to think that children will no longer be required to follow their parents' leadership, but this is just another development that stems from the *self-love* we studied at the beginning of Second Timothy 3:2. Paul vividly stated that society runs amuck in every sphere when it places *self* and *love for self* higher than anything or anyone else.

YOU CAN RECOVER YOUR GOD-ASSIGNED POSITION AS A PARENT

I want to tell you from Scripture that you absolutely have authority in the lives of your children. You have a God-given parental *responsibility* to raise them in the way they should go — and the Bible says that when you do it, they will not depart from it when they get older (*see* Proverbs 22:6). Your God-ordained authority in your home is not just a *right*; it is your God-given duty and responsibility. And you must exercise that authority according to biblical instruction — not only for the sake of your children, but also for the sake of generations to come.

◆

Your God-ordained authority in your home is not just a *right*; it is your God-given duty and responsibility. And you must exercise that authority according to biblical instruction — not only for the sake of your children, but also for the sake of generations to come.

◆

I'm amazed at the number of parents who feel they have no voice in their children's lives — even parents who have been saved for a long time. Many parents wrongly believe they have no right to tell their children what to do or what to believe! For example, they are very hesitant and reserved about telling their children they must go to church. These parents believe that to demand church attendance would be infringing upon their children's free will and individual rights. They hold to the notion that everyone should be able to make his own decisions — even a child, who is too young to make important life decisions by himself.

But a child *needs* training and guidance from his parents — and, believe it or not, he desperately craves it!

As a pastor and minister, I've actually said to some of the parents I've counseled over the years, "Do you give your child the freedom to choose whether or not he goes to school every day? No, you don't. You probably say, 'Get out of bed, brush your teeth, get dressed, and put on your shoes. You're going to school.' Why? Because you believe in school and in education. Therefore, you make school attendance a requirement." Then I've had to gently explain to these parents that since it would be irresponsible for them as parents to let their children miss school — *why would they let their children think it's acceptable to skip church*?

But in the last of the last days, the Holy Spirit says parental authority will come under assault and many children will become disobedient and disrespectful to parents. And often that attitude might be attributed to parents' abdication of their authoritative roles in the lives of their children.

But none of this has to be true concerning you and your family!

If you'll recognize the schemes and methods of the enemy — and steer yourself and your family clear of those things that are designed to steal, kill, and destroy (*see* John 10:10) — your family can be whole, healthy, and happy even in these last days. The enemy will try to oppress and take over the minds of people in this generation until they are given over to all kinds of extreme self-love, covetousness, boasting, pride, blasphemy, and disobedience. But those who make God's Word their priority and the Lord their refuge will enjoy peace, joy, strength, abundant life, and victory!

If your family has fallen victim to these perilous times — if your home is out of order or if your children no longer respectfully listen to what you say — you need a breakthrough and a drastic change. I can assure you from the Word of God that to reassume your position as the leader in your home and regain your children's obedience and respect *is* possible. You can turn things around in your home and family.

**If you'll recognize the schemes and methods of the enemy —
and steer yourself and your family clear of those things
that are designed to steal, kill, and destroy —
your family can be whole, healthy, and happy
even in these last days.**

First, ask God to forgive you if you have failed to assume or maintain your place of authority in your home. Then determine to consistently act on what God says in His Word pertaining to His divine order in the family — *and do it in a spirit of love.* It's possible to maintain a solid upper hand in your home while treating your children with tenderness and dignity. It's amazing how they will in time emulate your behavior and begin themselves to show honor where honor is due — to you as their parent and to your parental authority over them in the home.

This characteristic of "disobedient to parents" is widespread in the world today. Everywhere we travel in the world, we see children speaking disrespectfully to their parents and disregarding their parents' authority. Many assert that they don't want their "rights" violated by parents telling them what to do — and in certain cases, as mentioned earlier, the court system has even stood by children's rights to sue their parents. As I've stated, this has put the children in a superior position and weakened parents' ability to teach, to discipline, and to lead and guide their own children and their households.

Combining all the words we have studied so far, the *RIV* of Second Timothy 3:2 reads as follows:

Men will be self-focused, self-centered, self-absorbed, self-consumed, and in love with themselves more than anyone else. As a result of this self-love, they will be driven to obtain more and more and more. These boasters are so committed to their own agenda that they are willing to exaggerate, overstate the facts, stretch the truth, embellish a story, and even lie if it will get them the position, advantage, or goal they desire. They are arrogant, haughty, impudent, snooty, and insolent. They disdain, mock, slander, and speak ill of anyone who stands in the way of their ideology and freely use foul language. In this climate, parents will no longer be able to persuade, control, lead, or exercise authority over their own children....

These characteristics we've studied are all blaring prophetic indicators that the very last of the last days are upon us. Based on Scripture and the Greek word meanings we have studied thus far, take a moment to stop and consider: Is it not clear that the marks of a last-days society are on clear display in the world around you?

But just because this is what will happen in the very end of this age, that doesn't mean it must happen to you and me. We are in the world, but we are not *of* this lost world's system (*see* John 17:15,16). Since the Holy Spirit warned us of these things in advance, we must take heed to His prophetic words and take action to protect our families and homes from the taint and effects of these end-time conditions.

Instead of shrinking in fear at what is happening in the culture around us, this can be our greatest hour. We can live as overcomers if we will keep ourselves pure in God's love, maintain the moral code of God in our hearts and homes, watch over our mouths, diligently teach the Word to our children, and shine the light of Jesus into the darkness that has flooded nearly every corner of society. We can live above the evil that is besetting the world at the end of this age. People are looking for solutions to their deeply embedded moral dilemmas, and *we* have the answers they need. We must walk in the light and *be* the light others so desperately need to see.

◆

**Instead of shrinking in fear at what is happening
in the culture around us,
this can be our greatest hour.**

◆

CHAPTER 4

LAST-DAYS SURVIVAL GUIDE ACTION STEPS

TO PROTECT YOUR HEART, EYES, EARS, AND FAMILY

1. Be careful not to allow "floating ethics" into your life.

We've discussed what the Bible says about the widespread tendency in the last days to hurl away fixed ethics, or moral absolutes, and move to a "floating ethic" mode that is easily adapted as one deems it necessary. So I want you to ask yourself these questions and prepare yourself to receive God's answers:

- *Am I sticking with the Word of God and refusing to go the "floating ethics" way of the world in every arena of life, regardless of the consequences?*

Doing so may put you on a collision course with people you know who have gone astray or with a culture in decline. But God calls on you to be unmoving in your commitment to biblical truth. So ask yourself:

- *Am I staying rooted in the Bible?*

- *Or have I allowed myself to "float" regarding certain basic principles of the Bible that should be fixed forever in my heart and mind?*

Because the spirit of this age is so seductively leading people off track, I urge you to intentionally ask the Holy Spirit to awaken you to any area in which you have allowed your morals and beliefs to go "afloat" in any measure. If He begins to reveal what you need to see, commit yourself to doing whatever is necessary to get firmly anchored again in the truth of God's Word.

2. Be careful not to be duped by a deceived world in these last days.

Since the Bible says there will be a "falling away" at the end of the age and we are living in those times, we can know that we will see this degenerating process displayed all around us. It is this generation that is witnessing the effects of seducing spirits attempting to cause society to disconnect from most moral standards once held to be the common rule and view of society.

For this reason, it is wise for each of us to take time to examine our thinking and make sure we are sticking with the never-changing Word of God. We are the guardians of our own minds, so it is our responsibility to ensure that we are not being duped with the rest of the world as it is being modified to think in ways that God calls lawless. We must not allow the spirit of the age to deceive us, along with so many others, to think the Bible is an outdated relic of the past with no relevance to the modern world.

So set aside time to really think through what you believe. Ask yourself:

- *Is there any stance I have taken on a subject that may not agree with Scripture?*

- *Have any thoughts begun to creep in that cause me to wonder if the Bible is out of date or if I should perhaps be more "progressive" in the way I view certain subjects?*

The Word of God is sharper than any two-edged sword (*see* Hebrews 4:12). If you use it correctly, humbly setting yourself in agreement with it and allowing it to work in you, it will keep every hint of deception out of your life as it spiritually sharpens you.

3. Be careful not to be contaminated by the spirit of this age.

Those who live without a biblical foundation have chosen an unstable and unreliable path that floats on trends rather than on faith that is fixed in absolute truth. But those of us who stick with the Bible have a solid foundation.

As you take time to evaluate your spiritual walk, ask yourself:

- *Am I adhering to the fixed standard of God's Word in every area of my life?*

- *Have I made a rock-solid commitment to that standard — one that I will never budge from?*

If your answer is *yes* to those questions, prepare yourself for the possibility of being misunderstood in this life. The world may accuse you of being *antisocial, contrary, noncompliant, intolerant, narrow-minded, nonconformist, inflexible, obstinate,* and *uncompromising.* Regardless, stick with your commitment. *Refuse* to be contaminated by the spirit of the age.

Also ask yourself:

- *How do I respond when I feel hostility from those who don't agree with my unwavering stance of faith and conviction? Do I let it disturb me too deeply?*

Be careful not to be affected by the spirit of the age. Dig your heels into the bedrock of truth, and the Holy Spirit will reinforce you with the strength you need to endure victoriously to the end.

There is often a price for sticking with the truth. Ask yourself:

- *Am I willing to pay whatever price is needed to hold fast to the truth?*

- *Or have I been tempted to budge a little on the truth to protect myself?*

As the days proceed, this question will become more and more urgent and pertinent to the times, so it's good for us to examine ourselves on this question now.

4. Be careful about what you allow in through your ears.

In this chapter, I noted that scientific studies reveal that the use of profanity produces profane behaviors. Society today is inundated by foul language. Unfortunately, people hear so much of it that what was once shocking no longer has the same shock effect. Whether we realize it or not, we have become desensitized.

Evaluate yourself honestly:

- *What do I do when I hear foul language?*

- *Do I diminish its significance and pass it off, almost as unnoticed? Or does it grieve me to hear offensive words and nasty speech that should not be tolerated?*

- *Am I able to sit through foul language in a movie or television program without being deeply disturbed by it? Or do I get up and leave or change the channel to avoid letting that filth into my ears?*

Your ears are so important that even faith comes to you through your ear gates (*see* Romans 10:17). What you allow yourself to listen to determines what you think, what you believe, and what you accommodate in your life. So make a practice of asking yourself:

- *Is God pleased with what I am allowing in through my ears?*

Especially in these last days when verbal sewage abounds, be careful to ensure that you can always answer that question with a strong affirmative!

5. Be careful what you allow in through your eyes.

As we discussed in this chapter, Lot saw so much wickedness that transpired around him on a regular basis that he became numb and hardened to the evil that his eyes continually beheld. In fact, he became so calloused in his heart that he was able to live in the midst of it for an extended period of time. But the Bible says that by persistently hearing and seeing wrong images, he eventually *vexed* his righteous soul (*see* 2 Peter 2:7).

This word "vexed" is a translation of the Greek word *basanidzo*, which is the Greek word for *torture*. By constantly seeing sin all around him — and accommodating what he knew to be wrong — Lot subjected his mind and soul to unrelenting torment, which eventually reached the point of inner *torture*.

Especially in these last days, you must be careful what you allow in through your eyes. The devil wants to wage warfare against you — and if you allow evil images into your head through your eyes, you will open the gates for the enemy to attack you in your mind. What you look at has consequences, so be careful about what you allow in through your eyes.

As part of your self-evaluation, take some time to look through your entertainment archives and files. Ask yourself:

- *What do the films and the TV programs I've been watching say about my commitment to God and His Word?*

You are the guardian of your eyes, so be honest with yourself about what you are allowing to flood into your mind through your eyes.

6. Be careful to spiritually lead your family and children.

The Bible clearly forecasts that the home will come under assault in the last days. It even forecasts an unusual period when children will become *unpersuadable, uncontrollable, inconvincible,* or *unable to be led.* Parents will feel the loss of ability *to persuade, control, lead, or exercise authority over* their own children. But that doesn't have to be true of you!

Since we know a day is coming when children will deny their parents' right to lead them and will even assert their rights to make decisions for themselves without parental influence or intervention, we must take steps now to safeguard our homes to make sure this does not affect us.

The Bible categorically tells us that an assault on the home will occur in the last days. But if you will listen to the Holy Spirit, He'll steer you and your family clear of those things that are designed to steal, kill, and destroy so you and your loved ones can be whole, healthy, and happy in this critical hour. As you make God's Word your priority and the Lord your refuge, you and your family will be safeguarded, even in the midst of these tumultuous times.

Have you already experienced hardships in your family? If so, first seek God for forgiveness in any area that you have failed Him along the way. Then open your heart to receive the empowerment of the Holy Spirit to begin implementing His plan of restoration for your family.

In this area, as in the other areas mentioned earlier, honest self-evaluation is a crucial step in discovering God's ways to move forward. It may be painful, but it would be wise and healthy for you — and for your spouse, if you are married — to answer these questions to see how well you are providing spiritual leadership for your home.

- *How often do I read the Bible to my children or with my family?*

- *How often do I pray with my family?*

- *How often do I take time to help family members think through difficult subjects and see what the Scriptures say on important topics?*

One thing is an inescapable certainty — you must be careful to take your position as a leader to lead your family spiritually in these last days!

7. Be careful not to give way to a spirit of fear.

As noted above, shrinking in fear in the face of all that is happening in the culture around you is not the correct response. Instead of running for cover, you need to realize that this may be your greatest hour to help people around you who are in need.

As a part of a healthy self-examination, ask yourself:

- *Am I being proactive in sharing God's truth and light, or am I afraid to step out because of possible retribution?*

- *Do I find myself cowering in fear from what is happening in the world, or am I taking the posture that I can shine light into the darkness to help others find truth and freedom?*

- *What am I doing to help others? How am I becoming an instrument that brings healing and restoration to those who have been hurt by our times?*

Wringing your hands and giving in to fear helps no one. This is your opportunity to shine the light of Jesus into the darkness that has beset so many you meet every day in life. People are looking for solutions to their deeply embedded moral dilemmas, and *you* have the answers they need.

Especially in these last days, you must be careful not to give in to the fear of man. Instead, determine to seize every opportunity to wisely and lovingly speak truth to those who so desperately need your voice!

5

THE DARK CONNECTION BETWEEN 'UNTHANKFUL' AND 'UNHOLY'

In Second Timothy 3:2, Paul continued to expound on his prophetic insights regarding what will transpire in society at the end of the last days. He wrote, "For men shall be lovers of their own selves, covetous, boasters, proud, blasphemers, disobedient to parents...." These are the six words or phrases in this verse that we have covered so far. But there are two more words in the verse we have not studied. The rest of verse 2 says, "For men shall be lovers of their own selves, covetous, boasters, proud, blasphemers, disobedient to parents, *unthankful, unholy.*"

Before we proceed to discuss what the word "unthankful" means, we need to see what "thankful" means in the original Greek language of the New Testament. The Greek word translated "thankful" that is primarily used throughout the New Testament is *charistos.* The word *charistos* is a derivative of the word *charis*, which is the New Testament word for *grace.* However, when the word *charis* is transformed into *charistos*, it more fully expresses the idea of one whose heart is *thankful, grateful,* or *appreciative* for various reasons.

The Greek word *charistos* depicts *an inward awareness of having been fortunate or well-treated.* Thus, the word "thankful" — translated from *charistos* — projects the deep inward feeling of one who is *thankful, grateful,* or *appreciative* for what one has received or how one has been treated by others.

Let's look at those three words *thankful, grateful,* and *appreciative* for a moment. The word *thankful* is concerned with a person's attitude toward his good fortune rather than his feelings toward anyone responsible for it. It suggests that someone is relieved or pleased about a situation or a turn of events. Someone who is *grateful* realizes that someone else has helped him or treated him kindly, and he has warm feelings toward that person. Thus, the word *grateful* suggests more of an impulse to thank someone than *thankful* does. The word *appreciative* shows that a person recognizes the merits or appeal of something and expresses his or her recognition of it.

Thus, all of these — *thankfulness, gratitude,* and *appreciation* — are the expressions of a person who is *thankful* that he has experienced blessings in some form, is *grateful* toward the person or people who treated him kindly, and wants to express how *appreciative* he is for the kindness shown. All of this is included in the word "thankful," which is translated from the Greek word *charistos.*

UNTHANKFULNESS — WHEN THANKFULNESS IS CANCELED

But now let's look at what the Holy Spirit is referring to when He says society at large will become "unthankful" in the last days. The word "unthankful" is the Greek word *acharistos,* which is the word *charistos* with an *a* affixed to the front of it. In Greek, that little prefix *a* has a canceling effect. Although a person was once thankful, something has occurred and his thankfulness has been canceled. A person who was *thankful* has become *unthankful.* The meaning of *charistos* — the Greek word translated "thankful" — is radically altered when that little *a* is attached to the front of it. That little *a* literally changes its meaning from *thankful* to *unthankful*.

In other words, the use of the Greek word *acharistos* alerts us that although a thankful attitude previously prevailed, for some reason now the same person has *lost* his thankful, grateful, and appreciative attitude and is now *unthankful*. Thoughts of *unthankfulness, ingratitude,* and *unappreciativeness* now fill his heart and mind. This person is *not* thankful for the good he has experienced or for the blessing he has received. He is *not* grateful toward the person or people who have treated him kindly. He has become *unthankful*, filled with *ingratitude,* and *unappreciative* of what others have done for him. In other words, the Greek word *acharistos* pictures *an ingrate.*

The word "unthankful" is profoundly important. It is imperative that we understand what Paul was prophesying concerning a last-days age in which people will become so *unthankful, ungrateful,* and *unappreciative* that they feel *entitled* to everything.

A SOCIETY WHERE 'EVERYONE OWES ME'

When a person feels entitled to everything, he loses his thankfulness for nearly everything. Why should a person be thankful when he feels he is entitled to anything he is ever given? This sense of entitlement is destructive to individuals, and it leads society as a whole into a state of *unthankfulness* — exactly what the Holy Spirt prophesied would emerge in society at the end of the age.

Today society is filled with people who are ruled by a sense of entitlement. One writer correctly stated that such individuals have "an unrealistic, unmerited, or inappropriate expectation of favorable living conditions and favorable treatment at the hands of others."[3] The following quote is a brilliant statement about those who fit that description, listing the signs that indicate a person is ruled by a sense of entitlement. For example:

> "…These individuals will make infeasible demands of others around them, including relatives, friends, colleagues, lovers, etc. That's the first sign.

> "…When someone's disposition consistently changes when they fail to get their way, this is a clear indicator of entitlement. People who suffer from a sense of entitlement also tend to see the people around them as competition and struggle to compromise or negotiate on mutually beneficial agreements.

> "…Ultimately, the individual with a sense of entitlement takes, but they rarely give. They prioritize themselves over others at virtually all times and fancy themselves as superior to others.

> "…A sense of entitlement is one of the defining traits of a *narcissist*…."[4]

It is important to note the use of the word "narcissism" in this context. There are key signs to indicate that a person is narcissistic. In fact, one psychotherapist and author has identified what she calls the "seven deadly sins" of narcissism. They are as follows:

1. **Shamelessness:** Shame speaks of "the misery of a pervasive personal flaw." In narcissists, shame is so intolerable that the means have been developed not to experience it at all. They may come across as indifferent and amoral until a minor incident or social slight unmasks what they really are — extremely shame-sensitive without the ability to process shame in healthy ways.[5]

---

[3] Robert Porter, "*The Psychology Behind Sense of Entitlement*," March 11, 2020, betterhelp.com, https://www.betterhelp.com/advice/personality-disorders/the-psychology-behind-sense-of-entitlement/.
[4] Ibid.
[5] Sandy Hotchkiss, LCSW, *Why Is It Always About You?: The Seven Deadly Sins of Narcissism* (New York: FreePress, 2002), pp. 4-6.

2. **Magical Thinking:** Narcissists often create an alternate, romanticized reality they can manipulate and control in which they play an idealized role, using distortion and illusion known as magical thinking. A more hurtful way they can distort reality is to employ *projection* — a process by which they transfer to someone else whatever evokes shameful feelings in themselves.[6]

3. **Arrogance:** For a narcissist "…if someone else's stock goes up, theirs automatically goes down. Conversely, if they are feeling deflated, they can reinflate themselves by diminishing, debasing, or degrading someone else. This is the reason narcissists are often judgmental, perfectionistic, and power-hungry."[7]

4. **Envy:** A narcissist may try to use contempt, often unconsciously, to minimize a person's achievements, often presenting a laundry list of that person's flaws so the narcissist is restored to a superior position.[8]

5. **Entitlement:** Narcissists hold unreasonable expectations of particularly favorable treatment and automatic compliance from others because they believe they are uniquely special. Defiance against their will or what they want is to them an injury that deserves a display of rage or self-righteous aggression.[9]

6. **Exploitation:** For a narcissist, "exploitation can take many forms but always involves the using of others without regard for their feelings or interests. Often the other person is in a subservient position, where resistance would be difficult or even impossible. Sometimes the subservience is not so much real as assumed…. It may or may not involve deceit but quite often includes distortions of reality."[10]

---

[6] Ibid. pp. 7-9.
[7] Ibid., p. 11.
[8] Ibid., p. 15.
[9] Ibid., p. 20.
[10] Ibid., p. 25.

7. **Bad Boundaries:** Narcissists do not recognize that they have boundaries "…and that others are separate and are not extensions of themselves. Others either exist to meet their needs or may as well not exist at all. Those who offer the possibility of some sort of gratification will be treated as if they are part of the narcissist and will be expected, automatically, to live up to that person's expectations. In the mind of a narcissist, there is *no boundary* between Self and other."[11]

Whew! This list sounds a lot like the last-days society that the Holy Spirit forecasts in Second Timothy 3:2 — a society that will become self-focused, self-absorbed, and self-centered to the detriment of others. It's a society that does not understand boundaries, that lives for self-embellishment, and that is characterized by a pervasive sense of entitlement. In other words, when a person — or society itself — embraces a sense of entitlement, it produces a *"Me! Me! Me!"* attitude. Those who are consumed with self, as the Holy Spirit forecasts about society at the end of the age, will possess a sense of entitlement that has *self* at its heart. Whether these people are cognizant of it or not, they believe that "it's all about me."

A SOCIETY IN WHICH FEELINGS ARE KING

When people live with an unrealistic sense of entitlement, they rarely *feel* grateful for what they receive because they think it's theirs by right anyway. And no matter how much they receive, they expect more. They believe they are entitled simply "because" — regardless of their performance or having done anything to merit it. Furthermore, they are so skewed by their self-love and self-focus that they actually believe their "wants" are "needs" and misinterpret their "feelings" as "facts."

---

[11] Ibid., pp. 27-28.

Those with a sense of entitlement base what they believe on what they *feel* even if it does not match reality. For example, they may *feel* treated unfairly if they are not able to start out with the lifestyle it took their parents 30 years to achieve. They may *feel* they have a "right" to material things — assets, security, a home, a privileged lifestyle — that others have to work hard to attain. They may *feel* they have a right to entertainment and a life full of excitement and fun. And then they may *feel* that life is boring when nothing "exciting or entertaining" is happening.

People who believe they are entitled may *feel* the need for others to give them positive reinforcement and reaffirmation of their self-worth, whether or not they merit it. They also don't usually respond well to criticism, even when it is constructive. They usually *feel* an inherent "right" to question and challenge authority figures and institutions, as well as the ethics and legitimacy of people who run those institutions — especially if they *feel* that they have not received benefits they assume they are entitled to receive.

An entitlement mentality is a blight on any society that can eventually undermine a nation's economic stability, because it focuses on *taking*, not *giving*. Not only can this mindset erode a country's economic system, but it also hinders men and women from reaping the benefit of God's higher system of *effort and reward*. Since an entitlement mentality veers from the Lord's original intention and design, it has a detrimental, undermining effect on a person's soul that can skew the way he sees life, himself, others, and even God.

◆

**An entitlement mentality is a blight on any society
that can eventually undermine a nation's economic stability,
because it focuses on *taking*, not *giving*.**

◆

Please don't misunderstand me. I am *not* talking about people who need assistance and cannot help themselves because of some temporary setback or even a permanent disability. We are called to bear one another's burdens and to help the poor, thus fulfilling the law of Christ (*see* Galatians 6:2). Scripture commands us to help the poor — not only in our own nation, but also around the globe. It is difficult to fulfill our commission to preach the Gospel when people need the basics of food and water satisfied *first* before they can even hear us!

But it is clear that in recent years, Western nations are being groomed to live under a system of entitlement and benefits at the government's and taxpayers' expense. It's as if there has been a cultivated dependency mindset that has bridged generations, making the cycle of entitlement more entrenched into people's way of thinking as it has been perpetuated for years on end. How this has progressed so far and made such a mark on our culture would make for an interesting discussion that I'll not go into here. I believe many factors have contributed to the idea embraced by large segments of our population that little or no effort or work is required to obtain the things they crave.

**There has been a cultivated dependency mindset
that has bridged generations, making the cycle of entitlement
more entrenched into people's way of thinking
as it has been perpetuated for years on end.**

For example, as a society, we are rewarding hard work and excellence in workmanship less, instead of adopting the mentality that "everyone wins," no matter what. I'm sure you've seen firsthand or heard of situations in athletics in which one or two players couldn't be singled out for their outstanding performances because it might hurt the feelings or affect the psyches of the other team members. The result has been that every player receives a trophy "just for showing up," with no distinction made for those who excel.

All of this is a result of an attitude of *unthankfulness* and *entitlement*, which produces a narcissistic mindset that continually says, "What's in this for *me*?"

But in Second Timothy 3:2, the Holy Spirit uses the Greek word "unthankful" — the Greek *acharistos*. As I wrote earlier, that little *a* cancels a *thankful* attitude and turns it into the word "unthankful." This means at the end of the age, society — even though the population at one time exhibited the quality of *thankfulness* — will depart from a thankful attitude and gradually transition into a state of *unthankfulness*. Yes, we will see an *unthankful* attitude rise until its grip has seized society at the end of the age.

Many today are seeking their own rights and their own ways, and it is leaving them dissatisfied, empty, and disillusioned. Although those who fit this description are on an endless quest to please *self*, they have found true, lasting pleasure always to be just beyond their grasp. As much as these people possess — and as much as will be heaped on them in the form of benefits they didn't have to labor for — they don't feel thankful, because they feel *entitled* to it all. They have never learned the spiritual law that happiness is only obtainable where there is a *thankful heart*.

JESUS CALLED UNTHANKFULNESS 'EVIL'

Unthankfulness is so wicked that in Luke 6:35, Jesus connected it with evil. He said, "...Love ye your enemies, and do good, and lend, hoping for nothing again; and your reward shall be great, and ye shall be the children of the Highest: for he is kind unto the *unthankful* and to the *evil*."

Jesus' words position the characteristic of being "unthankful" in the same category as being "evil." This categorically tells us that an *unthankful* attitude is *evil* in God's sight. The way God sees it, it is in truth spiritually criminal not to be thankful for what we have in life, even if it seems like we have *little* compared to someone else's blessings.

Even if we believe we've worked hard and earned what we have, we *still* should be profoundly thankful that all we have was given to us by God. Our jobs and opportunities could have been given to someone else, but they were graciously given to us.

Others who need a job and a salary would be thankful to have your position and your income. There are people all over the world who do not have shelter, warmth, or clean water, but you likely have access to these blessings every day. When you remember that, it will help you to be *thankful* for what you have and for every blessing that comes your way.

Even if we believe we've worked hard and earned what we have, we *still* should be profoundly thankful that all we have was given to us by God. Our jobs and opportunities could have been given to someone else, but they were graciously given to us.

But unfortunately, we live in an end-time season when people are so *self*-focused, *self*-consumed, and covetous that they are rarely grateful for anything — and if they *are* grateful, that attitude is often short-lived and soon forgotten.

The people of the Western world in particular are so blessed that they take many of their blessings for granted. They don't realize how fortunate they are for what they have. Even though they may have needs, they live comparatively more blessed than the rest of the world. These lands *overflow* with material blessings. For example, statistics show that America's lowest income-earners are richer than most of the rest of the world. In fact, the typical person in the bottom 5 percent of the American income distribution is still richer than 68 percent of the rest of the world's inhabitants.[12]

The Bible commands us "be ye thankful" and "in everything, give thanks" (Colossians 3:15; 1 Thessalonians 5:18). Even if things seem to be going wrong all around us, we can stop to count our blessings! We may feel besieged by need at the present moment, but the fact is, we each have many reasons *to be thankful.*

Nevertheless, in Second Timothy 3:2, Paul said that many in the last days would become *un*thankful.

With our understanding of the original Greek words used by the Holy Spirit thus far in Second Timothy 3:2, the *RIV* of this verse reads as follows:

Men will be self-focused, self-centered, self-absorbed, self-consumed, and in love with themselves more than anyone else. As a result of this self-love, they will be driven to obtain more and more and more. These boasters will be so committed to their own agenda that they are willing to exaggerate, overstate the facts, stretch the truth, embellish a story, and even lie if it will get them the position, advantage, or goal they desire. They are arrogant, haughty, impudent, snooty, and insolent. They disdain, mock, slander, and speak ill of anyone who stands in the way of their ideology and freely use foul language. In this climate, parents will no longer be able to persuade, control, lead, or exercise authority over their own children. And although people were once thankful and appreciative, they will generally become void of gratitude and unappreciative of everything....

---

[12] Tim Worstall, "Astonishing Numbers: America's Poor Still Live Better Than Most of the Rest of Humanity," June 1, 2013, forbes.com, https://www.forbes.com/sites/timworstall/2013/06/01/astonishing-numbers-americas-poor-still-live-better-than-most-of-the-rest-of-humanity/#4a1af2854ef0.

Now it's time to proceed to the next characteristic that the Holy Spirit gives in this verse to depict society in the last days — *unholiness*. I will show you from the Bible the cause-and-effect nature of these last two characteristics in this verse. We will see that any person, nation, or society who has become *unthankful* is headed down a destructive path that will eventually lead them into a state of *unholiness*.

◆

Any person, nation, or society who has become *unthankful* is headed down a destructive path that will eventually lead them into a state of *unholiness*.

◆

UNHOLINESS IN THE LAST DAYS

In Second Timothy 3:2, Paul continued, "For men shall be lovers of their own selves, covetous, boasters, proud, blasphemers, disobedient to parents, unthankful, *unholy.*"

The word "unholy" in this verse is translated from the Greek word *anosios*. This word is based on the Greek word *hosios*, which depicts a person or group of people who are *reverent, respectful,* and *God-fearing*. But when an *a* is attached to it, this prefix has a canceling effect, which means what was once holy has become *unholy*, what was once reverent has become *irreverent*, and what was once God-fearing has *lost its fear of God*.

This word *anosios* can thus be translated *irreverent* and *disrespectful*. It depicts those who have *lost all fear of God* and whose way of thinking and outward actions have become *ill-mannered, impure, unclean, lewd, indecent, crude, coarse, vulgar, offensive,* and *rude*. It depicts words or actions that are *unholy, unsacred, impure, and unsanctioned by God.*

The Holy Spirit uses this exact word *anosios* in Second Timothy 3:2 to describe the *thinking* and *behavior* of society at the very end of the age. It depicts a group of people, a nation, or a society who once revered and honored what was holy, sacred, pure, and sanctioned by God, but they no longer do. They have let go of what they once revered as holy and sacred, and their *thinking* and *behavior* have become supportive of that which is *unholy, unsacred,* and *impure.* They have swapped positions and have embraced attitudes and actions that would *never* be sanctioned by God or the teachings of the Bible.

Thus, the Holy Spirit prophesies here that society will become *ill-mannered, impure, unclean, lewd, indecent, crude, coarse, vulgar, offensive,* and *rude* — and that people will develop a casual attitude toward words, actions, and behaviors that are *unholy, unsacred, impure,* and *unsanctioned by God.* It actually depicts a time with no "checks and balances." As the fear of God becomes more and more extinct, society will throw off moral restraint and engorge itself in areas that are condemned in the sight of God.

Romans 1:32 says, "Who knowing the judgment of God, that they which commit such things are worthy of death, not only do the same, but have pleasure in them that do them." This verse portrays a society that has knowledge of the Bible and is well-versed in what the Bible says. But because the people do not find that knowledge convenient or amenable to what they desire to do, they will not only discard it and put it aside, but they will also seek to encourage and promote unholy activities to others. In other words, there will be a global public-relations campaign to endorse sin and to encourage the unrestrained acceptance of every immoral lifestyle, regardless of how it conflicts with the time-tested, authoritative voice of God's Word.

◆

As the fear of God becomes more and more extinct, society will throw off moral restraint and engorge itself in areas that are condemned in the sight of God.

◆

When society throws off holiness and embraces unholy behaviors, it eventually causes a complete reversal of society — turning it from a godly, moral position to one that is godless and immoral. And at the end of the age, a proliferation of unholiness will penetrate deeper and deeper into society.

Think of it — we have seen things change radically even within the span of our own lifetimes. In just a few short decades, society has devolved from sanctioning open prayer in public schools to outlawing God altogether in those places. And abortion — the killing of nearly two billion babies worldwide in the last century — is now endorsed by governments around the world. Same-sex marriage, a concept totally ungodly and unholy according to the Word of God, is now law according to the U. S. Supreme Court. Now the whole situation has developed so profoundly that people are confused about genders and are submitting to surgical procedures to attempt to turn themselves into their "gender of choice."

In the Western world especially, there is a biblical foundation in society, and people generally know what God says so clearly about these things in Scripture. But man has chosen to walk a different route from what he once recognized and knew to be the right path. When God is ignored or removed, society begins the downward plummet into depravity. *This is precisely what is happening in our times.*

———◆———

**When God is ignored or removed,
society begins the downward plummet into depravity.
*This is precisely what is happening in our times.***

———◆———

As noted in the previous chapter, an evening of watching television reveals that *impure, ill-mannered, improper, unclean, indecent, coarse, vulgar, offensive, crude*, *lewd*, and *rude* behaviors are infiltrating every sphere of society. Even immoral conduct is now found in children's cartoons as part of a public-relations campaign to change the way children perceive what was once considered abnormal and perverse behaviors. What was once *vulgar* and *immoral* now fills the world of entertainment at every age-group level.

But just because you live in the last of the last days does *not* mean that you should be affected by this moral downslide. By making God's Word your standard and upholding it in your life, you can stay free from the spiritual corrosion that is eating away at the world today. What is happening to a lost society does *not* have to happen to you or your family. I remind you that you can build a wall of protection to keep yourself and your family safe even in these treacherous times.

To remain untouched by the moral degeneration we're seeing in society today, we must make the decision to keep our eyes on Jesus and live to please Him with our obedience to His Word. We must choose to make God's Word the guide for our hearts and never permit ourselves to entertain in our minds or find as funny those things that God deems "unholy."

———◆———

To remain untouched by the moral degeneration we're seeing in society today, we must choose to make God's Word the guide for our hearts and never permit ourselves to entertain in our minds or find as funny those things that God deems "unholy."

———◆———

Movies and sitcoms may make light of these kinds of lifestyles, but this condition isn't funny — it's *spiritually deadly and damning*. Unfortunately, *the world laughs while it goes to hell.* A lost society is oblivious to the deception that is dragging mankind lower and lower into depravity and judgment. There is nothing humorous or funny about this scenario.

But, you see, when man becomes "unthankful" — even ceasing to acknowledge God's goodness and to be thankful for His blessings — it triggers a moment when he begins to sink into decadence and to act "unholy." People become *self-focused* and *self-absorbed* — seeing themselves as the center of their universe.

And when a sense of entitlement rules society, the people in that society even begin to embrace the notion that they have a right to experience any form of sexuality they feel is right for them, with no fear of violating the law of God. Such people revolt against scriptures that confront their behavior and even seek *un*scriptural theological positions to affirm them instead of change them. They claim that the Bible — which is equivalent to the voice of God — has no right to infringe upon their feelings.

A Christian may not slide quickly into the depths the world has fallen into. But if unthankfulness works its way into the life of any believer — and as a result, he or she becomes dissatisfied, ungrateful, and unthankful — that person will begin to lose a healthy fear of God in his or her life. Once that happens, that person is susceptible to accommodating behaviors that God does not condone — and thus, the decline can happen to him or her as well.

◆

**When a sense of entitlement rules society,
the people in that society even begin to embrace the notion
that they have a right to experience
any form of sexuality they feel is right for them,
with no fear of violating the law of God.**

◆

146

THE PROCESS LEADING TO A REPROBATE MIND

There is a clear and defined process that occurs when a society chooses to throw off the eternal moorings of truth found in God's Word and go its own way. We can find that process in the first chapter of Romans.

In Romans 1:21, the apostle Paul broached this crucial subject by the Spirit, explaining with great clarity what happens when society turns from God. Paul wrote, "Because that, when they knew God, they glorified him not as God, neither were thankful; but became vain in their imaginations, and their foolish heart was darkened."

The word "knew" depicts *acquaintance* or *general knowledge*, not personal knowledge, such as the knowledge possessed by a person who knows Jesus Christ as his Lord and Savior. In this verse, the word "knew" pictures a society that previously possessed *a general acquaintance, a general knowledge*, or *a God-fearing attitude*. This lets us know that even if society was not predominately comprised of authentic Christians, at least the vast majority of people *recognized* and *acknowledged* God and His blessings upon them.

Paul used the word "knew" in the past tense, which indicates he was referring to a society that had *lost* its acknowledgment and sense of dependence upon God. The first part of this verse could thus actually be translated, *"Although they once had a general acquaintance with and knowledge about God and about things related to God...."*

So in verse 21, Paul was describing a society that in large part has arrived at the conclusion that a common acknowledgment of God is out of fashion with the times. As a result, people have progressively put God off to the side and out of sight. More and more, the societal trend is to stop giving Him the recognition that is due Him. This errant path that deviates away from man's dependence upon God triggers a widespread condition of spiritual and moral wandering that becomes more and more pronounced over time.

DARKENED MINDS AND FOOLISH THOUGHTS

Paul went on to describe the consequences of this destitute spiritual condition. When the vast majority in a society decides that the acknowledgement of God is no longer intellectually fashionable, people eventually become "vain in their imaginations."

The word "vain" is the Greek word *mataioo*, which means *ruined* and, in this case, depicts something that is *error-filled*. The "something" that is filled with error is the people's "imaginations." The word "imaginations" is from the Greek word *dialogismos*, a word that unmistakably refers to *mental activity* — a person's *reasonings*, *deliberations*, *calculations*, or *thinking processes*.

When these various Greek words are used together in the phrase "vain in their imaginations," a specific meaning is produced. Paul was explaining that when society sets God aside, *error* is released, eventually leading to *ruin* on multiple levels. It is like an inevitable "chemical reaction" that will always occur if the right elements are mixed together.

Scripture tells us that wisdom begins with the fear and knowledge of God (*see* Proverbs 1:7). It is an inevitable "cause-and-effect" pattern based on spiritual law. Thus, if society respects, recognizes, and acknowledges God, it results in enlightenment.

But the opposite is also true and carries with it its own inevitable cause-and-effect pattern. When the fear and knowledge of God is diminished and society begins to move away from Him, a spiritual "chemical mix" is produced that will always result in an environment where *intellectual nonsense* — conclusions that don't make either rational or spiritual sense — become the inevitable consequence.

Eventually error begins to breed and multiply, spilling into every sphere of society — courts, education, families, entertainment, business, government, and religion. The deceptive process continues until man's intellectual reasonings, untethered to God's eternal truths, has tainted all the deliberations, calculations, and thinking processes of the general population.

We each need to face this reality of what man is without God. When the knowledge and fear of God is removed, a vacuum is formed, causing intellectual and spiritual darkness to flood in and fill the void.

I'm not saying unbelievers are unintelligent. Obviously, the world has a great number of unbelievers who possess great mental capacity. But Paul stated that when intellectually brilliant people drift far from the truth, they eventually cast off restraint and pass into the realm of foolishness and deception. They see themselves as highly intelligent progressive thinkers. But because they reject the truth of Scripture and embrace the flawed conclusions of their own making, God says they actually become fools (*see* Romans 1:22). In fact, in verse 21, Paul wrote that "their *foolish* heart was darkened" as a result of turning away from God and His standards.

We each need to face this reality of what man is without God. When the knowledge and fear of God is removed, a vacuum is formed, causing intellectual and spiritual darkness to flood in and fill the void.

This word "foolish" is translated from a form of the Greek word *asunetos.* In actuality, it is the word *sunetos* with an *a* attached to the front of it. The word *sunetos* describes *supreme intelligence* or *conclusions and understandings supported with correlating evidence or facts.* It pictures *a person so mature in his thinking that he has the ability to accurately see a full picture.* But in Romans 1:21, this word *sunetos* has an *a* attached to the front of it, which has a reversing effect. Rather than portray *intelligence*, this word portrays a person who has *lost his intelligence* or who has *a lack of intelligence*.

Paul used this word *asunetos* to tell us what happens when people turn away from God: Rather than getting smarter, they regress and become more and more diminished and off-base in their reasoning, deliberations, calculations, and thinking processes. According to Paul's cogent argument, inspired by the Holy Spirit, a society that moves *away from* God always moves *toward* deceived, defective believing and reasoning processes that are dominated by the manipulative lies of demonic forces at work.

THE FOOLISH HEART OF A REPROBATE SOCIETY

Paul went on to say that a society that moves away from God acquires a "foolish *heart*." The word "heart" in Greek is *kardia*, which is the word for *the physical heart*. The use of this word at this juncture is very important, as you will see.

As you know, the heart pumps blood throughout the circulatory system of the human body. Its pumping action is so powerful that virtually every part of the body has blood in it. But in Romans 1:21, Paul didn't refer to the physical heart; rather, he used the word *kardia* to depict the collective "heart" of a people. In other words, in this context the apostle was talking about the very core that both receives and supplies the beliefs and values that fuel and define a lost society.

Paul revealed that when society moves away from God, its heart fills with *foolishness*. Then just as the human heart pumps blood into the various parts of the physical body, the heart of a wayward society will begin to pump *foolishness* and *flawed thinking* throughout its "circulatory system." Eventually every stratum of that society becomes touched with the destructive effects of the foolishness produced and disseminated when man separates himself from his Creator.

Paul says such a society will eventually become "darkened." That word "darkened" is a translation of the Greek word *skotidzo*, which denotes *physical* or *spiritual darkness*. But metaphorically it is used here to depict a world or society flooded with darkness that eventually spawns depravity, immorality, and a myriad of other ungodly behaviors.

As these God-rejecting societies sink deeper and deeper into this moral abyss, Romans 1:22 says the so-called leaders of the godless world will claim that the opposite is the reality. They will boast that society is on the cutting edge of a new future and a new order, free of past moral restraints. But that verse also reveals *God's* perspective of this baseless claim: "Professing themselves to be wise, they became fools."

The word "professing" and the tense used in this verse tells us that these alleged progressive thinkers *continually assert* that they are wise. These are people who never stop pushing their agenda or putting themselves forward as leading the way for the so-called "benefit" of the rest of society.

The people Paul was referring to in Romans 1 assert to be "wise," which is the Greek word *sophos*. This was the same word often used to portray *highly educated people*, such as scientists, philosophers, doctors, teachers, and others who were considered to be the super-intelligentsia of society. It depicts a class of individuals who believe themselves to be *clever, astute, brilliant, intellectually sharp*, or *especially enlightened*.

Paul again referred to this same category of so-called progressive thinkers in Second Timothy 3:2. In that verse, he called them "proud." This is a translation of the word *huperephanos*, a word that pictures a person or group of people who see themselves as intellectually advantaged and positioned above the rest of the crowd. It portrays *uppity, arrogant, haughty, high-and-mighty, impudent people who carry an attitude of insolence*. Such people believe they possess the right to decide what is right or wrong or what should be viewed as antiquated and out of fashion. This is a person or a group of people who could accurately be called *intellectual snobs*.

In Romans 1:22, Paul stated the reality — that these people are "fools." Forgive the bluntness of this statement, but the Greek word for "fools" is *moraino* — which is the word for one who is *mentally ill* or *mentally deranged*. It is the same word from which we derive the word "moron." This means that in Romans 1:22, when Paul wrote that these alleged intellectuals are "fools," he minced no words and made no apologies as he declared that such people are, in reality, intellectual *morons*.

**With all this in mind,
I'd like to share the *RIV* of Romans 1:21,22:**

Although society once had a general acquaintance of God, a general knowledge of God, and a reverence for things related to God, a time came when people found it no longer fashionable to give God His due reverence. Rather than be grateful to God for their blessings, they forgot who blessed them and ceased to be thankful. They turned from God, and as a result, they began to veer morally, which resulted in their thinking becoming laced with error that affected how they reasoned about everything. They alleged it was all right to believe things that are not supported by correlating facts and evidence, and eventually their conclusions became totally out of touch with reality.

A normal heart pumps blood, but the heart of a God-rejecting society pumps and proliferates foolishness until it is filled with darkness that eventually spawns depravity, immorality, and godless behaviors. The so-called leaders of a God-rejecting society constantly assert that they are brilliant intellectuals of a new way of thinking, even though it is difficult to fathom how they could

claim such a thing. Regardless of what they assert, their words and their ways of thinking make them sound like those who are mentally ill or mentally deranged. How could anyone think what they propose is normal? Make no mistake about it — those who think this way are clearly morons.

RELEASED TO REBEL AGAINST GOD'S WAYS

As Paul continued, he stated in Romans 1:28 that a God-rejecting society does not "like to *retain* God in their knowledge." Unlike the situation in Romans 1:21, this isn't a case of being only generally acquainted with God or His standards. These people really knew Him; they simply no longer wanted to *retain* that knowledge.

This is a depiction of a person or a group of people who were once familiar with God and His standard but who at some point find that standard inconvenient for the new morality they are bent on constructing. Because they no longer want to retain God in their minds and lives, Paul informed us in Romans 1:28 that "God gave them over."

Does this phrase mean that God abandoned these people or pushed them away, as some suggest? Scripture reveals that God holds out hope for everyone and is not in the habit of giving up on or abandoning anyone. *So what does this phrase mean?* The Greek words used in Romans 1:28 would be better translated, *"God released them."* God did not give them up or abandon them; He simply *released* them to follow their wayward inclinations because that is what they wanted to do.

God's Spirit will plead with people not to abandon truth and go another direction. But if society chooses to do so, He will *release* them to follow their inclinations. That is precisely what the words of Paul mean in Romans 1:28.

---◆---

God's Spirit will plead with people not to abandon truth and go another direction. But if society chooses to do so, He will *release* them to follow their inclinations.

---◆---

In verse 28, Paul described a God-rejecting society that ultimately develops a "reprobate mind." A common concept that comes to mind when we hear the word "reprobate" is of a person who is sick, disgusting, twisted, or perverted in some way. But in this verse, Paul used this word to describe an entire society that has deteriorated into this condition called *reprobate*. In Romans 1:28, he wrote, "...Even as they [society] did not like to retain God in their knowledge, *God gave them over to a reprobate mind....*"

I want to make it very clear from this verse what God did *not* do. This verse does not say God gave them a reprobate mind; it says He "gave them *over*" to a reprobate mind. The difference is very significant. The words "gave them over" is translated from the Greek word *paradidomi*, which means *to hand over* — or, in this case, *to release* or *to transfer*.

This means God will not hold society hostage against its will. Instead, He honors people's choices and *releases* them to follow the path of their choosing — even if they choose to follow their wayward instincts that He knows could have seriously damaging effects. When people do not want to retain God in their knowledge, He simply *releases* them to do as they wish. And as they walk away from God's spiritual laws and His well-established biblical principles, they put themselves in a position to become "reprobate."

A REPROBATE MINDSET IN THE MAKING

The word "reprobate" is translated from the Greek word *adokimos*. The word *dokimos* means *approved, fit, reliable,* and *trustworthy*. However, when an *a* is attached to the front of this word, making it *adokimos*, it reverses the meaning and instead depicts one who is *disapproved, unfit, unreliable,* and *untrustworthy.*

This depicts a society that has been exposed to a negative spiritual influence for so long — and in such heavy doses — that it has become *compromised, impaired, ruined,* and *no longer trustworthy.* This is the meaning of the word *reprobate* as used in the New Testament. And in Romans 1:28, it specifically depicts the collective mind of a society — or even the mind of an individual — that has become so tarnished, tainted, hardened, and both spiritually and mentally compromised that it loses its ability to arrive at sensible, godly conclusions.

Although God gives people marvelous minds worthy of great esteem, the word translated "reprobate" speaks of minds that have been damaged by continuous exposure to evil influences and by repeated bombardment with wrong ways of thinking. Consider the sobering implications revealed in Romans 1:28. A person's mind, created by God to gloriously function, can become *unfit* if it is regularly exposed to toxic environments and collective mindsets that deviate from and defy the truth of God's Word. That person can ultimately lose his or her ability to discern what is morally right and wrong.

That person's mind may remain brilliant in many respects, and the person who possesses that mind may be an exceptionally talented individual. Nonetheless, if that person's mind has become reprobate, it is now morally debased and twisted in its thinking. In God's view, such a person — or even an entire society — has lost the ability to think correctly and has become unfit to separate good from evil or to judge what is right and wrong.

This is why it is so important to guard what you expose your mind to. You also have a responsibility to teach your children and grandchildren how to guard their minds against immoral or negative influences. Help them understand the downward spiral that results from this type of destructive exposure — how it will dull their conscience and exact an increasingly damaging toll on their minds — minds that God intended from the start to work brilliantly and at full capacity.

This downward spiral that eventually positions a society to collectively embrace a reprobate mind is sadly the current state of affairs we find ourselves in today as we approach the close of this age. People's minds are being inundated with false information and a celebration of various forms of immorality, including a plethora of false propaganda about human sexuality.

This is a last-days attack of seducing spirits bent on modifying the collective mind of society and creating a way of thinking that is free of moral restraint. It's a demonic strategy that is both intentional and proactive, spreading its tentacles into every sector of society. Even people who grew up in church are being deceived to adopt mindsets that contradict God's truth and change how they view issues that *should* be set in stone in their lives.

Largely unaware of the danger, the people of this age ingest an unrelenting mental bombardment from every aspect of society of wrong people, wrong sources, wrong information, and wrong spiritual influences. It's all part of the satanic war being waged against the human race (including believers) to adversely affect people's thought processes, to undermine their core belief system, and to damage and disfigure their minds until they can no longer see what is *wrong* about *wrong*. Ultimately, this process results in people choosing sides that are opposed to those who adhere to long-held biblical truths.

As a result of the collective mind of society being modified — that is, seriously distorted and sin-damaged — that society will eventually end up "...do[ing] those things which are not convenient" (Romans 1:28). The words "not convenient" simply mean people will do things that are *not morally right or fitting*.

This is the satanic strategy that is actively operating in these end times. As God's people, we must be alert to the fact that Satan is loosing hordes of seducing spirits with doctrines of demons in these last days to lead an entire generation into delusion. Satan has launched a covert operation to seize minds — *especially young minds* — to lead them off track.

The enemy is using the voices of influential people in entertainment and the media to beguile and seduce. These pawns in Satan's evil game are those who already have been beguiled and seduced to believe a lie — and the lie they have swallowed themselves is propagated with ease to an unwitting audience being groomed to believe the lie.

God's people, we must be alert to the fact that Satan is loosing hordes of seducing spirits with doctrines of demons in these last days to lead an entire generation into delusion.

The devil's goal is to victimize a last-days generation and lead them into ways of thinking and behaviors that damage their minds and steal, kill, and destroy on as many levels as possible. (*Note:* I also write about this study of Romans chapter 1 in my book, *How To Keep Your Head on Straight in a World Gone Crazy*, which I encourage you to read as an aid and a powerful companion to this book you hold in your hands.)

THE PROGRESSION
FROM UNTHANKFUL TO UNHOLY

Romans 1:21 says all this began when mankind ceased to recognize God and glorify Him as God. That is *precisely* what we see in Second Timothy 3:2. Never forget that unthankfulness always leads to unholiness and to thinking and actions that are *ill-mannered, impure, unclean, lewd, indecent, crude, coarse, vulgar, offensive,* and *rude*.

In other words, the people who choose to forsake their knowledge of God and to be unthankful eventually become calloused and lose a sense of consciousness about their wrong attitudes and actions — to the extent that they begin to actively engage in them with pleasure. And to think, it all started with an attitude of unthankfulness!

Don't fall into this end-time mindset of unthankfulness. It is a trap the devil wants you to fall into because he knows where it will lead you — it will darken your mind and, ultimately, your *life*. You must resist it and determine to continually maintain an attitude of thankfulness, regardless of the circumstances surrounding you at the moment.

Whether our circumstances are good or not so good, the goodness and the character of God *change not* (*see* Malachi 3:6)! Therefore, it is *always* a good time to thank and praise Him for who He is — and it's *never* time to draw back and refrain from thanking and praising Him (*see* Hebrews 13:15)!

◆

**Don't fall into this end-time mindset of unthankfulness.
It is a trap the devil wants you to fall into because he knows
where it will lead you — it will darken your mind
and, ultimately, your *life*.**

◆

When people possess *thankfulness* and a *reverence* for God — when they recognize that He is the Source of their blessings — it causes them to live more uprightly and soberly. On the other hand, history shows that *unthankful* people are generally *not* God-fearing people.

When people lose their thankfulness and fear of God, they end up drifting far from their spiritual origins. A hatred of sin is lost, along with a dread of judgment. In fact, "judgment" — although there is such a thing as true, biblical judgment — becomes an unpopular, unwelcome subject. These people either want to hear that God is okay with everything they do, or they simply stop caring what He thinks about it.

When people lose their fear of God, they begin to *tolerate* what was once intolerable and ultimately *do* what they once condemned as wrong and displeasing to Him. It's simply a fact that when a person ceases to be thankful and loses his or her reverence for God, a process begins in which that person spiritually regresses and eventually become *unholy*.

**When people lose their fear of God,
they begin to *tolerate* what was once intolerable
and ultimately *do* what they once condemned
as wrong and displeasing to Him.**

Hence, the word "unholy" depicts a person or nation that has gone through a degenerative transformation. In some way, over a period of time, the people have slowly become *irreverent* and *disrespectful* and have *lost their fear of God*. Those who are in this dire spiritual condition venture into thoughts and activities that are unholy, with no fear of consequence or repercussion.

WHAT WE BELIEVE
AFFECTS OUR ACTIONS

A person's actions are deeply affected by what he believes. For example, if a person *believes* that he will give account to God for his life, that belief will affect the way he lives his life. He or she will live with eternity in view and with accountability in mind.

Conversely, if a person *doesn't believe* he will give account to God for his life, this belief will also affect his conduct. In essence, that person's mindset reduces him to living for temporal things — often on the level of a mere animal — and to doing things that are contrary to the Word of God with no concern for eternal consequences.

But, friend, judgment is a reality that every one of us will face. Believers will stand before the Judgment Seat of Christ, and unbelievers will stand before the Great White Throne Judgment (*see* Romans 14:10; 2 Corinthians 5:10; Revelation 20:11-15). One of the basic doctrines of the Church is eternal judgment (*see* Hebrews 6:2).

Knowing these truths — and staying ever aware of them — will greatly impact the way we live! Ignoring these truths will throw open the door for us to live in an unholy manner with no thought of accountability or of ever answering for our deeds.

It is so important that we understand that some form of judgment — a future accounting for our choices in this life — is a reality each one of us faces.

Living life without consequences, both temporal and eternal, is a hallucination. In understanding what lies ahead, we can seek God *today*, draw near to Him in love, and make choices for our lives accordingly.

———◆———

**It is so important that we understand
that some form of judgment — a future accounting
for our choices in this life — is a reality each one of us faces.**

———◆———

Let's take this one step further.

Many Christians believe that God loves them so much that He will ignore their sinful choices and never hold them accountable for their wrong actions or behavior. After all, they conclude, that would be far too unpleasant of an outcome to square with a loving God.

Certainly, God does love us — so much so that He gave His only Son for our salvation (*see* John 3:16). But the thought that in His love, He won't hold us accountable is an irresponsible view that produces irresponsible living.

Yes, God loves us. But that does *not* mean He condones the sin for which Christ died! If He did, Jesus' death would have been in vain.

---◆---

**Yes, God loves us.
But that does *not* mean
He condones the sin for which Christ died!
If He did, Jesus' death would have been in vain.**

---◆---

But I can assure you that Jesus' sacrificial death in our stead was *not* in vain! Without His death, we would be doomed to an eternal hell. His condemnation, death, and resurrection secured our release from the power of sin and gave us the ability to be made new by His Spirit so that we could stand, having been made righteous, before a holy God.

A *casual* approach to God is usually an *irreverent* approach that doesn't include the thought of accountability or of eternity. This explains why some Christians do things that are unacceptable to God without any sense of shame or conviction. They don't believe God will ever hold them accountable for their actions. Therefore, they do whatever they wish, believing that God will simply overlook it.

SOCIETY'S SLIPPERY SLOPE

This principle doesn't apply only to individuals; it also applies to society. For example, if society loses a fear of God and develops a casual attitude toward God and His holy instructions, it will be just a matter of time before it will begin to conduct itself in ways that violate God's moral code. And people will do it *blatantly* — with no fear of accountability for their actions. This total disregard for God's holiness can cause a person, a generation, or a nation to become *impure, ill-mannered, unclean, lewd, indecent, crude, coarse, vulgar, offensive,* and *rude.*

All of these ideas are included in the Greek word translated "unholy" in Second Timothy 3:2 that lists characteristics of the last-days age. This word suggests that those who practice these things have undergone an *ungodly transformation.* They have become something vastly different than what they were in the past.

Indeed, when God is put to the side in society, it will begin a slippery, downward slide into *unholiness.*

Think of the unholy transformation that has taken place in your lifetime — just in the media, for example. Blinded by Satan, a lost world is oblivious to the deception that is taking it lower and lower into depravity and judgment over the airwaves and Internet as well as in *every* facet of society.

Let me give you examples of what spiritual drifting in society can do. These points are presented here simply to demonstrate what happens when society becomes *self-focused, unthankful,* and *unholy* and ceases to be *God-*focused.

When you were growing up, could you have ever imagined that:

- Society would go from *praying* at the beginning of our day in school to *outlawing* references to God in school?

- Public recognition of God in educational institutions could result in *legal action?*

- Significant scriptures would be labeled as *hate language* and in some nations a Christian could be prosecuted for reading those scriptures — especially Romans 1 — publicly?

- Private business owners who use their own hard-earned profits to support Christian-based organizations would suffer *blasphemous attacks* and *boycotts* against their businesses?

- Small-business owners who refuse to do business with groups whose stated agendas violate their moral consciences and biblical convictions would be sued, threatened with violence and death, and put out of business — just because they believe the Bible?

- Religious freedom could come to mean freedom *from* religion or a *God-free* society?

These things were fantastical thinking a mere generation ago, but the Holy Spirit alerted us that a godless, immoral society would emerge at the end of the age. Did He tell us so we would hide from it? No, He told us these things in advance so we would be proactive in building our lives on the unshakeable foundation of the Word of God to avoid the sinking sand of selfishness that will rule society in the last days.

By giving heed to the Holy Spirit's warnings, we can build our lives to stand on solid ground. We'll escape the ground that is shifting beneath the feet of society today and empower our lives to be solid, stable, healthy, productive, and happy.

◆

He told us these things in advance so we would be proactive in building our lives on the unshakeable foundation of the Word of God to avoid the sinking sand of selfishness that will rule society in the last days.

◆

The *RIV* of Second Timothy 3:2 in entirety thus reads as follows:

Men will be self-focused, self-centered, self-absorbed, self-consumed, and in love with themselves more than anyone else. As a result of this self-love, they will be driven to obtain more and more and more. These boasters are so committed to their own agenda that they are willing to exaggerate, overstate the facts, stretch the truth, embellish a story, and even lie if it will get them the position, advantage, or goal they desire. They are arrogant, haughty, impudent, snooty, and insolent. They disdain, mock, slander, and speak ill of anyone who stands in the way of their ideology and freely use foul language. In this climate, parents will no longer be able to persuade, control, lead, or exercise authority over their own children. And although people were once thankful and appreciative, they will generally become void of gratitude and will be unappreciative of everything. Impurity will seep into society and cause it to become impure, ill-mannered, unclean, indecent, coarse, vulgar, offensive, crude, lewd, and rude.

The Holy Spirit foretold all of this to alert us to what would happen and to *awaken* and *prepare* us to live victoriously, even in the last days. And what the Holy Spirit prophesied nearly 2,000 years ago in Second Timothy 3:2 is coming to pass before our eyes, exactly as He foretold.

CHAPTER 5

LAST-DAYS SURVIVAL GUIDE ACTION STEPS

TO AVOID UNTHANKFULNESS AND UNHOLINESS

It's important to ask the following reflective questions to determine your own level of thankfulness. You must protect your heart at all costs from the godless attitude of entitlement that is making its way into the lives of so many people today.

I encourage you to take your time as you ask yourself these questions. Don't rush through them. As you read them, let them sink in deeply so the Holy Spirit can help you evaluate your spiritual condition and see what adjustments you need to make to stay free from the spirit of the world that is working with such virulence in society today.

1. Do you feel treated unfairly because you are not able to quickly achieve the lifestyle it took your parents' generation 30 or more years to achieve?

As I described in this chapter, an ungodly sense of *entitlement* veers from God's original design of effort — *work* — and reward. This mentality has an undermining effect on a person's soul and can skew the way he sees life, himself, others, and even God.

So it's important to ask yourself:

- *Have I allowed myself to be affected by the spirit of the age that says I inherently have a "right" to things that others had to work hard to get?*

The Bible teaches that even God rewards every man "according to his works" (*see* Psalm 62:12; Proverbs 24:12; Revelation 22:12). Although every born-again person will go to Heaven, everyone who goes to Heaven will not automatically receive equal rewards. The Bible teaches that some will receive greater reward and others lesser — all to be based on obedience to God's will during their earthly life.

If God Himself rewards us according to obedience and performance, then shouldn't it be safe to assume that what we earn and obtain in life should also not automatically come to us because we are "entitled" to it? The only thing we are entitled to is to live, to do something with our lives, and to lay hold of promises that are ours in Jesus Christ. Yet even our life's breath and our strength and ability to apprehend and fulfill God's will is a gift from our Creator. The truth is, *everything* is a *blessing* from Heaven for which we should be *grateful, thankful,* and *appreciative.*

So be honest as you ask yourself:

- *Do I exhibit gratitude for what God and others have done for me?*

- *What about my children and/or grandchildren? Do they have a feeling of entitlement, or do they understand that they need to work hard to be rewarded and to be thankful for what they have received in life?*

These are important questions because we are living in a last-days age when society will trend toward a mindset of entitlement and unthankfulness.

It is therefore important to probe your own heart to make sure an attitude of entitlement and unthankfulness has no place in you or in the lives of your family members. If you'll ask the Holy Spirit to help you be honest with yourself, He will graciously enable you to see if you need to make any adjustment in this area of your life.

And, really, even if we've determined before God that this is not a problem for us personally today, it is something that can creep in on any one of us at any time as the sway of the world grows stronger and stronger. We have to stay with the Word and in fellowship with Him to guard our hearts at all times and to stay on top of this spiritually so that this dark attitude doesn't subtly creep into our lives.

2. Do you require others to give you unending positive reinforcement and reaffirmation of your self-worth?

There is nothing wrong with needing encouragement from time to time. We all need it. I need it at times, and when I need it, I usually tell someone close to me that I need encouragement. But other people need positive reinforcement and encouragement as well.

Take stock of your life and ask yourself:

- *Do I expect others to pour encouragement into me all the time as if no one else needs it but me?*

If your answer is yes, it's time for you to start getting your eyes off yourself. You are too *self-focused*.

Philippians 2:4 says, "Look not every man on his own things, but every man also on the things of others." The word "look" in Greek is the word *skopeo*, the verb form of the word *skopos*, which pictures *an intense look* or *a scrutinizing look*. It is where we get the word "tele*scope*." A telescope enables a person to *zero in* and *focus* on an object that is distant. It is also where we get the word "micro*scope*." A microscope enables a person to take an *intense* and *penetrating look* at something that is very small and up close. But in Philippians 2:4, Paul uses the word *skopos* to mean we should not have a self-*scope*. In other words, we should not be constantly *zeroing in* on ourselves, so *self-focused* that we cannot see the needs of others around us.

Because we are living in the last days when society will be *self-focused* and *self-absorbed*, it's important to carefully evaluate your life to make sure you are not demanding that others provide nonstop positive reinforcement for you as if there is no one else who needed it. And if you find that you come up short in the evaluation, be assured that the antidote for such a problem is quite straightforward and simple: You simply need to get your eyes off yourself and begin to look around you for others who need encouragement and reinforcement as much as you do.

If you'll learn to think of others, it will free you from a great deal of inner struggles — and it will bring you joy to know you've made a difference in someone else's life. If you'll ask the Holy Spirit to help you change in this area — to become a giver and not just a taker in the area of positive reinforcement, encouragement, and affirmation of worth — He will enable you to become an amazing encourager for others who really need it.

3. **Do you feel that you have an inherent "right" to question and challenge authoritarian figures and institutions and the ethics of people who run them — especially if you feel you have not received benefits you believe you are entitled to receive?**

Because we are living at the end of the age, we are witnessing a time when disregard for authority is pandemic across society. The Bible clearly teaches that as the prophetic clock ticks toward the final countdown, widespread disrespect for authority will grow to become even more out of control and serve as a sign that we are reaching the cusp of this end-time age. As Christians, we must be awakened to what God says about authority so we do not fall prey to the spirit of the age. Just because the world wanders astray does *not* mean we should wander with it.

Many years ago, I wondered what Peter and Jude were referring to when they wrote that people at the end of the age would engage in speaking "evil" against authorities (*see* 2 Peter 2:11,12; Jude 1:9,10). The word "evil" is a translation of the Greek word *blasphemeo,* which signifies *derogatory behavior that involves nasty, shameful, or disrespectful speech.*

In these verses, Peter and Jude stated that even angels do not dare to speak disrespectfully to established authorities — yet at the end of the age, people will dare to do what even angels will not do. In other words, a full venting of disrespect will be unleashed in society as people engage in railing against all forms of established authority.

We are living in an hour when this is taking place. None of this is news to those of us who have been keeping up with the constant stream of ugly political discourse that populates our TV screens, computers, or mobile devices. People are railing against every imaginable position of authority, using every possible means of communication to bring a public platform to their fleshly rant. It's a clear example of the enemy's end-time strategy revealed.

However, it remains as true as ever that everyone who wants to do well in life must learn to cooperate with and respect those who have been invested with authority *and* learn to get along with others in life. In the majority of environments we live and work in — whether church, school, workplace, family, etc. — there is usually one who is the final authority, although there may be several others in a given area of life who are also in positions of authority over us (e.g., father/mother, senior pastor/pastoral team, employer/management team, principal/teachers, etc.). Regardless, we all must learn to work in harmony with whomever is over us in life.

Understanding biblical submission to authority and getting along with all forms of authority are essential if you want to do well at whatever station you are at in life. Those who refuse to cooperate with the authority figures they are subject to will never advance well in life unless they choose to change. If they decide to stay discordant and continue to refuse to submit to authority, it is likely they will be uninvited from participating in the future.

With this in mind, I urge you to do a self-evaluation of your attitude — and your mouth. Ask yourself:

- *Am I perceived as respectful or disrespectful by what others hear coming from my mouth?*

Make a decision to make any necessary adjustments in this area as soon as possible so you can remove yourself from the strong pull of rebellion toward authority that pervades this last-days society. You may disagree with an authority figure on some matter, but that does not give you the right to be disrespectful toward that person in authority over you — even when you're not in that person's presence. Disrespect is a manifestation of this end-time age. As a child of God, you surely do not want to fall into the trap of a wandering world that thinks it has a right to challenge authority figures in a godless, ugly manner.

4. Do you express thankfulness for what you have and for what others have done along the way to help you in life?

Here's an important question to ask yourself:

- *How long has it been since I stopped to thank God for what He has done for me or for the people who have been a blessing to me in life?*

In the last days when people will tend to be *ungrateful, unthankful,* and *unappreciative,* we must be intentional about being *thankful.*

In Ephesian 1:16, Paul wrote about people he was thankful for in his life. He said that he made it a point to always "give thanks" for them. The words "give thanks" comes from the Greek word *eucharisteo*, a compound of the words *eu* and *charis*. The word *eu* means *good* or *well*. It denotes a general *good disposition* or *an overwhelmingly good feeling* about something. The word *charis* is the Greek word for *grace* or *freely granted favor*.

When these two words are compounded into one, they form the word *eucharisteo*. This compound word describes *an outpouring of grace and of wonderful feelings that freely flow from the heart in response to someone or something*. This Greek word *eucharisteo* is the word Paul used in nearly all his epistles when he "gave thanks" for people.

In Colossians 1:3, Paul used the same Greek word when he wrote, "We *give thanks* to God and the Father of our Lord Jesus Christ, praying always for you." In First Thessalonians 1:2, he again used the same Greek word when he prayed similarly for the Thessalonian believers: "We *give thanks* to God always for you all, making mention of you in our prayers." In Second Thessalonians 1:3, he used this word again when he wrote, "We are bound to *thank God* always for you...."

The fact that Paul used the word *eucharisteo* when he prayed for people tells us that we must be thankful for the people God has put in our lives. Whenever we think of our closest circle of friends, a deep sense of gratefulness, thankfulness, and appreciation should well up within us!

So here's another important question to ask yourself:

- *When I pray, do I focus only on the "problem people" who bother me and steal my peace? Or do I always make certain to take the time to thank God for the faithful ones?*

The fact is, there are a lot of people who have been good to you along the way in life and you need to be intentional about being thankful for them.

Why not take a little time today to write down a list of all the people God has specially used to help you in life? Then stop to tell the Lord how grateful you are that He sent each one of them into your life. Stop for a moment and reflect on all God has done in your life through those who are closest to you. When you realize how kind people have been to you, it will help you to joyfully and unreservedly thank God for kindly placing helpful people in your life at key moments.

5. Do you have a serious attitude about sin and its consequences, or have you become too casual about godless behaviors that are not sanctioned by God?

The Holy Spirit prophesied that societal behaviors in the last days would become *ill-mannered, impure, unclean, lewd, indecent, crude, coarse, vulgar, offensive,* and *rude.* He also informed the Church ahead of time that people would develop a casual attitude toward words, actions, and behaviors that are *unholy, unsacred, impure,* and *unsanctioned by God.* Discarding the fear of God, society would throw off moral restraint and participate in things that are condemned in the sight of God.

Because we are living in the last days and are watching society become more and more tainted with these unholy traits, we need to make sure that we do not become *casual* about sin along with the rest of the world. A casual approach to sin is the reason some Christians do things that are unacceptable to God without any sense of shame or conviction. When a person loses the fear of God and develops a casual attitude toward sin, it's just a matter of time before that person begins to conduct himself or herself in ways that violate God's moral code.

Since the Holy Spirit prophesied that people would begin a slippery, downward slide into *unholiness*, it is wise for you to examine yourself with this question:

- *Have I become casual about any issues that God is NOT casual about?*

You do not need to be self-condemning, but a self-examination of this type may awaken you to areas where you have slipped in your convictions.

Let the Holy Spirit help you evaluate yourself. If you find nothing has slipped, then rejoice — but if you discover you have become a little casual about things God is not casual about, let the Holy Spirit put you back on course through His Word and prayer.

6. Do you ever seriously contemplate that eternity is in front of you and that you will give an account to God for your activities in life?

Because we are living in a last-days age when people will be self-focused and consumed with self-gratification, they often forget that eternity lies before them. In Second Corinthians 5:10, Paul reminded us, "For we must all appear before the judgement seat of Christ; that every one may receive the things done in his body, according to that he hath done, whether it be good or bad." It is always good for us to remember that eternity is in our future.

The word "appear" in Second Corinthians 5:10 is a translation of the Greek word *phaneros*. In this verse, it is a verb that means *to be apparent, revealed, visible,* or *manifest*. That means when you stand before the Judgment Seat of Christ, what you have done in your life will be clearly *revealed*. Also in this verse is the phrase "everyone" — the Greek word *hekastos*, meaning *all-inclusive; no one excluded*. It means *every* believer — which means that *you* will stand before Jesus to have your works evaluated.

In Matthew 25:19, Jesus taught that a day is coming in all of our futures when the books will be opened and He will "reckon" with us regarding how we lived our lives. The word "reckon" is a bookkeeping term that means *to compare accounts*, and it pictures *an accountant who put together a profit-and-loss statement and performed a thorough examination of the books.*

That means a day is coming when each of us will give an account for our lives. We will be evaluated to see what we did with the gifts and talents God gave us and whether we lived only for momentary pleasures or for eternal things. The fact that we are standing before Christ means we are *already* in Heaven, so an eternity in Heaven is not in jeopardy. However, *rewards* will be determined on the basis of that examination.

So ask yourself this question, and take some time to honestly assess the answer:

- *How often do I think of eternity — or am I primarily "now" focused?*

You must be intentionally cognizant of the reality that eternity is in front of you. If you do this, it will affect what you think, what you say, what you do, how you use your time, and how you spend your money. It will make you want to live your life with a view toward eternity.

7. Do you think Jesus finds you to be a grateful, thankful, appreciative person?

Finally, I simply ask you to present yourself with this question:

- *Do I think that Jesus — on the basis of what He hears me say and pray and the attitude I demonstrate in life — thinks that I am a grateful, thankful, and appreciative person?*

No one knows you better than Jesus. He watches you, listens to you, walks with you, and lives in you by His Spirit. As One who never leaves you nor forsakes you, He is your constant Companion. As such, no one knows you better than Jesus.

So ask yourself:

- *Does Jesus see me demonstrate gratitude?*

- *Does He see me being thankful for what I have in my life?*

- *Does He see me showing appreciation to others who have been a blessing to me?*

Jesus already knows the truth. This last action step is not for Him — it is for *you*. Be honest with yourself. If you find that you could be more grateful, thankful, and appreciative, ask the Lord to forgive you. Then take action to begin developing gratitude, thankfulness, and appreciativeness in your heart, attitude, words, and actions.

6

THE BREAKDOWN OF THE FAMILY, WIDESPREAD DIVORCE, COVENANT-BREAKING, AND THE DEVIL IN THE COURTROOM

We have already covered much of what the Holy Spirit forecasted in Second Timothy 3 — but there is more to learn. In this chapter, we will continue to dig further to see what else He had to say in Second Timothy 3 to help prepare God's people in the last of the last days.

First, however, I want to remind you of what we've seen regarding Second Timothy 3:1 and 2. Let's take in all we've discussed and then build from there.

From all we've learned thus far, the *RIV* of these two verses is as follows:

1. You emphatically and categorically need to know with unquestionable certainty that in the very end of days — when time has sailed to its last port and no more time remains for the journey — that last season will stand in the midst of uncontrollable, unpredictable,

hurtful, treacherous, menacing times that will be emotionally difficult for people to bear.

2. Men will be self-focused, self-centered, self-absorbed, self-consumed, and in love with themselves more than anyone else. As a result of this self-love, they will be driven to obtain more and more and more. These boasters are so committed to their own agenda that they are willing to exaggerate, overstate the facts, stretch the truth, embellish a story, and even lie if it will get them the position, advantage, or goal they desire. They are arrogant, haughty, impudent, snooty, and insolent. They disdain, mock, slander, and speak ill of anyone who stands in the way of their ideology and freely use foul language. In this climate, parents will no longer be able to persuade, control, lead, or exercise authority over their own children. And although people were once thankful and appreciative, they will generally become void of gratitude and will be unappreciative of everything. Impurity will seep into society and cause it to become impure, ill-mannered, unclean, indecent, coarse, vulgar, offensive, crude, lewd, and rude.

It's amazing to realize all the profound treasures of meaning that lay hidden just below the surface of the words in just these two verses! What a wealth of truth we've already gleaned to help arm and equip us for these last of the last days! But let's now go on to Second Timothy 3:3. There is much more to discover about what the Holy Spirit prophesied in this chapter to help prepare us to live as this age nears its conclusion.

DISJOINTED FAMILIES
AND THE DISINTEGRATION OF THE HOME

As Paul wrote under the inspiration of the Holy Spirit, he prophesied that the majority of people in the last days would become "without natural affection, trucebreakers, false accusers, incontinent, fierce, despisers of those that are good." In this chapter, we will look at the words *without natural affection, trucebreakers,* and *false accusers* to discover what these words mean, especially for those who live in the last of the last days.

The words "without natural affection" are derived from the Greek word *storgos.* This word *storgos* is a Greek word that depicts *devotion* and *commitment to one's family.* But in this verse, it is actually the word *astorgos.* When an *a* is added to the front of the word, it has a canceling effect; hence, it pictures *a lack of devotion to family, an absence of commitment to one's family, the deterioration of family relationships, the loss of family affection,* or *the breakdown of the family.* Furthermore, the word *astorgos* was a word that especially denoted individuals who had drifted so far apart that they had at last reached a point of irreconcilable differences between themselves. As a result, they found it was easier to part than to stay together.

The words "without natural affection" inform us that *the deterioration of traditional family and the home* will become pandemic as this age races toward its conclusion. The word *astorgos* unquestionably portrays *disjointed families* who have lost the *closeness* that was once exemplified in the traditional family. It no doubt portrays a day when individuals and families will drift far apart. As a result, differences that develop gradually between them over a period of time will become so difficult to fix that they will find it easier to keep drifting — or even to part — than to stay together and make things work out. That is the word that the Holy Spirit used in this verse to alert us that families at large in the last days will become disjointed and lose the closeness that was once a characteristic of the family unit.

It is a fact that today — all across societal stratum — families are under attack and are in a state of terrible deterioration. The Holy Spirit spoke clearly about this so that those who live in the last of the last days would be aware of this development and would take precautions to protect their families from this tragedy. We must have ears to hear what the Spirit is saying and respond with wisdom so that our families will remain free from this end-time attack.

If we pay heed to what the Holy Spirit says and build our homes according to God's Word, we can have strong families even in the last of the last days. Because we are living in this end-time hour, it is vital that a hedge is built around our marriages and families. If we use caution and exercise faith, we can do our part to withstand the spiritual attacks that are waged in the last days to tear families apart.

◆

**If we pay heed to what the Holy Spirit says
and build our homes according to God's Word,
we can have strong families even in the last of the last days.**

◆

We are all well aware that many marriages and families have already been torn apart. The devil has done his best to create devastating situations that have broken hearts, shattered children, and left families decimated financially. I know this well, for when my wife and I were first married, we led a large single-adult ministry that had a special emphasis on ministering to those who had suffered divorce. In those years, I learned about the trauma of divorce.

Almost no one *wants* to go through divorce. No one gets married to have a failed marriage with children torn between two separated parents. To this day, my heart goes out to those who suffer the trauma of divorce and as a result have become fractured.

Perhaps *your* family has experienced such a devastating attack. Or perhaps you are still together as a family, but you have lost the closeness you once knew as a family. Maybe you are just now beginning to sense that life is spinning out of control and that a disruption of some sort is about to encroach upon you and your family members. Or perhaps you are doing all you know to do, but your spouse seems to be headed in another direction that is deeply disturbing to you. It is very difficult when one spouse is committed to making a marriage work, but the other spouse is not. If that describes you, God is with you, and He will empower you to make right choices along the way.

Perhaps your family is strong, but you see your children or grandchildren suffering in their family life. It is difficult — to say the least — to watch a child, grandchild, or sibling go through hard times in their own families. It is especially difficult when you know that you could help them, but the door is not open for you to speak into their lives; you must remain silent on the sidelines because your counsel is not welcomed. In such cases, it is vital that you accept your silent role as a prayer partner to undergird them before the throne of God. As you stand in faith for your family members, God will move on their behalf and will eventually open a door for you to become the help you desire to be.

As I write on this subject, please know there is not even a hint of condemnation or judgment for anyone who has already experienced the deterioration of his or her family. But the Scriptures were written to warn us in advance of this development that will emerge in society in the last days so we would *respond*. Because these *are* the last days, it is obligatory that we do all we know to do to build a wall of protection around our homes and relationships so we don't succumb to the family-assaulting spirit of this age.

Today traditional families and homes are threatened by over-busy schedules, financial pressures, more than one job in a home, as well as multiple cars, televisions, digital devices, etc. Although some of these may appear to be blessings, these factors can create an entirely separate path for each family member if they are not properly managed.

---◆---

**Because these *are* the last days,
it is obligatory that we do all we know to do
to build a wall of protection around our homes and relationships
so we don't succumb to the family-assaulting spirit of this age.**

---◆---

If precaution is not taken, parents end up going in one direction while children go another direction — and often husbands and wives each have their own separate directions as well. Because of varying schedules, family members are rarely at home at the same time or eating a meal together. And when they are home, they are all looking at different TVs, computers, or gadgets in different rooms of the house. The family may technically live under one roof, but they do not truly share life because they are all going in different directions.

I'm not being negative; I'm being realistic about the challenges facing families today — challenges that did not exist even one or two generations ago when people lived simpler lives. Just know that this assault to pull the family apart is not happening only to you; it is happening to families everywhere across the globe. Because you care about the health of your family, it would be wise to evaluate the state of affairs in your home right now.

For example, be honest with yourself as you ask: *If things keep going the way they are right now, what will be the long-term impact on my family? Are we going to grow stronger or drift apart?*

The statistics in the following paragraphs are changing every year, so they will probably be out of date even before this book reaches you. But by looking at these facts, you will see how many developments in our age have contributed to the breakdown of the family — *including Christian families.* Much territory has already been lost on the home front. For the vast majority, the downward spiral has been unintentional. Regardless, much has been lost that can only be regained through repentance, smart decisions, and wise planning.

———◆———

It would be wise to be honest with yourself as you ask:
If things keep going the way they are right now,
what will be the long-term impact on my family?
Are we going to grow stronger or drift apart?

———◆———

The Holy Spirit prophesied the breakdown of the home, and it is happening right under our noses, just as He prophesied it would in the last days. But we can prevent that trend in our own homes and even recapture and restore what has already been lost.

Any parent or family has an opportunity to change a downward trajectory in their home life. They need only be willing to conduct an honest evaluation, allowing the Holy Spirit to be their Guide to help them arrive at truth and be willing to do whatever is necessary to make their families strong again. As they take steps along this path, they may see much repaired that has already been damaged and, in many cases, they may see their families become whole again.

The following are some facts, along with probing questions — *uncomfortable questions* — to help you make a truthful analysis about your own home life and what action steps you may need to take to recapture what has been lost and to make your family stronger than it has ever been. If your marriage and family have already been negatively affected, the Holy Spirit will also show *you* what action steps to take personally so you can become strong and healthy in your soul again. Only you know the answers to these questions.

I do not even suggest that I might be able to provide counsel on what your family should do. However, these are healthy questions to ask yourself.

The information that follows is based on 2019 U.S. statistics; however, these are similar to statistics found in the majority of Western nations. So here we go…

Television

Statistics show that in the United States, there are nearly three televisions per household. Many families today have a television in the family room, kitchen, bedroom, and often even in the kids' rooms. The day of the family sitting together to watch a TV program is almost gone. Instead, people gravitate to various television sets in different rooms of the house to watch what they wish, irrespective of the activities of the other family members.

Although you need not be against television in itself or against being financially blessed sufficiently to own several TV sets, you should ask yourself: *Do the multiple television sets in our home contribute to my family's spending time together, or do they contribute to pulling my family apart?*

Computers

More than one-third of American households have three or more computers in their homes. Do each of your children need one, or can you share among yourselves?

Although you certainly do not need to be against computers or against being financially blessed to own several of them, you should ask yourself: *Are all those computers contributing to my family's spending time together, or do they contribute to pulling my family apart?*

Digital Gadgets

Statistics show that the majority of Americans spend up to 12 hours a day in front of some type of screen and that the average person consumes five times more information every day than he or she did 50 years ago. How many members of your family have digital gadgets that distract them from interaction with each other?

Although you need not be against digital gadgets or being financially blessed to own several of them, you should ask yourself: *Are all those digital gadgets contributing to my family's spending time together, or do they contribute to pulling my family apart?*

Multiple Cars

More than 35 percent of American households have three or more automobiles. The fact is that life has become so scheduled and busy that it is challenging to live without multiple cars in one family. The father goes one direction; the mother goes another direction; and as kids reach the legal age to drive, they want their own vehicle so they can be free from depending on their dad and mom to take them everywhere they need or want to go.

Although you certainly need not be against cars or being financially blessed to own several of them, you should ask yourself: *Are those multiple cars contributing to my family's spending time together, or do they contribute to pulling my family apart?*

Mobile phones

Statistics show that more than one-third of Americans have three or more smart phones in their homes. This inevitably leads to family members being consumed with calls, texts, or social media. Family members often don't even talk to each other when they sit down for a meal because they are too busy reading, sending texts, or surfing the Internet.

How many mobile phones are there in your family? Although you need not be against mobile phones or being financially blessed to own several of them, you should ask yourself: *Are mobile phones contributing to my family's spending time together, or do they contribute to pulling my family apart?*

Internet

Statistics show that 90 percent of Americans regularly access the Internet. Nine out of every ten homes have access to the Internet. Further studies show that the average usage of the Internet is nearly seven hours per day per person of those who have access to it in their homes. This includes accessing the Internet on smart phones and every type of digital gadget. Life has become so intertwined with the Internet that we cannot easily live without it today.

How many hours does your own family spend on the Internet? Although you need not be against the Internet, you should ask yourself: *Are the hours my family members spend on the Internet contributing to our spending time together, or do they contribute to pulling my family apart?*

Social Media

How many people and families are addicted to social media? The latest statistics show the average social-media user spends two and a half hours a day on various social-media platforms. What effect do you think this has on family relationships and real-life friendships?

What would be the response of your family members if you required a forced fast from social media for a month? Why don't you try it and see what happens in your family during the time you shut it down? Although you need not be against social media, you should ask yourself: *Are the hours my family spends on social media contributing to our spending time together, or do they contribute to pulling my family apart?*

Extracurricular Activities

Statistics reveal that six out of ten children among average American households are involved in hours of extracurricular activities. These could include an endless list of school activities, sports, music, art, and so on. Although these activities are deemed important, what is required to get the kids to these activities often puts both financial stress and scheduling challenges on the family. It often leads to a disconnect between spouses because they don't see each other as a result of the time spent driving kids back and forth to events. Often these activities pull the family apart and frequently add nothing to their adult lives later on.

Although you need not be against extracurricular activities, you need to ask yourself: *Are the hours my family spends on extracurricular activities contributing to our spending time together, or are they a distraction that contributes to pulling my family apart?*

Sociologists have determined that all of these things I just listed are among the factors that have contributed to:

- Deteriorating marriages and spouses drifting apart as a result of lifestyles that are so fast-paced that husbands and wives don't regularly take time to interact in a meaningful way.

- Children who feel neglected or unwanted.

- Disorders in children who are rushed from one place to the next or who spend too much time watching television, computers, or digital devices rather than relating with parents and siblings.

Chemical Addiction

I must also mention the devastating role that addiction to prescribed medication and chemical addictions are producing in the family today. This has truly become a pandemic situation that is out of control. More than 50 percent of the American population annually misuses prescription drugs. Rising abuse of prescription opioids, which has led to heroin use, has fueled a record number of drug-related deaths.

This epidemic has forced the Center for Disease Control to issue a mandate that calls on physicians to look for other ways to alleviate pain before prescribing opioids and to limit the duration of the first prescription.[13] The consequences of this abuse have been steadily worsening and is reflected in increased treatment admissions, emergency-room visits, and overdose deaths.

Just ask any professional family counselor or experienced schoolteacher about the state of families and children, and the majority of them will tell you that the family today is under attack and in serious trouble. All the sociological studies and statistics irrefutably show that there is a downward trend for the traditional family and home over the past decades that is deeply disturbing.

But, thank God, there are those who are willing to wake up to this last-days development! Faithful believers who submit to the authority of the Scriptures and are willing to do whatever is necessary to build a hedge of protection around their homes do *not* have to fall victim to this destructive end-time attack on families. And if the enemy has already gained ground in their families, they can stand on God's Word and use their authority in the name of Jesus to *take back* that territory and recapture whatever has been lost! We'll look at addictive behaviors in greater depth in the following chapter.

---

[13] Jaime Rosenberg, "More Than Half of Americans Misuse Prescription Drugs," September 11, 2018, ajmc.com, https://www.ajmc.com/focus-of-the-week/more-than-half-of-americans-misuse-prescription-drugs.

---◆---

**Faithful believers who submit to the authority
of the Scriptures and are willing to do whatever is necessary
to build a hedge of protection around their homes
do *not* have to fall victim to this destructive
end-time attack on families.**

---◆---

MAKING THE DECISION TO REDEEM TIME

I want to encourage you that if you haven't taken the time with your family to build strength in each member individually and in the family as a whole — and if your family has suffered as a consequence — you can begin now to ask God to help you "redeem the time" (*see* Ephesians 5:16). He will show you how to make the necessary time to strengthen your family. And as you follow His leading, He will increase the positive impact of that time and fortify you and your loved ones to become a solid, robust family in Christ, devoted fully to Him.

Instead of living in regret about what you could have done better in the past, you can lay hold of this moment to make wise decisions about your present and future. If you simply live in a state of regret, that negative emotion will only make things even worse, dragging you down into a state of discouragement and self-condemnation. It's so much better to just lift your hands and rejoice that you still have an opportunity to redeem the time that has been lost! Don't let the devil lie to you and tell you that it's too late. It's *not* too late.

Ephesians 5:16 commands us to get busy "redeeming the time." Time can be either lost or wasted, depending on what we did with it. But if we have wasted or lost time or precious opportunities in our past, the end is not over! Ephesians 5:16 clearly says we can "redeem" time.

The word "redeem" in that verse is a translation of the Greek word *exagoradzo*. The word *agoradzo* is the Greek word for *a marketplace* that is cluttered with products and with a vast array of opportunities to spend far more time and money while shopping there than one ought to spend.

It was the same in the markets of ancient times as it is today. If a person wasn't careful, he could become lost roaming through the shops, wasting precious time. But that word *ex* means *out*. It's where we get the word *exit*. When *ex* is added to the word *agoradzo* to form *exagoradzo*, it paints the picture of finding what you need, purchasing it, and getting out of the marketplace quickly. In other words, do what you need to do and then make an *exit*!

But Ephesians 5:16 says we are to redeem the "time." That word "time" is a translation of the Greek word *kairos*. In this context, it refers to the brevity of time we have available and our need to be time-conscious in the way we conduct our lives. It depicts someone who is learning to make full use of time because he is conscious that his time is limited and he must use it wisely. Paul was saying that by implementing diligence and commitment, we can redeem time — or buy back time — that we have frivolously lost along the way.

The good news is this: If our lives have become cluttered and we've lost precious opportunities in any area — including time lost with our families — we can still *reverse* this condition. Through our recommitment to ourselves and to the Lord, we can buy back time that has been lost, wasted, or forfeited. And with the Holy Spirit's supernatural help, we can accomplish in *a short time* what we thought was forever lost. We can *redeem that time* and get back on course!

I want to encourage you — if your children are grown and you find yourself regretting your past attitudes and actions toward your family, God is still in the business of redeeming the time. If you'll seek His face and, if needed, seek counsel to help you get things back on track, God will honor your humility and your prayers. You can see God's power work to restore what has come under attack in your marriage and in the lives of your children.

---◆---

**Through our recommitment to ourselves and to the Lord,
we can buy back time that has been lost, wasted, or forfeited.
And with the Holy Spirit's supernatural help, we can accomplish
in *a short time* what we thought was forever lost.**

---◆---

I encourage you never to take the attitude that it's too late for your family or your loved ones. You can't change history or go back and relive seasons that are long past. But you can pray for God's will to be fulfilled in the season you're in now — and you can expect that He will work to restore hearts and lives according to His design and plan.

It is so important in these last days — regardless of the mistakes of our past or even our victories — that we commit ourselves as never before to obey God and what He has revealed in His Word, walking in every bit of light we receive as we seek Him. If we fail to honor and uphold the sacrificial work of Christ and His infallible Word, we risk falling in with the tide of the world and experiencing firsthand the fierce harshness that surrounds us in modern society. But if we stick with the immutable Word of God and let it be a lamp to our feet and a light to our path (*see* Psalm 119:105), it will lead us back onto the path of stability in every area of our lives — including our *families*!

If you have already suffered loss in your personal family, don't forget that there is still great opportunity for a divine turnaround! Our God is a Redeemer! He has the amazing ability to redeem what has been lost and to restore both time and opportunities that were lost along the way. And if you believe that you need someone to help you work through shattered emotions or brokenness, don't be afraid to find someone who is qualified to help you. God may heal your heart through a qualified person's godly counsel. There are gifted individuals He has prepared to help you make it through this personal trauma and get back on the path to wholeness.

It is so important in these last days —
regardless of the mistakes of our past or even our victories —
that we commit ourselves as never before to obey God
and what He has revealed in His Word,
walking in every bit of light we receive as we seek Him.

I want to make sure you clearly understand that the phrase "without natural affection" (*astorgos*) pictures *a lack of devotion to family, an absence of commitment to one's family, the deterioration of family relationships, the loss of family affection,* or *the breakdown of the family.*

By using the Greek word *astorgos*, the Holy Spirit is incontestably prophesying that the traditional family and home will come under severe attack in the very last of the last days. This first part of Second Timothy 3:3 could thus be translated, *"Love for and commitment to family will disintegrate...."* The good news is, we can guard against it!

TRUCE-BREAKING
AND THE VIOLATING OF COVENANT

But as Paul continued to forecast end-time societal characteristics in Second Timothy 3:3, he added that in the last days, people will become *"...truce-breakers, false accusers, incontinent, fierce, despisers of those that are good."*

The Holy Spirit adds the word "trucebreakers" to the list. The word "truce-breakers" is built on the Greek word *spondos*, which depicts *a covenant* or *those who are in some type of covenant with one another*. But in Second Timothy 3:3, the word is not *spondos*; it is the word *aspondos*. Remember, when an *a* is added to the front of the word, it has a canceling effect. Now it depicts *the undoing of a covenant* or *one who breaks a covenant*. The *King James Version* translated it as "truce-breaking," but it is actually the Greek word for *covenant-breaking*. It is very significant that it immediately follows the prophesied breakdown of the family at the end of the age. By using this word *aspondos*, Paul pictured the ultimate breakdown of covenant in the form of widespread divorce that will become rampant in a last-days society.

It's amazing to me that the word "trucebreakers" — translated from the Greek word *aspondos* — is the very word ancient Greeks used to describe relationships that had reached a point of *irreconcilable differences*. By using this word, the Holy Spirit prophesied that a season would emerge at the end of the age in which individuals in covenant relationship will drift apart until they reach a point of *irreconcilable differences* between themselves. These individuals will find that the less complicated solution is to walk away from the relationship — hence, *breaking their truce* or *breaking their covenant*.

I am well aware that some situations become so complicated that parting may be the only solution that remains viable in a covenant relationship. But in this verse, the Holy Spirit prophesied this to alert us so we would do all we can to guard against this tragic outcome in our own personal lives.

Remember, the phrase "without natural affection" forecasts the deterioration of the family. Then Paul built upon that point by telling us the extent to which this deterioration will go.

The word *aspondos* categorically means that *covenant-breaking* will become commonplace in the very last of the last days. And as noted earlier, the word *aspondos,* when applied to marriage, describes spouses who are no longer able to come to terms with one another. These are married couples who feel that they have become *incompatible* or that they have reached a point of *irreconcilable differences.* In this verse, Paul predicted a rampant outbreak of *divorce* in the very last of the last days.

THE SHORT- AND LONG-TERM RAMIFICATIONS OF DIVORCE

The introduction of *no-fault divorce* in the 1970s was a huge contributor to rampant divorce because it made the process easier than it had been in the past. Statistics show that the introduction of no-fault divorce opened the floodgates by allowing easier dissolution of marriages.

Often the relative ease in dissolving a marital union causes marriage agreements to be entered into with less-than-reverent attitudes about the sacred institution of marriage, although this is usually not the case for a couple who are both serious believers. This lack of reverence for the covenant of the marital union is especially prevalent among younger people who have not been reared in a godly environment. They know that they can rather easily "get out of it" if marriage doesn't meet up to their expectations.

◆

Often the relative ease in dissolving a marital union causes marriage agreements to be entered into with less-than-reverent attitudes about the sacred institution of marriage.

◆

Through the years since that law was passed, many spouses have experienced deep heartbreak from a divorce they never wanted and never dreamed would happen to them, and the "lovers of their own selves" syndrome prophesied by the Holy Spirit has been a great contributor to this moral mess. Because of the rampant self-centeredness in society today, many view marriage merely as a vehicle of self-gratification through romance and intimacy. In this new psychological approach to married life, one's primary obligation is not to one's family but to one's self. Hence, marital success is defined not by successfully meeting obligations to one's spouse and children, but by a strong sense of subjective happiness in marriage.

When the rule of personal happiness becomes the supreme dream, those who feel they are in unfulfilling marriages tend to feel justified in divorcing their spouse, acting on the modern ethic of expressive individualism. One social historian has observed, "The dissolution of marriage offered the chance to make oneself over from the inside out, to refurbish and express the inner self, and to acquire certain valuable psychological assets and competencies, such as initiative, assertiveness, and a stronger and better self-image."[14]

The result is that divorce has become a booming industry, especially since the 1970s. There are currently approximately 1.1 million divorces every year in the United States, and in some countries, the rate is even higher. One source estimates the divorce industry revenue will grow 1.2 percent annually, soon to exceed $11.3 billion annually. More than $40 billion is spent every year on child support and alimony, and there are currently more than 60,000 professional workers in this "industry" — administering dissolutions, facilitating negotiations, enforcing payment arrangements, etc.[15]

Meanwhile, this pandemic of divorce has also fueled the growth of government, as federal, state, and local governments spend more money on police, prisons, welfare, and court costs, trying to pick up the pieces of broken

[14] Barbara Dafoe Whitehead, *The Divorce Culture: Rethinking Our Commitments to Marriage and Family* (New York: Vintage Books, 1996), p. 5.
[15] "Family Law & Divorce Lawyers & Attorneys in the US Industry Trends," May 2019, IBISWorld.com, https://www.ibisworld.com/united-states/market-research-reports/family-law-divorce-lawyers-attorneys-industry/.

families. One study shows that the public costs of family breakdown exceed $112 billion a year.[16]

Since the 1970s, nearly 1 million children per year have watched their parents go through divorce — and it is statistically proven that children who are exposed to divorce are two to three times more likely than peers to suffer from serious social or psychological pathologies. Sociologists have concluded that 31 percent of adolescents with divorced parents dropped out of high school, compared to 13 percent of children from families with no divorce. Also, studies showed that 33 percent of adolescent girls whose parents divorced became teen mothers, compared to 11 percent of girls from continuously married families, and that 11 percent of boys who come from divorced families end up spending time in prison before the age of 32, compared to 5 percent of boys who come from intact homes.[17]

Researchers have also found that remarriage is not usually a healing balm for children of divorce. One leading sociologist found that "children whose parents have remarried do not have higher levels of well-being than children in lone-parent families."[18] Often the establishment of a step-family, or blended family, results in yet another move for a child, requiring adjustment to a new caretaker and new step-siblings — all of which can be difficult for children, who thrive on stability.[19]

Studies show that when children see their parents divorce for whatever reason — because they have drifted apart, because one or both parents have become unhappy, or because a parent left to pursue another partner — the kids' personal confidence in love, commitment, and marriage is often shattered. In the wake of their parents' divorce, children are also likely to experience

---

[16] W. Bradford Wilcox, "The Evolution of Divorce," (quoting economist Ben Scafidi), Fall 2009, nationalaffairs.com, https://www.nationalaffairs.com/publications/detail/the-evolution-of-divorce.
[17] Ibid.
[18] Andrew J. Cherlin, *The Marriage-Go-Round: The State of Marriage and the Family in America Today* (New York: Vintage Books, 2009), p. 22.
[19] Wilcox, "The Evolution of Divorce."

a family move, marked declines in their family income, a stressed-out single mother, and substantial periods of paternal absence. All of these are factors that put children of divorced families at risk. In other words, the great majority of divorces involving children in America are *not* in the best interests of the children.[20]

Sociologists estimate that if the United States enjoyed the same level of family stability today as it did in 1960, the nation would have 750,000 fewer children repeating grades, 1.2 million fewer school suspensions, approximately 500,000 fewer acts of teenage delinquency, about 600,000 fewer kids receiving therapy, and approximately 70,000 fewer suicide attempts every year.[21] Those are staggering statistics! Studies have also proven beyond a hint of doubt that divorce contributes to generational cycles of divorce.

We now know that adult children of divorce are 89 percent more likely themselves to divorce, compared to children who were raised in families with no divorce. Children of divorce who marry other children of divorce are *especially* likely to end up divorced. Of course, the reason children of divorce are more likely to end their own marriages is precisely that they have often learned all the wrong lessons about trust, commitment, mutual sacrifice, and fidelity from their parents.[22]

The fact is that within the Christian community, there is also a very high rate of divorce. This shows how the spirit of this age has penetrated the lives of God's people and the reason why those who are married must do all they can in these last days to build a hedge of protection around their marriages. Just to give an example, statistics show that approximately 35 percent of Christians have experienced divorce, which is similar to the percentage of non-Christians

---

[20] Ibid.
[21] Margaret McCarthy, ed., *Torn Asunder* (Grand Rapids, MI: William B. Eerdmans Publishing Co., 2017), p. 53.
[22] Nicholas Wolfinger, "Understanding the Divorce Cycle: The Children of Divorce in Their Own Marriages." 2005, researchgate.net.

in the same category.[23] Reports also show that 23 percent of Christians get divorced two times or more.[24]

WHAT TO DO IN LIGHT OF ALL OF THIS

First, what should you do if you are struggling in your marital relationship? God will use His Word, the power of His Spirit, and those who have the wisdom to help you bring healing and restoration to your marriage — *if* you both want it. It will take work, time, and willingness on the part of both you and your spouse. But with the help God provides, the two of you can see Him work a miracle in your marriage. You do not have to fall prey to the epidemic of divorce that is so rampant in the world today.

If you have already fallen victim to the heartbreaking ordeal of divorce, God's grace is present and available to restore you. He loves you. He cares deeply about the wound that this painful experience has inflicted in your soul — your mind, your will, and your emotions — as well as in the souls of your children. With the help of God and the empowerment of the Spirit, it is possible for you to fully recover from this trauma. *God is always present to help those who call and wait upon Him in time of need.*

It may not be you who has experienced divorce. Perhaps it is your child, grandchild, sibling, or another loved one who is dear to you. If you know someone who is going through this very heart-wrenching ordeal, let the Holy Spirit use you to pray for that person. Encourage the one who is experiencing such pain that he or she will come out on the other side of this struggle and discover God's redemptive plan. In some cases, with repentance, prayer, time, and qualified counseling, what seems lost can be restored.

---

[23] "Born-Again Christians Just as Likely To Divorce as Are Non-Christians," Barna.com, https://www.barna.com/research/born-again-christians-just-as-likely-to-divorce-as-are-non-christians/.
[24] Ibid.

I realize some situations do not seem fixable. One spouse may have a commitment to work through the problems and keep the marriage together while the other spouse remains unwilling to do what is right. The sad truth is that sometimes in this fallen world, the issues that can cause a broken marriage relationship just do not get worked out.

All you can do is your best, so I encourage you to give your marriage your best. That should be your focus. You cannot answer for another's heart or what your spouse is unwilling to do, but you *will* answer for your own heart and your own obedience to the Lord. Therefore, make sure you have done everything He has required of you so you are able to truthfully say you did all you knew to do to make your marriage work.

If you are looking back at a past divorce and you now realize that you also contributed to the failure of the marriage, it is important for you to acknowledge and repent for what you did wrong. Remember, God's arms are open wide to embrace you, forgive you, and restore you. Even more, He wants to give you a fresh revelation of the holiness and the blessing of marriage. The union between a husband and wife is His most precious gift of relationship besides the gift of a relationship with Himself through Jesus Christ.

The truth is, Jesus stands ready to breathe new life into *any* "dead" or hard places in your life. He wants to place you upright on your feet again so you can be a light and a witness for Him in the darkened world around you. *All you have to do is sincerely ask!*

MAKE THE DEVIL REGRET
HE EVER MESSED WITH YOU!

If you're still married, it's not too late to submit all areas of offense or hardness to Him and to believe Him for godly, lasting change. God's power is ready and willing *right now* to go to work on any marriage that is submitted to His Word, His authority, and His power. Never forget that God specializes in raising dead things back to life again.

**Jesus stands ready to breathe new life
into *any* "dead" or hard places in your life.
He wants to place you upright on your feet again
so you can be a light and a witness for Him
in the darkened world around you.**

The devil may have attacked you or your family, but just determine to see it as God sees it — as an amazing opportunity for you to take advantage of, armed with His strength and grace! You can become an instrument He can use to bring healing to those you love. *You can make the enemy sorry that he ever messed with you or your family!* With the Word of God as your guide, the Holy Spirit as your Teacher, and the support of brothers and sisters in the Christian community, you can rise above anything the enemy has waged against you, and you can live the rest of your life victoriously.

(To strengthen you in your journey in this area of marriage, I recommend my wife Denise's book *Who Stole Cinderella? The Art of Living Happily Ever After.* Don't let the title mislead you to think it is only for women, because Denise's amazing book has many strengthening truths to help husbands as well. Her book *The Gift of Forgiveness* is also a powerful tool to help empower your stance of faith.)

Perhaps you feel lonely at times because those you love are no longer near. Or maybe you feel stressed because of a lack of finances. Whatever you're facing right now, this is *not* the time for you to give up. On the contrary — it's time to jump back in the race and run with all your might to fulfill your God-given purpose and destiny!

God loves us so much that He *forewarned* us of these last-days events nearly 2,000 years in advance. He did it so we could prepare ourselves by drawing near to Him and walking by faith in the victory that was won for us in Christ's death and resurrection. We don't have to be dejected or afraid — *this is truly our hour on the earth to shine*!

THE WIDESPREAD BREAKING
OF ALL TYPES OF COVENANTS

I need to add that the Greek word *aspondos* in Second Timothy 3:3 does not *only* apply to the breaking of marital vows and divorce. The word is so all-encompassing that it could picture the breaking of *any* form of covenant — including business covenants, contracts, relational covenants, and marital vows. Please understand that the Holy Spirit uses this very specific word to inform us that at the very end of the age, there will be widespread *truce-breaking* on every imaginable level. Whereas a person's word or handshake was once considered to be a guarantee one could rely on, it will come to mean nearly nothing in the last of the last days.

The word *aspondos* could even depict the breaking of a deeply felt covenant bond between two or more friends. With life moving so fast, it is more difficult than ever to sustain a strong bond with the friends we are closest to, let alone maintain a deep relationship with those people. As the close of the age approaches, relationships will become "easy come, easy go" — reflecting the self-focused, self-absorbed spirit of the age that only sticks around for what is self-gratifying.

This Greek word *aspondos* could also refer to one who breaks a covenant with a local church. We can see that we live in a day when believers' commitment to their local church continues to grow weaker and weaker as people pull up roots and transplant themselves from church to church. And this is just one more example of what truce-breaking will look like in the very last days of this age. A disregard for covenant relationships will eventually infiltrate all facets of society — resulting in *en masse* divorce, contractual breaches of all kinds, and every other form of covenant bond being fractured or destroyed. Because this pattern will be so rampant, it therefore stands to reason that it will also try to infiltrate the Church.

**In light of all this,
the *RIV* of Second Timothy 3:3 reads this way:**

Love for and commitment to family will disintegrate, and divorce will become epidemic, with irreconcilable differences being a major factor in tearing families apart. In fact, every imaginable type of covenant will be regularly violated….

But where there is covenant-breaking, there is also widespread legal action and lawsuits — which leads to the next point Paul gave in his list of characteristics that will be indicative of society in the last of the last days. Pay close attention, because you will find this point very interesting. You will see again that the Holy Spirit was absolutely accurate in what He forecasted about society at the end of the age.

AN OVERLOADED COURT SYSTEM

In Second Timothy 3:3, Paul added his next point. He wrote that people in the last days will be "trucebreakers, *false accusers*…."

The words "false accusers" are translated from the Greek word *diabolos*, which is most often translated in the New Testament as *devil, accuser,* or *slanderer*. But as it is used in Second Timothy 3:3, it depicts *a court system that is overrun with accusing and slanderous lawsuits.*

The word *diabolos* — normally translated *devil* — in this particular verse portrays a court system that is overrun with lawsuits. Hence, the Holy Spirit shows us that in the last of the last days, people will feel as if the *devil himself* has been released with full force into the court system as an *accuser* and *slanderer*. Paul surely used this word to forewarn of a strange time at the end of the age when people would excessively *accuse* and *slander* each other, finding it easier to *sue* in a court of law than to sit down and work out their disagreements or difficulties.

The facts show that in our time, we are witnessing more litigation than ever before as people go about suing and being sued. That is exactly what the phrase "false accusers" forewarned us of in Second Timothy 3:3. It vividly warns us that in the last of the last days, the devil will find easy access into courts to *accuse* — and it will be a recurring pattern that increases more and more. That last season of the age will be a time when the legal system will become *overloaded* with lawsuits of all kinds as more and more people refuse even to *attempt* reconciling their disputes or differences.

Let me give you some statistics that are shocking. These are based on the current situation in the United States, but a similar pattern is transpiring as well in other Western nations. More than 100 million civil lawsuits are filed annually — and this is only *civil lawsuits*, which does not take into account other types of legal action. A nearly unfathomable $429 billion was spent in 2016 on costs and compensations in the U.S. tort system, which is equivalent to 2.3 percent of the gross national product.[25]

The possibility of being sued in America has made it one of the scariest places in the world to do business, because a person is always at risk of

---

[25] "Law Abuse Impact," U. S. Chamber Institute for Legal Reform, https://www.instituteforlegalreform.com/issues/lawsuit-abuse-impact.

someone suing him or her. As a result, America now has the most costly legal system in the world. Its legal system is so out of control that it impedes the ability to grow the economy and to even create jobs.

The impact of pervasive lawsuits in America — and the reputation of being easily sued — has made the nation unattractive for many international companies. This has put the U.S. at a competitive disadvantage.[26] One official report states that the effects of lawsuit abuse extend beyond America's borders. High liability costs make U.S. businesses less competitive internationally. Another study found that liability costs in the U.S. decrease manufacturing competitiveness.[27]

Fear of being sued has affected nearly every profession — and it has radically affected the medical profession. Defensive medicine now costs the United States $650 billion per year — which means approximately 26 percent of every dollar spent on medical care goes into protection against lawsuits. In addition, "a new study reveals that the cost of medical malpractice in the United States is running at about $55.6 billion a year — $45.6 billion of which is spent on defensive medicine practiced by physicians seeking to stay clear of lawsuits."[28]

Slander or defamation lawsuits are also much more prevalent in today's society — up 40 percent in some markets.[29] The worldwide associated costs of such lawsuits — counselors, doctors, professional help, detectives — is truly astronomical.

The potential of being sued is foreboding to a majority of Americans. In fact, a recent national survey shows that 87 percent of American voters view

[26] Ibid.

[27] Ibid.

[28] Rick Ungar, "The True Cost of Medical Malpractice — It May Surprise You," forbes.com, https://www.forbes.com/sites/rickungar/2010/09/07/the-true-cost-of-medical-malpractice-it-may-surprise-you/#3b7c971a2ff5.

[29] "Judicial Statistics, 2017: Issued Defamation Claims Up by 40%, Highest in Three Years," Inforrm's Blog, https://inforrm.org/2018/06/26/judicial-statistics-2017-issued-defamation-claims-up-by-40-highest-for-three-years/; Roy Greenslade, "23% Increase in Defamation Action as Social Media Claims Rise," October 20, 2014, theguardian.com, https://www.theguardian.com/media/greenslade/2014/oct/20/medialaw-social-media.

the number of lawsuits in the country as a problem and that 69 percent say there has been increased abuse of the legal system over the past decade. Furthermore, one in three voters — and 43 percent of small-business owners — report having either been threatened with or involved in a civil lawsuit. Only 14 percent of those who were part of a class-action lawsuit reported that they received something of meaningful value, such as a cashed check or redeemed coupon, as a result of the lawsuit. In contrast, four in five voters that had been involved in a civil lawsuit said that lawyers benefited the most from class-action lawsuits.[30]

The age of decency is dead. This is the age of slander and accusation.

A self-focused age of entitlement, as we saw in Second Timothy 3:2, lends credence to society's claim that an individual has a "right" to get all he or she can out of every situation. Of course, there are times when a lawsuit is required and valid, but Second Timothy 3:3 prophesies a day of inordinate suing as the devil goes wild in the legal system.

But today we are living in an age when employees sue employers; children sue parents; parents sue children; parents sue schools; patients sue doctors; different minority groups sue for reparations; and shoppers sue business owners. And more and more, Christian believers sue other believers — even though Paul wrote in First Corinthians 6:1 and 2, "Dare any of you, having a matter against another, go to law before the unjust, and not before the saints? Do ye not know that the saints shall judge the world? and if the world shall be judged by you, are ye unworthy to judge the smallest matters?"

The "I'm going to sue you" mentality is the type of low-level carnal Corinthian behavior that the apostle Paul pleaded with us as believers to avoid. Paul clearly stated that we should be able to work out any differences between ourselves. But in today's modern society, even believers often turn to the courts as a first recourse. It's true that heart-wrenching times do occur in which no

[30] "U.S. Legal System Is World's Most Costly According to a New Study," May 14, 2013, U. S. Chamber Institute for Legal Reform, https://www.instituteforlegalreform.com/resource/us-legal-system-is-worlds-most-costly-according-to-a-new-study.

other option is available but to turn to the courts for help — but this should never be a Christian's first choice or course of action!

We are living in a day when the devil is in the court system — weaponizing the law to accuse, attack, slander, vilify, and ravage others financially. There has been a descent into indecent behavior and the loss of ability to negotiate, to come to terms, to settle differences, or to decently solve disagreements with others. It's a day when people freely and readily turn to the courts almost without hesitation. The devil has used people to increase this trend that is running rampant throughout society to destroy lives.

The word "false accusers" is a translation of the well-known Greek word *diabolos*, normally translated *devil*. In Revelation 12:10, the devil is aptly described as *the accuser*. The name "Satan" additionally depicts the devil as the one who *accuses, slanders,* or *conspires against;* the *adversary.*

The very fact that the word *diabolos* is used in Second Timothy 3:3 tells us clearly what will happen in the last of the last days: The practice of *accusing* and *being accused* will get so out of control that it will seem as if *the devil himself* has infiltrated the courts and released his fury! And if we're honest with ourselves, we'd admit that this sounds similar to the world we live in today. (Even if you haven't experienced this kind of accusing in a court of law, you need only go to any social-media platform to witness a form of fierce accusing and public decrying that closely resembles *both the judge and jury of a courtroom!*)

But despite this disturbing trend, God wants *you* to keep your head on straight. He wants you as a serious believer to learn how to come to terms with others and to settle differences maturely.

We need to understand that there are times when it is better to be wronged than to wrong Jesus' reputation or our witness for Christ. There are times when it is better to trust God and refuse to sue for self-advantage or even self-defense. Let's not forget that forgiveness is a chief characteristic of the Christian message and the Christian life!

———◆———

**We need to understand that there are times
when it is better to be wronged than
to wrong Jesus' reputation or our witness for Christ.
Let's not forget that forgiveness is a chief characteristic
of the Christian message and the Christian life!**

———◆———

**Adding the Greek word *diabolos*
to this mix of divinely chosen words in Second Timothy 3:3,
the *RIV* of this verse thus far reads:**

Love for and commitment to family will disintegrate, and divorce will become epidemic, with irreconcilable differences being a major factor in tearing families apart. In fact, every imaginable type of covenant will be regularly violated, and the court system will be overwhelmed as people go overboard, suing and being sued....

TRANSFORMING THE PRESENT
AND SHAPING THE FUTURE

As I read Paul's list of signs that indicate the last of the last days is upon us, I am *astounded* at the accuracy of the Bible! Approximately 2,000 years ago, the Holy Spirit warned us in advance of these developments so we could safeguard our hearts and our homes and prevent these destructive trends from corrupting our families and our relationships.

You may have already experienced the damaging effects of these particular characteristics of modern society that were long ago foretold by the Holy Spirit. Although there's nothing you can do to change the past, the power of the Holy Spirit can transform your present and shape your future. Just because the devil has successfully waged and won attacks against you in the past does *not* mean he will be allowed to do it in the future!

God's redeeming and restoring power is always present to save and deliver. And as you keep your focus on Him, He will empower you to yield to His Spirit and take hold of His Word to stand your ground for a better tomorrow than you could have ever dreamed possible. God is a Specialist in turning broken lives that have suffered the enemy's attacks into marvelous, gleaming examples of His power and grace!

◆

**As you keep your focus on Him,
He will empower you to yield to His Spirit
and take hold of His Word
to stand your ground for a better tomorrow
than you could have ever dreamed possible.**

◆

CHAPTER 6

LAST-DAYS SURVIVAL GUIDE ACTION STEPS

TO PROTECT YOUR MARRIAGE AND FAMILY AND TO AVOID THE END-TIME THINKING OF THE ACCUSER

Before we go on to the next chapter, we must pause to ask some reflective questions. It's so important to take the time to determine the state of our families, our marriages, and our *attitudes* in this end-time season when people so freely accuse and sue one another.

I encourage you to not rush through these questions. Ponder them deeply so the Holy Spirit can help you evaluate what adjustments you need to make to protect your family, safeguard your marriage, and keep your life free from the spirit of the world that is working in society today. Pay careful attention to the questions that represent the action steps you need to take in the event that your family and marriage have already been negatively impacted by the devil's attack on families in this last season of the age.

1. What is the state of your family right now?

As we have seen, the Holy Spirit prophesied that in the last of the last days, many families will lose the closeness once exemplified in the traditional family and will begin to drift apart. It is a fact that today, all across the social stratum, families are under attack and in a terrible state of deterioration.

Since the phrase "without natural affection" informs us that *the deterioration of traditional family and the home* will become commonplace as the age races toward its conclusion, I want you to do your best to answer honestly as you ask yourself these questions:

- *Is my family strong, or are we beginning to be pulled apart?*

- *Is my family free of this assault that threatens our closeness — or can I see clear evidence that a war is being waged against my home to cause us to drift apart?*

- *Have I taken the time to seek God and receive His strategies for keeping my family strong in a world that offers so many avenues of distraction from quality time spent together?*

The Holy Spirit spoke clearly about this so we who live in the last of the last days would be aware of this development and take precautions to protect our families from this tragedy. We must have ears to hear what the Spirit is saying so we can respond with wisdom and keep our families free from this end-time attack.

If you take heed to what the Holy Spirit says and build your home according to God's Word, you can sustain a strong, godly family even in these last days. But because you *are* living in this end-time hour, it is vital that you build a hedge around your marriage and family. If you use caution and exercise faith, you and your family will withstand the spiritual attack being waged in the last days to tear families apart.

2. If you've strayed, what changes do you need to make to get your family back on course?

The Scriptures warn us that families will be assaulted in the last days, so you must respond by building a hedge of protection around your family. There is no need to be afraid, but this warning requires proactive steps. You must do all you know to do to build a wall of protection around your home and your relationships so you and your loved ones don't succumb to the family-assaulting spirit of this age.

As noted earlier, today traditional families and homes are threatened by over-busy schedules, financial pressures, multiple jobs in one home, and multiple cars, televisions, digital devices, etc. If all of these factors are not properly managed and precautions are not taken, they can create entirely separate paths for each family member. Parents go in one direction while children go in another — and often husbands and wives don't even go the same direction. Because of varying schedules, family members are rarely at home at the same time and rarely eat a meal together. And when they are home, they are all looking at different TVs, computers, or devices in different rooms of the house. The family may technically live under one roof, but they are not truly sharing life because they are each going in a different direction.

So ask yourself these questions:

- *When I look at my own family, do I see that we are all on the same page and headed in the same direction? Or are my family members so pulled apart by schedules that they are beginning to take separate paths?*

- *Do we regularly eat meals together as a family?*

- *Do we enjoy spending evenings together, even if it's watching a movie or a TV program together?*

- *Do we talk to each other when we are together, or is our family time constantly interrupted by text messages and alerts on social media?*

- *Are we doing more than living under the same roof? Are we truly sharing life together?*

- *What changes could we make to our daily schedules and to our choices in how we live that would help mend any "breaches in the wall" that are beginning to show up and help enhance our closeness as a family?*

How long has it been since you really made an evaluation of your home situation to see what is good, what is not so good, and what needs to be brought back into alignment with God's plan for your family? Besides your personal walk with Jesus, nothing is more important than the health of your family. It is wise to evaluate the true state of affairs in your home.

If you don't know what steps to take to build a stronger wall of protection around your home, I urge you to receive help from a trusted mentor or counselor who can teach you how to do it. It may feel humiliating to ask for help — but just stay willing to follow God's leading wherever He directs you along this path to strengthen your family. After all, if your body is sick, wouldn't you go to a doctor to get help? Likewise, if your family is sick, it's common sense for you to seek counsel from someone who is qualified to help you get your family back into a healthy state.

3. What steps are you taking to "redeem the time" that has already been lost?

Living in a state of regret changes nothing. In fact, it only produces negative emotions that make things even worse. We have seen that Ephesians 5:16 commands you to get busy "redeeming the time." That means if you have wasted or lost both time and precious opportunities in your past, you can "redeem" that lost time as God gives you new opportunities.

Time is a precious commodity. In context, it refers to the brevity of time you have available and urges you to be time-conscious in the way you conduct your life. It depicts someone who is learning to make full use of time because he is conscious that time is limited and he must use it wisely. Paul was saying that by employing diligence and commitment, you can redeem, or buy back, time that you have lost along the way — even time you *frivolously* lost.

The good news is this: If your life has become cluttered and you've lost precious opportunities in any area — including time lost with your family — you can still *reverse* this condition. Through your recommitment to the Lord and to His perfect will for your life, you can buy back time that has been lost, wasted, or forfeited. And with the Holy Spirit's supernatural help, you can accomplish in *a short time* what you thought was forever lost. You can *redeem that time* and get back on course.

If your children are grown and you find yourself regretting your past attitudes and actions toward your family — I want to encourage you that God is still in the business of redeeming the time.

So ask yourself:

- *Am I fulfilling my part to seek God diligently for His wisdom regarding my family?*

- *Am I ready and willing to do whatever God tells me to do, step by step, to redeem any time that's been lost and to help my family become all that He intends?*

- *What principles do I already know to do from God's Word that, if applied, would help build strong, loving relationships within my family? Am I walking in full obedience to those divine commands?*

God may lead you to seek out godly counsel to help you get things back on track. Just follow His plan, and He will honor your humility and your obedience. You can see God's power go to work to restore all that has come under attack in your marriage and in the lives of your children.

4. What is the state of your marriage right now?

If you have already become victim to the heartbreaking ordeal of divorce or separation, God's grace is available and present to restore you. God cares deeply about the wound that this painful experience has inflicted in your soul.

If this describes your situation, ask yourself:

- *Am I employing the full power of the Holy Spirit within to help me get free of all past hurts and offenses?*

- *Have I asked Him for wisdom concerning where to find support from qualified people who can help me fully recover from all past trauma?*

- *Is there anything God has asked me to do to help heal my relationship with my spouse (or my former spouse) that I have not been willing to do?*

It may take time to come out on the other side of the hurt you have experienced in the past. But as you seek Jesus diligently, you will find that He is the Healer of broken hearts — not the *patcher*, but the *Healer*!

Perhaps you are currently married but struggling in your relationship with your spouse. If that is your situation, healing and restoration is available to you — if you want it — through the truth of God's Word, the power of the Holy Spirit, and those qualified to help to whom He might lead you.

It will take time, work, and sustained commitment on the part of both partners in the marriage. But with the right choices made and the help God provides, you both can see Him work a miracle in your marriage. You do not have to fall prey to the epidemic of divorce that is so rampant in the world today.

So ask yourself:

- *Can I honestly say I have done my personal best to work on my marriage relationship and to make it all God intends and desires it to be?*

- *Have I diligently sought the Lord to know His perspective about my marriage?*

- *Have I allowed Him to talk to me about how I may have contributed to the problems?*

- *Have I acknowledged what I did wrong and humbly repented for it before God and before my spouse?*

As I said earlier, all you can do is your best, so *give* your marriage your best. You are not answerable for the unwillingness of a drifting spouse or for what another person is not willing to do. But you *are* responsible to do all you can do to ensure that you did your best to make it work.

You cannot answer for another's heart, but you will be confronted with your own heart.

Never forget that God does not condemn you, and His arms are open wide to embrace you, forgive you, and restore you. So if you are still standing in faith for God to work a miracle in your marriage and turn things around, remember that He specializes in raising dead things back to life again!

5. What are you doing to make the devil regret he ever messed with you?

It's time for you to make the devil regret that he ever touched you, your marriage, or your family. Regardless of the havoc the devil has tried to wreak in your home, God can turn the situation around and make you a mighty weapon in His hands to repel the enemy's attack!

If your marriage appears to be under siege, God is able to turn it around. He is certainly not behind the problem, but He is able to miraculously make something beautiful out of a bad situation. As Paul said, "…We know that all things work together for good to them that love God, to them who are the called according to his purpose" (Romans 8:28).

If the devil has attacked you or your family, it's time for you to make the enemy sorry he ever messed with you! With the Word of God in your heart, the Holy Spirit as your Teacher, and the support of those who are qualified to help you, it is possible for you to rise above anything the enemy has waged against you. Furthermore, you can press onward and live your life victoriously! This is not the time for you to surrender to discouragement and give up — it's time to give it your best! God wants you to fulfill the purpose and destiny He has appointed for you on this earth!

So ask yourself these questions:

- *What steps am I taking to blast the enemy by helping others who are in need?*

- *What am I doing to demonstrate victory over my circumstances, even in the midst of this attack?*

- *Have I consciously surrendered control to the Holy Spirit so He can show me how to deliver myself and my family from every attack?*

- *Am I willing to exercise my authority in Christ and wage an assault against the devil that will make him regret he ever messed with me?*

Your call as a believer is to become a shining example of God's grace and power that will make others stand in amazement. Whether or not you fulfill that call is entirely up to you and the choices you make along the way to adhere to God's Word and His way of confronting every obstacle and withstanding every attack.

6. What is your attitude about commitments and covenants?

As we saw earlier, the Holy Spirit prophesied that "truce-breaking" will become commonplace in a last-days society. The Greek word that the Holy Spirit used is so all-encompassing, it pictures the breaking of every form of covenant — including business covenants, contracts, relational covenants, and marital vows. The Holy Spirit let us know that there will be widespread *truce-breaking* on every imaginable level.

In the end of the age, relationships will be "easy come, easy go" as a result of the self-focused, self-absorbed spirit of the age that only sticks around for what is self-gratifying.

We've seen that truce-breaking in the very last days will infiltrate all facets of society — resulting in divorce, contractual breaches of all kinds, and every other kind of covenant-breaking. The word "truce-breaking" can even refer to one who breaks a covenant with a local church. Because this spirit of covenant-breaking will be so rampant, it therefore stands to reason that it will also try to infiltrate the Church.

This is such an important issue that it is wise for you to allow the Holy Spirit to honestly speak to you about it. Take some time to evaluate your own life in this area, and ask yourself:

- *Does my life show that I have fallen into this spirit of covenant-breaking — or that I am truly committed to keep my word to do all I can do to stay in covenant with the relationships God has placed in my life?*

- *Would others say I am a person of covenant — or that I am a friend who walks away in a time of need?*

- *Am I being faithful to the commitment I made earlier to my local church?*

- *Have I been faithful to my local church in good and bad times? Or am I among the many who uprooted and moved elsewhere when times got tough?*

- *Through my actions and my attitude, have I stayed in covenant or broken covenant with my church family — even though previously I was sure the Lord had led me to enter into that covenant?*

- *Would I want my children to be like me in this area of my life?*

The Holy Spirit knows if you are on track in this area of your life or if you need to make a self-correction. And if you do need to self-correct, He will show it to you and empower you to do it.

7. What is your attitude about suing another Christian and using the legal system to solve your problems?

In Second Timothy 3:3, Paul wrote that people in the last days will be "trucebreakers, false accusers…." We've seen that the phrase "false accusers" is translated from the Greek word *diabolos*, which is most often translated in the New Testament as *devil*, *accuser*, or *slanderer*. But as it is used in Second Timothy 3:3, it depicts *a court system that is overrun with accusing and slanderous lawsuits*.

We are living in times when even believers turn to the courts as a first recourse. It is true that there are situations where no other option is possible but to turn to the courts for help. However, the Bible clearly teaches this should *not* be a Christian's first choice.

We who live in this modern day know it to be true — the devil is in the court system, weaponizing the law to accuse, attack, slander, and vilify. *Accusing* and *being accused* is getting so out of control that it truly seems as if Satan himself has infiltrated the courts.

But God wants us as serious believers, to the best of our ability, to learn how to come to terms with others and settle differences maturely. We all need to understand that there are times when it is better to be wronged rather than to wrong Jesus' reputation or our witness for Christ. There are also times when it is better to trust God and refuse to sue for self-advantage or even self-defense.

So it would be very beneficial for you to honestly ask yourself:

- *What is my attitude about suing and using the courts as a first recourse, especially if people close to me are urging me to sue another party?*

- *Am I tempted to rush to a lawyer right away, or do I first earnestly seek the Lord, ask for others to help mediate if needed, and try to find a way to settle the issue maturely without turning to the legal system?*

There are moments when the legal system is required. But in this age when the devil has been unleashed to accuse, slander, and vilify others, it is imperative that we guard our hearts and our thinking. As the Church, we are not to fall into the debilitating, last-days pattern of accusing and being accused and then suing as a result!

7

'INCONTINENT' — WHEN SOCIETY CASTS OFF RESTRAINT

We've already discovered a great deal about what society will look like in the last of the last days. Let's start this chapter by taking into account the words we've studied in the last chapter from Second Timothy 3:3.

We've seen that the first part of this *RIV* verse can be interpreted as follows:

Love for and commitment to family will disintegrate, and divorce will become epidemic, with irreconcilable differences being a major factor in tearing families apart. In fact, every imaginable type of covenant will be regularly violated, and the court system will be overwhelmed as people go overboard, suing and being sued....

Now we must move to the next word that Paul listed in his prophetic projection about the close of the age. In Second Timothy 3:3, the apostle prophesied that people in the last of the last days will become "without natural affection, trucebreakers, false accusers, *incontinent*, fierce, despisers of those that are good." We have already looked at the words "without natural affection," "trucebreakers," and "false accusers." Now let's go on to unlock the original and applicable meanings of the word translated "incontinent" in this verse.

When one thinks of the word "incontinent," it usually brings to mind some form of *a lack of control*. In a medical sense, it describes a person who has lost control of his or her bladder or bowels and, as a result, experiences involuntary accidents. But the word "incontinent" can be used more widely to describe *any loss of control*.

To understand this word "incontinent" more fully, let me give you its original, historical meaning and then show you how it is applicable to the times we live in today. In English the word "incontinent" refers to *one who lacks moderation* or *one who lacks self-control in any or every sphere of life, resulting in indulgent behaviors.*

Now let's look at the original Greek word *akrates* that is translated "incontinent" in Second Timothy 3:3. This word *akrates* is derived from the word *kratos* — one of many Greek words that depicts *power*. But when an *a* is added to the front of it, that *a* has a canceling effect. Now rather than picturing *power*, the word shifts to picture a person or society who has *lost power over self* and therefore has *no self-control*. It refers to *the inability to exercise control, a lack of control, a lack of self-restraint, no willpower*, or *the inability to say no*.

This is the picture of a person or a society that has lost the ability to control itself and has abandoned self-restraint. The word "incontinent" — from the Greek word *akrates* — perfectly describes a person or group of people who live with an "I just can't say no" mindset that ultimately leads to destruction because it produces life with few boundaries and restraints.

◆

**An "I just can't say no" mindset
ultimately leads to destruction because it produces life
with few boundaries and restraints.**

◆

There are many issues with over-indulgence today — and it seems accurate to say that these particular problems are pandemic and proliferating by the day. Let's pause and look at the statistical facts to determine whether or not the majority of people today are "incontinent," as the Holy Spirit prophesied would occur in the very last of the last days.

I've given you the original meaning of the Greek word translated "incontinent." Now I will provide you with the applicable meaning this word has for you and me and why the Holy Spirit chose to use this word to depict society in the last of the last days. Read carefully. When you are finished with the following section, you can then decide if the word "incontinent" describes the vast majority of people in our age.

EXAMPLES OF 'INCONTINENCE' IN OUR WORLD TODAY

Before we proceed further, it is vital for you to see the connection between the word "incontinent" and the word "lasciviousness" listed as a work of the flesh in Galatians 5:19.

The word "lasciviousness" is translated from the Greek word *aselgeia* — a word that describes *excess* but primarily refers to *the excessive consumption of food* or *wild, undisciplined living that is especially marked by unbridled sex.* The behavior of "lasciviousness" is so destructive that Second Peter 2:6 lists it as the principal sin in the cities of Sodom and Gomorrah.

When we think of Sodom and Gomorrah, we usually think of cities filled with sexual perversion. Because the word "lasciviousness" — the Greek word *aselgeia* — also refers to *the excessive consumption of food*, we can conclude that in God's mind, it is just as perverted to overindulge in food as it is to engage in sinful sexual activities! *How does that make you feel about a lifestyle of unbridled overeating?*

Flesh that is not conquered by the Spirit of God has one aim in its fallen state: *total domination and destruction*. If permitted to run its full course, the flesh will consume the territory of a life once beautiful and transform it into an endless expanse of perpetual "badlands." This is the very opposite of God's process and intended outcome in a person's life. Lasciviousness produces a twisted, barren mess in every arena of life, which explains why God equates the word with *perversion*.

**If permitted to run its full course,
the flesh will consume the territory of a life once beautiful
and transform it into an endless expanse
of perpetual "badlands."**

Because the word "incontinent" refers to those who have lost self-control, it could depict:

- A person who has *no ability to stop eating*.

- A person who has *no ability to stop spending*.

- A person who has *no ability to restrain emotions*.

- A person who has *no ability to stop addictive behaviors*.

These various types of lack of restraint could all be depicted by the word *akrates*, which is translated "incontinent" in Second Timothy 3:3. So in the sections to follow, we will examine each of these forms of incontinence very factually and with ample documentation. Our goal is to determine if the characteristic of "incontinence" is currently affecting this last-days society as the Holy Spirit prophesied. I ask you to stay with me, even if you think it's an overload of information. If you will read the following facts and statistics, I believe you will see that we are indeed living in a last-days time frame in which self-control and self-restraint have been tossed to the wind, resulting in *indulgent behaviors* that are eventually wreaking destruction in lives on a massive scale.

Proverbs 29:18 (*KJV*) says, "Where there is no vision, the people perish...." Both the *New King James Version* and *American Standard Version* state it this way: "Where there is no revelation, the people cast off restraint...."

This verse is relevant for this discussion about casting off restraint. It tells us that when a person lacks any vision of what life should be or could be, he or she throws off self-control and self-restraint, which often causes that person to perish exactly as this verse says.

When a person lacks any vision of what life should be or could be, he or she throws off self-control and self-restraint.

Remember this as we look at examples of how a last-days society is throwing off restraint. Let's begin with the consumption of food and calories in our time. Get ready, because what you are about to read is *shocking*.

NO ABILITY TO STOP EATING

Before I dive into this section, I want to share an experience from my own life that was very unpleasant. Although I didn't enjoy it when it happened, God used it to produce a significant, necessary change in my life.

Years ago, my family confronted me about the fact that I had gained a great deal of weight. They knew I needed to do something about it for my health's sake. But as is usually the case with those who are overweight, I had looked at myself in the mirror long enough to become accustomed to what I saw and I did not see what others saw — that I was *seriously* overweight. I had dressed in black for years and felt that I had covered up my problem, at least to some degree. But my family saw the unhealthy condition I was in and loved me enough to confront me and help me take action to lose weight. I will forever be grateful for it.

To start my weight-loss program, I went to a doctor to be examined. As he filled out my chart, the doctor looked at my weight on the scale — and as he scribed the number on the chart, he mumbled the words "morbidly obese."

I couldn't believe what I'd heard. I asked him, "What did you say?"

He answered, "Sir, you are morbidly obese."

"I'm what?" I asked him again.

He answered, "Sir, you *are* morbidly obese."

If someone had slapped me, it couldn't have stunned me more. "Morbidly obese?!!"

The doctor was right, and I needed to hear it. Those words that were so difficult to hear pierced me in such a way that I made a quality decision to change my life right then and there.

The reason I am telling you this is that I want you to know I have a sincere compassion for those who struggle with their weight. There is not an ounce of judgment or condemnation in what you are about to read. The fact is that if you — or someone you know and love — are overweight or obese, you know that it is a prison in which one feels trapped and doesn't know how to get out.

But you can walk free of that prison!

For me, I personally needed to see and hear the truth. And I'm not alone. We often have to be confronted with truth as a catalyst to produce needed *change* — even if we don't like to hear that truth. That is exactly what happened to me, and I'm so thankful for it.

In this section, I am *not* trying to confront you, although you may feel confronted. I am simply attempting to give you an example of how the "incontinent" spirit of this age can negatively affect all of us. This self-indulgent throwing off of self-control and self-restraint is a symptom of these last of the last days.

◆

**We often have to be confronted with truth
as a catalyst to produce needed *change* —
even if we don't like to hear that truth.**

◆

**I remind you of the *RIV* interpretation
of Second Timothy 3:1:**

You emphatically and categorically need to know with unquestionable certainty that in the very end of days — when time has sailed to its last port and no more time remains for the journey — that last season will stand in the midst of uncontrollable, unpredictable,

hurtful, treacherous, menacing times that will be emotionally difficult for people to bear.

Remember, the Holy Spirit gave us this warning so we'd be wide awake and take preventive measures to keep ourselves and our families safe from the manifold types of harm that will be indicative of the last days. Society may throw off control and restraint when it comes to food consumption — a decision that can often prove fatal — but we must resist this destructive tendency in our own lives.

I want to use several examples to demonstrate how *a lack of self-control and self-restraint* is afflicting the world today. However, I will begin with the issue of the vast numbers of people who are overweight or obese today. Here we go — gear up for what you are about to read.

———◆———

**Society may throw off control and restraint
when it comes to food consumption — a decision that can
often prove fatal — but we must resist
this destructive tendency in our own lives.**

———◆———

THE SCALES DON'T LIE

Let's start with a worldwide view of this subject of obesity, looking at changes that began in the 1970s. According to the World Health Organization, worldwide obesity has nearly tripled since 1975. In 2016 — the date of the most recent analysis at the time of this writing — more than 1.9 billion adults 18 years and older in the world were *overweight*. Of that number, 650 million were *obese*.

That same 2016 report states that 41 million children under the age of 5 were overweight or obese and that more than 340 million children and adolescents ages 5-19 were overweight or obese. One updated study from 2017 shows that 39 percent of adults, ages 18 years and over, were overweight and 13 percent were obese. As alarming as these statistics are, they are not current, and experts believe the numbers are now much higher.[31] The facts prove that the Western world is overweight and gripped with a mushrooming condition of morbid obesity.

But what does the term "overweight" actually mean? Forgive the technical answer, but if a person has a BMI (Body Mass Index) of 18.5-24.9, that person is generally considered to be at a *normal* weight. When a person's BMI is between 25 and 29.9, that individual is generally considered to be *overweight*. It is true that one may be technically overweight due to muscle mass, but this is the exception to the common reasons that people are overweight.[32]

But what about the "obese" category? What does this term refer to? If a person has a BMI (Body Mass Index) exceeding 30, they are defined as *obese*. Research shows that approximately 70 million adults in America fit in this category.

I don't want to focus only on the United States, but statistics for this nation are the most available and proven to be true. So let's look at statistics regarding the overweight and obese in the United States. A recent study stated that 160 million Americans are overweight or obese. That's about *one-half* of the entire adult population! Think of that number — *160 million*! Yet this actually doesn't take into account the 30 percent overweight or obese individuals who are under the age of 20, so the actual totals are much higher.[33]

---

[31] "Obesity and Overweight," April 2020, World Health Organization, www.who.int/news-room/fact-sheets/detail/obesity-and-overweight.

[32] "How Much Should I Weigh for My Height and Age?," Medical News Today, www.medicalnewstoday.com/articles/323446.php.

[33] "The Vast Majority of American Adults Are Overweight or Obese, and Weight Is a Growing Problem Among U.S. Children," IHME, http://www.healthdata.org/news-release/vast-majority-american-adults-are-overweight-or-obese-and-weight-growing-problem-among.

According to the most recent report from the CDC (Center for Disease Control) issued in 2018 (also not current), 42.4 percent of all adults age 20 and older in America were overweight or obese.[34]

Being overweight presents a risk of developing a number of health conditions, but the obese are the most greatly endangered. The website of the CDC states that people who are obese are at increased risk for many serious diseases and health conditions, including:

- High blood pressure (hypertension)

- High LDL cholesterol, low HDL cholesterol, or high levels of triglycerides (dyslipidemia)

- Type 2 diabetes

- Coronary heart disease

- Stroke

- Gallbladder disease

- Osteoarthritis (a breakdown of cartilage and bone within joints)

- Sleep apnea and breathing problems

- Some cancers (endometrial, breast, colon, kidney, gallbladder, and liver)

- Mental illness, such as clinical depression, anxiety, and other mental disorders

- Body pain and difficulty with physical functioning

---

[34] CDC: Prevalence of Obesity 42.4 Percent in 2017 to 2018," February 27, 2020, MedicalXpress.com, https://medicalxpress.com/news/2020-02-cdc-prevalence-obesity-percent.html.

- Low quality of life

- Many causes of death (mortality)

The CDC further states that obesity and its associated health problems have a significant economic impact on the health-care system. Medical costs associated with being overweight or obese may involve both direct and indirect costs. Direct medical costs include preventative, diagnostic, and treatment services related to obesity. Indirect costs relate to mortality and morbidity costs, including a decrease of productivity. Those who are overweight or obese as a whole are more often ill, absent from work, and lose physical mobility that hinders their ability to function normally in life.

But in addition to these costs, data also shows that obesity affects the ability of the armed forces to recruit new men and women. In 2007-2008, 5.7 million men and 16.5 million women who were eligible for military service exceeded the Army's enlistment standards for weight and body fat.[35] In other words, millions of young men and women are *too overweight or obese to serve in the armed forces.* Because that statistic is from 2007-2008, experts know the numbers are now much higher. This national plague of obesity is producing destruction on countless levels in personal lives, but this statistic demonstrates its detrimental effects even on a national level. In a very real sense, it means overweight and obesity is becoming a national-security issue!

THE SOURCE OF OVERWEIGHT AND OBESITY

The fundamental causes of overweight and obesity are an increased intake of unhealthy foods, widespread overeating, a decrease in physical activity, and the sedentary pace that characterizes so many people's workplaces, schools, and lives. Let's look at each of these in order.

---

[35] Fritz Dufour, MBA, DESS, *The Adult Obesity Epidemic in the United States: A Comprehensive Approach* (2018), p. 37.

Unhealthy Foods

As I told you earlier, the issue of weight has been a struggle for me at various times in my life. Part of my problem through the years has not only been too much intake, but also eating incorrectly. My wife loves to eat like a rabbit and has tried to convince me through the years to eat all kinds of "green things" that I personally do not enjoy and have no desire to eat. My attitude through the years was, *Denise can eat like a rabbit all she wants, but that is not my idea of enjoying food!* Nonetheless, I have had to adjust that attitude, learn how to eat more correctly, and not give in to the pull of this modern society to overindulge in unhealthy foods.

Statistics reveal that this struggle to eat correctly affects a large percentage of the population, with a majority eating wrongly. Research shows that people who struggle with weight usually eat too many processed foods, indulge in too many carbohydrates, ingest too much sugar, do not eat enough whole foods, and engage in a lot of unhealthy yo-yo dieting.[36] This type of fad dieting has been proven not to have lasting results, but instead to often produce a worse situation in the long term.

It is true that a small percentage of cases of obesity are caused by certain health conditions. However, the majority of cases can be traced to a common root cause: a widespread surrender to the cravings of the flesh and the abandonment of self-control and self-restraint, leading to a lifestyle of self-indulgent eating.

The Center for Disease Control reports that almost 40 percent of Americans eat fast food during any given 24-hour period. To be specific, 45 percent of those from 20 to 39, almost 38 percent of those ages 40 to 59, and 24 percent who are over 60 fit in this category.[37]

---

[36] "9 Reasons You May Be Gaining Weight Unintentionally," Healthline.com, www.healthline.com/nutrition/unintentional-weight-gain#1.-You-eat-too-many-highly-processed-foods.

[37] "Almost 40% of Americans Eat Fast Food on Any Given Day, Report Says," time.com, https://time.com/5412796/fast-food-americans/.

Although it seems the diet and wellness industry is booming with popularity, recent data states that 90 percent of adults don't eat enough fruits and vegetables and obesity rates continue to tick upward. The popularity of fast and processed foods suggests that Americans may not always be following through on their intentions to eat healthier.[38]

The U.S. weight-loss market is now worth a whopping $72 billion a year, but the number of dieters has fallen, largely as a result of the push for "size acceptance."[39] While the number of those who are overweight and obese grows larger, the actual number of people trying to lose weight has declined as the message being communicated more and more is that people must learn to accept themselves as they are.

———◆———

Although it seems the diet and wellness industry is booming with popularity, recent data states that 90 percent of adults don't eat enough fruits and vegetables and obesity rates continue to tick upward.

———◆———

Those who struggle often say they'll fix it with exercise or by joining a fitness club or gym. In the United States alone, the fitness industry is worth billions annually. There are nearly 40,000 gyms and approximately 37,000 health clubs that generate $28 billion annually.[40] That sounds good, but when you dig deeper, you find that 82 percent of gym members go to the gym less than 1 time per week; 22 percent completely stop going 6 months into their membership; and 31 percent say they never would have paid had they known

---

[38] Ibid.

[39] "The $72 Billion Weight Loss and Diet Control Market in the United States, 2019-2023, February 25, 2019, businesswire. com, www.businesswire.com/news/home/20190225005455/en/72-Billion-Weight-Loss-Diet-Control-Market.

[40] "Health and Fitness Club Companies by Revenue in the United States 2018," statista.com, www.statista.com/statistics/922841/us-health-clubs-by-revenue/.

how little they would use it.[41] Billions of dollars are spent on good intentions that are never realized.

Widespread Overeating

Let me give you more "wake-up facts." In the 1970s — before the rampant increase of those who are overweight or obese began — the average caloric intake of an adult in the United States was 2,077 per day, which is about the right amount of calories needed. Even today it is recommended that men in their 30s should eat around 2,200 calories and moderately active women require about 1,800 to 2,200 calories each day for a healthy weight maintenance. Sedentary women only need around 1,600 calories to maintain their weight.

But Americans today are consuming nearly *double* the daily amount of calories that are needed — *nearly 4,000 calories a day*. In short, the biggest contributor to excess weight and obesity is simply *overeating*. This fatal trend doesn't occur only in America; it is also being witnessed in much of the Western world. An overview shows that America is eating itself into health problems, physical immobility, and impaired lifestyles that could be avoided if self-control and self-restraint were put into place.

Can you see how the spirit of this age is producing a widespread condition of "incontinence" that is producing widespread destruction?

**An overview shows that America is eating itself
into health problems, physical immobility,
and impaired lifestyles that could be avoided
if self-control and self-restraint were put into place.**

---

[41] "Are Gym Memberships Worth the Money?," January 5, 2019, TheHustle.com, https://thehustle.co/gym-membership-cost.

Since the mid-1970s, food portions have changed dramatically. My family is made starkly aware of this issue of food-portion sizes when we entertain a foreigner in America. Those from abroad nearly gasp when they see how much food is served on one plate. They even ask "why" would any restaurant serve such large portions of food to a single individual.

Research shows that portion sizes began to grow in the 1970s and have continued in sync with the ever-increasing sizes of bodies. Food companies, restaurants, and fast-food chains promote larger items. Restaurants use larger dinner plates and sell larger muffins or provide endless complimentary bread. Pizzerias sell larger pizzas, and fast-food companies sell larger burgers, larger portions of French fries, and larger drinks.

Industry experts predict portions will continue to grow larger because that is what clients want. This has even affected car manufacturers, who must install larger cup holders in new cars to accommodate the larger sizes of cups. Mountains of evidence show that the portions of foods and beverages have rapidly increased over the past decades and that, in fact, larger portions have become typical.

Furthermore, people eat out much more than they did in the past. Competition has become so fierce between restaurants and fast-food chains that larger portions of food are offered to obtain a larger market share of diners. Many restaurant owners report that customers want more and more food for their money. Consumers increasingly choose restaurants on the basis of larger food portions, which they view to be a better bargain. This view is contributing to the intake of excessive calories, which adds to the obesity epidemic.

Think how many restaurants today have "all you can eat" buffets or salad bars. These "all you can eat" bars are frequently filled with people who are already overweight or obese but who prefer eating at such places because it is cheaper and they can consume all they want.

People often allege they are going to an "all you can eat" salad bar because they are dieting. However, many items that entice the eaters are high in calories. And after piling gobs of calorie-laden salad dressing on top of their heaping portions of salad — along with croutons and bacon bits — the entire notion of eating less or being moderate is tossed aside. Because this type of restaurant offers a "salad bar" and portrays the notion of a healthier option, people deceive themselves into thinking they are doing well in their eating habits, even as they keep going back for multiple servings.

Decreased Physical Activity

What about a decrease in physical activity? Let me ask — does the neighborhood where you live even have sidewalks? Relatively few new neighborhoods have sidewalks because people no longer use them.

Most households have cars (as we saw earlier, up to three cars per household), so people simply do not walk as they once walked. Since the advent of cars, the number of neighborhood schools, stores, and churches have continued to decrease until they nearly no longer exist. People drive long and unwalkable distances to reach stores, schools, and other locations that are part of their daily or weekly routine.

Walking has almost become a thing of the past. If you see someone out walking, you can surmise they have intentionally decided to walk. In most places in America, there is no reason to walk unless you are trying to get exercise. Most people use their legs to walk from the chair to the kitchen, to the bathroom, to the bedroom — or they walk to the car to drive somewhere.

People are so out of the habit of walking that even when they drive to the store, to the mall, or even to church, they drive circles around the parking lot to look for a space closer to the entrance so they won't have to *walk*. They often sit in their cars in the parking lot, waiting for a space to become available closer to the door so they don't have to *walk* further to the entrance.

Does this sound familiar to you?

Inactivity — a lack of regular, physical movement — is a great contributor to weight gain, obesity, life-crippling immobility, and health problems that would generally disappear if people would simply become more mobile. The problem of overweight, obesity, and immobility is so out of control that malls and groceries stores provide motorized carts to assist those who can no longer walk sufficiently to shop for their needs as they motor around to purchase food and goods. It is worth noting that in other parts of the world where cars are less available and where people are required to walk as part of normal life, the percentages of the overweight and obese are radically lower.

Do you recall when it was an unusual sight to see obese individuals riding in motorized carts? But now it seems those carts are all around us. In fact, I was recently in an American grocery store and felt like I had to dodge motorized carts as I walked the aisles.

Certainly it is right that such devices are provided for those with physical challenges, and I don't hold a shred of judgment for people who are overweight or obese. Many are overweight or obese for real medical and physical reasons. But the scenario I am describing did not exist on the scale it does today a generation ago.

◆

**Inactivity — a lack of regular, physical movement —
is a great contributor to weight gain, obesity,
life-crippling immobility, and health problems
that would generally disappear if people
would simply become more mobile.**

◆

Sedentary Workplaces and Schools

The workplace environment has also changed. Now people sit for hours in front of computer screens without moving much during their work day. Not only is staring at a screen for hours mentally unhealthy, it contributes seriously to weight gain and the loss of physical mobility. The common practice of daily sitting for hours in front of a computer screen while drinking soft drinks and eating snacks is another huge factor in the burgeoning weight gain that is being witnessed among Western populations today.

Due to budgetary challenges, even in most public schools, gym classes have been eliminated. As a result, many children have less physical activity than they had years ago. Plus, millions of children are sitting for hours in front of TVs, computers, and digital gadgets rather than spending time engaged in physical activity at home and in their neighborhood.

Factor in the wrong eating habits that result from parents working and the kids fending for themselves in terms of what they eat till mom and dad get home (often eating too much fast food), and you discover why experts tell us that the physical size of children is growing rapidly in the Western world. Young children as a whole do not physically move as they did before the age of technology invaded their spaces!

OTHER DILEMMAS CONNECTED TO OBESITY AND BEING OVERWEIGHT

Accommodating a large population is a serious challenge. For example, airlines are faced with the dilemma of what to do with the expanding size of passengers. This epidemic of obesity has had a substantial impact on airplanes, trains, and all other forms of public transportation.

Certainly those who are larger must be accommodated, but think of how this affects the transportation business. At present, nearly every form of transportation is in the process of retrofitting seats and aisle widths to accommodate the growing size of passengers. The airline industry is struggling with this issue, asking such questions as: Should individuals who are larger be required to purchased two seats? Should they be charged more if providing a larger seat for them means someone else cannot be seated? Does this open the airline to a lawsuit?

The situation has become so serious that some have suggested a "fat tax" to compensate for lost seating due to accommodating physically larger people. Absolutely no one should ever be "fat-shamed," but the truth remains that this situation has created a real and serious challenge for transportation companies that rarely existed just a few decades ago. And the trends indicate that the physical size of the population will only get larger in the future. On so many levels, the prospect is dire.

Then there is the issue of public venues — theaters, public auditoriums, and even churches — that are faced with how to seat the growing size of the public. Even in churches, wise planning is required to scatter larger, oversized seats in various places of the auditorium to seat church members who can no longer fit in normal-sized seating. Every pastor wants every person to come to church as Scripture commands, but learning how to accommodate a myriad of body sizes can be a challenge to a local church.

---◆---

**The trends indicate that the physical size
of the population will only get larger in the future.
On so many levels, the prospect is dire.**

---◆---

Even the fashion industry has had to make changes to accommodate the growing size of the population. They have resized everything in a process called "vanity sizing." The intent is to reduce the real-life measurements in order to make those wearing larger sizes feel better about their clothing size. A graph in a *Good Housekeeping* article reveals:

- A women's size 20 in 1970 was made to fit a woman with a 33-inch waist. In 2011, that same dress size 20 was worn by women *with 40-inch waists.* That's a 7-inch increase for one dress size in approximately four decades.

- A women's size 16 in 1970 was worn by women with 29-inch waists; in 2011, that same dress size accommodated women with 36-inch waists.

- A women's size 12 in 1970 was worn by women with 26-inch waists; in 2011, a women's size 12 was worn by women with 32-inch waists.

- A women's size 8 in 1970 was worn by women with approximately 24-inch waistlines. In 2011, that same size 8 accommodated women with about 30-inch waists — an expansion of about 6 inches within that same dress size.

As I've stated, most brands have applied "vanity sizing" to their clothing labels, making these items sound smaller than they actually are in order to make customers "feel better" about their size.[42] But make no mistake — this is a delusion that isn't helping anyone in the long term.

LASCIVIOUSNESS

I remind you that this word "lasciviousness" is a translation of a Greek word that refers to the *excessive consumption of food* or *wild and undisciplined*

---

[42] Penny Travers, "Chart Shows Shocking Change in Clothing Sizes," August 17, 2015, GoodHousekeeping.com, www.goodhousekeeping.com/uk/fashion-beauty/a556302/chart-shows-shocking-change-in-clothing-sizes/.

living that is especially marked by unbridled sex and was listed as the principal sin of the cities of Sodom and Gomorrah. Again, it was one of the chief reasons why God destroyed Sodom and Gomorrah — and this word includes *the excessive consumption of food*! From a linguistic point of view, this means that in God's mind, it is a *perversion* to overindulge in food.

I believe that when you honestly assess the damaging effects of excessive eating and what it does to a person or to a nation, you will better understand why God would view this as a perverting act that destroys human life. As I told you earlier, God delivered me from the bondage of this stronghold, so I address this subject from a compassionate point of view and as one who knows firsthand how destructive it is on multiple levels. If you or someone you know is currently struggling with the issue of excessive eating, be assured that it is *not* a life sentence. It may take time to overcome this habit, but I am a living witness that freedom *is* possible.

**When you honestly assess the damaging effects
of excessive eating and what it does to a person
or to a nation, you will better understand why God
would view this as a perverting act that destroys human life.**

In Second Timothy 3:3, we are emphatically told that a last-days society will become "incontinent" — translated from the Greek word *akrates* — depicting *a loss of self-control*. But, again, this does *not* have to be you!

As noted, it could depict a person who has no ability to stop eating, to stop spending, to restrain emotions, or to stop giving in to addictive behaviors. Now that we've seen one example that clearly demonstrates *a loss of self-control* and *a loss of self-restraint*, let's look at another vivid example that makes it clear we are living in the midst of a last-days generation that is "incontinent."

But before we proceed, I want to share an important reminder: Remember that all works of the flesh can be forgiven — but before forgiveness comes, sin must be acknowledged. *This is God's requirement.*

Once you confess your sin, God will forgive you. From that moment forward, you can be set on a route to freedom and move on with your life! If your "incontinence" has created problems at home for your spouse, your family, or anyone else, pray for God's grace to be upon your loved ones to forgive you and upon you to ask for their forgiveness. Then begin to take whatever steps are necessary to make your life healthier than ever before.

◆

**Remember that all works of the flesh
can be forgiven — but before forgiveness comes,
sin must be acknowledged. *This is God's requirement.***

◆

I remind you that the word "incontinent" in Second Timothy 3:3 — the Greek word *akrates* — depicts *a lack of self-control and self-restraint.*

**The *RIV* version
of Second Timothy 3:3 thus far reads:**

Love for and commitment to family will disintegrate, and divorce will become epidemic, with irreconcilable differences being a major factor in tearing families apart. In fact, every imaginable type of covenant will be regularly violated, and the court system will be overwhelmed as people go overboard suing and being sued. People will generally lose the ability to say no and will be unable to control their instincts in nearly every area of life....

NO ABILITY TO STOP SPENDING

Because the word "incontinent" depicts those who have lost self-control, it could also specifically describe *a person who has a fiscal lack of control or the inability to say no to self-indulgent spending.*

We saw in Chapter 5 that a pervasive sense of "entitlement" will be indicative of a last-days society. As noted in that chapter, the Holy Spirit forecasted a *self-focused, self-absorbed, self-centered* society in the last days that will be filled with people ruled by a sense of entitlement who do not understand boundaries and live for self-gratification. These people will want what they want *when* they want it, with no regard for the value of patience or, in the case of covetousness and the mismanagement of money, the consequences of accrued debt to obtain it before the time.

As we discussed earlier, the word "incontinent" absolutely refers to *the inability to exercise control, a lack of control, a lack of self-restraint, no willpower,* or *the inability to say no.* And I remind you once again that the word "covetous" depicts *an insatiable desire to always have more and more.*

◆

**The Holy Spirit forecasted a *self-focused,
self-absorbed, self-centered* society in the last days
that will be filled with people ruled by a sense of entitlement
who do not understand boundaries
and live for self-gratification.**

◆

A serious end-time societal condition is revealed when we connect the meaning of the word "covetous" to that of the word "incontinent." We find a prophetic warning that a pernicious and pervasive fiscal lack of control will emerge in the very last of the last days. As a self-entitled society throws off all restraints, people will be hurled into excessive living, exorbitant spending, and mindless consumerism.

Anyone could fall into this trap, and there is no judgment if you are among those who have succumbed to the spirit of the age when it comes to the handling of money. But if you have fallen into the trap of self-consumption — if you are never satisfied and always wanting *more* — you must heed the Holy Spirit's voice as He tries to wake you up. He wants you to realize that the enemy is trying to drag you into a financial cesspool that has the potential to ruin you financially and put undue stress on your family and relationships.

If you or someone you know is caught in the trap of debt and lack, just know that this, too, is *not* a life sentence. It may take time and your sustained obedience to the wisdom of God, but freedom *is* possible.

◆

**If you have fallen into the trap of self-consumption —
if you are never satisfied and always wanting *more* —
you must heed the Holy Spirit's voice
as He tries to wake you up.**

◆

A LACK OF FISCAL RESTRAINT

Remember, these warnings were not given to scare anyone, but to help each of us know what is coming at the end of the age so we can take precautions to guard ourselves from falling into end-time traps. Let's proceed to see if the word "incontinent" that is used in Second Timothy correctly describes the financial situation in society today.

The world as a whole — especially Western nations — has generally thrown off fiscal restraint. However, I cannot focus on all the ailments of every country in the world, so I will stay close to home (for many of my readers) and focus on the United States. As the world's richest nation, the United States should be in the best shape of all. So let's look at the facts and see if even America is fulfilling the Holy Spirit's prophecy about society becoming "incontinent" at the end of the age.

For the next few paragraphs, we'll focus on the debt in both the national and personal spheres of America. Get ready. This is shocking information.

At the time of this writing, the U.S. government's public debt exceeds $23 trillion — the highest it has ever been. That amounts to $69,999 for every person, young and old, $179,695 for every household, or $792,000 for every single U.S. tax-paying citizen. *In fact, the U.S. debt is so out of control that it now exceeds its gross domestic product.*

It is important to understand that these were the most recent statistics as of the end of 2019, so these shocking facts were already out of date by the time this book was sent to the printer. The U.S. national debt is growing at a rate of approximately *$45,000 per second*, so it is impossible to print current debt numbers that are accurate. [43]

As a result of this exponential growth of debt, the Congressional Budget Office projects the U.S. national debt will reach at least $30 trillion by 2030. Even the government has become "incontinent" and, as a result, is selling the next generation into debt slavery.

But it's not only the government. Americans as a whole are digging deeper into debt. In fact, the total household debt in the United States — including mortgages, auto loans, and credit-card and student debt — climbed to $14

---

[43] Drew Desilver, "5 Facts About the National Debt," July 25, 2019, PewResearch.org, https://www.pewresearch.org/fact-tank/2019/07/24/facts-about-the-national-debt/.

trillion in 2019.[44] The average American has a credit card balance of $4,293, and total credit-card debt is also at its highest point ever — surpassing $1 trillion.

◆

Even the government has become "incontinent" and, as a result, is selling the next generation into debt slavery.

◆

In a recent survey, more than 1 in 3 people — which nationally equates to 86 million Americans — said they're afraid they'll max out their credit card when making a large purchase, and most of those polled considered a large purchase as anything $100 or more.[45] The fact that most of those surveyed view a $100 expenditure as a large purchase shows how much debt is already piled on their credit cards and how closely they are living to the edge.

DROWNING IN DEBT

Even though the median U.S. household income is $61,372, a majority of Americans are living from paycheck to paycheck and spending everything they earn.[46] This is a prescription for disaster. In fact, this is madness!

Americans are drowning in debt! As difficult as it is to comprehend, the total mortgage debt rose to a staggering $9.4 trillion; total auto debt passed $1.3 trillion; student-loan debt sadly reached a record $1.48 trillion; and credit-card debt is unimaginably between $1 trillion and $1.5 trillion.[47]

---

[44] Richter Felix, "This Is What Nearly $14 Trillion of Household Debt Looks Like," November 25, 2019, World Economic Forum, https://www.weforum.org/agenda/2019/11/u-s-household-debt-climbs-to-13-95-trillion/.

[45] John S. Kiernan, "91 Million Americans Fear Maxing Out Their Credit Cards on Large Purchases," January 28, 2020, WalletHub.com, https://wallethub.com/blog/large-purchases-survey/57193/.

[46] G. E. Miller, "The Shocking Percentage of Americans That Live Paycheck to Paycheck," January 21, 2019, 20SomethingFinance.com, https://20somethingfinance.com/percentage-of-americans-living-paycheck-to-paycheck/.

[47] "Key Figures Behind America's Consumer Debt," Debt.org, https://www.debt.org/faqs/americans-in-debt/.

And the lure to get more credit cards never stops as credit-card companies mail or email offers for new credit cards to lure you into their trap. They may try to get your attention by saying you are "preapproved" for a 0%-interest credit card or a valuable sign-up bonus or that they want to offer you their fancy "gold" or "platinum" card. But what they don't blatantly tell you is the information they hide in tiny print, hoping you won't read too closely.

Often credit-card companies offer cash bonuses or several thousand airline miles for simply opening an account. However, you'll usually need to spend a certain amount within a specified time period to qualify for the cash or the promised airline miles.

Be careful about using credit cards. Although you may intend to pay off your balance each month, most people do not. Over a period of time, most consumers usually get pulled into accumulating a terrible burden of debt and regretting that they ever started down the path of depending on credit cards.

Eleven percent of American teenagers already have their own credit cards. When most of us who are adults were teenagers, we didn't even know what a credit card was! But according to *U.S. News and World Report*, banks and credit-card companies pay schools more than $1 billion annually to gain access to students' names and addresses so they can lure students to get their first credit card.

◆

Be careful about using credit cards.
Although you may intend to pay off your balance each month,
most people do not. Over a period of time,
most consumers usually get pulled into accumulating
a terrible burden of debt and regretting that they ever started
down the path of depending on credit cards.

◆

Most teens get into deep trouble with credit cards by using them for routine spending. Teen "shopaholics" are at special risk because they use "retail therapy" to get over mood swings. This often becomes an addictive behavioral pattern that quickly gets these teens into big financial trouble.[48]

Statistics show that more than half of college students get their first credit card as freshmen — and more than 80 percent owe more than $3,000 by the end of their senior year. It is shocking, but more people between the ages of 20 to 24 years declare bankruptcy than graduate from college, and much of it is due to the wrong use of credit cards![49]

Students with minimal financial experience buy into the idea of making a "minimum payment" — not realizing how quickly the amount of interest that builds up on unpaid balances each month. The average back-to-school expenditure runs about $3,400, which takes 39.5 years to pay off in minimum payments at 18-percent interest, incurring an additional $9,100 in interest alone.[50]

Outstanding student-loan debt has also tripled in the last decade and has now exceeded $1.5 trillion. Education has become so expensive that a college education is now the second-largest expense an individual is likely to make in a lifetime, second to purchasing a home.[51] Projections are that as much as 40 percent of borrowers will likely default on their student loans by 2023.[52] Of those who file for Chapter 7 bankruptcy protections, 32 percent of them carry student-loan debt.[53]

---

[48] "Why Teens Get in Trouble With Credit Cards," crchealth.com, https://www.crchealth.com/troubled-teenagers/credit-cards/.

[49] Ibid.

[50] Ibid.

[51] Jessica Dickler, "Consumer Debt Hits $4 Trillion," February 19, 2019, cnbc.com, https://www.cnbc.com/2019/02/21/consumer-debt-hits-4-trillion.html.

[52] Judith Scott-Clayton, 2018 Brooking Institution Report, "The Looming Student Loan Default Crisis Is Worse Than We Thought," January 11, 2018, brookings.edu, https://www.brookings.edu/research/the-looming-student-loan-default-crisis-is-worse-than-we-thought/.

[53] Mike Brown, "Study: For Those Filing for Bankruptcy, Student Loan Debt Lingers On," 6/11/19, lendedu.com, https://lendedu.com/blog/student-loans-bankruptcy/.

What is equally unthinkable is that more than 3 million senior citizens in the U.S. are still paying off their student loans. That's right — 3 million Americans aged 60 and older owe more than $86 billion in unpaid student loans that they are trying to pay off with social-security benefits![54]

MAKING MORE AND HAVING LESS

The fact is that Americans are making more than ever before, but they feel like they have less. The majority do not have an emergency fund, are not saving for their child's college education or for their own retirement, and are constantly worried about their financial situation. But because they want to live the American dream, they feel they are entitled to have everything they want. So instead of practicing restraint, they borrow too much and exercise little or no self-restraint. They put themselves into devastating circumstances as they regularly eat out, go to the movies, overspend on clothes, take vacations, and purchase newer cars at the expense of future needs. Financial-management experts state the problem is not usually a lack of money, but exorbitant spending and using money in undisciplined and self-indulgent ways.[55]

For example, what would be wrong with learning to be satisfied with the house you have right now rather than going into deeper debt for a larger one? Is your house really that unsatisfactory? But America is famous for its cars, restaurants, theme parks, fashion — *and big houses.* Because of what foreigners have seen in movies, they usually think of America as the land of big houses.

Houses in the U.S. are among the largest in the world, and the sizes keep growing larger and larger. At present, the average size of a house in America

---

[54] Kelly McLaughlin, "3 Million Senior Citizens in the U.S. Are Still Paying Off Their Student Loans," May 3, 2019, businessinsider.com.
[55] "This Is How You Know You're Living Above Your Means," August 16, 2018, WashingtonPost.com, https://www.washingtonpost.com/business/2018/08/16/this-is-how-you-know-youre-living-above-your-means/.

has more than doubled since the 1950s.[56] But although Americans are already living in the world's biggest houses, a recent study has found that 43 percent of Americans surveyed are not pleased with the size of their current home and would prefer something larger.[57] About 29 percent of people in homes larger than 3,200 square feet stated that they would like to get a bigger house.

But let's also dig a little deeper into the state of car debt in the United States. As stated earlier, the outstanding auto-loan debt held by Americans was more than $1.2 trillion at the end of 2019.[58] The facts show that at least 84.6 percent of new vehicles purchased in the United States in 2019 were financed.[59] This means about 35 percent of American adults rely on auto loans to pay for their cars.[60] Because most car owners purchase newer cars to replace their current car before it is paid off, they end up in perpetual debt for their vehicles for most of their lives.

As mentioned earlier, Americans are drowning in debt and are living from paycheck to paycheck while earning more than ever before. Many have sold themselves into financial slavery by going into debt on TVs, furniture, computers, clothes, knickknacks, and other material things that quickly lose their appeal.

For example, when the financial crisis hit the United States in 2008, I wondered how it would affect the number of people who eat in restaurants. But the restaurants remained packed in spite of the fact that people were financially struggling (unlike the more recent crisis in which so many restaurants were

[56] Margot Adler, "Behind the Ever-Expanding American Dream House," July 4, 2006, npr.org, https://www.npr.org/templates/story/story.php?storyId=5525283.

[57] Andrew Soergel, "Go Big and Go Home: Many Americans Want a Larger House," February 26, 2015, USNews.com, https://www.usnews.com/news/blogs/data-mine/2015/02/26/trulia-survey-many-americans-want-a-bigger-house.

[58] Jenn Jones, "Auto Loan Statistics 2020," January 10, 2020, LendingTree.com, https://www.lendingtree.com/auto/debt-statistics/.

[59] M. Szmigiera, "Share of New U.S. Vehicles With Financing 2017-2019," April 2, 2020, statista.com, https://www.statista.com/statistics/453000/share-of-new-vehicles-with-financing-usa/.

[60] Niall McCarthy, "Over 100 Million Americans Have Auto Loans," January 4, 2019, statista.com, https://www.statista.com/chart/16520/the-number-of-car-loan-accounts-in-the-us-by-year/.

required to temporarily shut down). Do you know why? They were eating on credit cards.

The amount of consumer debt connected to eating out is enormous. The most recent statistics show 81 percent of restaurant customers pay with a credit or debit card, and restaurant owners report that only 19 percent of customers pay with cash.[61] Within hours of eating that delicious meal, the food passes through a person's system and is flushed away. It becomes nothing more than a memory soon forgotten, yet it can cost that person interest payments for years.

In Second Timothy 3:2, Paul said people in the last days would be "lovers of their own selves, covetous," which portrays people who are *self-focused, self-centered, self-absorbed, self-consumed,* and who live with *an insatiable desire to always have more and more.* Then in verse 3, Paul added the word "incontinent," which depicts the *inability to exercise control, a lack of control, a lack of self-restraint, a lack of willpower,* or *the inability to say no.* Paul's use of these words clearly forecasted a fiscal lack of control that would emerge in the very last of the last days.

If you have yielded to the spirit of the age that says you can have whatever you want, whenever you want it with no consequences, there is no condemnation against you. This is simply a snare of the current world system — a pattern that multitudes have become entangled in, producing long-term financial havoc and stress in their lives and in their relationships.

But you — and anyone else you know — can get free of any financial trap if you choose God's way and allow Him to change you. This behavior is a work of the flesh that can be forgiven and overcome. Once again, sin must be acknowledged, but once it has been confessed, God will forgive you and empower you to move into a life of freedom!

---

[61] Kristen Gramigna, "The Cost of Being a 'Cash-Only' Restaurant," June 2015, FSRmagazine.com, https://www.fsrmagazine.com/expert-takes/cost-being-cash-only-restaurant.

**To review, the word "incontinent" in Second Timothy 3:3
depicts a lack of self-control and self-restraint,
and the *RIV* version of this verse reads:**

**Love for and commitment to family will disintegrate, and divorce
will become epidemic, with irreconcilable differences being a
major factor in tearing families apart. In fact, every imaginable
type of covenant will be regularly violated, and the court system
will be overwhelmed as people go overboard suing and being
sued. People will generally lose the ability to say no and will be
unable to control their instincts in nearly every area of life....**

NO ABILITY TO RESTRAIN EMOTIONS

In Chapter 5, we saw what Second Timothy 3:2 forecasts: that society in the last days will become *self-focused*, *self-absorbed*, and *self-centered*. It will be an end-time world that does not understand boundaries and that lives for self-embellishment with a sense of entitlement. Now let's see how all of these characteristics of an end-time society pertain to a lack of emotional restraint.

Those who are consumed with self-will possess a sense of entitlement — even believing that they have an inherent right to express their emotions however they wish, regardless of how it sounds, who it hurts, or how destructive it is to themselves or others. And whenever an individual or society throws off emotional restraint in this way, the result is ill-mannered, impolite, uncivil behavior.

THE PANDEMIC OF INCIVILITY

Uncivil behavior is defined as being rude or as engaging in antisocial speech or behavior. This can include rude gestures, vulgar language, offensive manners, continual interrupting, and loudly having private discussions in public spaces.[62]

One *national survey* found that 70 percent of Americans believe uncivil behavior has reached epic proportions. It is so widespread that 43 percent of Americans reported to expect an experience with it in the next 24 hours. Another recent poll reports nearly 50 percent of those surveyed said they were done with political conversations because of the incivility and bullying that followed. Another recent poll found that Americans claim to encounter uncivil behavior on average 17.1 times per week, or 2.4 times every day.[63]

Another report brings further light to the dire state of civility in America. It said 50 percent of American parents report that their children have experienced uncivil behavior at school. Approximately 69 percent of Americans have either stopped buying from a company or have reevaluated their opinion of a company because someone from that company was uncivil in their interaction. Further, 58 percent have advised friends, family, or co-workers not to buy certain products because of uncivil, rude, or disrespectful behavior from the company or its representatives. Finally, 69 percent of Americans report that cyber-bullying is getting worse, and 72 percent worry about children being cyber-bullied.[64]

The Impact on Politics

A recent study shows that 80 percent of Americans believe that the growing trend of unrestrained emotional behavior in politics has become a debilitating problem in our national conversation.[65] Research has linked political

---

[62] Shelly D. Lane and Helen McCourt. "Uncivil Communication in Everyday Life: A Response to Benson's 'The Rhetoric of Civility,'" *Journal of Contemporary Rhetoric*, Vol. 3, No. 1/2, 2013, pp. 17-29.

[63] Weber Shandwick, "News — Civility in America 2013: Incivility Has Reached Crisis Levels," webershandwick.com. Retrieved 2016-11-01.

[64] Ray Williams, "The Rise of Incivility in America," raywilliams.ca, https://raywilliams.ca/the-rise-of-incivility-in-america/.

[65] Daniel Cox and Robert P Jones, PhD., "Americans Say Elections More Negative Than Past, Lack of Civility as Major Problem," November 11, 2011, ppri.org, https://www.prri.org/research/americans-say-elections-more-negative-than-past-lack-of-civility-as-major-problem/.

incivility to reduced trust in the legitimacy of political candidates, political polarization, and policy gridlock. Examples in political discourse include, but are not limited to, name-calling, derisive or disrespectful speech and vulgarity, intentional lies, and misrepresentation of truth and facts.[66] One poll states that 58 percent of Americans expect the ugly behavior in politics to get worse.

The Impact on Journalism

Because of the Internet — and online media platforms where people are bolder to express themselves than in face-to-face encounters — online ugliness is also becoming more prominent and hostile. According to the Pew Research Center (PRC), 73 percent of online adults have seen someone being harassed in some way, and 40 percent have actually experienced it. In a general poll of Internet users, 92 percent believe that interaction on the Internet emboldens people to be more rude and aggressive compared with their face-to-face experiences. In fact, a Pew Research Center survey found 70 percent of 18-to-24-year-olds had experienced harassment on the Internet.[67]

The Impact on the Workplace

Disrespectful behavior has become commonplace in the workplace too.[68] According to recent data, 98 percent of all employees report experiencing this type of negative behavior in the workplace, with a sharp increase in frequency over the past several years.[69]

At an annual meeting of the American Psychological Association, researchers reported that workplace incivility is on the rise.[70] Such behaviors are

---

[66] Tony M. Massaro and Robin Stryker, "Freedom of Speech, Liberal Democracy, and Emerging Evidence on Civility and Effective Democratic Engagement," April 18, 2012, SSRN, https://papers.ssrn.com/sol3/papers.cfm?abstract_id=2042171.
[67] Ray Williams, ibid.
[68] Lynne M. Andersson, Christine M. Pearson, and Christine L. Porath, *Assessing and Attacking Workplace Incivility, Organizational Dynamics*, Vol. 29, No. 2, pp. 123–137, © 2000 Elsevier Science, Inc.
[69] Christine Porath and Christine Pearson, "The Price of Incivility," *Harvard Business Review*, January-February 2013, https://hbr.org/2013/01/the-price-of-incivility.
[70] Lois. M. Collins, "Incivility Turning More Workplaces Toxic," August 10, 2011, *Deseret News*, https://www.deseret.com/2011/8/10/20208714/incivility-turning-more-workplaces-toxic.

characteristically rude and exhibit a lack of regard for others.[71] Examples of this ugly behavior can include making insulting comments, spreading false rumors, and engaging in social isolation.

One researcher of organizational behavior at the University of Maryland says, "When it comes to incivility, there's often a snowballing effect. The more you see rudeness, the more likely you are to perceive it from others and the more likely you are to be rude yourself to others."[72]

This snowball effect is having a tremendously negative effect in the workplace, since a culture of rudeness can cause employees to be chronically distracted, less productive, and less creative.[73] For example, one survey found that 48 percent of victims intentionally reduced their work effort (resulting from the fallout of offense, strife, etc.), 38 percent intentionally decreased the quality of their work, 66 percent experienced reduced job performance, and 78 percent reported reduced levels of commitment.[74]

There is no question that this ever-growing proliferation of ill-mannered behavior lowers trust, sparks feelings of anger, fear, and sadness, and even leads to depression. But the "snowball is rolling," and professional researchers are struggling in vain to find ways to stop the spreading effects of uncivil, rude, and unrestrained emotional responses.[75]

This out-of-control behavior is pandemic. In fact, another survey found almost 50 percent of all U.S. workers report that they have experienced or witnessed some kind of bullying — verbal abuse, insults, threats, screaming, sarcasm, or ostracism. Studies now estimate that the annual costs of bullying in the workplace is more than $200 billion (resulting from more people

---

[71] Lynne M. Andersson and Christine M. Pearson (July 1999). "Tit for Tat? The Spiraling Effect of Incivility in the Workplace," *The Academy of Management Review*, Vol. 24, No. 3, July 1999, pp. 452-71.

[72] "Why Are We Being So Rude to Each Other?," June 26, 2018, WashingtonPost.com.

[73] "When We Fight Fire With Fire: Rudeness Can Be as Contagious as the Common Cold," June 26, 2018, WashingtonPost.com, www.washingtonpost.com/news/speaking-of-science/wp/2018/06/26/when-we-fight-fire-with-fire-rudeness-can-be-as-contagious-as-common-cold-research-shows/.

[74] Porath and Pearson, "The Price of Incivility."

[75] "When We Fight Fire With Fire: Rudeness Can Be as Contagious as the Common Cold."

calling in sick to avoid situations, etc.). As bad as this sounds, it's not the full picture. The Workplace Bullying Institute reports that 40 percent of the targets of bullying never told their employers.[76]

The Impact on Families

"Incontinent" emotions — that is, unrestricted emotions — are also affecting the family. Because the family is losing its ability to negotiate with each other, it is leading to massive expenditures in the offices of marriage and family counselors.

If your marriage needs counseling, you would be wise to admit that you need help and find someone to help you.

But the facts show that marriage and family counseling is a burgeoning industry. Today there are more than 50,000 marriage and family therapists who treat individuals, couples, and families nationwide.[77] As a result of unmanageable emotions at home, revenue for the marriage and family industry was projected to reach $18.6 billion annually by 2019.[78]

The average fee for seeing a family counselor is between $60-$120 per hour, depending on where one lives. Because few insurance companies cover costs associated with family counseling, those who need it often must come up with cash to pay the counselor. This frequently adds more stress to the pre-existing emotional situation, because many don't have the available funds to continue seeing the counselor as long as is needed. Many who need help start out well and have good intentions, but they fail to continue therapy because they simply cannot afford it. This can add a sense of failure and frustration that often compounds the problems at home.

---

[76] Ray Williams, "The Rise of Incivility in America."

[77] "Employment Outlook and Career Guidance for Marriage Family Therapists," careersinpsychology.org, https://careersinpsychology.org/employment-outlook-guidance-marriage-family-therapists/.

[78] "Psychologists, Social Workers, and Marriage Counselors in the U.S. Industry Trends (2015-2020)," March 2020, IbisWorld.com, https://www.ibisworld.com/united-states/market-research-reports/psychologists-social-workers-marriage-counselors-industry/.

The Impact on Everyday Life

People are also experiencing increasing levels of this emotional lack of restraint in their everyday lives as "outrage speech." This unrestrained verbiage includes name calling, insulting, character assassination, mockery, and other types of emotional displays.[79]

It's even evident on the road in the form of "road rage." CNN reports that road rage has been on the rise for years. In fact, it has become so serious that fatal car crashes linked to aggressive driving climbed nearly 500 percent in 10 years, according to the National Highway Traffic Safety Administration.

One news organization that tracks gun violence found the incidents of drivers who pulled out a gun in a threatening manner or fired a gun at another driver or passenger rose from 247 in 2014 to 620 in 2016. Although this statistic is now outdated, in the first six months of 2017, they tracked 325 incidents — nearly two a day. It's difficult to believe that people on such a wide scale could be so emotionally out of control — but these are hard facts!

The American Automobile Association's Foundation for Traffic Safety found that nearly 80 percent of polled drivers said they expressed serious aggression, anger, or road rage while driving at least once in a year.[80]

- 51 percent of respondents admitted they tailgate on purpose. That's *104 million* drivers willing to take the risk of riding another driver's car bumper!

- 47 percent of those polled admitted they yell at other drivers. That's *95 million* hollering hotheads ready to spew defamatory remarks at other drivers!

[79] Sarah Sobieraj and Jeffrey M. Berry, "From Incivility to Outrage: Political Discourse in Blogs, Talk Radio, and Cable News," February 8, 2011, Taylor & Francis Online, https://www.tandfonline.com/doi/abs/10.1080/10584609.2010.542360.
[80] Tamra Johnson, "Nearly 80 Percent of Drivers Express Significant, Anger, Aggression, or Road Rage," July 14, 2016, AAA Newsroom, https://newsroom.aaa.com/2016/07/nearly-80-percent-of-drivers-express-significant-anger-aggression-or-road-rage/.

- 45 percent of drivers admitted they honk in anger or annoyance. That's *91 million* angry, honking drivers on the road!

- 33 percent or 67 million drivers admitted they gesture obscenely at other drivers. That's *49 million* drivers ready to make obscene gestures at other drivers they're upset with!

- 4 percent of drivers admitted to actually getting out of their cars to confront other drivers. That's *8 million* hotheaded drivers willing to go to those lengths to vent their anger!

- 3 percent of drivers are guilty of ramming another car on purpose. That's *6 million* drivers capable of using their vehicles as a weapon if they get angry enough!

But wait — there's more!

- 6 percent admitted they threw objects.

- 6 percent admitted they actually got in a physical altercation with another driver.

- 5 percent admitted they deliberately sideswiped another vehicle.

- 5 percent forced another driver off the road.

This out-of-control road rage not only results in ugly confrontations, but people's lives have been lost as a consequence. In 2006, there were 80 fatal crashes related to road rage, but that number grew 500 percent in 9 years. It may be difficult for us to fathom, but from 2013 to 2017, 136 people were actually killed in firearm-involved road-rage incidents. The American Automobile Association (AAA) linked more than 12,500 injuries to driver violence out of 10,000 car accidents since 2007.[81]

[81] Taylor Covington, "Road Rage Statistics in 2020," February 25, 2020, TheZebra.com, www.thezebra.com/road-rage-statistics/.

There is nothing normal about what you have read in this section regarding the inability to say no to acting on wrong, negative emotions. But the Holy Spirit prophesied clearly that people living in the last-days society would become "incontinent" in the last days. He unquestionably forecasted the epidemic of emotional explosions we are witnessing on so many fronts in this day.

This horrible, unrestrained behavior has an accumulated negative effect on any person over a period of time. It makes one more susceptible to heart disease, diabetes, a weakened immune system, insomnia, and high blood pressure. It consumes huge amounts of mental energy and clouds a person's thinking, making it harder to concentrate or enjoy life. It can also lead to stress, depression, and other mental-health problems.

---◆---

The Holy Spirit prophesied clearly that people living in the last-days society would become "incontinent" in the last days. He unquestionably forecasted the epidemic of emotional explosions we are witnessing on so many fronts in this day.

---◆---

Lashing out alienates your colleagues, supervisors, or clients and erodes their respect. It causes lasting scars in the people you love most and gets in the way of friendships and work relationships. Explosive anger makes it difficult for others to trust you, to speak honestly to you, or to feel comfortable around you. And such behavior is especially damaging to children.[82]

As ugly as this type of destructive behavior is, it is simply a work of the flesh — and as is true regarding all works of the flesh, it can be conquered by the Spirit of God. All who are tempted to give in to emotional impulses — to

---

[82] "Anger Management," helpguide.org, https://www.helpguide.org/articles/relationships-communication/anger-management.htm.

throw off emotional self-control or self-restraint — and who think they have an "inherent right" to express whatever they feel at any given moment are walking down a path that leads to disastrous consequences. But as with any work of the flesh, if sin is acknowledged and these individuals are willing to change, the flesh and emotions can be brought back under control as they submit their mind, will, and emotions to the Lordship of Jesus Christ.

NO ABILITY TO STOP ADDICTIVE BEHAVIORS

But as destructive as it is to lose one's ability to control his or her emotions, perhaps the most heartbreaking of all "incontinent" behaviors are those connected with addictive behaviors. We already covered the addictive consumption of food — but let's look at other addictive behaviors that have become so widespread in these last days of the present age.

◆

As destructive as it is to lose one's ability to control his or her emotions, perhaps the most heartbreaking of all "incontinent" behaviors are those connected with addictive behaviors.

◆

There is a broad array of destructive addictions, including addiction to alcohol, drugs, food, gambling, pornography, sex, the Internet, social media, video games, shopping, risk-taking behavior, etc. The facts show that addiction is raging out of control, impacting millions of lives, and killing thousands of people every year. Addiction destroys marriages, friendships, and careers and threatens a person's basic health and safety.

As noted several times already in this chapter, the word "incontinent" depicts *the inability to exercise control, a lack of control, a lack of self-restraint, no willpower*, or *the inability to say no*. It pictures a person or a society that has abandoned self-restraint and lacks moderation and self-control in every sphere of life, resulting in self-indulgent behaviors.

MIND-ALTERING SUBSTANCES: THE FLESHLY ATTEMPT TO 'FIX ONESELF'

But in the last section of this chapter, I want us to see how society has thrown off restraint in regard to various addictive substances. Before we begin to see how widespread alcohol and drug abuse has become, I want to point out the meaning of the word "witchcraft" in Galatians 5:20. This word is a translation of the Greek word *pharmakeia*, which is where we get the phrase "pharmaceutical drugs" or the word "pharmacy." In the New Testament, it was the Greek word used for *medicines or drugs that inhibit a person's personality or change his behavior.* We would call these *mind-altering drugs.*

When the Early Church was being established in the First Century, pagans embraced demonic religions that used drugs to alter the state of one's mind. You see, heathen worshipers came to pagan temples to find relief from a wide spectrum of sicknesses, mental-stress factors, and a myriad of other personal problems. Rather than confront the true needs of the heathen worshipers and identify real solutions for their problems, the priests of these pagan religions poured hallucinogenic drugs into vials of wine, stirred it all together, and then gave the mixture to the worshipers to drink.

After the recipients were medicated and under the influence of these mind-altering drugs, the priests would send them home, telling them that they would feel better. However, once the drugs wore off, the worshipers found themselves facing the same or even worse problems.

The only way these seekers found continuing relief from their problems was to return again and again to the pagan temples to receive more doses of these mind-altering drugs, which gave the people temporary relief but offered no permanent solution. The priests were powerless to heal and incapable of solving anyone's problems. All they could do was continue to offer the worshipers more drugs, thus temporarily altering the state of their minds and giving them a brief respite from their problems and pain. However, in the long run, the drugs offered by the priests only prolonged the pain of those they pretended to help.

How does this apply to you and me today?

The flesh still doesn't know how to fix itself. It will try to convince a person to ignore his problem, to hide it with some superficial covering, or to drink alcohol or take drugs to make himself feel better. The alcohol or drugs may give that person a brief hiatus from reality — but when the effects wear off, he will still have the same problems to deal with that he had before.

If your doctor has prescribed medication for you, be faithful to take your medication. But don't let your flesh tell you that you can keep covering up your problems with temporary solutions. Those temporary solutions will eventually wear off or run out — and when they do, the same issue you faced before will resurface again.

◆

The flesh still doesn't know how to fix itself.
It will try to convince a person to ignore his problem,
to hide it with some superficial covering,
or to drink alcohol or take drugs
to make himself feel better.

◆

Based on Galatians 5:20, we find that the misuse of drugs — at least in God's mind — is the equivalent to witchcraft. But like any work of the flesh, this, too, can be dealt with victoriously by the Spirit of God in the life of any believer who is willing to subject himself to the Holy Spirit's control.

But let's go on to see exactly how society has dived head-first into the widespread abuse of alcohol and of both prescription drugs and illegal drugs in our age.

The Impact of Alcohol

Facts show that alcohol is the most widely abused substance in the world today. Alcohol abuse includes drinking-related behavior that may cause people to physically endanger themselves or others; get into trouble with the law; experience difficulties in relationships or jobs; and fail to fulfill major obligations at work, school, or at home.

A mere generation ago, alcohol was not so available as it is today. It was primarily purchased in alcohol stores. But today alcohol is evident everywhere. It can be purchased at grocery stores, convenience stores, kiosks, malls, most restaurants, and in nearly every hub or venue of commercial transportation. My intention with this subject is not to focus on the United States, as this is a worldwide problem. However, statistics from the U.S. are most readily available, so let's see both worldwide facts and statistics from the U.S. regarding the impact of alcohol.[83]

- Every year worldwide, alcohol abuse is the cause of 5.3 percent of all deaths (or 1 in every 20 deaths).

- Nearly 300 million people worldwide have an alcohol-use disorder.

- Recent statistics show that 30 Americans die every day in an alcohol-related car accident, and six Americans die every day from alcohol poisoning.

---

[83] "Statistics on Addiction in America," Addiction Center, www.addictioncenter.com/addiction/addiction-statistics/.

- About 15 million American adults have an alcohol-use disorder. That's about 6 percent of the population at the time of this writing, and the trend continues to spiral upward.

- In 2017, 2.4 million Americans between the ages of 18 and 25 started to drink alcohol. However, statistics show that alcohol consumption generally begins between the ages of 12 and 17.

The Impact of Drugs

But today millions of people struggle with addiction. Studies show that more than 50 percent of the American population annually misuses prescription drugs.[84]

Many are addicted as a result of prescription medication that unintentionally resulted in addiction. But there are also millions of people who are addicted to *analgesics, depressants, stimulants*, and *hallucinogens*. Analgesics are narcotics such as *heroin, morphine, fentanyl*, and *codeine*, among others. Depressants include *alcohol, barbiturates, tranquilizers*, and even *nicotine*. Stimulants include *cocaine, methamphetamine*, and *ecstasy*, among others. Hallucinogens include *LSD (acid), peyote (mescaline), psilocybin (magic mushrooms), marijuana, ketamine, phencyclidine (PCP)*, and *salvia divinorum (diviner's sage)*, among others.

- Almost 21 million Americans have an addiction to at least one drug.

- Drug-overdose deaths have more than tripled since 1990.

- Recent statistics show that alcohol and drug addiction cost the U.S. economy over $600 billion every year.

- About 20 percent of Americans who deal with depression or an anxiety disorder also additionally have a substance-abuse disorder.

---

[84] Jaime Rosenberg, "More Than Half of Americans Misuse Prescription Drugs," September 11, 2018, AJMC, https://www.ajmc.com/focus-of-the-week/more-than-half-of-americans-misuse-prescription-drugs.

- The problem is so widespread that 90 percent of people who have an addiction started to drink alcohol or use drugs before they were 18 years old, and Americans between the ages of 18 and 25 are most likely to use addictive drugs.[85]

The Impact of Misused Prescription Drugs

There are a myriad of causes for the misuse of prescription drugs. Often it is related to health, stress, work, family, relationships, and finances. Frequently because people do not know how to manage their situations or emotions, they are turning to prescription medication in record-setting numbers to find peace and to help control their feelings.

Prescription opioids have especially garnered national attention because it has fueled a record number of drug-related deaths. Opioids are a special concern because they are an ingredient in many pain-relieving medications. In 2017, doctors issued 191,218,272 opioid prescriptions, a slight decline from the 200,000,000 opioid prescriptions that they issued every year from 2006 to 2016. Since 1999, the sale of opioid painkillers has increased by 300 percent.

This epidemic is so serious that the Center for Disease Control issued a mandate for physicians to look for other ways to alleviate pain before prescribing opioids and to limit the duration of the first prescription.[86]

- Approximately 130 Americans die every day from an opioid overdose.

- From 1999 to 2017, 399,230 Americans lost their lives to opioids.

- In 2017 alone, 47,600 fatal overdoses occurred that involved at least one opioid.

---

[85] "Statistics on Addiction in America."
[86] "More Than Half of Americans Misuse Prescription Drugs."

- Approximately 20 to 30 percent of people who take prescription opioids misuse them.

- Approximately 10 percent of people who misuse prescription opioids become addicted to them.

- Approximately 2.1 million Americans have an opioid-use disorder.[87]

The Impact of Illegal Drugs

A generation ago, when we thought of drug abuse, we often thought of heroin users whose arms looked like they were nearly rotting from dirty needles or hippies whose minds were wasted on LSD. But today drug abuse — even the use of heroin — has moved into the mainstream.

Heroin is a powerful, addictive opioid — especially heroin mixed with fentanyl — and it is a major contributor to the opioid epidemic.

- In 2017, approximately 494,000 Americans over the age of 12 were regular heroin users.

- In 2017 alone, 886,000 Americans used heroin at least once.

- Approximately 25 percent of people who try heroin once go on to become addicted.

- In 2017, 81,000 Americans tried heroin for the first time.

- More than 15,000 Americans died from a heroin overdose in 2017.

- In addition, drug violations count for a large proportion of incarcerations in local, state, and federal facilities and represent the most common arrest category.

---

[87] "Statistics on Addiction in America."

Marijuana is becoming increasingly legal throughout the United States for medical reasons. However, it is still widely used as a recreational drug and may be addictive and cause serious health problems. Studies show that:

- Between 30-40 million Americans smoke marijuana every year.

- In 2017, 1.2 million people between the ages of 12 and 17 and 525,000 Americans over the age of 26 used marijuana for the *first time*.

- As unthinkable as the following statistics seem, studies also show that in 2018, 13 percent of eighth-graders, 27 percent of tenth-graders, and 35 percent of twelfth-graders had used marijuana at least once in the past year.

- Approximately 30 percent of those who regularly use marijuana have a marijuana-use disorder.

Cocaine is so addictive that some cocaine users become addicted after using the drug only once. Its continued use can damage organs, produce mental disorders, and cause respiratory failure. Studies show that:

- Approximately 5 million Americans are regular cocaine users.

- According to a 2017 survey, 2.2 million Americans used cocaine at least once that previous month; cocaine was involved in 1 out of every 5 overdose deaths in 2017; and the percentage of cocaine-related overdose deaths increased by 34 percent between 2016 and 2017.

- Americans between the ages of 18 to 25 use cocaine more than any other age group. In 2017, 1 million Americans over the age of 12 used cocaine for the first time, and in 2018, almost 4 percent of twelfth-graders admitted to having used cocaine at least once in their lives.

Methamphetamine is a controlled substance that has a high potential for abuse, addiction, and overdose. Although methamphetamine has been proven to be highly addictive and dangerous, studies show:

- Approximately 774,000 Americans are regular users of methamphetamine.

- Of that number, approximately 16,000 of these users are unimaginably between the ages of 12 and 17.

- In 2017, approximately 195,000 Americans used meth for the first time.

- The number of fatal meth overdoses nearly tripled from 2011 to 2016.

Hallucinogens are illegal, mind-altering drugs that carry great risk of hallucinations, impaired judgment, and reckless behaviors. Although these risks are well-known, studies show that:

- Approximately 1.4 million Americans are hallucinogen users.

- In 2017, 1.2 million Americans — a number that includes 344,000 minors between the ages of 12 and 17 — used a hallucinogen for the first time.

- As recent as 2018, even 2 percent of twelfth-graders admitted to trying a hallucinogen.

Inhalants are readily available because they are usually household objects like nail polish, glue, hair spray, leather cleaner, and spray paint, but they can have permanent mind-altering or brain-damaging effects. These solvents, gases, and aerosol sprays are inhaled by people to get high and can cause a person to lose consciousness or develop an addiction.

- More than 23 million Americans have tried an inhalant at least once in their lives.

- Approximately 556,000 Americans are regular inhalant users.

- Almost 9 percent of twelfth-graders in 2018 admitted to using an inhalant.

- Inhalants contribute to approximately 15 percent of deaths by suffocation every year.[88]

The Impact on Families and Children

As a result of the widespread consumption of alcohol and misuse of prescription drugs and illegal drugs in today's society, thousands of families have suffered greatly from the havoc wreaked by addicted family members. This has contributed to a deepening disintegration of the family unit because of the confusion and disconnection these addictions produce in relationships.

In fact, research shows that children who grow up in environments of addiction struggle deeply within themselves with brokenness. If the children don't succumb to addiction themselves, they often isolate themselves from others as a form of self-protection, which also contributes to the disintegration of the family.

As of 2017, approximately 8.7 million children aged 17 or younger in U.S. households were living with at least one parent who had a substance-abuse problem. This shows the breadth of the problem. And when one considers the additional "baggage" that often accompanies substance abuse — including mental illness, poverty, and domestic violence — it becomes clear that the situation for the children who live in these households is horrific.[89]

---

[88] "Statistics on Addiction in America."
[89] "Report Reveals That About 1 in 8 Children Lived With at Least One Parent Who Had a Past Year Substance Use Disorder," August 24, 2017, SAMHSA, https://www.samhsa.gov/newsroom/press-announcements/201708241000.

It is common knowledge that those with substance-abuse problems often struggle financially. This can create a lower socioeconomic status that produces increased difficulties in academic and social settings and in functioning within the family unit.

One reason addiction is associated with financial crisis and poverty is that many addictive behaviors are used as a form of escapism. This means that those who are addicted spend exorbitant amounts of money on these substances to escape from the realities of life.

Because those with addictions often have health problems, mental struggles, and emotional imbalances, addicts also miss work, which contributes to the overall dysfunction of their financial situation. Their responsibilities at home are also often overlooked, leaving other family members to compensate. This causes imbalance in the home structure and even chaos — and, at times, a lack of needful attention to a family's financial affairs as a result.

As the downward spiral progresses, the financial side effects begin to snowball with bad credit, missed payments, debts, and late fees. The addict slides into deeper poverty, with a host of other problems propelling the decline — such as marital troubles, divorce, loss of job, and possibly arrest and criminal charges. In short, the impact of addiction creates a never-ending, losing battle for financial survival that often leads to financial ruin.[90]

Studies show that children in these struggling families are at risk of parental abuse or neglect and often suffer from indirect consequences, such as living with inadequate household resources. Research has found that children of parents with an alcohol-use disorder are at greater risk for depression, anxiety disorders, problems with cognitive and verbal skills, and parental abuse or neglect. Research has also shown that children of parents who have a drug-use

---

[90] Jessica Bosari, "The Cost of Addiction on Families," June 19, 2012, Forbes, https://www.forbes.com/sites/moneywisewomen/2012/06/19/the-cost-of-addiction-on-families/#7fb8d8145097.

disorder are at higher risk for mental and behavioral disorders and functional impairments.

To deal with this situation, these children often eventually begin self-medicating themselves as a way of trying to deal with their unresolved pain and their wounded self-worth and self-esteem. As a result, the next generation also often limps through life, struggling with substance abuse.

The facts show as many as 20 percent of current abusers grew up in abusive households themselves. Thus, the long-term impact this has upon children cannot be overstated.

Ask any professional family counselor or experienced schoolteacher about the state of families and children, and the majority of them will tell you that the family today is under attack and in serious trouble. All the sociological studies and statistics irrefutably show a downward trend for the traditional family over the past decades that is deeply disturbing.

But, thank God, there is great hope for those who are willing to wake up to this last-days development and submit to the authority of the Scriptures! They do not have to fall victim to the downward pull of addiction and its disastrous consequences on the rest of the family. They can surrender their lives fully to the Lord Jesus Christ and begin to *take back* the territory the enemy has taken! They just have to be willing to do whatever is necessary to build a hedge of protection around their homes and to recapture what has been lost.

◆

**Thank God, there is great hope for those
who are willing to wake up to this last-days development
and submit to the authority of the Scriptures!**

◆

A BURGEONING DETOX AND REHABILITATION INDUSTRY

Because of this "incontinent" situation where restraint has been thrown to the wind, new industries have emerged to try to help cope with the problem. For example, today in the United States, rehabilitation centers for drugs, alcohol, and other types of addiction are so numerous that the industry is bringing in approximately $35 billion annually!

There are 14,000-plus treatment facilities, and this number is growing. Approximately 2.5 million persons go to these rehabilitation centers for treatment — not only for alcohol and drug abuse, but also for all types of unrestrained addictions, such as sex addiction, gambling, Internet addiction — and the list goes on and on.[91]

But the detox and rehabilitation industry has become so varied that one can choose which one he or she wishes to go to based on personal preference or income. Basic programs run approximately $5,000. But an individual could choose a high-end detox/luxury rehabilitation center that offers the full gamut of services — acupuncture, aromatherapy, equine therapy, golf, spa treatments, pools and hot tubs, massage therapy, nutritional counseling, music therapy, expressive arts therapy, exercise therapy, gourmet meals, private rooms, and exercise facilities.

That person will pay between *$30,000-$65,000* for a month-long stay! Yet the disappointing reality is that 40-50 percent of those who go through detox and rehabilitation relapse back into substance abuse and have to return to undergo treatment all over again.

The flesh cannot fix itself, but through the power of His Spirit and His Word, Jesus *can* bring deliverance, hope, and new life.

---

[91] Leah Miller, "Benefits of Long-Term Drug Rehab Facilities and How To Find One," May 13, 2020, National Rehabs Directory, https://www.rehabs.com/treatment/120-180-day-long-term-rehabilitation/.

A WORLD WITH NO RESTRAINT

To do justice to the word "incontinent" and the many ways it is manifesting in this last-days society, we could keep discussing a seemingly endless list of areas where people in this present age have lost self-control, abandoned self-restraint, and given in to the whims of the flesh. This chapter is by no means comprehensive. However, based on what you have read, what are your own conclusions? More and more:

- Are people losing restraint with *food*?

- Are people losing restraint with *spending*?

- Are people losing restraint with *emotions*?

- Are people losing restraint with *addictive behaviors*?

If your answer is yes, remember what the Holy Spirit prophesied in Second Timothy 3:3 — that people in the last days would become "incontinent," lacking self-control and self-restraint.

Let's review again the *RIV* version of Second Timothy 3:3 — at least to the point we have discussed so far:

Love for and commitment to family will disintegrate, and divorce will become epidemic, with irreconcilable differences being a major factor in tearing families apart. In fact, every imaginable type of covenant will be regularly violated, and the court system will be overwhelmed as people go overboard suing and being sued. People will generally lose the ability to say no and will be unable to control their instincts in nearly every area of life....

Consider the last part of the interpretive version above: *"...People will generally lose the ability to say no and will be unable to control their instincts in nearly every area of life…."* Does that sound like the society we are living in today? If so, you can know that this scripture is a divine alert for us! God wants us to know that we are living in the last of the last days — right at the end of the age before Jesus wraps everything up!

CHAPTER 7

LAST-DAYS SURVIVAL GUIDE ACTION STEPS

TO AVOID AN 'INCONTINENT' ATTITUDE IN YOUR LIFE

Because this is the end of the age, it is easy to fall into traps of vice that the devil has set for a last-days society. But if you'll take the following action steps, your deliberate pursuit to stay honest with yourself and to stay true to God's Word will help you avoid any display of incontinence in your personal life. These steps will help you stay spiritually alert to any area in which you have become susceptible to the spirit of this delinquent age. If these action steps are not already established habits in your walk with God, you should begin to implement them immediately in order to stay spiritually garrisoned even in the most troublesome of times.

As in every chapter so far, these action steps are simple to follow. And if you'll open your heart to the Lord and determine to faithfully implement them, they will awaken you to areas that need change.

1. Confront yourself about your real condition.

The word "incontinent" in Second Timothy 3:3 pictures a person or society who has *lost power over self* and hence has *no self-control*. It describes *the inability to exercise control, a lack of self-control, a lack of self-restraint, no willpower,* or *the inability to say no.* It perfectly describes a person or people who have the "I just can't say no" attitude that ultimately leads to destruction because it produces life with few boundaries and restraints.

After reading this chapter, now it's time to personalize what you have learned by looking at your own heart to make an honest examination. Ask yourself:

- *Am I living with self-control and self-restraint — or do I show a lack of exercising self-restraint in my inability to say no to myself regarding unhealthy desires?*

I realize this is not an enjoyable question to ask yourself — especially if you already know the answer and it isn't one you're thrilled about accepting. There is no escaping the fact that heart conviction can be uncomfortable.

But if you see a need for change in your personal life, God isn't responding with judgment or condemnation. That type of response does nothing to help change you! The Holy Spirit will convict you of the need to improve in this area, and it will be your responsibility not to ignore it. When He convicts you, He also gives you the power that is necessary to make needed changes!

So today ask the Holy Spirit to help you conduct a sincere examination of yourself. As you do, ask yourself:

- *Have I fallen into a pattern reflective of an out-of-control end-time society? Or am I free and on track?*

2. Confront yourself about the way you are eating.

We've seen that in one survey, 1.9 billion adults 18 years and older in the world are *overweight* and that 160 million Americans are overweight or obese.

But I encourage you to take the painful step of personalizing these statistics by asking yourself:

- *Where do I fit in this number? Am I overweight or obese?*

More than 50 percent of the American population is overweight or obese. That means if you live in the United States, there is a 50-percent chance, based on this statistic, that *you* are overweight or even obese. If that is true concerning you, it means you don't feel your best; you don't look your best; and you certainly don't feel good about yourself when you put on your clothes and look in the mirror. And when you meet people, you may even wonder if they're thinking that you are overweight. *Ugh! I understand that feeling.* Friend, it's time to take action.

- First, confess to God that you have not properly managed your eating habits. Ask Him to give you the wisdom and power you need to get things in balance.

It may be difficult to get started, but once you have begun losing weight, you'll feel better about yourself — and you'll be much healthier!

- Second, if you don't know which steps to take to get out of bondage in this area, ask someone you trust to help you.

I guarantee that there is someone close to you who has already faced this battle and gotten victory in this area of his or her life. Ask that person for help and make yourself accountable to him or her. If you'll do this, it will help you! If you need to go to a doctor to get help, take that step. Just do whatever you need to do to get the ball rolling on good body management!

God has a good plan for your life and a long race for you to run. For you to finish your race, you have to take action to get yourself in shape. If you don't, you could jeopardize your ability to finish your race well. I know you don't want that to happen, so right now ask the Holy Spirit to give you the courage needed to assault this problem head-on and to walk into freedom!

As you eat every meal, remember the wisdom found in First Corinthians 10:31: "Whether therefore ye eat, or drink, or whatsoever ye do, do all to the glory of God." Before you eat, always ask yourself:

- *Can I eat this kind of food and this portion of food to the glory of God?*

I have personally found that confronting myself with this question helps keep me focused and on track when it's time to eat — and I believe it will help you too.

3. Confront yourself about your sedentary lifestyle.

This action step can be tough, but it is really important. If you're overweight and out of shape, it's going to require a change in your thinking and in your habits of physical movement to get you into better shape.

Look at your life. Ask yourself:

- *How often do I physically move?*

- *Do I sit all day long?*

- *Do I work many hours in front of a computer?*

- *How often do I get out of the house and walk?*

- *Am I willing to do what is necessary to make a change in this area of my life for the sake of my health?*

Never forget that your body is an instrument given to you by God — but to keep it working in good shape, you have to *use* it and *move* it.

When I started to lose weight, I knew that I also needed to start physically moving. I needed to physically exercise, but I didn't know how to get started. So I began to work with a trainer who knew all about the body and physical exercise. But for this man to help me, I had to be willing to submit to him and recognize that he knew more than I knew about exercise and fitness. I never argued or refused to obey this man; I just did what he told me to do, whether I understood it or not. He had authority to speak to me, and I had made a decision to listen and to obey.

Little by little, I began to move more freely, and today I do exercises every morning with enjoyment. I feel better, and I know it is prolonging my life. In fact, I feel better today than at any other time in my entire life. But this process began with a decision to find someone who could help me, to submit to that person's knowledge and experience and obey his recommendations, and to keep moving consistently day after day, whether I felt like it or not.

How about you? Are you really ready to change in this area of your life? Don't cut your life short by not taking care of the physical vessel God gave you to live in. Find someone qualified to help you; follow his or her instructions; and stay faithful to the task. Little by little, day by day, you'll begin to gain more freedom in movement. And you'll be so thankful that you made the decision to increase your level of physical exercise!

4. Confront yourself about how you spend your money.

The word "covetous" depicts *an insatiable desire to have more and more.* The Scriptures give us a prophetic warning that society will throw off restraint in the last days — feeling entitled to everything — and as a result, many will be hurled into mindless consumerism.

If you have fallen into this trap, there is no judgment toward you at all. However, you must be willing to hear the Holy Spirit's voice in your spirit as He works to *wake you up.* The Holy Spirit wants you to recognize the enemy's agenda as he tries to drag you into a financial cesspool that has the potential to ruin you financially and drag you into the slavery of debt.

Perhaps you've gotten into financial trouble because of things that were beyond your control. Sometimes that happens. Maybe you had to help a child or a parent or you lost your job and it affected your ability to keep up financially. Those things do happen in life, but the Holy Spirit has the wisdom you need to make adjustments to get over the hump and to experience more financial freedom. So ask yourself:

- *How do I fare when I analyze my income versus my expenditures?*

- *Am I willing to do what is needed to self-correct and bring my affairs back into order financially?*

Working to find answers to these questions is always painful. However, your efforts will produce good fruit if you will do what is necessary to establish a workable budget designed to get your finances back to a healthy balance.

My wife and I have had to cut back many times, and it has never been easy. But it has always borne good fruit, and we've been glad we did it.

Hebrews 12:11 (*NLT*) says, "No discipline is enjoyable while it is happening — it's painful! But afterward there will be a peaceful harvest of right living for those who are trained in this way." Living on a budget may be hard to do at first, but this self-discipline will produce marvelous fruit and an ever-increasing measure of financial freedom.

If you've done wrong in the way you've spent your money, quickly confess it as sin and receive the cleansing work of the blood of Jesus as part of your strategic plan to get back on track. First John 1:9 says, "If we confess our sins, He is faithful and just to forgive us of our sins and to cleanse us from all unrighteousness." By quickly confessing sin and submitting to the cleansing power of Jesus' blood, you'll stay free of self-condemnation. This will keep your heart pliable, and you'll be in an effective position to bind the devil off your finances and to give freely into the work of God's Kingdom as He directs!

5. Confront yourself about your emotions.

God gave you emotions to help you feel passionate, alive, and joyful. He even gave you emotions to alert you when something is wrong. But your emotions don't need to be controlling you! As long as you are the one controlling your emotions, they can be a mighty blessing. However, if you let your emotions take over and manipulate you like a puppet, you'll end up as a slave to your emotional whims — up one day and down the next.

But Second Timothy 3:2 forecasted that the last-days society will not understand boundaries and will throw off restraint of every kind — including emotional restraint! This will put people in jeopardy of losing so much in terms of relationships, opportunities, and personal joy.

People in the last days will think they have an "inherent right" to express whatever emotion they may feel at any given moment, regardless of its negative impact on themselves or on others. That is why it's imperative that we make sure we have not fallen into this vicious trap along with the rest of the world.

God wants you to experience a life of joy, so it is essential that you understand where you are in this area of emotions. Today I urge you to analyze your life and your emotional behavior over the past few years. Ask yourself:

- *Am I in charge of my emotions — or are my emotions in charge of me?*

- *Do I say things when I'm frustrated or upset that I would never want anyone to say to me?*

- *Do I exercise respect in the way I speak to others? Or do I freely say whatever I wish because I think I have a right to do it?*

For you to enjoy life and enjoy others — and for others to also enjoy you — you must deal with this question head-on. If the Holy Spirit shows you that this is an area in which you need to make a change, don't moan and groan about mistakes of the past that you can't do anything about. Simply ask for forgiveness and repent. Then commit yourself to the process of self-correcting in this area of your life. You can trust the Counselor who resides within to help you get the victory!

6. Confront yourself about negative addictive behaviors.

In this chapter, we've seen that we're living in a world of addictions — to food, alcohol, drugs, gambling, pornography, sex, the Internet, social media, video games, shopping — and the list goes on and on. Addictions of all types are raging out of control, destroying marriages, friendships, and careers, and threatening the health and safety of society as a whole.

When we talk about addiction, we're talking about self-indulgent behaviors that have gotten out of control. So ask yourself:

- *Are there any behaviors, acts, or attitudes that have gotten hold of me and are robbing me of the good life God wants me to have?*

The answer to that question could be something as small as watching too much TV or being in the unhealthy habit of participating in gossip. But no matter how inconsequential that bad habit seems, it is destructive to your walk with God and your ability to fulfill His plan for your life. So if *any* type of addiction has the ability to control your decisions, your actions, or your thoughts on any level, it's time for you to break free of that addiction and to step into the freedom Jesus Christ intends for you to experience in your life!

This action step involves *confronting yourself.* Set aside time to scrutinize your life. Thoughtfully and honestly ask yourself:

- *Are there any areas of my life in which I am living in bondage?*

It's possible that you've lived with a self-indulgent, negative behavior so long that you don't even see it anymore. So ask the Holy Spirit to help you see areas in which you need to enjoy more freedom. Then repent for allowing bondage of any kind in your life — or addiction to *anything* that is displeasing to the Lord — and with His help, begin to develop a plan to walk out of that behavior.

The Holy Spirit is inside you, and He will empower you to do what is right. If you need help from someone else to walk into full freedom in that area, find someone you trust to talk to about your need to change. Ask that person to pray with you and to help hold you accountable to carrying out the decision that Jesus has alerted you that you need to make!

7. Confront yourself about your vision or lack of vision.

We saw that both the *New King James Version* and *American Standard Version* says, "Where there is no revelation, the people cast off restraint..." (Proverbs 29:18).

When people have no revelation of what God has created them to be or to do, they are reduced to a rather low-level existence in life. In fact, when they lose their sense of purpose, they become slothful and begin to cast off restraint, permitting things in their lives that they know are *not* permissible in the eyes of God. This is often why people eat wrong, spend wrong, tolerate addictive behaviors, and allow emotions to pull them down and control them.

So you need to ask yourself:

- *What is God's plan for my life?*

- *Have I lost touch with the purpose God placed me on this earth to accomplish?*

If your answer is yes to that last question, you can safely conclude that it's a primary factor in the reason you're struggling with self-control regarding your weight, finances, behaviors, and/or emotions.

Furthermore, you should ask yourself these important questions in your time of self-evaluation:

- *Do I have a vision for improving my eating habits and my overall health?*

- *Do I have a vision for healthy finances and freedom from debt?*

- *Do I have a vision for strengthening my emotional balance?*

- *Do I have a vision for walking in an increase of self-control and self-discipline in my life?*

These are not sideline questions; they are very important questions with which you need to confront yourself and answer truthfully. God already knows the truth, so your honesty is not for Him — it's for you. You'll never change in these areas until you see and accept the truth. But when you see the truth, the Holy Spirit will begin to help restore your vision in these crucial areas of your life!

If you have a difficult time asking yourself these questions — and answering them honestly — find a faithful, loving, trusted friend you can ask to help you complete this personal inventory. When divine vision for your personal growth begins to flood back into your life again, you'll be so glad you chose to press through and do it!

8

FIERCE, DESPISERS OF THOSE THAT ARE GOOD, TRAITORS, HEADY, HIGH-MINDED, LOVERS OF PLEASURE MORE THAN LOVERS OF GOD

In Second Timothy 3:3 and 4, Paul continued to describe what society will look like in the last of the last days. People will become "without natural affection, trucebreakers, false accusers, incontinent, fierce, despisers of those that are good, traitors, heady, high-minded, lovers of pleasures more than lovers of God...." In this chapter, we will continue examining these words to see how they apply to those of us who are living in the last of the last days. Let's start with the word "fierce" and the phrase "despisers of those that are good."

The word "fierce" is a translation of the Greek word *anemeros*, which is formed from the word *hemeros* — a word which means *civilized, cultivated, cultured, gentle, mild, polished, tame,* or *well-behaved.* But when *hemeros* becomes *anemeros* — as Paul used it in Second Timothy 3:3 — it pictures a person or society that is *cruel, fierce, harsh, savage, uncivilized, vicious,* or *violent.*

When most of us think of barbaric practices in history, our minds are often riveted to some despotic ruler who was responsible for the torture and slaughter of thousands of people. Or we might think of a particular period of history, such as ancient Rome, when society as a whole embraced many monstrously barbaric practices.

I've traveled to many Roman stadiums and theaters where barbarism and atrocities occurred during the imperial period in the form of cruel entertainment that the population loved. The ancient Romans packed those venues, stomping their feet and cheering with glee as blood was spattered and spilt in the arenas below. It is hard to fathom the unimaginable tortures and religious persecution that took place in these locations, especially against early Christians who had come to believe on the name of the Lord Jesus Christ as the Church was born in the midst of a pagan environment.

I think of the gladiators who fought one another to the death, and the ravenous lions and other wild beasts that ripped people from limb from limb and devoured them — *flesh, blood,* and *bone* — right in front of the crowd. With each victim felled by the savage weaponry of a gladiator or the pounce of a starved, vicious beast, the audience would cheer and applaud loudly, while those who were dying writhed about in their own blood.

Some people have seen glimpses of similar scenes in various movies as they were growing up. For example, who could ever forget the scenes from the movie "Spartacus" in which barbarians mercilessly killed each other as Romans spectators roared with delight?

In early history — from Rome, to the Middle East, to the northern shores of Africa, and all the way to Spain and to Britain — scenes of this kind of Roman violence were performed and enjoyed in the stadiums as entertainment.

Throughout the empire, adoring crowds erupted with *thrilled delight* at the sight of the shedding of human blood. In fact, such bloody spectacles provided the most popular form of amusement of that time! Although the Romans claimed to be the great, sophisticated educators and "civilizers" of the world in their day, they were actually monstrously *barbaric* in many ways.

ARE WE LIVING IN THE MOST BARBARIC SOCIETY IN HUMAN HISTORY?

But in our own time — at a time in modern history when we seem to be so sophisticated — we have taken the barbaric behavior of the ancient world to a new, unprecedented level. We may seem to be more sophisticated. But in reality, we no longer have to visit stadiums and other venues to experience violence and bloodshed, because now we bring huge doses of violence directly into our homes through television, digital devices, and the Internet. Although the means by which we receive our entertainment may be more technologically sophisticated, this generation is as barbaric, or even more so, than previous generations. It is simply barbarism manifesting in a different form.

We can look back at ancient Roman society and wonder how they tolerated such savagery and cruelty. Yet in Second Timothy 3:1-4, the Holy Spirit pointed His prophetic finger toward the future and prophesied that in the last of the last days, violence would become *even more* widespread and commonplace in society. And we are seeing this come to pass.

This present generation has seen so much brutality as entertainment on screens in front of them that they have become numb to its hideousness. Today people purchase tickets to movie theaters to watch scenes of human carnage play out before their eyes as thrilling entertainment.

So I ask you — if we regularly feast our eyes and emotions on enacted scenes of human bloodshed, does that really make us more civilized, even though more sophisticated, than the ancient world that once reveled in the live scenes played out before them?

Although the means by which we receive our entertainment may be more technologically sophisticated, this generation is as barbaric, or even more so, than previous generations. It is simply barbarism manifesting in a different form.

In my book *How To Keep Your Head on Straight in a World Gone Crazy*, I write about the numbing effects that evil has on a mind that is continually bombarded by it. In that book, I used the example of Lot. Lot was a righteous man who dwelled in the evil environment of Sodom for so long, he became numb to the evil in the city until it didn't bother him as it once did.

The Bible says that Lot was a "righteous man" who was "vexed with the filthy conversation of the wicked." The word "vexed" is a translation of the Greek word *kataponeo*, which is a compound of the words *kata* and *poneo*. The word *kata* carries the idea of *domination*, and the word *poneo* means *to work to the point of exhaustion*. But when these words are compounded, the new word denotes *total exhaustion*. It can actually be translated *to wear out, to tire out, to break down*, or *to bring to a place of total and complete exhaustion*. The use of this word lets you know that the activities of Sodom began to wear out, break down, and exhaust Lot's strength to resist it.

Even the strongest believer can be worn down by the constant onslaught of evil surroundings. This is the reason why God urges His people to "flee" from evil (*see* 2 Timothy 2:22). Unfortunately, Lot stayed in that depraved environment so long — living in the midst of it, hearing and seeing its evil effects day by day — that he finally succumbed to it. In fact, in some fashion, Lot became an accepted part of that polluted environment by occupying his own seat at the city gates.

**Even the strongest believer can be worn down
by the constant onslaught of evil surroundings.**

Likewise, current statistics prove that if a person watches enough violence on television, his sensitivity to violence will become dulled and he will become numbed to acts that would otherwise prick his conscience and vex his soul. The same statistics reveal that if a person watches enough pornography, in time that person will lose his sensitivity to the wrongness of this behavior; once again, he will become *numb* to it.

This is what happened to Lot. He watched and heard so much wickedness in the activities that transpired around him on a regular basis that he became *numb* and *hardened* to the evil of it. Eventually Lot became so calloused to the wrong around him that he was able to live in the midst of it for an extended period of time.

But today this calloused, "vexed" condition has infected an entire generation whose souls have been continuously bombarded by *anemeros* images — that is, by "fierce" images and behaviors, exactly as the Holy Spirit foretold in Second Timothy 3:3. This time, however, the violence is not in Roman stadiums but in temperature-controlled movie theaters, in the privacy of our in-home TV rooms, or on our children's devices that they stare at for hours on end.

Consider these facts:

- The escalation of violence in entertainment is now so widespread that by age 18, a child will have seen more than 200,000 acts of violence on television and witnessed more than 40,000 simulated murders.[92]

- The average seventh-grader watches more than 4 hours of television per day — with more than 60 percent of the programs containing violence.[93]

- The same average seventh-grader plays electronic games 4 hours per week — with more than 50 percent of games categorized as "violent."

- In most of the industrialized world, 90 percent of homes with children have more than one television, not to mention video-game equipment, a personal computer, and high-tech cell phones with the capability of showing movies. This means parents can watch television in one room while their children sit unsupervised in another room with access to "entertainment" that projects violence into their young minds.

- Violent video games have created a thirst for violence. In fact, statistics now reveal the majority of children select "fantasy violence" as their favorite type of video games.

- Further studies reveal that the more frequently children practice fantasy acts of violence on video games, the more likely it becomes that they will carry out real acts of violence.

---

[92] Sandra L. Bloom, *Creating Sanctuary: Toward the Evolution of Sane Societies* (New York: Routledge, 1997), p. 204.
[93] *Marketing Violence to Children: Hearing Before the Committee*, United States Congress, Senate, Committee on Commerce, Science, and Transportation, 2001.

- These games are so similar to the programs used in real military training that one expert has stated, "We're not just teaching kids to kill; we're teaching them to like it." Advertising boldly tells children, "Let the slaughter begin!" and awards them points for each person slaughtered during the game.

- The desensitizing effect of these words and images on young minds is proven to numb them to the seriousness of brutal acts committed against others.

- Today's music is filled with violence. All we have to do is listen to popular music or stroll down the aisle of almost any music or computer-game store to have this truth confirmed.

- The average teenager now listens to more than 10,500 hours of music during the years between the seventh and twelfth grades — much of which is violence-related.[94]

- This means violent words and acts are being routinely poured into the minds of teenagers under the guise of music. This destructive influence is very difficult for parents to control, and many of them have no idea what their children are listening to on the radio, CDs, and the Internet.

- As a result of the widespread use of the Internet, youth are regularly exposed to violent words, violent music, violent images, and pornography. There are literally *thousands* of websites specifically dedicated to foster racial hate, bigotry, violence, and pornography to the younger generations.

---

[94] Joshua Leeds, *The Power of Sound: How To Be Healthy and Productive Using Sound* (New York: Healing Arts Press, 2010).

- Research shows — beyond any shadow of doubt — that violence in the media has a direct link to youth violence. One expert stated it well: "To argue against it is like arguing against gravity."[95]

In this present-day culture, this escalation of violence has spread beyond the Internet and the screens of movie theaters, television, digital devices, and computers. It is now infiltrating society as "shooters" take aim at innocent people in public venues across the nation. One would think in this time when terrorism and bloodshed is so widespread that people would shun such entertainment. In reality, the opposite is true. Entertainment based on violence has only increased in popularity, and great masses of people are finding pleasure in thrillers filled with carnage. Just as the ancient Romans had a taste for blood, modern society pays money to sit and be entertained by murder, barbarism, and bloodshed.

As society is more and more obsessed with images of violence, it is seeping into the mainstream. Anyone with spiritual eyes opened is aware that violence is on the increase.

But the Church was forewarned long ago. The Holy Spirit prophesied that violence — from the Greek word *anemeros* — would indeed escalate in the end of the age, and we who were born in this end-time generation are witnesses to the unfolding prophetic fulfillment of this truth.

◆

**As society is more and more obsessed
with images of violence, it is seeping into the mainstream.
Anyone with spiritual eyes opened is aware
that violence is on the increase.**

◆

---

[95] Judith Levine, *Shooting the Messenger: Why Censorship Won't Stop Violence* (New York: Media Coalition, Inc., 2000), p. 2.

Once a Christian leader told me to make time to go see a movie that he "raved" about. When I went to see it, I was so shocked that I walked out of the theater in the middle of the movie. There was so much blood-letting and killing in the movie that it grieved me. I wondered how this person could recommend it when it so blatantly glorified killing.

You should not expose your mind, emotions, and imagination to such violent, bloody images. Yet the cinemas are *filled* with such entertainment.

Unfortunately, scores of Christians who regularly pay to watch movies with this type of violence are searing their minds with the dark images contained in them. And just as Lot became desensitized to Sodom's evil environment, many are becoming numb to the horror of violence. Their minds have been bombarded by such images for so long, it has become "no big deal." As I've drawn near to the Lord over many years, I have come to see these types of movies as deeply grieving to my spirit.

**Many are becoming numb to the horror of violence.
Their minds have been bombarded by such images for so long,
it has become "no big deal."**

And what about children? How have *they* become affected by the images of violence that bombard them?

Do you allow your children to view violent acts and images in the media, disregarding the negative impact it has on their minds, emotions, and souls? Do you really want your children to watch endless hours of bloodshed through various media or to listen to it in secular music? Have you considered how it desensitizes them and affects their relationship with the Holy Spirit?

But there is another way in which violence has escalated that is both shocking and alarming. I believe the following information illustrates perfectly how *uncivilized* society has become in our time. Stay with me, and I believe you'll understand why I have chosen to make a point from the following subject.

VIOLENCE AGAINST SOCIETY'S MOST DEFENSELESS HUMAN BEINGS

Some years ago, the Holy Spirit impressed me to address the subject of *abortion* in our Moscow church. I had never spoken on that subject, yet I knew the Holy Spirit was compelling me and that this was a message my congregation needed to hear. When I began to study for this message, I came to understand why the Spirit had impressed it upon me so strongly.

Before I cover the statistics you are about to read, I want to say that if you have ever terminated the life of a child — or if you know someone who has done this — there is forgiveness in Jesus Christ. Just as there is forgiveness for every grievance against God, there is forgiveness for this wrong decision of aborting an unborn baby. If you will ask God from your heart to forgive you, you can be assured of His promised forgiveness (*see* 1 John 1:9). Because He loves you so deeply, He will forgive you, cleanse you from all unrighteousness, and heal every broken place in your soul so the enemy cannot use it against you.

But as painful as it is to state the enormity of the cost in lives and personal destinies that abortion has exacted upon mankind, I believe it is necessary. As believers, we can't just hide our heads in the sand like ostriches and pretend this holocaust of human life hasn't been an ongoing horror in our world over this past century right up to the present day.

As I prepared to minister to my congregation, my research began with the actual number of abortions that had occurred in the world since the earlier years of the Twentieth Century. Because I was speaking to my own congregation in Moscow when I first delivered this message, I decided to start my research with a study of how many abortions had occurred in the Soviet Union.

- Because accurate numbers of abortions were not kept in the Soviet Union before 1957, I started counting from 1957 to the collapse of the Soviet Union in 1991. In those 34 years, I found that approximately 306,457,000 abortions were performed in the Soviet Union.[96] This number is *larger* than the entire population of the USSR when the USSR dissolved in 1991.

- Then I turned my attention to China to see how many abortions have been performed there. However, because records for the numbers of abortions performed in China before 1970 were unavailable, my research had to begin with 1971, when the best information became available. Those records revealed that from 1971 to 2020 — a span of nearly 50 years — 489,936,650 abortions were carried out in China.[97]

- Let me help you comprehend that number. The current population of the United States is approximately 328 million. This means from 1971 to 2020, China aborted the equivalent of the entire population of the United States — *and nearly 162 million more.* That second number is almost equivalent to the entire populations of Canada and Mexico combined! So if you add the 328 million and 162 million abortions carried out in China, the total number of infants killed in the womb during that time period is actually approaching the equivalent of the entire human population from the Arctic to the southern border of Mexico! That is the magnitude

---

[96] Alexandre Avdeev, *The History of Abortion Statistics in Russia and the USSR from 1900-1991* (Paris: University of Paris, January 1995), pp. 64-65.

[97] William Robert Johnson, "Historical Abortion Statistics, PR China," JohnstonsArchive.net, http://www.johnstonsarchive.net/policy/abortion/ab-prchina.html.

of the number of babies who were aborted in China in an almost 50-year span of time.

- Then I turned my attention to the United States to see how many babies had been aborted since 1973 when abortion was legalized by the Supreme Court in the famous case of Roe v. Wade. Since 1973, nearly 62 million abortions have been performed in the United States!

- But hold on — the most solid information shows that the world-wide number of abortions over the last 40 years (1980-2020) is estimated to be close to 2 billion. Think of that horrifying landmark number modern society has reached — *2 billion abortions* carried out globally in a span of 40 years!

- To help you grasp that number, try to imagine this: If *all* the people were killed who are currently living in North America, Central America, and South America — *plus* all of Europe, Russia, and Australia! — the total number of deaths still would not amount to the number of babies who have been aborted worldwide in the last 40 years!

- Although these statistics are already mind-boggling, by the time you read this, they will be outdated, because 125,000 abortions are carried out every day worldwide.[98]

Although some contend that the world today is technologically more advanced and more sophisticated, this slaughter of nearly *2 billion babies* shows that we are *not* more civilized; rather, barbarism is escalating on an unthinkable scale. Infants are routinely brutally burned to death by chemicals injected into a mother's womb or torn to pieces in the womb by medical forceps.

---

[98] "Abortions Worldwide This Year," Worldometer.com, https://www.worldometers.info/abortions/.

Almost every minute of every day in sterilized hospitals and clinics around the world, this barbaric act occurs. This is worldwide savagery of the worst kind that makes all other holocausts and genocides pale in comparison. This is murder on a scale so massive that no fiction writer could have ever imagined it. Yet this is *reality* in our present-day age.

So although we may think the mass killings that occurred at the hands of Nero, Domitian, Hitler, Stalin, or other cruel leaders were barbaric and cruel — a fact that no one would argue with — those barbaric times do not come close to the magnitude of the horrific cost of lives that abortion providers as a whole are responsible for — murdering nearly *2 billion babies* through the act of abortion. This is the mass annihilation of those who cannot scream, who cannot be heard, who cannot defend themselves, and whose mutilated bodies are thrown into garbage cans, sold for parts to the highest bidder, or recycled to be used in shampoos or cosmetics.

When godly advocates raise their voices against this genocide, those who are pro-choice often portray them to be narrow-minded, right-wing fanatics. These advocates for life are attacked with a vengeance by the pro-choice faction that wants to intimidate, silence, and render powerless the opposition and retain the legal right to terminate the life of a child.

Make no mistake — this present generation is tainted with the blood of innocent children. And one could argue that this generation as a whole is largely guilty of the most heinous and barbaric behavior perhaps in the entire history of mankind because of the murder of these 2 billion unborn children.

In Second Timothy 3:3 and 4, Paul stated that society in the last days will become "fierce," translated from the Greek word *anemeros*, which I tell you again pictures a person or society that has become *cruel, fierce, harsh, savage, uncivilized, vicious,* or *violent.*

Just as the Holy Spirit prophesied, a last-days society has developed a great fascination with violence and, as a result, is possibly becoming the most violent generation to ever live on the earth. I have only highlighted a few ways that this word "fierceness" has emerged in society — *media violence* (which statistically leads to increased real-life violence) and *abortion*. As you read on, you will likely think of other ways that society in our times has become increasingly violent and uncivilized.

Just as the Holy Spirit prophesied,
a last-days society has developed a great fascination
with violence and, as a result, is possibly becoming
the most violent generation
to ever live on the earth.

'DESPISERS OF THOSE THAT ARE GOOD'

But Paul went further in Second Timothy 3:3, stating that many in society at the close of the age will become "despisers of those that are good." This phrase is the next prophetic characteristic that the Holy Spirit tells us will become an end-time reality. But what does "despisers of those that are good" mean?

The phrase "despisers of those that are good" is a translation from a very strange Greek word — the word *aphilagathos*. This rarely used and very odd word is used to depict *a land where laws seem to primarily defend and protect the rights of offenders — or those who are evil or immoral — rather than the rights of good people, often leaving the good with no defense.* This word is so unusual that it is used only here in the New Testament when the Holy Spirit prophesies what society will be like at the end of the age.

Many today believe we are living in a time when society fights to defend offenders and even make excuses for them, while at the same time often leaving the rights of victims and law-abiding citizens in jeopardy. Perpetrators and those who harm innocent people are often protected and given "sanctuary" while the victims are left with very little sympathy and very few rights. Although that practice seems to belie common sense, this is precisely what Paul prophesied in this verse would occur at the end of the age.

Society today is filled with moral dilemmas. It seems there are a plethora of laws to protect law-breakers and a wide range of instances in which criminals are aggressively protected and are even released to go free while their innocent victims suffer. Certainly, everyone wants every person to have a fair legal defense, but often in our time, it is increasingly difficult to prosecute offenders. But according to Second Timothy 3:3, the world in the last days will not only be *violent* and *savage*, it will also become *morally confused* as to what is right or wrong. It wouldn't be a difficult task for you to think of other ways this has application to the world we live in today.

**When all these Greek word meanings are considered,
the *RIV* of Second Timothy 3:3 reads as follows:**

Love for and commitment to family will disintegrate, and divorce will become epidemic, with irreconcilable differences being a major factor in tearing families apart. In fact, every imaginable type of covenant will be regularly violated, and the court system will be overwhelmed as people go overboard, suing and being sued. People will generally lose the ability to say no and will be unable to control their instincts in nearly every area of life. People will become savage, and it will eventually feel like there are no laws to protect the innocent.

AN AGE OF HOPELESSNESS —
OR AN AGE OF ABOUNDING POWER AND GRACE?

It may seem like we live in an age of hopelessness amidst a fallen world that has run amuck. Yet these are the days we were appointed by God to live in, and He has not abandoned us to turbulent times. We have the Word of God to keep us firmly founded and the Holy Spirit as our Teacher, Mentor, and Guide. We also have other brothers and sisters in the Christian community upon whom we can lean for support and receive help when it is needed. With all that God has provided, we are well able to live victoriously for Him in these last times!

It's not time for you to throw in the towel in despair in difficult days. Instead, there's never been a better time to throw up your arms and *shout* your victory! You and I are called by God to be part of a chosen generation at the end of the age. This is history's greatest opportunity to share the Good News of Jesus Christ and to help bring in a last-days harvest of souls before the age concludes. *What a privilege God has given us!*

We must arm ourselves with God's Word and the weapons of warfare He has provided. Then we must allow the Holy Spirit's power to flow through us so we can each run our race with endurance all the way to the end! And before we conclude this spiritual race and make the big exit, we must do all we can to tell the Good News of Jesus Christ to people we encounter so we can take as many people with us to Heaven as possible. *Amen!*

I want to encourage you to renew your commitment to live your life according to the truths set forth by the Bible, to continually reinforce yourself in the Spirit, and to take a bold stance against any part of society's moral code that is in conflict with the Word of God. When everything else teeters and passes away, the Bible and its unchanging truth is the sure foundation that will remain. So make the decision that, no matter what, you will align yourself with its immutable principles and hold fast to the eternal and powerful promises of God!

TRAITORS — FAIR-WEATHER FRIENDS

But wait — there is still more that the Holy Spirit adds in His prophetic list of characteristics that will be indicative of society in the last of the last days. The Spirit also foretells that much of society will become "traitors, heady, high-minded, lovers of pleasure more than lovers of God; having a form of godliness, but denying the power thereof: from such turn away" (2 Timothy 3:4,5).

The word "traitors" in verse 4 is a translation of the Greek word *prodotes*, which is a word that specifically denotes *one who is a traitor to an oath; one who betrays or abandons a friend; a lack of commitment to oaths or relationships; one who is treacherous in the context of an oath or a relationship; a fair-weather friend.*

By using the word *prodotes* — translated here as "traitors" — the Holy Spirit warns that in the last of the last days, a lack of commitment to relationships will develop and proliferate throughout society *en masse*. Friendships will not be what they used to be.

Being *self-lovers*, people in society will make themselves their own *first* priority. If they're faced with having to personally sacrifice something to keep their commitment to someone else, their response will tend toward breaking off the relationship that requires the commitment. People who fit this description are often called "fair-weather friends." As long as the "weather" is good in the relationship, he or she will be there. But if storms arise or the relationship is no longer convenient for that person, the solution is to walk away. This is what the Holy Spirit prophesied we could expect to see at the end of days.

These "traitors" are likely people who seem to be friends as long as things go well. But the moment the relationship hits a bump or a problem is encountered along the way, they break their oath of friendship. In this sense, they are faithful to keep an oath only as long as it doesn't personally inconvenience them or cost them more than they had planned when they first made their oath. Thus, the oath was on shaky soil even when it was first made. It really shows the *lack of commitment to relationships* that will come to exist *en masse* in the last of the last days.

Simply ask people today to honestly assess the level of relationships they have in their lives. You may be shocked to hear that so many feel a great deficit in the area of relationships. Even more surprising is the realization that vast numbers have felt abandoned by people they once really thought were friends. This "shallowness factor" or lack of commitment is a prime sign that we are coming close to the end of this age before Jesus comes for His Church.

The Greek word *prodotes* demonstrates the lack of commitment and the shallowness of relationships that will develop between individuals at the end of the age. Most people who read these words will agree inwardly that this characteristic is the case today. It is just a fact that commitment to relationships is not what it was some years ago.

If you have *five friends* who have been in your life for *five years* — and who *remain* as friends to this present day in your life — you are blessed. Statistics actually reveal that most people do not have five relationships that have lasted longer than five years. Relationships in modern society often end in disappointment. The Holy Spirit prophesied that this would be indicative of the last of the last days.

There are many contributing factors that produce shallow, short-lasting relationships. For example, years ago, people lived in the same house, on the same street, and attended the same church for years. Neighbors knew each other and the kids on the street knew each other. But today people frequently move from place to place, making it difficult to make and maintain stable relationships.

Today people not only relocate from one home or apartment to another, but they also frequently change jobs, and the relationships they made in the former workplace are often forgotten as they move to a new place of employment. Unfortunately, people are not even committed to their churches as they once were. They move from church to church, leaving behind people to whom they had supposedly felt a deep commitment. All of these factors have affected the quality of long-term relationships that once existed between people.

This mobility was not possible before the advent of the automobile and highways. Before that, people walked or traveled by horse and carriage — which made their world very small. But with the arrival of new technologies, people began to move far and wide. Even their need to attend a "local" church was largely removed, since people could drive to attend a church that was a great distance from their neighborhood. The development of sophisticated highways and transportation eliminated the need for people to attend a church in the neighborhoods where they had been raised and where they once served.

All of these wonderful technological advancements have ultimately contributed to the ease with which people change locations, change jobs, change churches, and so on. They are also reasons why so many feel a shallowness and a lack of longevity in their relationships. The Holy Spirit prophesied that this would happen at the end of the last days.

If you have been personally disappointed or hurt by shallow relationships, ask the Holy Spirit to heal your heart. God does not want you to live in brokenness for the rest of your life. In fact, He wants to lead you to other godly people who, like you, are seeking deep and meaningful relationships.

HEADINESS AND EMOTIONAL INTEMPERANCE

After the characteristic of "traitors" or lack of commitment in relationships, the Holy Spirit then adds to the list of signs that will become more and more prevalent in the very last days. He says that near the close of the age, people will not only become "traitors," but they will also become "heady" (v. 4).

The word "heady" in this verse is a very poor translation of the Greek word *propetes*. This is a word that depicts people who are *wholly given to violence, who enjoy violence, and who have become known for their violent, reckless, rash, emotional intemperance*. The Holy Spirit is prophesying of a time to come when people would be given to violence and unable to control their tempers.

We have already seen that violence is the hottest-selling ticket today on the Internet, in music, and in video games. We are also witnessing the long-term impact on society as acts of violence steadily increase in every part of modern culture. In Chapter 7, we learned that instances of "fierce" road rage and random shootings in public places are increasing. These are examples of the reckless, impulsive acts of madness that the Holy Spirit warns will take place at the end of the age.

If Jesus tarries and future historians look back on *our* time, what will they write about *us*? Will they remember us the way we remember the Romans and their taste for violence? The Holy Spirit was forecasting that violence in the last of the last days would become more and more widespread, until both man's lust for violence and his acts of violence became more prevalent on the earth than at any other time in human history since the earliest days of the Bible.

I believe this is precisely what the Holy Spirit intended to say in this verse as a warning to prepare the Church. Unfortunately, it's true that this present "civilized," "sophisticated," and "technologically advanced" generation has become the generation that is most "wholly given to violence" in human history. Violence is glorified on television, on the Internet, in music, and in video games, and violence is the hottest-selling ticket at the box office. Children across the world *play to kill* with video games that realistically emulate murder. The long-term result is evident, as actual acts of violence are increasing in every part of society today.

As I've stated several times, God is not in the business of scaring us, but He does want to prepare us so we can insulate ourselves and our families against the madness that will assault society as it nears the end of time. As He makes us aware of what's going to happen in a lost society that no longer lives according to godly standards or moral absolutes, we are then empowered to protect ourselves and our children and grandchildren from the ever-growing influence of violence that is occurring around us. This is why it would be wise for each of us to take a good look at our lives to see if we have become affected by this alarming and growing trend of "headiness" and violence in our culture.

**As He makes us aware of what's going to happen
in a lost society that no longer lives according to
godly standards or moral absolutes, we are then empowered
to protect ourselves and our children and grandchildren
from the ever-growing influence of violence
that is occurring around us.**

I truly believe that if we will listen to the Holy Spirit, we will hear His voice pleading with us to turn off violence in our homes — through *all* forms of media. He wants us to maintain hearts free from the desensitizing rot and decay that is occurring in these last of the last days. The degenerative effect of violent words and images on children, teenagers, and adults is unfathomable — and this is even before taking into account the destructive influence that such sights and sounds have on the rest of society, including increased acts of crime.

Everything you are reading in this book simply presents a common-sense response to what the Holy Spirit prophesied would occur at the end of the age just before Jesus returns. But let's focus here on the Holy Spirit's specific warning regarding this quality of being "heady."

It would be wise for each of us to take an honest look at ourselves to see if we have become affected by this alarming trend that reveals an increasing appetite for violence in our culture. And what about our children or grandchildren? How might they have become affected? Do we allow them to view violent acts and images, forgetting the negative impact it will have on their minds and emotions? Do we really want our children to watch endless hours of bloodshed through various forms of media? And by the way, don't overlook the violence that is broadcasted for hours every day in cartoons to the very youngest among us!

If the Holy Spirit is speaking to your heart, I urge you to respond to Him. Since we are indeed approaching the end of the age, it is imperative that we respond to His warnings and keep ourselves clear of the clutter that, along with the lost world around us, can cloud and confuse our minds and harden our hearts.

In light of all these things, I must ask you:

- If you took an honest look at your media cabinet or your digital storage of movies, television programs, songs, and so forth, how many do you think Jesus would be willing to watch or listen to with you? Is it time for you to go through and discard everything that would grieve the Holy Spirit?

- Is the Holy Spirit speaking to you to stop tolerating violent scenes and soul-desensitizing messages in your life and in the lives of your loved ones? If so, what action are you going to take to obey Him? Why not "clean house" and remove the movies, programs, and music you have that would grieve or offend Him and desensitize your own soul to the things of God?

———◆———

**Since we are indeed approaching the end of the age,
it is imperative that we respond to His warnings
and keep ourselves clear of the clutter that,
along with the lost world around us,
can cloud and confuse our minds
and harden our hearts.**

———◆———

Proverbs 4:23 says, "Keep thy heart with all diligence; for out of it, are the issues of life." It is imperative that each of us set a guard over our hearts, minds, and emotions and that we do not allow evil to gain access to us. To do this, God says we have to get serious about the matter and become very *diligent* in our pursuit!

HIGH-MINDED

Then the Holy Spirit adds the next word in Second Timothy 3:4 to describe many in a last-days society. He says many will be "high-minded" — a word translated from the Greek word *tuphoo*. This is a description of *one who is inflated with pride* or *one who is puffed up and clouded by his own sense of self-importance*. It comes from the Greek word *typhoo*, which is where we get the word *typhoon* — something very important to note!

Think about what happens when people are informed that a typhoon or hurricane is coming. They begin preparing for its arrival by picking up and putting away things that could be damaged or destroyed. Windows are boarded up;

vehicles are moved to higher ground; and loved ones are taken out of harm's way. The closer the storm gets, the darker the skies become and the more violent the winds rage. Everything looks ominous and foreboding.

By using the word *tuphoo*, translated here as "high-minded," the Holy Spirit is telling us that in the end of days, there will be moments when it will look like society is rapidly degenerating right before our eyes into one huge mass of people who arrogantly deny God and are self-inflated with pride. It will seem almost like a typhoon when massive dark clouds, destructive winds, and heavy rain are moving in from the sea and over the landscape.

When such a violent storm arrives, everything is affected *except for those who have taken appropriate shelter or who have fled from the storm*. But the good news is that typhoons or hurricanes never last long! They are short-lived and eventually pass. Just as they blow in, they also blow out.

As we've viewed the sudden shifts in political and moral climates over the course of recent years, we've probably all had the feeling that dark clouds are filling the horizon. We've seen things occur that most of us have never seen before in our lifetime. And many of us have thought, *It seems like the very atmosphere is changing, and it doesn't look as if it's going to stop.*

By using the word *typhoo*, the Holy Spirit plainly warns us that *many* people, within many spheres of society, will emit a proud, God-defying atti-tude. This is especially true of those who fit the category of intellectual elitists, disdaining those of us who hold to the immutable truth of the Bible. God's Spirit warns us that at the end of the age, this intellectually snobbish attitude will try to blast onto the scene in full strength, much like the dark clouds and destructive winds of a typhoon.

But although typhoons bring great destruction, they always eventually pass from the scene, leaving the task of rebuilding to the inhabitants of the impacted region. Likewise, it may seem that an evil society comprised of evil people is going to have a lasting impact — but these times will pass when the King of kings returns with His people to establish His Millennial reign on the earth (*see* Revelation 19:11-20:6)!

Instead of "hunkering down" and trying to hide from these "signs of the times," it's our time to shine as bright lights in a sin-darkened world.

The stormy season of the very last of the last days is when we are needed most — and we have the power of the Holy Spirit to empower us to face any challenge and to conquer any foe. It's never a question of *if* we will win this battle; it's only a question of *when* we'll win.

Never forget — in the end, the Lord *will* come to set up His Millennial reign, and we will have the great honor to reign with Him (*see* Revelation 20:6). Ultimately, the victory is ours to claim! *Amen!*

'WHEN, WHY, HOW' — ASKING THE RIGHT QUESTIONS

Through these prophetic verses, the Holy Spirit is encouraging us. His message is that regardless of how things look in the world around us, the situation is *temporary*. This current culture is a *temporary culture*.

We may question *when* things are going to change or *why* things are not changing when we think they should change. But the bigger question should be this: *How should we live and conduct ourselves in times when ominous, dark clouds are blowing in — changing the face of nations and the very atmosphere around us?*

The Bible is clear on the matter. It instructs us on how to ensure that we're equipped to live victoriously and make a difference in this world in the last days. It is *not* an instruction manual on how to hunker down and try our best just to survive.

◆

We may question *when* things are going to change
or *why* things are not changing when we think they should change.
But the bigger question should be this:
How should we live and conduct ourselves in times
when ominous, dark clouds are blowing in —
changing the face of nations
and the very atmosphere around us?

◆

For example, if you have children, how do you raise them in the midst of modern society's *typhoon* situation? What are you as a parent to do in these perilous times in which pride, insolence, and animosity toward the things of God seem to hold sway in politics, in the media, and on college campuses across the nation?

We must raise our children "in the nurture and admonition of the Lord" (*see* Ephesians 6:4) and teach them how to cultivate a relationship with God for themselves that is personal and intimate. We should train them in such a way — and live godly lives before them — that they'll know how to separate themselves from these perilous conditions as young children and adolescents and also later after they grow into adulthood and leave home.

While our children are living with us, we must take responsibility for instructing them in how to guard their hearts and minds from the treachery of the world we're living in. It's our job to shield them from harm — spirit, soul, and body — and to teach them how to protect themselves and to walk accurately on the right path in the midst of the crooked and perverse world that surrounds them.

These are exactly the times we're living in now — times that are perilous, marked by twistedness and perversity. The words of the Holy Spirit are being fulfilled before our very eyes, so we need to be especially alert to what He has said. Although we live *in* this world, Jesus said we're not *of* the world (*see* John 17:14-18). We must make every effort to steer clear of the world's attitudes and teach our children and grandchildren how to do the same.

The events that the Holy Spirit is describing in these verses may seem overwhelming when we read it and deeply understand it, but He reminds us that just as a typhoon passes, these events will also eventually pass. And those who have taken shelter in Jesus will be safe!

**The words of the Holy Spirit
are being fulfilled before our very eyes,
so we need to be especially alert to what He has said.
We must make every effort to steer clear of the world's attitudes
and teach our children and grandchildren
how to do the same.**

**With all this in mind,
the *RIV* of this first part of Second Timothy 3:4 reads:**

People will find it easy to walk away from commitments and to easily throw away relationships. They will become reckless, impulsive, and known for their enjoyment of violence. They will become full of pride and inflated with a sense of their own self-importance — to the extent that it may end up feeling like society is being hit by a typhoon; however, those menacing winds of change will eventually blow out like a storm that comes and goes.

A LOVE OF PLEASURE
THAT SUPERSEDES A LOVE FOR GOD

But now let's look at the last phrase in verse 4, where Paul wrote that people will become "…lovers of pleasures more than lovers of God." These words are packed with insight about what will happen to society in the last days, including trends that will negatively emerge among many Christians.

The phrase "lovers of pleasure more than lovers of God" is translated from the Greek word *philodonos*, which is comprised of the word *philos*, meaning *love*, and the word *hedone*, meaning *pleasure*. The word *hedone* is the root of the word *hedonism*, which denotes *individuals who give themselves to the unbridled and unrestrained seeking of pleasures of any type.*

Thus, the word *philedonos* — translated here as "lovers of pleasure" — means *to live for the fulfillment of one's pleasure*. It is a picture of *people who are completely preoccupied with their own self-gratification* or *people who make personal happiness their highest aspiration in life.* The dictionary says a *hedonist* is a person who believes the pursuit of pleasure is the most important thing in life. Thus, *he is a nonstop pleasure-seeker.* Hedonists are self-centered, self-focused, self-consumed, and self-obsessed.

When verse 4 says that people will be "…lovers of pleasure more than lovers of God," even the words "more than" are very important to note. This phrase is translated from the Greek word *mallon*, which means *more than* or *more than what it is compared to.* This word involves the ranking of comparison with something else — in this case, the higher and more important priority over the lower and the less important.

So when Paul wrote that the people would be "lovers of pleasure more than lovers of God," he was *not* saying these people won't love God. Rather, his intended meaning was that their love of pleasure would have *a higher rank than* and would *exceed* their love for God.

To be clear, God's highest call for you is not that you are happy. Just seeking pleasure and having happiness is not His greatest will for you. His greatest will for your life is that you truly love Him and are *obedient*. If you are wholeheartedly doing God's will, you will find joy in doing it.

Never forget this: Every form of happiness is both temporary and an unreliable measuring stick for determining how pleasing we are to God or for how well we are walking in obedience to Him. But according to Second Timothy 3:4, the unending, unobtainable pursuit of happiness will become a chief goal of people at the end of the age. In fact, Paul says that the love of pleasure will become so widespread that people will be more devoted to *pleasures* and to *the pursuit of their own happiness* than to their love for God and their pursuit of *Him*.

The fact is that there has never been a generation in history with more material possessions and comfort than this present generation. Yet in spite of our abundance of goods and ongoing pursuit of pleasure, the worldwide happiness index is at the lowest point on record — especially in industrialized nations where wealth abounds. As believers, we cannot let the errant doctrine that we are entitled to be "happy" drive our lives. Pleasing God and obeying His Word must be our heart's cry!

**As believers, we cannot let the errant doctrine
that we are entitled to be "happy" drive our lives.
Pleasing God and obeying His Word
must be our heart's cry!**

But when the Holy Spirit speaks of "lovers of pleasure more than lovers of God" in Second Timothy 3:4, He is forecasting a society living to attain personal pleasure or happiness as the very highest aim or aspiration in life. You might even say it depicts a wandering world that is obsessively addicted to happiness and to the attainment of pleasure.

BELIEVERS, BEWARE!

Paul prophetically declared in Second Timothy 3:4 that society in the last days will become consumed with themselves to the point that they'll be driven to unparalleled levels of selfishness.

It's not just the unsaved population that is susceptible to an unbalanced love of pleasure and an overemphasis on "self." Many Christians are so obsessed with comfort that they don't want to be asked to do anything that would inconvenience them or jeopardize their comfort. As the decades have passed, this condition has greatly affected churches, where it has become more and more difficult to find people who are willing to serve in church as volunteers.

Furthermore, teachings abound that make it "sound" like God's greatest and highest will for your life is that you are happy. But I'll say it again: Being "happy" is not God's ultimate will for your life. If you *are* happy, that is great. But God's ultimate will is that you do what He asks you to do, regardless of whether or not your obedience makes you happy.

The attainment of happiness is a delusion that is part of the great deception of the last days — with people in mad pursuit of a dream that is unattainable or unsustainable because it is only a fleeting emotion. In fact, I would encourage you to do a study in the Bible of the word "happy." You'll find that the *only* way we can be truly happy is by doing what God has asked us to do. Every other form of happiness is temporary and an unreliable measuring stick in determining how well we are pleasing God.

But according to Second Timothy 3:4, the unending pursuit of happiness will become the chief goal of people at the end of the age — even of many who profess to be Christians. The reason we know that Paul was talking about Christians can be found in the use of the phrase "lovers of pleasures *more than* lovers of God." According to this phrase, the people Paul was talking about will have an affection for God, but their love of pleasure or happiness will *exceed* their love for God. That doesn't mean they won't love God. It simply means they will love pleasure *more than* they love God.

When Paul wrote that people will be "lovers of pleasures more than lovers of God," the words "more than" were used to draw a drastic comparison between two points. In other words, it doesn't mean these Christians won't love God; it simply means that they will love the pursuit of their happiness and the pleasures of life *more than* they love God. Although they may claim to know Christ, their devotion to pleasures will *far surpass* their devotion and service to Him and to His Church.

**The people Paul was talking about
will have an affection for God,
but their love of pleasure or happiness will *exceed*
their love for God. That doesn't mean they won't love God.
It simply means they will love pleasure *more than* they love God.**

ACTIONS SPEAK LOUDER THAN WORDS

I don't know any Christian who would openly confess that he loved pleasures more than he loved God — but *a person's actions speak louder than his words.* Actions reveal the truth about what a person loves and values most. As

I just noted, pastors all over the world can testify that people are becoming less and less willing to serve in the local church. *This is an indication of how the Church at large can be influenced by a last-days demonic agenda.*

Oh, we must care deeply about those matters that mean most to God! Especially as we draw near to the time of Jesus' return, we must do everything we can to guard our hearts and keep them free from selfishness and greed so we can remain focused on His coming. We must set our hearts and minds on Jesus and keep our priorities aligned with His Word so that when He comes, He will find faith in our hearts that we nourished and nurtured as we waited in anticipation of His appearing (*see* Luke 18:8; 2 Timothy 4:8).

The fact is, soon everything in this world will pass away. Only those things that were done in obedience to Jesus will last for eternity. In light of this awesome truth, it's imperative that we examine our hearts to determine our true spiritual condition. If we find areas that need improvement and we are willing to yield to the Holy Spirit's leadership, He will help us know how to bring correction to those areas in our lives that are out of harmony with Him.

◆

**We must set our hearts and minds on Jesus
and keep our priorities aligned with His Word
so that when He comes, He will find faith in our hearts
that we nourished and nurtured as we waited
in anticipation of His appearing.**

◆

As I've said before, there's a reason the Holy Spirit wants us to know that we know, *of a certainty*, that these things will indeed come to pass (*see* 2 Timothy 3:1). He wants us to know them in advance for a reason! But He's not enumerating all these last-days signs to *scare* us; He's letting us know what to expect in order to *prepare* us for what's ahead. He is doing His part to ensure that we won't be overcome by the evil that will develop in the world in the last of the last days.

So in conclusion and with all we've discussed in mind, the following is the *RIV* of Second Timothy 3:4 in its entirety:

People will find it easy to walk away from commitments and to easily throw away relationships. They will become reckless, impulsive, and known for their enjoyment of violence. They will become full of pride and inflated with a sense of their own self-importance — to the extent that it may end up feeling like society is being hit by a typhoon; however, those menacing winds of change will eventually blow out like a storm that comes and goes. Meanwhile, people will become fixated on the unobtainable pursuit of happiness and pleasure even more than they love God.

CHAPTER 8

LAST-DAYS SURVIVAL GUIDE ACTION STEPS
TO AVOID THESE END-TIME TENDENCIES AND TRENDS

In this chapter, we have seen the amazingly accurate prophetic statements the Holy Spirit made regarding society in the very last of the last days. For those of us living in this generation, it is evident that we're in the season when time has almost reached its last port and only a sliver of time remains for the journey. At this very end of the age, society will drift far off course in many serious ways. But just because the world drifts off course does *not* mean *you* or *your family* should drift off course!

We see that the Holy Spirit emphatically and categorically prophesied that society at the close of the age would be filled with:

- Many who have become "fierce" — that is, uncivilized and savage in many aspects.

- "Despisers of those that are good" — that is, those who will cause it to seem like laws protect only the offenders, and law-abiding citizens will be left without defense.

- "Traitors" — that is, "fair-weather friends" who specialize in shallow relationships.

- Many who are "heady" — that is, those known for being both reckless and rash and given to an intemperate enjoyment of violence.

- Those who are "high-minded" — that is, those who defy God and are filled with their own self-importance, producing a pervasive sense of foreboding that a spiritual typhoon is filling the horizon.

- Those in society and even many in the Church who have become "lovers of pleasure more than lovers of God" — that is, addicted to the pursuit of their own happiness more than they desire to pursue God Himself.

So I want you to honestly ask yourself the following seven questions. Examine yourself to see if you have been affected by any of these characteristics that we've discussed in this chapter so you can build a wall of protection around yourself and your family against the onslaught of destructive tendencies and trends that continue to grow in intensity in this last-days society.

1. **"Have I become numbed in my response to images of violence, or does such graphic violence still trouble me?"**

We live in a world today that is filled with images of violence. Violence is pervasive throughout society — in the movies, in the news, and throughout the Internet. Because it seems to be infiltrating every realm of the society we live in, we must be careful not to allow ourselves to become numb to violence until it no longer disturbs us as it once did in the newness of our walk with Jesus.

Can you say that violent and graphic images still disturb you, or have you become so desensitized to them that such images no longer bother you as they once did?

Certainly there is no reason to feel self-condemned. But if you see that your tolerance level for violence and bloodshed — even in entertainment — is greater than it once was, it is entirely possible that your soul has become calloused in this area of your life. That is not a small thing. The calloused soul is a serious condition, because the person who possesses such a soul finds it more difficult to hear the tender voice of the Holy Spirit.

I ask you today to reflect on your own level of sensitivity to things that grieve the Spirit of God. See if you have become affected by this trend toward violence in the world around you. If you find that you have become too tolerant of images that are offensive to the Spirit of God, I urge you to take time to ask the Holy Spirit to soften your heart. Then make the decision to eradicate such images from your own realm of visual contact.

2. "Have I considered how Jesus would feel about the movies I watch?"

I know this is not an enjoyable question, but it is an important question for you to answer. Remember that the Holy Spirit lives inside you — and you subject Him to the things you allow to go into your mind through your eyes and your ears.

Can you honestly say that the Holy Spirit is pleased by the things you are subjecting Him to that you watch in movies, on TV, on digital devices, or on the Internet? Can you imagine asking Jesus to sit on the sofa next to you to watch the things you are watching, or would you be embarrassed to ask Him to join you? The truth is that Jesus is always with you, and you are subjecting Him to whatever you are watching.

I know you don't want to grieve Jesus and the Holy Spirit who dwells within you. So I encourage you to take some time today to evaluate what you need to eliminate from your viewing habits. If it isn't something you'd want to invite Jesus to watch with you, you don't need to be watching it anyway.

3. **"Have I allowed my children or grandchildren to watch images of violence that could possibly sear their conscience and desensitize them?"**

Even cartoons today are filled with graphic violence and disrespect. The devil is clearly targeting children because he wants to desensitize them to these carnal things from an early age.

What are your children or grandchildren watching on television, on their gadgets, or on the Internet? Do you know what they are focused on when they watch their screens or play their digital games? Would Jesus commend you for being a faithful guardian over your children or your grandchildren in this area? Or would He reprove you for allowing them to be tainted with soul-destroying images and attitudes?

It is easy to let children sit in front of the TV and digital gadgets as a way to keep them occupied. However, you have a God-given responsibility to be a guardian over their young souls. What they put into their eyes and minds will eventually produce a harvest in their lives. Are you absolutely certain what they are watching as entertainment will produce a good result?

I urge you today to deeply ponder this question. What have you been allowing the children under your charge to take into their eyes, their ears, and their minds? If you find that you've been too lenient in this area, it's time for you to self-correct and begin to take your responsibility as guardian very seriously. It's better for you to take action now than to have to repent later when the children produce a bad harvest from the violence and the wrong attitudes and actions in the movies and the games you allowed them to engage in as entertainment.

4. **"Have my friendships with others become more shallow over time? Am I possibly viewed by some as a fair-weather friend?"**

For many reasons we discussed in this chapter, relationships have become shallower and more short-term for many people. Maybe that's a trend you can relate to. You may even feel that your closest friends have drifted away because they have moved, changed jobs, or switched churches and didn't maintain their relationship with you. Or they may have experienced a change in marital status, and your relationship was negatively impacted because the friendship was forsaken — something that often happens today.

I suggest you take the time to explore this question further by asking yourself these questions:

- *Have I experienced this sense of loss in the area of close relationships with friends?*

- *If so, what kind of deficit has this created in my life?*

- *Who is my closest friend? To whom do I turn in times of need? To whom do I turn when I feel a need to do something with someone I trust?*

- *Do I have a friend I can spend time with and with whom I can open my heart with no fear of my trust being compromised?*

- *Just as important — to whom am I a friend these days? Can someone else say he or she looks to me as a trusted confidant and friend?*

- *Have I been able to maintain close relationships with others, or have I been affected by the spirit of the age to the extent that I have become unreliable as a trusted friend?*

People everywhere — including you — need close and trusted relationships they can depend on for years and years. These relationships are precious gifts. Do you have them in your life? Can someone else say that *you* are that trusted friend they need?

The Church today is filled with lonely people who are lacking in this very important area of close relationships. So I urge you to take this question seriously and conduct an honest, thorough evaluation of your own relationships.

Even if the world has drifted in this area of close, long-lasting relationships, God wants *you* to be among those who are rich with faithful friends and who are counted as faithful friends to others.

5. "Have I felt like the horizon before me in society is getting darker and darker?"

If your answer is yes, there is a simple reason for what you've been sensing. It *is* growing darker and darker, just as the Holy Spirit prophesied it would be at the end of the age. But rather than wring your hands while you worry and fret, this is your opportunity to *rise and shine* and show the power and the love of God to those around you (*see* Isaiah 60:1)!

Take some time to honestly answer this question:

- *In what ways am I shining the light of the Gospel to those I know who are in darkness and who are making wrong decisions right now?*

It is entirely possible that God is waiting on you to step up and shine the light of Jesus Christ into their lives to help them see more clearly what is right and wrong. If you don't know how to do that, the Holy Spirit certainly does. If you'll lean on Him and follow His instructions, He will show you how to shine the light to those who so desperately need it.

Here are some other important questions to ask yourself:

- *Who are the people I know who really need me to shine the light to them?*

- *Can they depend on me to lovingly show them the way?*

- *Can they count on me to speak the truth to them in love?*

- *Or have I been failing them as God's voice and as a family member or friend?*

As time goes on, darkness will continue to creep into many people's lives. However, this means the light you possess will be easier to see if you are willing to let yourself shine out to the world around you.

Are you allowing the Holy Spirit to use you as a light-bearer to people you know who really need the light? This question will become more and more important as time goes by, so I urge you today to examine your heart to see if you are hiding your light under a bushel or if you are allowing the Holy Spirit to shine the light of God's Word and of Jesus' love through you to others.

6. "Have I allowed the driving force in my life to become the pursuit of happiness, or is obedience to God still my chief passion?"

You don't want to rush through this question, because this is about sustaining your first love for Jesus (*see* Revelation 2:4). It is vital that you conduct an honest self-examination and ask yourself:

- *Considering how I live my life each day, which is greater — my desire to please God in all that I do, or self-gratification?*

To help yourself answer accurately, I suggest that you take an honest look at your calendar, your checkbook, and your service at church. Where is the majority of your time and money being spent? This is a real-life indicator of what is truly motivating your life. How often do you attend church, and how often do you faithfully volunteer in some way to help others?

I made this statement earlier: God's highest call for you is not that you are happy. His greatest will for your life is that you are *obedient*.

When you read that statement, do you agree or disagree with it? Does it aggravate and frustrate you, or does it confirm and resonate with what is already in your heart?

Take a few moments to pray as David prayed: "Search me, O God, and know my heart; test my thoughts. Point out anything you find in me that makes you sad, and lead me along the path of everlasting life" (Psalm 139:23, 24 *TLB*). Listen for what the Holy Spirit speaks to you. If He shows you any areas in which you need improvement, repent and surrender those things to Him, taking any action steps He reveals.

7. **"Has the message gotten through to me that Jesus does not want to scare me, but He does want to prepare me to live in victory in these last days?"**

Second Timothy 1:7 states that God never gives anyone a spirit of fear; therefore, we know that God is not in the business of scaring anyone. However, as a loving Father, He does want to prepare every one of us for what we need to know to stay sound, healthy, and free from the evil that is lurking in the world at the end of the age.

John 1:5 says that the darkness doesn't have the power to overcome the light of God inside you and me. However, we have a responsibility to make sure we do not allow darkness to have a voice in our lives. We must live according to the light of God inside us so it can radiate its glorious and powerful presence *through* us to those around us.

Although you do not need to be afraid, God does want you to wake up and to be continually vigilant because the devil really is as a roaring lion who walks about, seeking to find those he can devour (*see* 1 Peter 5:8). For you to avoid the enemy's attacks, you must learn to keep your eyes open spiritually, stay in tune with the Spirit of God, stay in close fellowship with a local church, and stay under protective spiritual authority.

With all of that in mind, this is a good time to thoughtfully ask yourself:

- *Am I taking all the necessary steps so I don't become assaulted by the evil that is working in the world today?*

This is so important that I urge you to thoroughly evaluate how you are taking precautionary steps to make sure you are not being affected by the spirit of this end-time age.

And now I leave you with this final question to ask yourself before we move on to the next chapter:

- *Can I honestly say that I am diligently working on my spiritual life and that I am making good spiritual progress?*

This question is of paramount importance to the longevity of your spiritual health, so I urge you to really take it to heart.

In conclusion, I want to add a word of encouragement. You've done well if you didn't skip over or take lightly any of these Action Step questions. If there were some questions that left you feeling like you've fallen short, just take a moment to ask God for forgiveness, which He gives freely. He will help you find a plan of action so you can make needed corrections that will strengthen your spiritual health and help you navigate the challenges of this last-days season that looms on the horizon.

And now let's go on, for there is more to learn from Second Timothy 3!

9

THE LAST-DAYS MASQUERADE AND A FINAL SHOWDOWN

In this chapter, we will examine the *final characteristics* that the Holy Spirit enumerated concerning a last-days society. So far we've seen that the Holy Spirit gave us a prophetic heads-up in Second Timothy 3 regarding *the very last of* the last days. We have discussed certain specific characteristics revealed in these verses that will mark society as the age approaches its conclusion.

The characteristics of an end-time society at large will generally become:

- Lovers of their own selves

- Covetous

- Boasters

- Proud

- Blasphemers

- Disobedient to parents

- Unthankful

- Unholy

- Without natural affection

- Trucebreakers

- False accusers

- Incontinent

- Fierce

- Despisers of those that are good

- Traitors

- Heady

- High-minded

Now let's examine the *final characteristics* in Second Timothy 3:1-13 that will emerge in a last-days society as they are enumerated by the Holy Spirit in this portion of Scripture. This does not necessarily mean that this represents an all-inclusive list; however, these last characteristics do conclude the list given by the Holy Spirit in this particular section of Scripture.

AN APOSTATE CHURCH IN THE LAST DAYS

We have seen that when Paul wrote about end-time events in his second epistle to Timothy, he forecasted an astonishing sequence of changes that will come about in society at the very end of the age. Although there will be a great outpouring of the Holy Spirit on those in the Church who are hungering for it, the apostle also prophesied that chief among the elements of this seismic shift in society would be an extremely serious spiritual defection that takes place within a large segment of the Church.

In Second Timothy 3:5, Paul wrote, "Having a form of godliness, but denying the power thereof: from such turn away." The word "form" is the Greek word *morphosis*, and it means *an outward shape* or *form*. This verse prophetically states that many in the last days — including this portion of the Church Paul alludes to — will have all the right words and forms in their religious practices. However, these same people will lack the power of God because they will "deny" its operation.

To explain what this means, let me begin by using the example of a mannequin to make my point. Today mannequins nearly look human. Some are so developed that they would outwardly pass for a real human being to a casual onlooker. I've personally had the experience of turning to speak to someone in a store, only to discover it was a mannequin! It had such a dimensionally accurate outward "form" that it passed momentarily for a real human being. The form was correct, yet it was nothing but an empty form with no life.

This mannequin example vividly depicts the idea presented by the word "form" in Second Timothy 3:5. The Holy Spirit is foretelling that some religious groups at the end of the age will have a "form" of godliness, but they will lack the inner power that makes godliness real. It will *look* good and even *sound* good, but at the end of the day, it will be devoid of spiritual power and will lack spiritual effectiveness.

The word "godliness" is a translation of the word *eusebeia*, which in this case denotes *piety* or *religiosity*. This "outer form" used to depict this notion could possibly include clerical clothing, religious styles, religious actions, religious phrases, religious symbols, and other external religious trappings that people associate with someone or something that is *religious* or even *spiritual.*

On the other hand, this modern age offers countless, multi-generational streams of ministry outside the traditional denominations. Therefore, the "outer form" of a minister might not fit our stereotypical image of "religious" attire and trappings at all.

In truth, it all boils down to the condition of the heart for any minister or believer in any part of the Body of Christ. The outer attire and trappings may seem convincing; the personality of the person claiming to be spiritual may be appealing. But if that person's inner life is devoid of the life of God, he or she has only the "form of godliness" to dispense to the world.

**The Holy Spirit is foretelling that
some religious groups at the end of the age
will have a "form" of godliness, but they will lack
the inner power that makes godliness real.**

In the context of verse 5, the Holy Spirit is saying that there will be people at the end of the age who possess all the external paraphernalia of godliness — the right words, the right symbols, and the right actions. They may wear religious clothing or have a cross draped around their necks and a Bible in their hands. They may even have a strong social-media presence with pious-sounding posts. But these people will be like "spiritual mannequins" dressed up in religious clothing — having the outward "form of godliness" but lacking the inward, life-giving power of God.

Imagine a mannequin dressed like a minister — in religious attire with a gold-chained cross draped across its chest — posed with a Bible in its hands. A good mannequin artist could dress it to bear a striking resemblance to a real minister of the Gospel. In fact, someone might even actually mistake this mannequin for being a real minister. It would certainly have all the right outward trappings. Yet it would be nothing more than a shell — a form dressed in religious clothes. (*Note:* This is not to say there is anything inherently wrong with wearing religious attire. For some very godly ministers, it is simply their custom or preference to do so.)

---◆---

**These people will be like "spiritual mannequins"
dressed up in religious clothing —
having the outward "form of godliness"
but lacking the inward, life-giving power of God.**

---◆---

By using this illustration, Paul was prophesying by the Holy Spirit that a time would come at the end of the age when some within the Church would dress themselves in religious paraphernalia or "look the part" — but, like mannequins, would be empty shells, inwardly lifeless. Paul also wrote that these particular individuals would "deny" the power of authentic godliness. The word "deny" in this context means *to reject* or *to renounce*. By using this word, Paul forewarned of a time when this particular category of spiritual leaders, confronted with truth and power but no longer embracing it, would reject and rebuff its operation.

This is the Holy Spirit's prophetic warning found in Second Timothy 3:5 — that the end of the age will see apostasy emerge inside the Church. It will dress itself in the guise of the Christian faith, but like a mannequin, it will contain no life or power. When confronted with the true power of the Gospel that can transform lives, this particular category of what the world calls a "Christian" will "defect" from God's truth and embrace a lie. This is a picture of *an apostate Church.*

When I was a young man reading this verse, I wondered, *Who could this possibly refer to?* I knew of no denomination that denied outright the basic doctrines of the Bible, so it seemed like a far-fetched idea to me at that time.

But today this is no longer an unlikely concept. We are living in a strange age when "spiritual mannequins" are all around us — whether dressed in religious garb or sitting in our pews. They speak in religious terms; they even use Bible language and symbols. But because they have stepped away from the Scriptures and from the authentic power of God, they are not true, living witnesses of the Gospel of Jesus Christ; they are simply hollow shells that imitate the real Church.

In fact, Paul wrote that this last-days apostate Church will be guilty of "denying the power thereof." The word "denying" in Second Timothy 3:5 is the Greek word *arneomai*, which means *to deny*, *to disown*, *to reject*, *to refuse*, or *to renounce*. It means a time will come when some spiritual leaders will *reject* and *rebuff* the genuine operation of God's power. When confronted with the true power of the Gospel that can transform lives, these "defecting" individuals will reject God's truth and embrace a lie.

◆

The end of the age will see apostasy emerge
inside the Church. It will dress itself
in the guise of the Christian faith,
but like a mannequin, it will contain no life or power.

◆

Many traditional denominational churches were born in revival and in the power of the Spirit. They were pioneered by men and women who believed the Bible and gave their lives for the preaching of the Gospel. But not all traditional churches have stayed loyal to their original, God-given message and mission. Although their doctrinal tenets and creeds remain largely unchanged, the actual practice of their faith represents a shocking departure from those foundational truths of the Bible.

In order to meet the new cultural norms that exist in modern society, errant denominations have gradually moved in the direction of modifying the

Gospel wherever needed to avoid controversy or to better "fit in." As a result, a watered-down Gospel is being presented in these "last of the last days" that marginalizes sin and does not recognize the need to repent. Instead, those who propagate this false Gospel suggest that the real problem with human beings is psychological or medical and can be treated by acceptance, inclusion, right conditioning, and even medication.

**Many traditional denominational churches
were born in revival and in the power of the Spirit.
They were pioneered by men and women who believed
the Bible and gave their lives for the preaching of the Gospel.
But not all traditional churches have stayed loyal
to their original, God-given message and mission.**

This trend to throw open the doors to every possible lifestyle — no matter how unscriptural — under the banner of God's love and tolerance is creeping into historical denominational churches all across the world. Truly we are living in an end-time society when "spiritual mannequins" have become the order of the day in large segments of the Church.

A DEPARTURE FROM THE FAITH

We are seeing the departure from the faith that Paul prophesied, and it is snowballing with the passing of time. At first, this departure was a slow drift. However, the trajectory has become more pronounced in recent years, accelerated over the past several decades by influential portions of the historical Church choosing to abandon the clearly stated, foundational truths of the Bible.

I am thankful for the strong spiritual heritage that many traditional denominational churches have forged within the Church at large. Of those denominations that were born in a strong move of the Spirit, there are still those that contend for the faith and pour multiplied millions of dollars into worldwide evangelism.

The denomination in which I was reared is a strong example of this latter category. I am myself the by-product of this denomination, which not only fervently teaches the Bible, but also tirelessly gives and labors to fulfill the Great Commission around the world. But today even this denomination is under intense pressure to modify itself to meet current social norms, even if they are contrary to the teaching of Scripture.

◆

Of those denominations that were born in a strong move of the Spirit, there are still those that contend for the faith and pour multiplied millions of dollars into worldwide evangelism.

◆

It is true that many traditional churches have stayed loyal to their original God-given message and mission. Yet although the historical tenets of some traditional denominational churches remain largely unchanged, the actual practice of their faith represents *a shocking departure* from those foundational truths.

Ironically, those same foundational doctrines that are being dismantled in actual practice often remain intact within the manuals and creeds of these denominations. Yet those tenets were originally written in part to define the framework and substance of their faith — to *defend and keep the faith*!

This trend to try to avoid controversy and "fit in" has gone so far that the apostle Paul would be hard-pressed to recognize the Gospel message in what is preached from the pulpits of many of these denominational churches. The pure truths of Paul's epistles have largely been replaced with an alternate gospel of inclusion. This "form of godliness" within the modern-day Church emphasizes social justice and social action on a wide range of societal problems instead of offering the life-transforming power of God that accompanies genuine repentance from sin and dead works and that can transform a society from the inside out.

The result of these many modifications is a watered-down gospel that is presented in these last days as truth. But it is, in fact, a "mannequin" of a gospel — one that marginalizes sin and does not recognize the need to repent, Instead, as mentioned earlier, behavior that was once commonly acknowledged as sinful is now labeled a psychological or medical issue.

The need to be washed in the blood of Jesus and transformed by the power of the Holy Spirit is not even on the radar of these particular denominations. This ominous departure from the truth of Jesus Christ has swung so far that now these denominations are promoting *inclusivity* as if *that* is the message of the Church in this hour.

An example of this ominous departure can be seen in the Washington National Cathedral in Washington DC. The leadership of the National Cathedral proudly states that it is a long-time supporter of the full inclusion of lesbian, gay, bisexual, and transgender people in the life of the Church and considers LGBTQ equality one of the great civil rights issues of the Church in the Twenty-First Century. (*Note:* LGBTQ is the acronym for "Lesbian, Gay, Bisexual, Transgender, and Queer.")

The Washington National Cathedral website states, "As one of the nation's most iconic faith communities, Washington National Cathedral strives to be a house of prayer where all are welcome. As we live into that expansive, inclusive identity, we at the Cathedral want to be as clear as we can be that all means all. Every person is loved by God. We can preach that from the pulpit, but the most emphatic way we can say it is to live it by uniting same sex couples in marriage at the altar in our Cathedral."[99]

◆

**This ominous departure from the truth of Jesus Christ
has swung so far that now these denominations
are promoting *inclusivity* as if *that* is
the message of the Church in this hour.**

◆

Certainly it's true that every person is loved by God. In fact, mankind was so loved from the beginning that God sent His Son Jesus to die as the ultimate Sacrifice for sin in order to reconcile us to Himself and purchase our eternal freedom (*see* John 3:16). But equally true is Ephesians 5:5, which tells us that fornicators, unclean persons, covetous, and idolaters have no inheritance in the Kingdom of Christ and of God. Ephesians 5:12 stresses that it is a "shame" to even speak of such things among God's people, let alone to bring those sinful ideas and lifestyles in as an accepted part of the church.

Celebrating same-sex wedding ceremonies at our altars is a slap in the face of Scripture. Everyone should be loved and respected, regardless of his or her lifestyle choices. All must be seen as precious souls for whom Jesus died and who can be changed by the power of God. But our responsibility to love and respect a person does not mean we are required to endorse everything that person does.

I wish the example of the National Washington Cathedral was an unusual case, but it's not. This trend to throw open the doors to every possible lifestyle,

---

[99] Gary Hall (Former Dean), "LGBT Advocacy," https://cathedral.org/initiative/lgbt-advocacy/.

no matter how unscriptural, under the banner of God's love and tolerance is creeping into historical denominational churches all across the world. This movement is attempting to infiltrate nearly every major denomination with a demonic pressure to conform to the new social norms. Churches are under increasing pressure to accept and endorse same-sex marriage at the altars of their churches — even though it is a clear violation of Scripture.

The creeds of most traditional denominations are similar and remain, for the most part, historically correct. However, in practice, certain denominational churches have *stepped away from* — and in some cases have actually *denied* — what their biblical creeds state. They have departed from God's immutable truth in order to accommodate a society in sin rather than to confront it as His prophetic voice.

This is certainly not true of all traditional denominational churches, but the evidence is very clear: Liberal, progressive thinkers are negatively affecting the way many churches practice their faith. Even more grievous to contemplate is the fact that this departure from basic truths of the Bible is occurring in denominations that were once considered to be holdouts for the true Gospel and the power of God. The same could also sadly be said for some non-denominational and non-traditional churches as well.

Paul declared that apostasy would arise in the Church at the end of the age. It would dress itself in the guise of the Christian faith, but like a mannequin, it would contain no life or power.

Have you ever encountered a "spiritual mannequin" in the form of a denomination, a local church (denominational or otherwise), or a Christian leader? The Holy Spirit will help you discern what is truly of Him and what is merely dressed in religious garb (*see* 1 John 2:26,27). You will know the "hollow shell" from the real — and you will be responsible for your response to that knowledge. The apostle Paul was inspired by the Holy Spirit to write, "…From such turn away" (2 Timothy 3:5).

**Paul declared that apostasy would arise
in the Church at the end of the age.
It would dress itself in the guise of the Christian faith,
but like a mannequin, it would contain no life or power.**

As I note in my book *How To Keep Your Head on Straight in a World Gone Crazy*, a departure of this magnitude takes place *slowly* over a period of time and can often go unnoticed until the departure has swung *far* from the foundations of Scripture. Seducing spirits with doctrines of demons have gradually lured believers away from a rock-solid position on Scripture in order to accommodate the moral mess in the world rather than to change it (*see* 1 Timothy 4:1). It's a little here, a little there — a small modification here, a minor alteration there — until finally a church or a denomination that started out blazing hot with the fire of God becomes a hollow shadow of its former glory, an outward form with no power.

This drift begins so gradually that those who are in the process of departing from the faith will probably not even realize what is happening. But little by little, bit by bit, over a period of time, these people are involved in a transition that is moving them *away from* what they once believed and adhered to — and *toward* a very different positioning before God.

Eventually this process of departure reduces a church or denomination to little more than a humanistic goodwill organization that lacks the power of God and endorses only the portions of Scripture that society finds comfortable. As a result, people stream into hell, rarely confronted in life with the truth they need in order to repent and be regenerated by the power of the Holy Spirit.

This drift begins so gradually that those who are in the process of departing from the faith will probably not even realize what is happening.

This modern-day "departing from the faith" that I've just outlined didn't explode on the scene overnight while the Church slept. It began as a slow drift in some religious circles. However, over the past decades, the pace has accelerated until today it often manifests as a blatant rejection of Scripture if a particular issue is at all in conflict with the modern moral mindset.

The pressure to modify faith has existed from the very inception of the Church Age. Pressure still exists today to dilute the faith to be more accommodating to the lost world. This is nothing new. *But we must not allow that pressure to accomplish what the enemy has designed it to do.* It is not *our* faith; it is the Lord's. We do not have the right to adapt the faith — only to *keep* it.

We must therefore refuse to deny the faith — the eternal truths and time-tested doctrines of the Scriptures. We must protect that faith, guard it, and hold tight to it, even if it requires giving our lives for it.

It is indeed possible for a church to become a thriving religious organization with little or no operation of the Bible or the work of the Holy Spirit. In fact, the Holy Spirit Himself warned us of this danger in Second Timothy 3:5, where He states that there would be a *rejection* of the Bible and of the true power of God in the last of the last days — not in all churches, but in many places.

◆

**The pressure to modify faith
has existed from the very inception of the Church Age.
Pressure still exists today to dilute the faith
to be more accommodating to the lost world.
This is nothing new.
*But we must not allow that pressure
to accomplish what the enemy has designed it to do.*
It is not *our* faith; it is the Lord's.
We do not have the right to adapt the faith —
only to *keep* it.**

◆

In Second Timothy 3:2-4, Paul says we are to "turn away" from such people and such churches. The words "turn away" are a translation of the Greek word *apotrepo*, which is a compound of the words *apo* and *trope*. The word *apo* means *away*, and *trope* depicts *a turn*.

When these two words are compounded, they form the word *apotrepo*, which means *to turn away from* and depicts *a mental, spiritual, or physical turning*. The Greek tense is so strong that it cannot be misunderstood. Paul was urging his readers to withdraw from this atmosphere immediately.

The Holy Spirit is *commanding* us in this verse to mentally and spiritually turn away from spiritual mannequins that have the right spiritual form but lack the genuine, life-changing power of Christ. But because the word *apotrepo* also depicts *a physical turning*, we can know that if need be, we must also *physically turn away* and *remove ourselves* from that apostate environment. The message of this verse can thus be stated, *"If you're a part of an apostate group, detach from them mentally and spiritually, and, if need be, physically remove yourself from their company."*

**With all this in mind,
the *RIV* of Second Timothy 3:5 reads:**

Although they may possess an outward form of religiosity, they will rebuff, refute, refuse, and reject the authentic power that goes along with genuine godliness. I urgently tell you to mentally, spiritually, and physically turn away and remove yourselves from such people.

How about you? Have you become a spiritual mannequin? Are you just going through the religious motions — talking the talk and looking the part? Or are you truly loving and serving God with all of your heart, all of your soul, all of your mind, and all of your strength?

And what about the church you attend? Are you a part of a religious denomination that retains correct doctrine in its historic creeds but has in practice departed from those historical tenants of faith to become more compatible with a world that is morally wandering in these last days?

No one is immune to becoming a mere "form of godliness." Even the most sincere and devoted believers can gradually become spiritual mannequins over time.

------------◆------------

**No one is immune to becoming
a mere "form of godliness."
Even the most sincere and devoted believers
can gradually become spiritual mannequins over time.**

------------◆------------

It is up to you to keep the fire of your relationship with Jesus stoked and burning brightly. How do you do this? By pulling away daily to spend time in His presence and in His Word. I encourage you to invite the Holy Spirit to breathe new life into you every day, and you will truly begin to thrive in this end-time age!

WHAT DOES 'CREEP INTO HOUSES' MEAN?

Second Timothy 3:6, Paul went on to say, "For of this sort are they which creep into houses, and lead captive silly women laden with sins, led away with divers lusts."

The phrase "of this sort" refers to those who have a *form* of godliness but deny the power of authentic godliness. According to Paul, these end-time truth modifiers will attempt to "creep into houses" at the end of the age.

The words "creep into" are a translation of the Greek word *enduno*, which in this case means *to dress in a disguise by wrapping oneself in a garment.* It describes the *stealth operation* of one who wears a disguise to make himself or his message more appealing so he or it can gain access into people's private spaces. The word "houses" in this verse is a translation of the Greek word *oikia*, which describes *households*, *homes*, or *residences*. This depicts a clandestine or an *undercover* operation to gain access into people's homes.

In years past, the idea of "creeping into houses" left many wondering what Paul meant. This is an example of how words once difficult to understand can mean so much more with the passing of time. From the vantage point of our present, high-tech age, we see that the Holy Spirit was likely referring to the age of the technology when radio, television, cable systems, and the Internet create an environment that makes "creeping into houses" very easy.

For example, at the time I am writing this chapter, there are approximately 4.33 billion people who are active Internet users in the world. This means approximately 57 percent of the world's population has access to the Internet.

Even those who live in remote places on the planet can tap into a seemingly limitless source of information and media through all kinds of devices, including computers, tablets, and cell phones. This must be what the prophet Daniel alluded to when he said that "knowledge shall be increased" in the last days (*see* Daniel 12:4).

On one hand, we would all agree that this easy digital access to information has created wonderful possibilities. However, it has also opened the floodgates for nonsense to "creep into houses," just as the Holy Spirt foretold in Second Timothy 3:6. Because of this nonstop infiltration of information, we must use caution about "what" and "who" is channeled into our devices and into the privacy of our homes.

In fact, this makes Paul's words in First Thessalonians 5:12 about knowing "who" ministers to you even more important. Paul warned, "And we beseech you, brethren, to know them which labour among you...." The word "know" in this verse is a translation of the Greek word *oida*, which means to *fully perceive* or *fully comprehend*.

Paul used this word to tell us that we should really know something about those we allow to speak into our lives and permit access into our private spaces. Since this was true 2,000 years ago when Paul wrote that verse, how much more true is it today when so many are looking for ways to "creep into houses" via various media?

It is extremely important for you to know "who" is speaking the Word of God to you through the various media that is coming into your home or private space. Are you sure you know who they are? Are you confident in them? Do you know what they really believe on topics that are non-negotiable to you? Don't wait until you are tainted, defiled, or vexed in your soul to find out what they *really* believe concerning basic doctrine and the moral absolutes of the Bible!

---◆---

**It is extremely important for you to know "who"
is speaking the Word of God to you through the various media
that is coming into your home or private space.**

---◆---

God has entrusted you to be the guard of your ears, your eyes, and your mind. Especially in these days when there is an inundation of new and unfamiliar voices being broadcasted into people's private spaces, it is imperative that you take Paul's admonition to heart to *really know* who you are allowing to speak into your life.

WHAT DOES 'SILLY WOMEN LADEN WITH SINS' MEAN?

It is in the context of these last of the last days when the floodgates of information have been opened — and a deluge of new voices, new personalities, and new ideas are flooding into people's private spaces — that Paul specifically prophesied the next part of verse 6. He stated that the devil would attempt to "lead captive silly women." These are strange words to our eyes and ears, so let me walk you through their meaning in the original Greek so you can understand what the Holy Spirit is saying to us.

The words "lead captive" comes from an old Greek word used to depict a moment when an enemy would *thrust the point of a spear into the back of a captive to push him in any direction he wished him to go.* It came to denote the idea of *manipulation by mental or spiritual suggestion.* It can present the idea of a person mentally or spiritually manipulating people to get them to do what he or she wants. Thus, the Holy Spirit foretold a time would come when the devil would begin to manipulate people with information that creeps into their homes under the guise of help.

The words "silly women" seem offensive to our modern mind, so we must understand what Paul meant. These words are a translation of the Greek word *gunaikarion*, which describes *needy women* or *weak women*. It is absolutely true that women in the First Century were less educated than men. Education was simply not available to most women at that time in history. However, it is unlikely that the word *gunaikarion* in this verse is about women being foolish or ignorant. This word more than likely refers to women who feel an acute sense of need in their lives. For this reason, this phrase could be accurately rendered *"needy women."*

The Holy Spirit foretold a time would come when the devil would begin to manipulate people with information that creeps into their homes under the guise of help.

But as Paul continued, he described these particular women as being "laden with sins." The word "laden" is a translation of the Greek word *soreuo*, which depicts *one who feels burdened, loaded, or overwhelmed*. The word "sins" is a translation of the Greek word *hamartia*, which means *to miss the mark of what was hoped for*.

In this context, this phrase "laden with sins" actually depicts *personal failures*, *problems*, or *disappointments* in life. It describes women who feel disappointed, frustrated, and overwhelmed. The high hopes they'd nurtured for life, marriage, family, or career didn't happen as they had dreamed. So here in verse 6, the Holy Spirit prophesies that certain women at the end of the age will feel particularly vulnerable and overwhelmed by life. The inference is that this vulnerability will cause these women to become targets of manipulation.

Paul continued by writing that these women will "be led away with divers lusts…." The phrase "led away" is a translation of the Greek word *ago*, which means *to lead*, but it often depicted animals that were led by a rope tied around their necks and that followed wherever their owner led them. It pictures *being led by a gentle tug or pull*. It is also the root for the Greek word *agon*, which describes *a conflict* or *a struggle of the human will*. It seems the Holy Spirit is warning of the vulnerability of women who wrestle on many fronts in life and whose hearts and emotions are easily tugged on because of inner struggles.

The word "lusts" is a translation of the Greek *epithumia*, a word that pictures a person's *deepest longings*. These would include longings of every type, some of which originate from an area of brokenness or deficiency in a person's life. It could include a deep desire for help that might come in a variety of forms, whether it's counsel for troubled marriages or broken relationships, for better health, for more finances, etc.

The use of this Greek word indicates that many women will be desperate to find help — and often, unsafe voices will appear to tug on their hearts and manipulate their emotions to lead them in a wrong direction in the guise of help. It paints a picture of women in a weakened, vulnerable condition within the privacy of their homes. With access to media and the Internet, they sincerely and desperately search for answers to their pain and their inner struggles — and then suddenly something speaks to their sense of need.

With the modern proliferation of radio, television, Internet, and a sundry of digital devices, it is now very easy to see how wrong voices can "creep" into anyone's private space. All it requires is the simple click of the button on your TV remote, your computer, or your cell phone — and, suddenly, those who wish to speak to you are right in the middle of your house, your family, your head, and your heart.

So the Holy Spirit essentially prophesied that the devil would offer false help to frustrated women who feel overwhelmed with disappointments concerning their marriage and relationships, their finances, and their dreams. Of course, we know that such a vulnerable state is not exclusive to women. Certainly men can also harbor brokenness or unresolved issues that give access to the "creeping in" of wrong voices and negative influences. Nevertheless, it is no random accident that the Holy Spirit warned that certain women would be a special target of deception at the end of the age. The devil is well aware that if he can find an inroad to influence the minds of women, it will open the door for him to "creep into homes" and begin to influence entire families.

**It is now very easy to see how wrong voices
can "creep" into anyone's private space.
All it requires is the simple click of the button
on your TV remote, your computer, or your cell phone —
and, suddenly, those who wish to speak to you
are right in the middle of your house,
your family, your head, and your heart.**

Of course, our modern means of communication sets the stage for great blessing as well. We thank God for the wonderful ministry that is now coming into homes and people's private spaces because of technology.

My own ministry reaches people through these avenues. Many of my personal friends also minister through the various forms of media, and I am so thankful that we all have the ability to reach into the heart of people's needs right where they live with the life-transforming truth of God's Word.

Nevertheless, Paul warned us all to be especially careful about incorrect voices that would try to creep right into the midst of our home environments, and especially into the homes of those seeking answers for the complexities of their lives. And he foretold by the Spirit of God that this would happen in the last days — specifically to vulnerable women.

In Second Timothy 3:6, Paul sounded the alarm regarding Satan's desire to exploit women at the conclusion of the age. It's true that Satan wants to exploit both men and women — but in this context, Paul's message comes through loud and clear: Those with wrong messages will come on the scene, seeking to pull on the heartstrings of certain, more vulnerable women with the aim of influencing them to go in a wrong direction. And isn't that just like the enemy to try to exploit a person's pain, weaknesses, and vulnerability?

According to the Holy Spirit's warning, there will be a certain category of women who are influencers in the home whom the enemy will attempt to lure and lead into a web of deception. The devil is the ultimate opportunist, and he will seek to take advantage of an end-time situation in which many women feel frustrated and disappointed in life and in their family situations and will go in pursuit of help. These women will be targeted by those who creep into their spaces with erroneous answers.

Just look at what is being said on daytime talk shows or written in publications targeting a female audience. You will discover a deluge of propaganda bombarding women today to modify what they believe and to lead them into a more "progressive" way of thinking that is completely contrary to the teaching of Scripture. The devil knows that women are powerful influencers — *very* powerful. That's the reason he seeks them as a primary target.

**The devil knows that women
are powerful influencers — *very* powerful.
That's the reason he seeks them
as a primary target.**

The truth is, women in general are demonstrably more diligent than are men in their search for answers to life's problems. But the category of women referred to in Second Timothy 3:7 are those who will be "ever learning, and never able to come to the knowledge of the truth." The word "ever" is the Greek word *pantote*, which means *at all times* or *endlessly*. In this context, this pictures those who are desperately seeking for answers but are searching in the wrong place or hearkening to the wrong voices — or their hearing is obscured, and they are hearing these false voices through the filter of their pain and disappointment.

What a vivid reminder of why it's so important for the Church to raise its voice and herald clear answers in these last days for people who are struggling. If the Church does not raise its prophetic voice to speak as God's spokesman in these times, other voices will fill the vacuum.

This should also prompt you to evaluate your own life in this regard. Here's an important question to ask yourself and then to thoughtfully ponder the answer: *What can I do better to speak more effectively to the needs of those around me?*

**If the Church does not raise its prophetic voice
to speak as God's spokesman in these times,
other voices will fill the vacuum.**

**Putting the meanings of these words together,
the following is the *RIV* of Second Timothy 3:6,7:**

These sorts of people project themselves as "help" with the intention of gaining access into people's homes to manipulate

them — especially targeting some sincere women who feel over-whelmed by frustrations and disappointing failures in life and whom the manipulators find easier to influence because they have so many unmet longings. These women are endlessly doing their very best to gain insight needed to help them navigate life, but they are perpetually unable to come to right conclusions based on truth.

As Paul continued in this passage of Scripture, he gave us a concrete scriptural example of those who have a "form of godliness but deny the power thereof." To do this, the apostle used an example from Old Testament history regarding two well-known enemies of God.

WHO WERE JANNES AND JAMBRES?

In Second Timothy 3:8, Paul wrote, "Now as Jannes and Jambres withstood Moses, so do these also resist the truth: men of corrupt minds, reprobate concerning the faith." According to Paul, those who have a "form of godliness" will be similar to Jannes and Jambres. So who were Jannes and Jambres?

Jewish intellectuals who lived in the ancient city of Alexandria, Egypt, wrote that Jannes and Jambres were the two leading sorcerers in the book of Exodus who attempted to "withstand" Moses. As residents of Alexandria, these Jewish intellectuals had access to Egypt's historical records. By studying the ancient archives, they identified Jannes and Jambres as the sorcerers who opposed Moses (*see* Exodus 7:11,22; 8:6,7).

In fact, Jannes and Jambres were so well-known in the ancient world that even Pliny the Elder wrote about them.[100] The historian Eusebius also wrote about these two men.[101] The noted theologian Origen wrote about them as

---

[100] Pliny, *Natural History*, 30:11.
[101] *Præparatio Evangelica*," ix.8.

well.[102] In addition to these sources, "the names Jannes and Jambres appeared frequently in other Jewish, Christian, and pagan sources in Arabic, Aramaic, Greek, Hebrew, Latin, Old and Middle English, and Syriac."[103]

Paul wrote, "Now as Jannes and Jambres withstood Moses, so do these also resist the truth: men of corrupt minds, reprobate concerning the faith" (2 Timothy 3:8). The word "resist" is translated from the Greek word *anthistemi*, which means *to stand against* or *to stand in opposition*. It demonstrates the attitude of one who is *fiercely opposed* to something and therefore determined to do everything within his power to *resist it, stand against it, withstand it,* or *defy it.*

Paul says these evil end-time influencers will have "corrupt minds." However, the Greek tense causes it to be better translated "corrupted minds" — meaning that they will have minds that have "become corrupted" over a period of time.

The word "corrupt" is the Greek word *kataphtheiro*. This is a compound of the word *kata*, which means *down*, and the word *phtheiro*, which means *corruption, degeneration,* or *deterioration*. Hence, the word depicts individuals whose minds have become "corrupted" — that is, *their minds have progressively moved downward into a state of collapse, deterioration, and ruin.*

WHAT DOES 'REPROBATE' MEAN?

In Second Timothy 3:8, Paul wrote, "Now as Jannes and Jambres withstood Moses, so do these also resist the truth: men of corrupt minds, reprobate concerning the faith." Although they were Egyptian sorcerers, as these two men embraced spiritual delusion, their minds progressively moved into a state of degeneration and deterioration until they became "reprobate concerning the faith."

---

[102] *Against Celsus.*
[103] David Noel Freedman, ed., *The Anchor Bible Dictionary, Vol. 3* (New York: Doubleday, 1992), p. 638.

The word "reprobate" is translated from the Greek word *adokimos*. The word *dokimos* means *approved*, *fit*, *reliable*, and *trustworthy*. But when an *a* is attached to the front of this word, making it *adokimos*, the meaning is reversed and the new word instead depicts one who is *disapproved*, *unfit*, *unreliable*, and *untrustworthy*.

This depicts a society that has been exposed to a negative spiritual influence for so long — and in such heavy doses — that it has become *compromised*, *impaired*, *ruined*, and *no longer trustworthy*. This is the meaning of the word *reprobate* as used in the New Testament. And in Romans 1:28, it not only pertains to the collective mind of a society, but also to the mind of an individual living within a society. Whether collective or individual, this mind has become so *tarnished*, *tainted*, *hardened*, and both spiritually and mentally *compromised* that it loses its ability to arrive at sensible, godly conclusions.

Consider the sobering implications revealed in Romans 1:28. Although God gives people minds worthy of great esteem, the word translated "reprobate" speaks of minds that have been seriously damaged by long-term, continuous exposure to evil influences and by a continual bombardment of wrong thoughts. A person's mind, created by God to gloriously function, can thus become *unfit* if it is regularly exposed to toxic environments and wrong types of thinking. It can lose its ability to discern what is morally right and wrong.

That same mind may remain brilliant in many respects, and the person who possesses that mind may be a marvelously talented individual. Nonetheless, if that person's mind has become reprobate, it is now morally debased, unfit, and twisted in its thinking. From God's perspective, such a person — or even an entire society — has lost the ability to think correctly, to separate good from evil, or to judge what is right and wrong.

We are living in a day when people's minds are being inundated with false information and a celebration of various forms of immorality, including a deluge of counterfeit propaganda about human sexuality. We are witnesses to a last-days attack of seducing spirits, bent on modifying the collective mind of society and creating a way of thinking that is free of moral restraint.

This modification process is spreading its tentacles into every sector of society. Even people who grew up in church are now becoming affected. Many are changing how they view certain moral issues that *should* be set in stone in their lives, grounded on the rock-solid truth of God's Word.

This has come to pass as a result of an unrelenting mental bombardment by wrong people, wrong sources, wrong information, and wrong spiritual influences. It's all part of a demonic strategy being waged against the human race (including believers) to adversely affect people's minds and to damage and distort their way of thinking until they can no longer see what is *wrong* about *wrong*. Ultimately, this process results in people choosing sides that are opposed to those who adhere to long-held biblical truths.

As a result of the collective mind of a last-days society being mentally modified — that is, seriously ill-affected and sin-damaged — more and more people within that society will begin to "...do those things which are not convenient" (Romans 1:28). The words "not convenient" simply mean people will do things that are *not morally right or fitting*.

◆

We are witnesses to a last-days attack of seducing spirits, bent on modifying the collective mind of society and creating a way of thinking that is free of moral restraint.

◆

The devil knows he just needs to find a point of access into the mind of a person or into the collective mind of a society. If he succeeds in finding that inroad, it won't be long until the behavior of that person or the overall behavior of that society will conform to a new and deceptively appealing way of thinking — one that is far from the well-established, time-tested standards God clearly states in the Bible.

As God's people, we must be alert to the fact that Satan has launched a covert operation to lead society off track in this hour, loosing seducing spirits with doctrines of demons assigned to lead an entire generation into delusion. The enemy is using the voices of influential people in the media and educational institutions — those who already have been beguiled and seduced to believe a lie. His goal is to victimize a last-days generation and lead them into ways of thinking and behaviors that damage their minds and steal, kill, and destroy on as many levels as possible.

I remind you of Isaiah 5:20 (*NASB*). It speaks of a coming day when people "...call evil good, and good evil; who substitute darkness for light and light for darkness...." This forecasts a time at the close of the age when society will become reprobate and lose its ability to discern the difference between right and wrong — even to the point of justifying bad as good and good as bad. This is the day in which you and I live — an end-time moment that the Holy Spirit specifically warned us about.

◆

**As God's people, we must be alert to the fact
that Satan has launched a covert operation
to lead society off track in this hour,
loosing seducing spirits with doctrines of demons
assigned to lead an entire generation into delusion.**

◆

We are already living in the age of the reprobate!

MINDS THAT BECOME CORRUPTED
OVER A PERIOD OF TIME

But Paul said these individuals will be reprobate concerning "the faith" (2 Timothy 3:8). That means their minds will no longer think correctly when it comes to the faith. But wait — because the phrase "the faith" includes a definite article, this is not talking about raw faith, such as faith for miracles. The definite article in the Greek text tells us that the phrase "the faith" instead refers to *the long-held, time-tested teaching of Scripture* or *the non-negotiable doctrines and tenets of the Christian faith.*

First Timothy 4:1 is another important text where the Holy Spirit spoke of the future: "Now the Spirit speaketh expressly, that in the latter times some shall depart from the faith, giving heed to seducing spirits, and doctrines of devils." In this verse, the Holy Spirit categorically forecasts that in the conclusion of the last days, a breeding ground for error will fester not only in the secular world, but also within the Church. And as we discussed earlier, we are seeing this even in this day. Already in the Christian world are many spiritual leaders who seek a dangerous truce with the world under the guise of inclusiveness and compromise.

These leaders may have once held strong doctrinal positions. But over time, they began to shape their beliefs to meld with the changing moral climate of society — and in the process, they produced a Gospel message very different from the one presented in the Bible. Along the way, they embraced compromising positions and allowed their thoughts to be affected with the errant mindsets that promote such positions. Their minds thus became progressively more "corrupted" until they actually came to believe and embrace the nonsense they promoted.

This is the destructive track that much of the Church is on as man's natural reasoning strives to reach a generation who is unfamiliar with the Bible and considers the dictates of the Word restrictive and out of date. Regrettably, we must call this what it is: *a departure from Scripture*. That is what Paul was referring to in Second Timothy 3:8 when he stated that these individuals would be reprobate concerning "the faith."

◆

Man's natural reasoning strives to reach a generation who is unfamiliar with the Bible and considers the dictates of the Word restrictive and out of date. Regrettably, we must call this what it is: *a departure from Scripture*.

◆

The Holy Spirit is forewarning believers of a dangerous, demonic plot that the Church will have to contend with in the last of the last days. There have been many attacks against the Church throughout its 2,000 years of history. But the Holy Spirit sounds the alarm that this end-time attack will be unlike previous ones and will be especially severe. Yet this last-days assault against the Church will be so insidious that the Holy Spirit spoke in advance about it in absolutely clear, unmistakable, and definite words.

FALSE TEACHING SPREADS LIKE A SPIRITUAL DISEASE

Paul went on to say, "They shall proceed no further: for their folly shall be manifest unto all men, as theirs also was" (2 Timothy 3:9).

Pay attention to the word "proceed" in this verse. It is a translation of the Greek word *prokopto*, which means *to advance* or *to make progress*, but this very word was used medically to denote *the advancement of spreading disease*. Paul used this word to tell us that people who are "reprobate concerning the faith"

356

will spread their ungodly belief system until it is like a disease out of control if they are not stopped.

Understand that it only takes a few spiritual leaders getting off track to affect larger segments of the Church. Never forget that physical infections begin at the microscopic level with a relatively small number of contagions and that many are often very treatable if they are addressed in their early stages. However, if they are left untreated, infections can quickly grow out of control and lead to serious physical complications or even death.

Likewise, when spiritual infection finds its way into the Church, it quickly begins to multiply inside unless it is swiftly addressed and *stopped*. Ultimately, if these destructive forces — these doctrines that are scripturally errant — are allowed to propagate within a local church, they will gain strength and spread to the entire congregation.

A spiritual leader who is infected with false doctrine is only one person — but because he is an influential person who touches many lives, it is likely that others will be contaminated through his touch. His diseased influence will spread like germs until it infects people who gather to worship.

If correction doesn't come to the errant leader's life, his words and teachings have the potential to become food that makes others sick. Because his influence is strong, it is likely that those who are close to him will pick up whatever has contaminated him and become infected with the same spiritual problems. The point is that it doesn't take too many erring individuals to transmit sickness to an entire church body when they hold positions of influence.

But Paul was telling us that the "spiritual disease" of these leaders will progress no further because "...their folly shall be manifest unto all men..." (2 Timothy 3:9). The word "folly" is the Greek word *anoia*, which comes from the Greek word *nous* — the word for the *mind*. But that little *a* attached to the front of it has a canceling effect. This means it is no longer the picture of a normal mind; instead, it means *mindless*. The *King James Version* translates the word as "folly," but it more accurately depicts the idea of *madness, irrational thinking,* or *brainlessness.* Here we find that error develops from one stage of "bad" to a worse stage of "bad." In fact, it eventually becomes so extreme that people can begin to recognize the lunacy of its conclusions.

This is why Paul said that what these leaders espouse and promote is so ridiculous that it will eventually become "manifest" to all men. The word "manifest" is a translation of the Greek word *ekdelos*, which means *to become obvious* or *to become unmistakably clear.* Hence, these errant leaders' lunacy will eventually grow out of control. And a time will come when many will be able to clearly see that what these degenerate individuals are believing and peddling is sheer madness.

**Putting the meanings of all these words together,
the *RIV* version of Second Timothy 3:8,9 reads:**

Now as Jannes and Jambres fiercely opposed and defied Moses, these also will be fiercely opposed to and will defy the truths of Scripture. They will be men with minds that have been ruined — defective, malfunctioning, and reprobate concerning the teachings of Scripture. But the advance of spiritual disease they spread will be halted, and their irrational way of thinking — their lunacy, madness, and spiritual nonsense — will become unmistakably clear to all men, as theirs also was.

A FINAL SHOWDOWN AT THE END OF THE AGE

In Second Timothy 3:9, Paul tells us that Jannes and Jambres resisted, stood against, withstood, and defied God's power. And just as Jannes and Jambres withstood Moses, at the end of the age there will be well-known personalities — religious, social, and political — who will emerge on the scene to oppose the Gospel and present an alternative message. It will be a part of the end-time, worldwide mutiny that Paul prophesied about in Second Thessalonians 2:3 (*see* pages 90-91).

Friend, the Scriptures makes it clear that this last-days development *will* occur. But Paul said that just as Pharaoh's sorcerers were unable to compete with the power of God, so, too, these end-time wanderers will be unable to compete with His mighty power.

Herein is a prophecy of a final showdown at the end of the age — one in which the power of God will prove to be unbeatable in the face of evil. Sinister forces are already gathering like a dark, foreboding storm on the horizon. Before this final contest of powers is over, society will experience the effects of these devastating winds of revolutionary change to a greater and greater degree.

The demonic lies that fuel this spiritual typhoon will attempt to creep not only into homes, but into universities and into new laws that will negatively impact God's people. These so-called progressive leaders will do everything they can do religiously, socially, and politically to modify and defy the teachings of Scripture and to actually deny the true operations of God's power. A sophisticated counter-gospel will be offered, mingled with a dangerously wayward political system.

But in the end, God's power *will* show up. And just as Jannes and Jambres were ultimately revealed as a threat to God's purposes, end-time enemies of the faith will be exposed and overshadowed by the power of God, and the Church will emerge victorious. Paul was prophesying in Second Timothy 3:8 and 9 that as the power of God worked through Moses to confront the powers of evil in his day, that same divine power will flow mightily through a remnant in the last-days Church. And as God's power is made manifest, the folly of warped ideologies and last-days doctrinal nonsense will become evident for all to see. Just as Moses' rod "swallowed" the rods of Jannes and Jambres (*see* Exodus 7:12), God's power will ultimately devour and humiliate the power of the enemy.

But Paul also prophesied that the activities of evil men — those with a form of godliness but who deny the power of it — will spin further out of control as time passes. In Second Timothy 3:13, he wrote, "But evil men and seducers shall wax worse and worse, deceiving, and being deceived."

The word "wax" is again a translation of the Greek word *prokopto*, the word we have already seen that was used medically to depict *the spreading advancement of disease*. This lets us know that the apostate Church will become sicker and sicker as time passes — going from bad to worse — or as Paul said, they will go about "deceiving and being deceived."

The word "deceiving" is a translation of the Greek word *planao*, which pictures *a wandering from an established moral path* or *one who has veered from a solid path*. This very word was used historically to picture *a lost animal that got so lost that it could not find its way back home*. By using this special word, Paul informed us that some will become so spiritually misleading — and they will wander so far off track — that they will not be able to find their way back without help. Instead, Paul wrote, they will go about "deceiving and being deceived." This means they will not only spread deception, but they will also buy into it themselves and become the by-products of the delusion that they themselves promote.

**With all that we've discussed in mind,
the *RIV* of Second Timothy 3:13 reads this way:**

**But these wicked men — real, bona fide frauds who masquerade
as spiritual leaders — will lead people off track as they spread
their deadly teachings and put people under their magic spell.**

Over time, they will go from bad to worse, deceiving and being self-deceived by the nonsense they communicate to others.

In these last of the last days, God calls on you and me to speak clearly and authoritatively from His Word — holding tightly to what the Scripture says and not to what a wandering end-time society will attempt to dictate or direct. In order to avoid being taken captive by the infectious deceptions that pretenders will try to peddle, we must keep our minds renewed daily with the Word of God, stay connected in a vibrant, on-fire church that accurately teaches the Scriptures, and stay filled with the Holy Spirit.

We have now come to the conclusion of the characteristics that the Holy Spirit prophesied would emerge in society in the last of the last days. Read the following carefully and digest the full impact of what the Holy Spirit has said to you and me in these verses!

The following is the full *RIV* version of Second Timothy 3:1-9,13:

1. You emphatically and categorically need to know with unquestionable certainty that in the very end of days — when time has sailed to its last port and no more time remains for the journey — that last season will stand in the midst of uncontrollable, unpredictable, hurtful, treacherous, menacing times that will be emotionally difficult for people to bear.

2. Men will be self-focused, self-centered, self-absorbed, self-consumed, and in love with themselves more than anyone else. As a result of this self-love, they will be driven to obtain more and more and more. These boasters are so committed to their own agenda that they are willing to exaggerate, overstate the facts, stretch the truth, embellish a story, and even lie if it will get them the position, advantage, or goal they desire. They are arrogant, haughty, impudent, snooty, and insolent. They disdain, mock,

slander, and speak ill of anyone that stands in the way of their ideology and freely use foul language. In this climate, parents will no longer be able to persuade, control, lead, or exercise authority over their own children. And although people were once thankful and appreciative, they will generally become void of gratitude and will be unappreciative of everything. Impurity will seep into society and cause it to become impure, ill-mannered, unclean, indecent, coarse, vulgar, offensive, crude, lewd, and rude.

3. Love for and commitment to family will disintegrate, and divorce will become epidemic, with irreconcilable differences being a major factor in tearing families apart. In fact, every imaginable type of covenant will be regularly violated, and the court system will be overwhelmed as people go overboard, suing and being sued. People will generally lose the ability to say no and will be unable to control their instincts in nearly every area of life. People will become savage, and it will eventually feel like there are no laws to protect the innocent.

4. People will find it easy to walk away from commitments and to easily throw away relationships. They will become reckless, impulsive, and known for their enjoyment of violence. They will become full of pride and inflated with a sense of their own self-importance — to the extent that it may end up feeling like society is being hit by a typhoon; however, those menacing winds of change will eventually blow out like a storm that comes and goes. Meanwhile, people will become fixated on the unobtainable pursuit of happiness and pleasure even more than they love God.

5. Although they may possess an outward form of religiosity, they will rebuff, refute, refuse, and reject the authentic power that goes along with genuine godliness. I urgently tell you to mentally, spiritually, and physically turn away and remove yourselves from such people.

6. These sorts of people project themselves as "help" with the intention of gaining access into people's homes to manipulate them — especially targeting some sincere women who feel overwhelmed by frustrations and disappointing failures in life whom the manipulators find easier to influence because they have so many unmet longings.

7. These women are endlessly doing their very best to gain insight needed to help them navigate life, but they are perpetually unable to come to right conclusions based on truth.

8. Now as Jannes and Jambres fiercely opposed and defied Moses, these also will be fiercely opposed to and will defy the truths of Scripture. They will be men with minds that have been ruined — defective, malfunctioning, and reprobate concerning the teachings of Scripture.

9. But the advance of spiritual disease they spread will be halted, and their irrational way of thinking — their lunacy, madness, and spiritual nonsense — will become unmistakably clear to all men, as theirs also was....

13. But these wicked men — real, bona fide frauds who masquerade as spiritual leaders — will lead people off track as they spread their deadly teachings and put people under their magic spell. Over time, they will go from bad to worse, deceiving and being self-deceived by the nonsense they communicate to others.

In the final chapter that follows, we will look at God's solution to help us remain spiritually robust so we can thrive as we fulfill our part in His purposes at the close of this age. God inspired Paul not only to identify the problems that would assault a last-days generation, but also to outline what is needed for us to successfully navigate the end-time waters we are called to sail upon in our times!

CHAPTER 9

LAST-DAYS SURVIVAL GUIDE ACTION STEPS

TO PROTECT YOURSELF FROM ERROR THAT TRIES TO CREEP INTO YOUR PERSONAL SPACE

Because this chapter is filled with especially thought-provoking material, I believe it would be wise for you to take some time to ponder and digest what you have just read.

God has given you the responsibility to protect yourself and those you love. The following action steps are therefore designed to help you think through what you need to do to block all wrong voices from finding access into your space. They will also help you identify and eradicate every wrong voice that has already found its way into your life and into the lives of those you love.

You can see why these action steps are so important to take seriously. So I encourage you to take the time to reflect on the following questions as you ask them of yourself. Do your best to come to an honest, personal conclusion on each one.

1. **"Whom do I think of when I read about a 'form of godliness but denying the power thereof'"?**

When you read about those in the last days who will have a "form of godliness" but deny the power of it, does anyone immediately come to your mind?

Do you know anyone who fits the description of a spiritual mannequin? In other words, do you know of any spiritual leader or group — or even an individual — in the Christian world who may be adorned with all the right words and who may have an outward appearance of being spiritual, but who lacks the authentic power of God that goes along with genuine godliness?

After you've pondered the answer to those questions, make the matter personal. Instead of dwelling only on others who fit this description, what about *you*?

Ask yourself:

- *Did I allow the power of God and the gifts of the Spirit to operate through me more in the past than I do in my present walk with the Lord?*

- *Have I in some way become a spiritual mannequin that verbally and outwardly looks right but no longer operates in the power of God?*

- *Have I personally fallen prey to the trend to update or modify the faith so I can better "fit into" a society that is changing its foundational moral code?*

These may be difficult questions to ask yourself, but they are wise ones to ask. After all, the Holy Spirit forewarned that this will be the tendency that develops in the last-days generation — and you are now part of that last-days generation.

If you find it difficult to honestly answer each of these questions with a resounding *no*, it is time for you to get honest with God about your situation. Allow the Holy Spirit to examine your heart. Make sure your ears are open to hear what He has to say to you.

It is certain that if the Holy Spirit has something to say to you, He only wants to help you. So determine to stay absolutely honest with yourself as you ask yourself these questions as well:

- *Do I have ears to hear what the Holy Spirit wants to say to me about my own spiritual condition?*

- *Am I willing to allow the Holy Spirit to examine my heart and my life regarding these important questions?*

2. "Is there any particular person or group I need to 'turn away from' after reading this chapter?"

Many people attend churches that are right on target in creed but *in practice* have stepped away from the clear teaching of Scripture. In Second Timothy 3:5, the apostle Paul has a strict admonishment for believers who find themselves in this type of detrimental church environment: They are to spiritually, mentally, and physically remove themselves from that spiritually negative situation and relocate to a body of believers who are holding fast to the Scriptures and the power of God.

I encourage you to take the time to seriously assess your own life regarding this matter, and then ask yourself this question:

- *Since this is what the Bible commands, what does this mean for me personally?*

Perhaps all is well for you on this account because you attend a church that is committed to the Bible and open to God's power working in your midst. But what if your church or denomination does *not* fit that description? What if the spiritual company you are connected with has stepped away from the foundational doctrines of the Bible and has progressively modified itself to fit the world's degenerating moral culture? What are you going to do with Paul's admonition to spiritually, mentally, and physically remove yourself from that environment?

This is not *my* personal recommendation — rather, *it is the command of Scripture.*

Your spiritual life and that of your family is so very important. What you pour into yourself or allow to be poured into loved ones under your charge will eventually produce a harvest. So ask yourself:

- *If I keep myself and my family in the spiritual environment we are in at the present time, what kind of harvest will it produce in us in the future?*

Everything is at stake when it comes to being in the right or wrong spiritual environment.

With all this in mind, it's now time to ask yourself this question:

- *Am I committed to a church or denomination that fosters love for the Bible, faith in the infallible and immutable Word of God, and the operation of God's power?*

If you cannot answer *yes* to that question, you need to face the very real possibility that you are in the wrong place. God has said in His Word that He requires you to relocate to a safe place where these things will be nurtured in your life and in the lives of those you love. Be assured that He will lead you to the right place as you seek Him for guidance.

One day when you face trouble and need a foundation to stand on, that critical moment will reveal if, by your past decisions, you received all you needed to face the fires of life. If you are in a church or denomination that is pouring faith-filled teaching into you, you'll be equipped to face anything. But if you are in a church or denomination that isn't teaching you to stand on the Scripture and walk in the Spirit by faith, you will be ill-prepared to overcome when you encounter the next challenge or hardship.

So ask yourself this:

- *What is the Holy Spirit prompting me to do personally in response to Paul's admonition in Second Timothy 3:5?*

I encourage you to keep seeking the Lord until you know what He's asking you to do and how He's asking you to do it. This is vital in order to accurately position yourself and your family for the serious days ahead.

3. "Whom am I allowing to infiltrate my private space?"

The Holy Spirit forecasted that a time would come at the end of the age when evil would "creep into houses." With the development of technology, it is so much easier for all kinds of voices to "creep" into your personal spaces. That's why it is very important to ask yourself:

- *Whose voices am I allowing to enter my private space and speak into my life through various forms of media and digital devices?*

God commands you to know those who minister to you (*see* 1 Thessalonians 5:12). So what do you really know about those voices you've allowed on your TV, computer, or other devices? Who is really speaking into your life? Do you know where they stand on matters that are (or *should* be) non-negotiable to you? Are you allowing someone who is safe to speak into your spiritual life, or are you permitting someone who is possibly spiritually corrupted to influence you?

God has made you the guardian of your eyes, ears, and brain. This is a sacred trust. Your mind is the central control center of your life, so whoever influences your mind will ultimately affect your entire life.

So ask yourself:

- *Am I satisfied that safe voices are speaking to me?*

- *Have I done my homework to know who they are, what they believe, and the true nature of their affiliations?*

If you are confident that you are receiving teaching from safe voices with whom God has connected you, stick with them and support them. They need your help and financial support, and you need what they have to give you.

Always do your due diligence in these matters, ensuring that you really know who is speaking to you. Remember, you are the "watchman on the wall" of your mind and of your heart, from which flows the very issues of life (*see* Proverbs 4:23).

4. "Who comes to mind when I think about those whose minds have become corrupted over a period of time?"

On this topic of spiritual leaders whose minds have become corrupted over a period of time, I can definitely think of some leaders who once walked in the purity of God's Word, but over time they have veered to embrace so-called alternative "truths." When I see where these leaders have landed in their belief system, it is difficult to comprehend how they could have ended up in such errant positions. What is even more shocking is that their minds have become so affected by nonsensical thinking that they *adamantly* believe the nonsense they espouse and promote!

Do you know anyone whose mind has been tainted and corrupted over a period of time? It doesn't have to be a spiritual leader. It might be a parent, a spouse, a friend, a sibling, or someone you know who once worshiped alongside you at church but over time slowly drifted into a misguided belief system that is unthinkable to you. People who fit this description are actually espousing what they once believed was wrong — and many of them are even more adamant about the unscriptural positions they have embraced than those people who have *never* believed in the God of the Bible!

It is deeply disappointing and personally hurtful to see someone veer from his or her faith to embrace the deceptive nonsense that is becoming popular in society today. But through Paul, the Holy Spirit prophesied this would occur in the last of the last days.

If you know a person (or a group of people) whose mind has been corrupted by the popular thinking of our modern society, ask yourself this question:

- *What steps am I taking in prayer to see those who are currently walking a path of deception turn around and be restored?*

If you see a problem with deception in a person's life, it isn't enough to wring your hands and worry about it. God expects you to move into action to intercede for that person. Jude 23 says you are to reach into the fires of destruction to see such people delivered. One of the best ways you can do that is by praying for them.

The people you're praying for may not want to hear what you have to say, but they cannot stop you from praying for them. It is possible that their deliverance will be won because you stood in the gap to intercede for them. (I encourage you to read Chapter 11 in my book *How To Keep Your Head on Straight in a World Gone Crazy*. It specifically shows you how to intercede for people in your life who are in trouble.)

Are you praying for those you are concerned about? If not, take this action step as the Holy Spirit's charge to add those people to your prayer list. Recognizing the need and the fact that just wringing your hands or talking about it will not change a thing. *But when you begin to pray, God moves!* He will begin to work in people's lives in response to your prayers of faith, helping them see the deception that has drawn them away from His eternal truth.

5. "Whom do I think of when I consider people who have refused to budge from the non-negotiable doctrines of the Christian faith?"

We can easily think of people who have become apostate in their beliefs. But who comes to mind as those who have remained steadfast and unchanging, holding fast to the non-negotiable, central truths of Scripture? It's not enough to think only of those who have made devastating spiritual errors. We need to recognize the rock-solid examples of spiritual leaders and friends who have dug their heels into Scripture and into the power of God and have refused to ever budge from what the Scriptures teach!

These faithful warriors for Christ need others like you to voice and show your support for their righteous stance. And within that number, those who are ministers of the Gospel need people like you to join them as partners and friends, sowing into their work for the Kingdom and encouraging them to press ahead as they shine the light of God's Word into a world that is increasingly dark.

Ask yourself these questions:

- *Who comes to mind when I think of people who are bright and shining lights — true examples of spiritual stability whom I can always count on to be scripturally dependable and spiritually stable?*

- *What individuals "shine as lights in the world" and "hold forth the truth," as Philippians 2:15 and 16 says, for others to see and to follow in the midst of a society that is diluting and distorting truth?*

It would be healthy for you to actually make a list of those you know who qualify as faithful contenders for the faith. Even more, it would be an excellent idea for you to take time to express your thanksgiving to them and to even begin to partner with them in the ministry.

Everyone needs a boost of encouragement! Why not think of ways you can give that boost to such brave and consistent soldiers in the faith? Strengthen them in their fight of faith as they provide such a valuable example of solid spiritual leadership for you and for others!

6. "Whom do I know who is qualified to help me discern if what I am listening to is healthy or unhealthy for my spiritual life?"

With so many new faces and voices entering our private spaces these days through so many different forms of media, it is important for you to feel safe with those you are listening to. If you don't know how to discern between safe or unsafe voices, ask yourself this question:

- *Who is a person in my life to whom I can turn for help in discerning whether the people I'm listening to are healthy or unhealthy for my spiritual life?*

There has never been a more important time for you to be connected to people who are strong in the Word of God and whose sense of discernment is trustworthy. So ask yourself these questions as well:

- *Do I have such trustworthy individuals in my life?*

- *Am I a member of a church that is a safe haven for me?*

- *Do I trust the spiritual leadership of my pastor or spiritual leader?*

If you cannot answer these last three questions with a solid *yes*, then here is the next question you should honestly ask yourself:

- *Why am I still going to a church that is not a safe haven for me, sitting under leaders I can't trust to spiritually lead me?*

If that is your situation, you need to find the voice of a shepherd you are willing to follow, just as Jesus taught in John 10:4,5. Certainly there is no such thing as a perfect pastor, just as there is no such thing as a perfect church member. But you need to have a solid sense of confidence in whomever you have entrusted with the role of leading you spiritually in a local church.

I urge you to find that person or persons whose discernment you trust when you have questions about the spiritual diet you are ingesting. Ultimately, the Holy Spirit is your Guide. But as you learn to let Him lead you in life, He surrounds you with the right people to help you when you are having trouble discerning between healthy and unhealthy spiritual food.

7. "Whom do I know who needs to read this chapter?"

When we read a chapter like this one, we often think of someone who needs to read the truth it contains. Maybe you know someone who is starting to go in a wrong direction. Ask yourself these questions:

- *Is there someone I know in need of having their eyes opened to the process of deception they have bought into?*

- *Could the discussion in this chapter possibly be the help needed to get that person I know back on track again?*

- *Is the Holy Spirit leading me to give a copy of this book to that person so I can let the book do the speaking for me — especially the material in this particular chapter?*

We are living in a time when friends and family members need to speak up and speak out to help their loved ones stay on course. Sometimes knowing what to say is difficult. A book like this can do the job for you. That's why I've included this last action step — to consider using this book as a tool to "stay the plague" of spiritual infection in the lives of people you know who are susceptible to deception and the devastating effects that will inevitably ensue as a result of that kind of spiritual contamination.

You could give this book to someone who fits this description either personally or anonymously, whatever way seems to be wisest as you are led by the Holy Spirit. And as you get this book to those who are vulnerable to the deception of this age, it will provide an open door for the Holy Spirit to come through, wielding His mighty sword of the Word to attack any error they are being tempted to embrace and thus *eradicate* it from their lives!

10

HOW TO VICTORIOUSLY NAVIGATE LAST-DAYS STORMY WEATHER

As we come to the close of this book, it has become clear through our discussion that turbulent winds will blow through society at the very end of the age. Scripture prophesies that these spiritual tempests will spread out across the entire world with far-reaching consequences.

For us to catch a glimpse of what it may be like to live through a last-days spiritual storm, we'd do well to consider the patterns and effects of a hurricane. As a hurricane approaches, its impending presence can be felt by the torrent of pounding rain and the rising sea tides that precede it. These raging rains and swelling tides can be sufficiently deadly by themselves — but they are merely *symptoms* of the real storm that is still gathering strength and preparing to hit land.

As the massive storm pushes the sea toward land, the swell of the waves grows higher and usually strikes the land *before* the devastating winds of the actual hurricane. When these rising tides hit the shore, everything in their path is in danger of being ravaged with catastrophic consequences.

Hurricanes consist of multiple belts of rain and wind that pound the land in sequence, one after another, with relatively brief pauses in between each violent phase. Individuals who are caught in the tempest but don't understand how hurricanes behave may wrongly assume that the storm is calming down after each belt passes. Yet more belts of rain and wind are inevitably on the way to strike with equal or even greater intensity.

When the eye of the storm arrives, the sky may appear blue and clear, giving the illusion that the storm has passed. In this brief moment of calm, some find a false sense of security in thinking the storm is over. Yet in reality, the fiercest impact of the entire storm system is still approaching — *on the backside of the eye wall as the hurricane continues to move inland.*

Some people mistakenly assume that the worst has passed during the eye of the storm. They emerge from their places of safety, not realizing that the hurricane is far from over, and consequently they place themselves in harm's way. Much of the physical and human loss in a hurricane results from people mistaking this temporary calm as a sign that the storm has passed. Because they misread the signs overhead, they face the full force of the hurricane's backside unprepared. Many get swept away in the ensuing floodwaters or hit with deadly debris that would have had no effect on them if they had stayed in a place of safety just a little longer.

Yet this is still not the full picture of a hurricane's impact. Another major outcome of hurricanes is the turbulent weather systems they create in their wake, which affect huge geographical regions. These storms often spawn tornadoes that angrily sweep across large swaths of land or produce torrential downpours that cause widespread, devastating floods and destroy homes, farmland, and buildings far from where the hurricane first struck land. By the time the storm system has run its course, hundreds or even thousands of square miles have been affected and many people have been displaced, have suffered damage to their personal property, or are missing or deceased.

I believe this accurately describes the various effects we may feel as we live in a tumultuous last-days environment. As we've seen from the Word of God, we are in the last of the last days, and the spiritual weather is becoming stormier and stormier. We know that according to the Holy Spirit's prophetic predictions, a spiritual storm will slam against society with devastating consequences at the very end of the age. There may be times when we think the worst has passed and that the storm is over — but the strongest winds are still on the horizon before us.

At times we will feel the full force of the turbulent spiritual winds, whereas at other times, it will feel like there has been a pause from pressure. This temporary pause will give the incorrect impression that the worst is over. But we must always keep in mind what the Holy Spirit has clearly prophesied: that a dramatic change in society will occur at the end of the age, which will cause the winds of opposition to rise up against the Church with serious consequences.

◆

According to the Holy Spirit's prophetic predictions, a spiritual storm will slam against society with devastating consequences at the very end of the age. There may be times when we think the worst has passed and that the storm is over — but the strongest winds are still on the horizon before us.

◆

As I told you at the beginning, this is why I have written this book. We must wake up and become spiritually prepared to not only survive, but to *thrive* during the stormy season that lies ahead as we sail through to the last port in this last-days season.

Just as a hurricane affects large geographical areas far from where it first hits land, the spiritual storm that will strike in these last days will affect large sections of society. In fact, according to the Holy Spirit, by the time this last part of the storm system has run its course, every part of the world will be affected.

Between now and the time of Jesus' triumphant return, society will race toward a cataclysmic collision with end-time events. Even now the spiritual climate is dramatically shifting. Yet you and I have been chosen by God to live in this crucial hour — and as part of His Church, we have a spiritual inheritance to lay hold of that will empower us to live as overcomers in the midst of the storm. As we listen to what the Holy Spirit is saying and prepare ourselves by standing on the promises of God's Word, we can expect to experience the empowering strength of the Spirit of might upholding us and seeing us through to victory in every situation.

**You and I have been chosen by God
to live in this crucial hour — and as part of His Church,
we have a spiritual inheritance to lay hold of
that will empower us to live as overcomers
in the midst of the storm.**

In the past chapters, we've studied the long list of all the signs that will characterize society in the last of the last days. One might be tempted to become alarmed or concerned as the weight of all that is being revealed hits home. But remember what I have emphasized throughout the pages of this book: The Holy Spirit's intent was never to *scare* us but only to *prepare* us. He pulled back the curtain of time and gave us a glimpse of what was to come in order to show us:

- How to overcome personally in the midst of it.

- How to protect ourselves and those we love.

- How to help others position themselves in a place of sustained victory in Christ in the midst of great peril and pain.

In Second Timothy 3:1-9, we've seen how Paul outlined the various types of turbulence that will be experienced by those of us who live in the last-days society. But as he kept writing, Paul also included a powerful reminder that we have everything we need — including every promise God has given us — to successfully make it through the rough waves of this season. So let's continue on to discover God's "navigational instruments" that He has provided for us to utilize so we can make it successfully to our ultimate destination without becoming a casualty of this age!

THE POWER OF A PERSONAL EXAMPLE

Paul gave instructions to Timothy that are also crucial to us because they provide God's divine solution for living victoriously in the midst of dark, negative events that many will face in the environment of the last days. After hearing what is coming in the future, Timothy may have wondered if he had the strength of spirit required to overcome in such a last-days stormy season. We may wonder the same thing about ourselves when we read Paul's words in Second Timothy 3.

But Paul backed up for a few moments and began to personally remind Timothy of how he himself had victoriously endured perilous times in his own life. Paul wanted the younger minister to take his personal example as proof that Timothy, as well as every other believer, could come through the most perilous of times victoriously.

Timothy had served closely alongside Paul for many years and had seen the Word of God and the power of the Holy Spirit sustain the apostle throughout many difficult circumstances. This is why Paul wrote to him, "But thou hast fully known my doctrine, manner of life, purpose, faith, longsuffering, charity, patience, persecutions, afflictions, which came unto me at Antioch, at Iconium, at Lystra; what persecutions I endured: but out of them all the Lord delivered me" (2 Timothy 3:10,11).

Paul used himself as the example to demonstrate how anyone can survive and even thrive in perilous times. The apostle knew that if he could be victorious in doing what he had done for the Kingdom, given the intensity of the battles he had faced, anyone could do the same. So drawing on his own personal example, Paul told Timothy, "But thou hast fully known..." (v. 10).

The words "fully known" are a translation of the word *parakoloutheo,* a word that depicts *one who has closely followed someone else with the intention to replicate his or her life.*

The first part of the word is from the Greek word *para*, which speaks of *closeness* and portrays the side-by-side relationship that Timothy enjoyed with Paul. By using this word, Paul emphatically reminded Timothy that from a very close proximity through many years, the younger man had been close enough to observe moments when Paul was assailed from without.

Timothy also witnessed how the apostle remarkably overcame in the midst of each one of those onslaughts time and time again. Paul used this word *parakoloutheo* to remind Timothy that he had closely observed how God's Word and the power of the Holy Spirit had been sufficient to empower, sustain, and give Paul, his mentor and spiritual example, the strength to overcome in every situation, regardless of the enormity of the challenge.

---◆---

**Paul used himself as the example to demonstrate
how anyone can survive and even thrive in perilous times.
The apostle knew that if he could be victorious
in doing what he had done for the Kingdom,
given the intensity of the battles he had faced,
anyone could do the same.**

---◆---

It's important to identify whom God has placed in your own life to fulfill this role of mentor and spiritual example, just as Paul filled that role in Timothy's life. So I suggest you take a moment to ask yourself these questions:

- *Is there anyone to whom I am close enough to observe this kind of personal victory in his life?*

- *Is there a leader whom I respect and admire so greatly that I'd want to emulate his example as an unwavering warrior in the fight of faith and endeavor to be like him in my own walk with Christ?*

- *Is there one certain leader producing the type of fruit in his life that I long to see generated in my own life?*

- *If so, who is that leader?*

You may wonder if it's right to follow someone so closely that you actually start emulating him or her. But the Bible is replete with scriptures that instruct us to be followers of spiritual leaders. One such instance is Hebrew 6:12: "That ye be not slothful, but followers of them who through faith and patience inherit the promises."

It's important to note that this scripture says we are to be "...*followers* of them who through faith and patience inherit the promises." The word "followers" is taken from the Greek word *mimetes*, from which we derive the English words "imitate," "mimic," and "mime." However, the best translation of this word is actually the word "actor."

Therefore, the command to "follow" isn't referring to a casual type of following. Rather, it implies an intentional study of the deeds, words, actions, and thoughts of another person (how that person thinks) in an attempt to fully understand that person and then to replicate his attributes in one's own life.

This type of focused, deliberate following enables a person to think like his subject, walk like his subject, mimic his subject's movements, make the vocal intonations of his subject, and act like his subject in a masterful way. However, this can only be achieved by those seriously committed to the act of *replication*.

Of course, in a serious disciple's commitment to act, mimic, or replicate a respected spiritual leader, his full focus is on replicating the leader's godly character and his walk with Christ. That is the process and the result of true discipleship. With all this in mind, we could actually translate this phrase: *"…But skillfully and convincingly act like those who through faith and patience inherit the promises."* In other words, the disciple is to do it in such a way that he too — through faith and patience — inherits the promises of God!

A good actor studies the character and life of another for the purpose of portraying that person on a stage or on film. In the process, the actor obtains every bit of information he possibly can about the person in order to better portray him in his acting role. Then the actor begins to practice acting just like that person — trying to talk like him, think like him, and even walk and dress like him. If the actor acts long enough and consistently enough, the character role he is playing can actually become a part of the actor's own identity. That's the power of acting!

---◆---

**In a serious disciple's commitment
to act, mimic, or replicate a respected spiritual leader,
his full focus is on replicating the leader's godly character
and his walk with Christ. That is the process
and the result of true discipleship.**

---◆---

It is for this very reason that Paul reminded Timothy, "But thou hast fully known...." The Greek actually means, *"You have followed closely in order to replicate my life."* Paul wanted to remind Timothy that the younger man had witnessed a good example and that if he would replicate what he had seen Paul do, he could have the same victorious results. And that principle applies today to anyone willing to "follow closely" so that he can "fully know."

Paul continued by reminding Timothy, "But thou hast fully known *my doctrine....*" The word "doctrine" is translated from the Greek word *didaskalia*. It depicts *teaching that is applicable to one's life.* Paul's doctrine — all of which was solidly founded on God's words as revealed to man — was not only theological, but it was also his very foundation and the reason he was able to overcome every circumstance. Doctrine — that is, what Paul believed, embraced, and acted upon — was the bedrock of his life.

In Matthew 7:24-27, Jesus spoke of this bedrock of eternal truth that is the essential foundation of every believer:

Therefore whosoever heareth these sayings of mine, and doeth them, I will liken him unto a wise man, which built his house upon a rock: And the rain descended, and the floods came, and the winds blew, and beat upon that house; and it fell not: for it was founded upon a rock. And every one that heareth these sayings of mine, and doeth them not, shall be likened unto a foolish man, which built his house upon the sand:

And the rain descended, and the floods came, and the winds blew, and beat upon that house; and it fell: and great was the fall of it.

Jesus warned that rain, floods, and winds *will* come in life. But if a person has built his life upon the solid foundation of God's Word, he can survive any storm, because all that he is and possesses is built on that immovable rock.

On the other hand, if a person has built his life on a bad foundation, it is like building a house on sinking sand. When the rains, floods, and winds come to beat upon that person's life, he will experience great loss because his shaky faith won't be sufficient to hold him in place.

———◆———

**Jesus warned that rain, floods, and winds *will* come in life.
But if a person has built his life upon the solid foundation
of God's Word, he can survive any storm,
because all that he is and possesses
is built on that immovable rock.**

———◆———

But if your faith is built on solid rock, you can withstand *any* storm. That is the importance of having right and wrong doctrine in your life!

Paul's doctrine — what he believed — was so powerful and rock-solid that it held him through every circumstance in life, enabling him to withstand all the rains, floods, and winds that came against him. In his epistle, he reminded Timothy of this truth to encourage the young man that those who have a rock-solid faith can outlast any storm. That is why Paul said to Timothy, *"You know my doctrine."* He wanted Timothy to be reassured that his rock-solid faith had carried him through — and that it would carry anyone through who is established on such a foundation. For those living in perilous times, this is a very important message!

But Paul next reminded Timothy, "But thou hast fully known my doctrine, *manner of life....*"

The words "manner of life" are translated from the Greek word *agoge*, which is used by Paul to depict how he had *conducted himself* in various experiences in life. The use of this word lets us know that there were no secrets between Paul and Timothy and that Timothy had been close enough to personally witness the effect of Paul's doctrine in the way he lived and in the way he had braved multiple perils in his own life. As a close observer and pupil, Timothy was near enough to Paul to see how his leader's faith and doctrine carried him victoriously through every imaginable kind of situation. By using the words "manner of life," Paul was in essence saying, *"Timothy, the proof of my doctrine is evident in the way I have lived my life and have victoriously survived everything I have faced."*

Paul then added, "But thou hast fully known my doctrine, manner of life, *purpose....*"

The word "purpose" is a translation of the word *prothesis*, which depicts *a purposeful plan*. This lets us know that Paul's life had not been happenstance; rather, he had lived very purposefully. Paul knew he was born for a purpose and had consecrated his life to the fulfillment of that divine plan. Regardless of the bumps he encountered along the way, the apostle had held fast to the vision God had given him (*see* Acts 26:19). Paul reminded Timothy that if *he* could stay steadfast and on track with his God-given assignment and purpose, then Timothy — and anyone else — could do it too.

Then Paul went on to write, "But thou hast fully known my doctrine, manner of life, purpose, *faith....*" The word "faith" is the Greek word *pistis*, and the very nature of this Greek word for "faith" implies *a powerful force that is forward-directed and never in retreat*. Paul was telling Timothy that his own faith was aggressive and always forward-directed. The apostle possessed such a powerful faith that he had never retreated or surrendered. On the contrary, he had continued to press forward, regardless of opposition and even in the face of multiple assaults orchestrated against him.

———◆———

**Paul knew he was born for a purpose
and had consecrated his life to the fulfillment of that divine plan.
Regardless of the bumps he encountered along the way,
the apostle had held fast to the vision
God had given him.**

———◆———

Because Timothy was so close to Paul, the younger man had personally observed this unbendable and unbreakable faith in his mentor. Paul reminded Timothy how he had seen faith work in his own life and then stressed that the same faith would enable Timothy — or anyone else who put their trust in Christ — to make it through any season of life.

Paul continued, "But thou hast fully known my doctrine, manner of life, purpose, faith, *longsuffering*...." In the apostle's ministry, he had seen many people do things that disappointed him. But rather than let it sour him, Paul had supernaturally been able to extend *longsuffering* to others, even in the face of disappointment. Timothy had been close enough to his mentor to see the demonstration of this quality on many occasions, so Paul reminded him that God's power was enough to sustain him, even if others failed him or did things that were disappointing to him.

The word "longsuffering" is a translation of the Greek word *makrothumia*, which depicts *the patient restraint of anger*. It can be translated *forbearance* or *patience*. Longsuffering is likened to a candle with a very long wick that can burn an extended period of time. A person who possesses this quality is ready to *forbear* and *to suffer long* as he *patiently waits* for an event or result to transpire.

Paul used his own example to tell Timothy that, when it comes to fulfilling the will of God for one's life, it doesn't matter what other people do or what disappointments may come in relationships. Regardless of those factors, each person is faced with the choice to surrender to the Holy Spirit. As Timothy made that right choice, he would be sustained by the powerful fruit of longsuffering.

**When it comes to fulfilling the will of God for one's life,
it doesn't matter what other people do
or what disappointments may come in relationships.
Regardless of those factors, each person is faced with the choice
to surrender to the Holy Spirit.**

What a powerful message for those who will live in the last of the last days and who may see many people commit acts that are far below their expectation of them!

Paul next reminded Timothy, "But thou hast fully known my doctrine, manner of life, purpose, faith, longsuffering, *charity....*"

The word "charity" is a *King James Version* translation of the Greek word *agape*, which is actually the New Testament word for *the love of God*. It depicts *a love that gives even if it's never responded to, thanked, or acknowledged. It knows no limits or boundaries in how far, wide, high, and deep it will go to show that love to its recipient.* It is a *self-sacrificial love that moves one to action.*

Paul reminded Timothy that this was the type of love that had worked in his life and in many different circumstances. It is certain that in Paul's own ministry, others had failed him and responded in ways that were below his expectation of them. But because *agape* love worked so profoundly in Paul's life, he was able to keep on loving, even when his actions of love were not responded to, thanked, or acknowledged.

Divine love knows no limits or boundaries in how far, wide, high, and deep it will go to show that love to its recipient. It was that kind of love that enabled Paul to be self-sacrificial for others.

In the last days when society — and even many in the Church — will be prone to be selfish and self-seeking, it is imperative that we learn to function in this type of high-level love. Paul reminded Timothy that if he, Paul, could love even difficult and disappointing people, Timothy could too. And the same is true for you and me!

Divine love knows no limits or boundaries in how far, wide, high, and deep it will go to show that love to its recipient. It was that kind of love that enabled Paul to be self-sacrificial for others.

Paul further wrote in Second Timothy 3:10, "But thou hast fully known my doctrine, manner of life, purpose, faith, longsuffering, charity, *patience....*" The word "patience" is an unfortunate translation of the Greek word *hupomone* which would be better translated "endurance." It pictures *the ability to stay or to remain in one's spot; the ability to keep a steadfast position;* or *the attitude of one who has resolved to maintain territory that has been gained at any cost.*

In a military sense, this word *hupomone* was used to picture *soldiers who were ordered to maintain their positions even in the face of fierce combat*. It means *to defiantly stick it out, regardless of the pressure mounted against the one who is holding fast.* Hence, it pictures *staying power* or *"hang-in-there" power. It is the attitude that holds out, holds on, outlasts, perseveres, and hangs in there, never giving up, refusing to surrender to obstacles, and turning down every opportunity to quit.* It pictures *one who is under a heavy load but refuses to bend, break, or surrender because he is convinced that the territory, promise, or principle under assault rightfully belongs to him.*

Paul faced unremitting persecution. Every day he and many other believers were confronted by hostile powers that were arrayed against them. Culture, pagan religion, government, unsaved family and friends — all these forces were arrayed against them, putting constant pressure on them to forfeit their faith and return to their old ways.

I want to point out that the Early Church called this type of "patience" the "queen of all virtues." Early Christians believed if they possessed this one virtue, they could survive anything that ever came against them. It is this same virtue that is sustaining believers today who live in godless regions of the world — and this virtue is exactly what *you* need to victoriously outlast the pressures and ordeals you may be dealing with today.

The determination inherent in the word *hupomone* is clearly seen when it was used in a military sense to picture soldiers who were ordered to maintain their positions even in the face of fierce combat. Their order was *to stand their ground and defend what had been gained.* To keep that ground, they had to be courageous to do whatever was required — *no matter how difficult or long-lasting the assignment.* Their goal was to see that they survived every attack and held their position until they had outlived and outlasted the resistance. These soldiers had to indefinitely and defiantly stick it out until the enemy forces realized those soldiers couldn't be beaten, thus deciding to retreat and go elsewhere.

Although the *King James Version* translates this Greek word *hupomone* as "patience," a more accurate rendering would be "endurance." Two accurate ways to translate the word in our modern vernacular would be *staying power* or *hang-in-there power*. Both of these translations adequately express the correct idea about *hupomone* — because this is an attitude that never gives up! It *holds out*, *holds on*, *outlasts*, and *perseveres*.

The Early Church called patience the "queen of all virtues" for good reason. Believers knew that as long as they had this character quality working in their lives, it wasn't a question of *if* they would win their battles — it was only a question of *when*.

Hupomone — that is, *endurance, staying power, hang-in-there power* — is one of the major weapons you can wield to outlast any difficulty or time of stress and pressure that comes your way.

◆

**The Early Church called patience
the "queen of all virtues" for good reason.
Believers knew that as long as they had this character quality
working in their lives, it wasn't a question of
if they would win their battles —
it was only a question of *when*.**

◆

Paul reminded Timothy that if he as his leader could walk in this supernatural force in *his* day and time, so could Timothy — and so can anyone else. Especially for those of us who live at the end of the age, it is imperative that we possess and walk in this unbeatable force!

Then continuing on in Second Timothy 3:11, Paul wrote, "Persecutions, afflictions, which came unto me at Antioch, at Iconium, at Lystra; what persecutions I endured: but out of them all the Lord delivered me."

The word "persecutions" is a translation of the Greek word *diogmos*, which is a derivative of the word *dioko*, a hunting term that denoted *the actions of a hunter who strives to follow after, to apprehend, to capture, or to kill an animal.* It means to *strategically hunt* or *pursue* an individual or a group of people. It depicts *a well-planned strategy to track down in order to abuse, hurt, or apprehend.* Paul used this word to remind Timothy (and us) that much of what happened to the apostle had been the intentional evil devices of people who wanted to do him harm. The word "persecutions" — the Greek word *diogmos* — affirms that people had intentionally tried to harm Paul along the way.

Furthermore, Paul added the word "afflictions" to this statement about persecutions. The word "afflictions" is a translation of the Greek word *pathema*, a word that depicts all types of *suffering* but really speaks of *emotional struggles* or *mental agony* as a result of circumstances or what others have done. The use of this word means that circumstances and even other people had put Paul through a lot of emotional and mental grief. Nonetheless, it had all passed and he had remained unaffected, secure in the love of God and possessing a sound mind in spite of it all.

What a powerful testimony! If Paul could remain unaffected when difficult circumstances or opposition arose from without, that means anyone can remain unaffected. This is a strong and pertinent message for those of us who live in perilous times and who may feel let down and disappointed by people who we believed were with us or for us!

That word "endured" is a translation of the Greek word *hupophero*, which is a compound of *hupo* and *phero*. The word *hupo* means *under*, and the word *phero* means *to bear*. When compounded, the new word means *to bear up under as one who is under a heavy load*. However, it is used to depict a strong undercurrent of a river that carries one downstream to a place of safety and away from danger.

Although Paul had experienced many negative assaults, the power of God had always transported him along safely to his next destination. In fact, when Paul was referring to all the things he had faced and overcome, he declared, "…Out of them all the Lord delivered me." (2 Timothy 3:11). The word "out" in Greek is the word *ek*, which depicts an *exit* or an *escape* from difficult circumstances. The word "all" is all-encompassing. This was Paul's declaration — that he had *escaped* from *every single event* as the Lord miraculously "delivered" him.

The word "delivered" comes from the Greek word *hruomai*, a word that means *to rescue, to deliver, to snatch or even to drag out of danger*, or *to save in the nick of time*. This depicts *an intervention* or *a rescue operation intended to snatch a person out of physical or spiritual peril*.

Paul's message was clear — that if *he* could experience such delivering power time and time again, that same power will work for anyone who will believe it and embrace it. As Timothy read Paul's dreadful litany of societal ills that would develop in the last days, the younger minister possibly would have wondered how anyone would be able to escape it all unharmed. This, then, led to Paul's declaration that God's intervening and delivering power will work for *anyone* who is willing to cooperate with it.

**Although Paul had experienced
many negative assaults, the power of God
had always transported him along safely
to his next destination.**

That's God's promise to those of us who have been chosen to live in this last-days perilous period. We can expect to experience His delivering power and to escape the negative effects of a last-days stormy season!

This, of course, doesn't mean the devil won't *try* to affect us. He will do his best to drag the entire world and even the Church into his snare. Paul was open-eyed about the devil's attempts to attack even the godly. This is why the apostle went on to write, "Yea, and all that will live godly in Christ Jesus shall suffer persecution" (2 Timothy 3:12).

The words "shall suffer persecution" is a future form of *dioko*, which is again the hunting term to denote the actions of a hunter who strives to *follow after, capture,* or *kill* an animal, and depicts a well-planned strategy to *track down in order to abuse, hurt, or apprehend.* This lets us know that Paul was not naïve about the devil's tactics. He forewarned Timothy — and those of us who live at the end of the age — that there would be hardships to endure before it is all over. But just as Paul was supernaturally aided by the delivering power of God, we will also experience His intervening power in our lives if we will stay on track and refuse to be moved by what we feel, hear, or see.

THE POWER OF STAYING ON TRACK

After Paul reminded Timothy of how God's Word and power had always sustained him in the past and never failed him, the apostle went on to explain the necessary requirement for overcoming in any season of life. In Second Timothy 3:14, Paul wrote, "But continue thou in the things which thou hast learned and hast been assured of, knowing of whom thou hast learned them."

The word "continue" is a translation of the Greek word *meno*, which means to be *unwavering* and *unmoving.* It depicts *a resolute decision to remain steadfast* and pictures *one who refuses to budge even in the face of pressure.* It describes *one who holds his ground even to the point of fighting back* and projects the idea of *one who firmly endures and is immovable, unshakable, and consistent in what he believes.* By using this word, Paul instructed Timothy — and you and me — to *continue* in what we believe and to resolve that regardless of what is happening around us, we will not change our positions or abdicate our faith when it comes to what the Bible teaches!

◆

**Just as Paul was supernaturally aided
by the delivering power of God, we will also experience
His intervening power in our lives if we will stay on track
and refuse to be moved by what we feel, hear, or see.**

◆

As you will see in the paragraphs that follow, something significant happens when a believer holds fast to the Word of God like that and consistently continues in it. That strict adherence to the Word of God is the trigger that releases the power of God into the life of that believer. Paul knew this, which is why he urged Timothy to "continue in the things thou hast learned."

The words "thou hast learned" is a form of the Greek word *manthano*, a word that depicts *a relationship between a pupil and his teacher*. Since Paul had been Timothy's teacher, he used this word to remind Timothy of his relationship with him. The apostle then added, "But continue thou in the things which thou hast learned and hast been assured of, knowing of whom thou hast learned them." The words "hast been assured of" is a form of *pistoo*, a Greek word that refers to something that a person has found to be *irrefutably reliable, true, trustworthy*, and *worthy of being established* in one's life.

Paul reminded Timothy, "knowing of whom thou hast learned them." The words "of whom" are translated from the word *para*, and it depicts the *close relationship* that existed between Paul and Timothy. The word "learned" is again *manthano*, the Greek word that pictures the relationship between a pupil and his teacher. Paul reminded Timothy that everything the younger man knew about faith, he had learned as a pupil walking alongside the apostle himself. Through Timothy's up-close observation of Paul's life, he had seen that these principles and truths were irrefutably reliable, true, trustworthy, and worthy of being established in his own life.

The *RIV* of Second Timothy 3:14 reads as follows:

But you continue consistently, firmly, steadfastly, and unmoving in the things you learned at my side as a pupil. By your close observation of me and my life, you know for a fact that what you've been taught is unequivocally true, reliable, and worth being incorporated into your own life. You saw all of this in me, and as a result of your close, up-front observation of my life, you know it is true.

In addition to Paul's powerful role and influence in Timothy's life, Timothy had also been powerfully influenced by a godly mother. In Second Timothy 3:15, Paul wrote, "And that from a child thou hast known the holy scriptures, which are able to make thee wise unto salvation through faith which is in Christ Jesus."

The word "child" in this verse is translated from the Greek word *brephos*, a word that pictures *an infant* or *a child who is still nursing at his mother's breast*. From the record in Acts 16:1, we know that Timothy's mother was a Jewish woman who had come to faith in Christ. Apparently she had become a Christian either before Timothy was born or when he was "still nursing at his mother's breast." Taking advantage of his tender and teachable age, his mother schooled Timothy in the "holy Scriptures" from the time he was an infant.

Paul reminded Timothy that even when he was a nursing child, his mother gave him a heavy dose of respect for the "holy Scriptures." This shows the important role that a godly mother plays even in the life of a babe in her arms.

The words "holy Scriptures" in Greek is *hiera grammata*. The word *hiera* comes from the root word *hieros* and describes something that is *sacred, set apart,* or *holy.* It is the word used in the Old Testament Septuagint to describe the *sacred, consecrated,* and *set apart* instruments that were used in various elements of Old Testament temple ritual and worship. Once those manmade instruments were consecrated, they were considered sacred and placed in a holy category — forever *set apart,* never to be used again for common purposes.

The word "scriptures" is translated from the word *grammata,* which is the plural of the Greek word *gramma.* The word *gramma* depicts not only every letter of the alphabet, but it also includes even the marks above or below each letter, along with every tiny jot or mark in the text. All the ink on the page falls into the category of the word *gramma.*

By using the word *grammata,* Paul let us know that every letter, character, jot, and mark — even the smallest scribble in the Bible, and, in fact, all the ink on every page — is holy, sacred, and filled with the awesome and remarkable power of God. We also learn that Timothy had been taught to believe this truth ever since he was an infant.

Paul further added that these amazing, awesome, remarkable Scriptures are so powerful that they "are able to make thee wise unto salvation." The phrase "which are able" is translated from the word *dunamis,* which is the very specific Greek word for *power* and carries the idea of *explosive, superhuman power that comes with enormous energy and produces phenomenal, extraordinary, and unparalleled results.*

**Even the smallest scribble in the Bible,
and, in fact, all the ink on every page — is holy, sacred,
and filled with the awesome and remarkable power of God.**

But wait — the word *dunamis* is also the very word used to depict *the full might of an advancing army*. In this verse, Paul intentionally used this word to let us know that when the Bible is believed and embraced and its power is released into a person's life, it produces powerful, impressive, incomparable, and "beyond human" results. The Holy Scriptures are so powerful that when the door to one's heart is opened and God's words are given a grand reception, the power in those divine words is released to march forth like an advancing army that drives back every trace of evil and takes new territory for God's rule in a person's life!

In fact, Paul says the supernatural ability inherent in the Scriptures has the power to make one "wise" unto salvation. The word "wise" is a translation of the Greek word *sophidzo*, which depicts the process required to obtain *special insight*.

When used in a non-biblical context, this word *sophos* portrayed highly educated people, such as scientists, philosophers, doctors, teachers, and others who were considered to be the super-intelligentsia of society. It depicts a class of individuals whom the world would call intellectually brilliant, sharp, clever, astute, smart, or especially enlightened. It described those considered to be intellectually impressive and a cut above the rest of society. Paul intentionally used this word to affirm that when the Scriptures are believed, embraced, and acted upon, they have the power to transform someone to become wise, even intellectually a cut above the rest of society!

◆

**The Holy Scriptures are so powerful that when the door
to one's heart is opened and God's words are given
a grand reception, the power in those divine words
is released to march forth like an advancing army
that drives back every trace of evil and takes
new territory for God's rule in a person's life!**

◆

But Paul specifically said wise "unto salvation." Even the word "unto" is important in this verse. It is translated from the Greek word *eis*, which gives the idea of something that is *progressive*. The more a person embraces the Scriptures, the more he will progress forward "into" the fullness of all that salvation is intended to be. The word "salvation" is translated from the Greek word *soteria*. It depicts not only *eternal salvation*, but *present deliverance and wholeness in every part of life.*

This means the Bible itself contains the saving and delivering power of God. And if you'll believe it, embrace it, and act upon it, the latent power in His words will be released to cause you to progressively experience more and more deliverance, healing, and wholeness in every area of your life!

We've seen that in the last of the last days, people's lives will be assaulted, twisted, and negatively affected by the moral craziness that grips a wandering society. But this is the hope that God presents to us: that even in the midst of such perilous times, any person who has been negatively affected can be restored if he or she will believe, embrace, and act on the Holy Scriptures! His delivering, healing, miraculous power that is resident in His Word is ready to be released into the life of *any* person who will simply believe, embrace, and act on what He has said.

---◆---

**The Bible itself contains
the saving and delivering power of God.
And if you'll believe it, embrace it, and act upon it,
the latent power in His words will be released
to cause you to progressively experience more and more
deliverance, healing, and wholeness in every area of your life!**

---◆---

THE POWER OF GOD IN THE SCRIPTURES

This is why Paul made his next statement in Second Timothy 3:16,17: "For all scripture is given by inspiration of God, and is profitable for doctrine, for reproof, for correction, for instruction in righteousness: that the man of God may be thoroughly furnished unto all good works."

The word "inspiration" is translated from the Greek compound word *theopneustos, a* compound of the Greek words *theos*, which means *God*, and *pneuo*, which is where we derive the words *spirit* or *breath*. When compounded, the new word means *God-breathed*. However, there is *much, much more* to this word that you absolutely *must* understand. The following paragraphs will help you grasp the truth that God's presence is actually *held inside* the Scriptures — to be unlocked and experienced by anyone who is willing to dive deep into them.

---◆---

**God's presence is actually *held inside* the Scriptures —
to be unlocked and experienced by anyone
who is willing to dive deep into them.**

---◆---

THE *CREATIVITY* OF HEAVEN

Let's focus on the Greek word *pneuo* for a moment. It is the foundation for the word *pneuma*, which is the word used in the Old Testament Greek Septuagint to describe the *creative power* that God released to create the world and to make Adam a living soul.

The word *pneuma* carries a profound range of meanings, including *life, force, life-force, energy, dynamism, and power*. The Jews considered the *pneuma* to be the *powerful force* of God that created the universe and all living things — and the *force that continues to sustain creation*. In the Old Testament, the *pneuma* of God would sometimes move mightily upon a person, *enabling* him to do supernatural feats.

Indeed, this word *pneuma* is the very word used in Genesis 1:2, where we are told that the Holy Spirit brooded upon the face of the deep and then released creative power to bring order to the chaos that covered the face of the earth at that time. When the *pneuma* of God was released in that moment, such a torrent of creative power was released that restoration came into the world in a split second of time. Unimaginable levels of divine and creative power were unleashed in that instant when the *pneuma* of God moved upon the face of the deep!

The Greek word *pneuma* is also the word used in the Old Testament Septuagint to describe that moment when God *breathed* into Adam, and, in a split second, the man became a living soul (*see* Genesis 2:7). Adam lay on the ground, perfectly formed, but had no life in him. Until he was touched by the creative *pneuma* of God, he was little more than a mannequin made of clay. But when God's *pneuma* — that is, His creative power — entered into Adam's nostrils, the man was awakened to become a living soul.

So in both instances in the opening chapters of Genesis, we discover that the word *pneuma* is used to depict the creative power of God and the breath of the Almighty that gives life! Keep this in mind as you recall everything Paul wrote about in Second Timothy 3. In this prophetic chapter that we've been studying, Paul clearly enumerated all the dark, malevolent characteristics that will mark the last of the last days.

The *pneuma* of God moved upon the earth with creative power to restore a world that had become chaotic. In a similar fashion, the last-days society will be full of people who have been traumatized and wounded and who desperately need the *pneuma* of God.

When the *pneuma* of God that is locked inside the Scriptures is believed, embraced, and acted upon, its latent creative powers are unleashed to bring restoration to anyone who has been negatively affected by life. And even if a person feels numb as a result of chaotic and hurtful life experiences, the divine *pneuma* of God that is resident in the Scriptures has the power to revive that numbed soul to become a living, thriving soul once again!

As mentioned earlier, this word *pneuma* is a form of the word *pneuo*, which is used in the word *theopneustos* to describe the "inspiration of God" in connection with the Scriptures. This lets us know that *creative power* is contained in every page and in every mark of ink contained in the written Word of God.

So when the Bible tells us that all Scripture was given by "inspiration of God," it's telling us beyond all doubt that Scripture itself carries within it the very *creative power* and nature of God Himself!

---◆---

**Even if a person feels numb
as a result of chaotic and hurtful life experiences,
the divine *pneuma* of God that is resident in the Scriptures
has the power to revive that numbed soul
to become a living, thriving soul once again!**

---◆---

THE *MUSIC* OF HEAVEN

But wait — there is still more to this Greek word *pneuo* that you must understand. The word *pneuo* also communicates the concept of *the dynamic movement of air.* For instance, it can mean *to blow,* as *to blow air* or *to blow air through an instrument to produce a distinct musical sound.*

For example, in ancient times when a musician wanted to play a musical instrument, such as a pipe or flute, he would lift the instrument to his lips and *breathe into it* to produce a musical sound. The breath he breathed into that musical instrument was called *pneuo,* which is the same word we are looking at right now.

Although the musical instrument was perfectly formed, it was unable to produce beautiful music by itself. The instrument was totally dependent on the breath of a musician in order to come alive and produce the sound of beautiful music. If there was no breath, there was no musical sound to be enjoyed. But if a musician lifted that instrument to his lips and breathed into it, suddenly it would begin to produce melodious sounds for hearers to enjoy. The mere breath of the musician could change an atmosphere when breathed into a pipe or flute.

The word *pneuo* is the Greek word that describes a musician's breath when breathed into a pipe or flute. But here in Second Timothy 3:16, Paul used this word to describe God's musical presence in the Scriptures!

Just as a musician would blow into an instrument to produce a distinct sound, God's Spirit mightily moved on those who wrote the Scriptures. And in those divine moments, these individuals temporarily became the instruments through whom God expressed His heart and His will. They were the writers, but God was the Great Musician who, over centuries of time, breathed upon each one, His chosen instruments. It was in this way that the Bible became God's message delivered through human writers to you and me.

And today, in the same way, the Word of God can still release the sounds of Heaven into your life. When the breath of God in the Scriptures is received, embraced, and acted upon, that *pneuma* can begin to produce beautiful, new sounds in your life that supersede all the old sounds you've been hearing.

Perhaps you are tired of the mood swings and the unpleasant sounds that swirl around at times in your head, your life, or your home. If so, know that it can all be changed in a moment as you unlock the music of Heaven that lies "latent" inside your Bible, releasing the power of God's unchangeable Word through your own mouth!

**The Word of God can still release
the sounds of Heaven into your life.
When the breath of God in the Scriptures
is received, embraced, and acted upon,
that *pneuma* can begin to produce beautiful, new sounds
in your life that supersede
all the old sounds you've been hearing.**

This means depression can go, mood swings can be positively changed, and the unpleasant sounds in your life or home can be altered! You just have to tap in to the power of God that is resident in your Bible and bring that power into your private space through the words of faith in His Word coming through your own heart and mouth.

If you will unlock and release God's Spirit — His *pneuo* that is locked inside the Scriptures — He will change the sounds in your life completely, and you will be invaded with the sounds of Heaven!

THE *FRAGRANCE* OF HEAVEN

But there are also places where the word *pneuo* is used in ancient Greek literature to depict *a fragrance*. We can deduce, then, that just as the *pneuo* of God can change the sounds in our lives, it can also change the "odors" in the atmosphere around us! And because the word *pneuo* can carry this idea of *a fragrance*, we can know that the Word of God also holds within it *the fragrance* of Heaven.

If you are tired of the "stink" in your life — in your home, your relationships, or any other area — know that it can all be changed. When you receive, embrace, and act on the Scriptures, your obedience will unleash the fragrance and aroma of Heaven in every area of your life.

People buy a lot of difference fragrances for their homes, yet their Bibles sit untouched and unopened. But the truth is, nothing will change the "odors" of wrong words and attitudes and of stale, carnal living in their homes more quickly than opening the Word of God and acting on it. That Word — once received, embraced, and acted upon — releases heavenly fragrances to replace the foul smell of strife, frustration, and carnality that have lingered too long in people's lives.

◆

**Nothing will change the "odors"
of wrong words and attitudes and of stale, carnal living
in people's homes more quickly than opening
the Word of God and acting on it.**

◆

What I want you to see is that the *breath* of God is resident within the Scriptures! That means God's *creative* and *restorative power*, *the music of Heaven*, and the *perfume* or *aroma* of Heaven are all locked up inside your Bible. If you find yourself lacking in *any* area, you can release the Word of God — which is infused with the very breath of God — into your life.

- The *creative ability* of God is available to you through His Word to change situations and circumstances.

- When you bring the Scriptures into your home and speak them out of your own mouth, they bring the *music* of Heaven into that place.

- If you will release the Word of God into a situation that's "stinking," the *perfume* of Heaven will eradicate the smell of whatever it is you're dealing with.

The very atmosphere and conditions of your home, your marriage, your children, your health, and your finances can be changed through the breath of God contained in the Scriptures and released through your mouth!

All of this can be found in this word *pneuo*, the Greek word translated "inspiration" in Second Timothy 3:16. All Scripture is given by inspiration of God — which means *the very breath of God Himself* is inside the Bible!

By the Spirit of God, Paul was speaking to us today — to the generation who would be living in the last of the last days on earth just before Jesus returns. Paul was telling us that the very *creative power*, the *music* of Heaven, and the *aroma* of Heaven itself can invade our lives and utterly change what we experience in our time on this earth from this moment on!

◆

**The very *creative power*, the *music* of Heaven,
and the *aroma* of Heaven itself can invade our lives
and utterly change what we experience
in our time on this earth from this moment on!**

◆

THE EXAMPLE OF A BALLOON

Let me give you another illustration to demonstrate the power contained in the Scriptures. Suppose you have a balloon that has never been inflated. If you pick up that balloon and begin to blow air into it, it will begin to take shape, and eventually the balloon will assume a new form. If you continue to blow more air into the balloon, little by little it will continue to expand and grow bigger and bigger.

In a similar way, God took human language and lifted it to His lips and began to breathe into it in order to impart divine revelation to mankind. And just as a balloon expands a little at a time as a person continues to breathe into it, God continued to breathe revelation into the hearts of men chosen for the task, little by little over vast periods of time. And the Scriptures continued to grow larger — until finally a moment came when the Old and the New Testaments were complete.

To expound on my balloon illustration a bit, I want you to imagine someone lifting a balloon to his lips and blowing into it to inflate or expand it. Once he is finished, he ties a knot at the opening of that balloon so that it retains its shape.

But let's think a minute about the contents of that expanded balloon. At first, you might say it is filled with air. But upon deeper examination, you would find that it holds much more than mere air. Something else besides air is trapped inside — the very breath of the person who blew into it. In fact, if you were to have the contents inside that balloon scientifically analyzed, you'd find the DNA of that person's breath. The balloon would contain the *very substance* of the person who breathed into it!

In much the same way, when God took human language and lifted it to His lips, He breathed on the writers as they wrote and the Scriptures began to take form. That's what Paul meant when he wrote that the Bible was given to us by the *inspiration*, or the *breath*, of God Himself.

Initially man had only the first five books of the Bible. But then God began to breathe His revelation into the hearts of other individuals ordained to record what they heard — and man's knowledge of God grew broader. God then breathed again and again upon the prophets of the Old Testament, and revelation continued to expand. Again God breathed, and His inspired words were penned by chosen writers of the First Century to reveal and unfold the New Covenant, purchased by the redemptive act of His Son.

**When God took human language and lifted it to His lips,
He breathed on the writers as they wrote
and the Scriptures began to take form.**

Through the years, the knowledge of God kept growing and growing and growing — much like a balloon expanding to its fullest capacity. Finally, God breathed upon the man named the apostle John, and the book of the Bible ordained to be the last was written. The divine gift of the Holy Scriptures to man had been completed, at which point God "tied a knot on the end of the balloon." From that moment till today, mankind has possessed a Book that isn't just human words *about* God — *it actually contains the very presence of God Almighty!*

This means every one of *God's* words carries the *creative power*, the *perfume*, and the *music* of Heaven. When we release these words into our lives and act on them, they bring dynamic change into our homes, our families, our churches, our jobs, etc.

Just as a person ties a knot in the bottom of a balloon to trap the air when he finishes inflating it, God "tied a knot" on the end when He finished breathing out revelation that was destined to be contained in the Scriptures. And just as a balloon is filled with the DNA of the person who used his breath to inflate the balloon, the Scriptures — the Word of God — are filled with the divine breath of God.

This means the Bible is not just a book like any other book; *the Bible is a book that actually contains God Himself!*

Do you really grasp the magnitude of this? God didn't just breathe *on* the Scriptures — He breathed *into* them. God is *in* the Bible — His life and substance and all that He is in power, creativity, music, and fragrance. *God Himself* is contained in the pages of the Bible! That's why it's such a shame that people have Bibles all over their homes — in the bathroom, in the kitchen, in their bedroom, and even in their car — yet they don't pick up their Bible to read it and unlock the powerful presence of God that resides within!

When God breathed out the Scriptures, every word, every paragraph — *every part of it* — was infused with His divine presence. There's not a word in the Bible that is void of the presence and power of God. And by meditating on and studying God's Word, we begin to release the presence of God that is in the Bible directly into our lives.

◆

**God didn't just breathe *on* the Scriptures —
He breathed *into* them. God is *in* the Bible —
His life and substance and all that He is in power,
creativity, music, and fragrance. *God Himself*
is contained in the pages of the Bible!**

◆

This is why I teach the Scriptures verse by verse and even word by word. Every word, every character, every jot and tittle (*see* Matthew 5:17) in the

Scriptures is filled with divine power — because God Himself is contained inside the Bible.

This is also why Satan takes such a fierce stand against the Bible. The devil is adamantly opposed to the propagation of the Bible because he knows its power. Satan knows that anyone who takes hold of *this* Book — who reads it, receives it, meditates on it, and acts on it — will experience the very life and being of God impacting his or her life for good.

You rarely hear of groups trying to remove the books of other religions from public schools — because the devil doesn't care whether those books are propagated. There's no life of God resident in those works. They contain no power to transform human life and thereby threaten the enemy's kingdom.

**The devil is adamantly opposed to the propagation
of the Bible because he knows its power.
Satan knows that anyone who takes hold of this Book —
who reads it, receives it, meditates on it, and acts on it —
will experience the very life and being of God
impacting his or her life for good.**

And it doesn't matter the condition of the society you live in. When the Word of God is working in you, it will heal you, remove the hidden scars in your soul, and undo anything that a calloused world or society has done to you. What a word for us to claim, especially for us who are living at the end of an age that is destined to be known as perilous times!

The Word of God carries creative, restorative power that can deliver us from every power of darkness and infuse our lives with the music and aroma of Heaven. Everything we need is in God's Word. If we would simply unlock it and release what's in it, it would supply answers to every problem we face and provision for every one of our needs.

When Paul wrote that "all scripture is given by inspiration of God," he was reminding Timothy — and every believer till the end of the age — that if a person has the Bible, he possesses the greatest source of life-giving power and energy that exists in this earthly realm! A person simply needs to delve into the Word — tapping deeply into its internal resources and allowing the life of God in it to flow up, out, and into every part of his being. And in that moment, enough divine power will be released to change what needs to be changed in that person and in any difficult situation he is facing.

◆

**Everything we need is in God's Word.
If we would simply unlock it and release what's in it,
it would supply answers to every problem we face
and provision for every one of our needs.**

◆

THE MIRACULOUS POTENTIAL
OF THE HOLY SCRIPTURES

Next, we will see that Paul listed all the ways that the Scriptures will bring benefits to the one who receives it, embraces it, acts on it, and taps into its inherent power. In Second Timothy 3:16, Paul stated, "All scripture is given by inspiration of God, and is profitable for doctrine, for reproof, for correction, for instruction in righteousness, that the man of God may be thoroughly furnished unto all good works."

It is essential to understand the meaning of the word "profitable" in this verse. It is a translation of the Greek word *ophelimos*, which is a word that has multiple meanings, including something that is *an absolute requirement, essential, mandatory,* or *obligatory* and, if embraced, will be *beneficial, profitable,* and to one's *advantage.*

This word *ophelimos* categorically tells us that God's Word must be viewed as being an absolute requirement, essential and mandatory in one's life. Furthermore, anyone who believes it, embraces it, and acts upon it will experience immeasurable benefits that are to his or her advantage. Because the Bible actually contains God's presence and power, it is loaded with supernatural and divine benefits.

As already noted, it can release the creative power of God into any person's chaotic life or situation. It has the ability to replace discordant sounds in any person's life or situation with the sounds of Heaven. It can supernaturally release the fragrance of Heaven to replace any stinking smell in a person's life or situation.

But for these wonderful benefits to be realized, the Bible must be embraced as *ophelimos — an absolute requirement, essential, mandatory,* and *obligatory.*

Paul then specifically stated that the Bible is mandatory for "doctrine." What does the word "doctrine" mean in this context? It is a form of the word *didaskalia,* a Greek word which pictures *well-packed teaching that has full applicability for every part of one's life.*

This means Scripture is not to be relegated to simply being a book about theology. Rather, it is full of God's wisdom that has practical application for every question and situation life could ever present us. People often ask if that is actually possible — if it can be said that the Bible truly addresses every question. The answer is *yes.*

The Bible answers every question directly, or it answers every question by principles that are demonstrated in Scripture. A person may not enjoy the answers, but the answers are there.

The Scriptures are jam-packed with the answers we need — and that includes the answers we desperately need for tricky problems that are rampant in a last-days society. God's Word provides answers to even life's most difficult problems — as long as one is willing to search it out and then walk in obedience once the answer is found.

———◆———

**Scripture is not to be relegated
to simply being a book about theology.
Rather, it is full of God's wisdom that has practical application
for every question and situation life could ever present us.
People often ask if that is actually possible —
if it can be said that the Bible truly addresses every question.
The answer is *yes*.**

———◆———

When a believer opens his heart to the Word of God, the Scriptures often bring correction. This is why Paul said, "For all scripture is given by inspiration of God, and is profitable for doctrine, for reproof, for correction...."

This particular word for "correction" is very important — and its meaning is probably not what you think. It is *especially important* for a last-days society — and even a last-days Church — that has been assaulted on so many fronts at the end of the age.

But before I delve into the meaning of this word "correction," first let's quickly review the *RIV* (*Renner's Interpretive Version*) of Second Timothy 3:1-7 so we can see why the Church and society at the end of the age will need the Word of God to bring "correction."

The *RIV* of Second Timothy 3:1-7 shows Paul prophetically stating:

1. You emphatically and categorically need to know with unquestionable certainty that in the very end of days — when time has sailed to its last port and no more time remains for the journey — that last season will stand in the midst of uncontrollable, unpredictable, hurtful, treacherous, menacing times that will be emotionally difficult for people to bear.

2. Men will be self-focused, self-centered, self-absorbed, self-consumed, and in love with themselves more than anyone else. As a result of this self-love, they will be driven to obtain more and more and more. These boasters are so committed to their own agenda that they are willing to exaggerate, overstate the facts, stretch the truth, embellish a story, and even lie if it will get them the position, advantage, or goal they desire. They are arrogant, haughty, impudent, snooty, and insolent. They disdain, mock, slander, and speak ill of anyone who stands in the way of their ideology and freely use foul language. In this climate, parents will no longer be able to persuade, control, lead, or exercise authority over their own children. And although people were once thankful and appreciative, they will generally become void of gratitude and will be unappreciative of everything. Impurity will seep into society and cause it to become impure, ill-mannered, unclean, indecent, coarse, vulgar, offensive, crude, lewd, and rude.

3. Love for and commitment to family will disintegrate, and divorce will become epidemic, with irreconcilable differences being a major factor in tearing families apart. In fact, every imaginable type of covenant will be regularly violated, and the court system will be overwhelmed as people go overboard, suing and being sued. People will generally lose the ability to say no and will be unable to control their instincts in nearly every area of life.

People will become savage, and it will eventually feel like there are no laws to protect the innocent.

4. People will find it easy to walk away from commitments and to easily throw away relationships. They will become reckless, impulsive, and known for their enjoyment of violence. They will become full of pride and inflated with a sense of their own self-importance — to the extent that it may end up feeling like society is being hit by a typhoon; however, those menacing winds of change will eventually blow out like a storm that comes and goes. Meanwhile, people will become fixated on the unobtainable pursuit of happiness and pleasure even more than they love God.

5. Although they may possess an outward form of religiosity, they will rebuff, refute, refuse, and reject the authentic power that goes along with genuine godliness. I urgently tell you to mentally, spiritually, and physically turn away and remove yourselves from such people.

6. These sorts of people project themselves as "help" with the intention of gaining access into people's homes to manipulate them — especially targeting some sincere women who feel over-whelmed by frustrations and disappointing failures in life whom the manipulators find easier to influence because they have so many unmet longings.

7. These women are endlessly doing their very best to gain insight needed to help them navigate life, but they are perpetually unable to come to right conclusions based on truth.

This passage in Second Timothy 3 makes it clear that the last-days society will exist within a messed-up world desperately in need of a course correction. Those words lead right up to the word "correction" in Second Timothy 3:16. In Greek, it is the word *epanorthosis*, which means *to correct, to set straight, to erect, to set upright,* or *to put back on an even level.* This word "correction" therefore depicts the supernatural ability of the Word of God *to lay hold of a person who has been knocked flat by life and, through correction, set that person upright on his feet again*!

That is good news in a world where today so many challenges threaten to knock people down. People have been hurt *before* they came to Christ, and people have been hurt *after* they came to Christ. But believers' hearts and minds are to be infused with the Word of God. And as they let that Word work inside them, it doesn't matter how many times they've been knocked flat by life, Scripture has the power to put them upright on their feet again.

The Scriptures are profitable and powerful to rectify you and your circumstances — to *correct* you and put you back on your feet again — when they are released into your life by faith!

God's very breath resides in every word of the Scriptures. That means each word holds the power to make you strong, keep you strong, enlighten you, change your circumstances, and even pick you up off the ground and correct your course if you've been knocked flat on your back by the trials of life.

God's very breath resides in every word of the Scriptures. That means each word holds the power to make you strong, keep you strong, enlighten you, change your circumstances, and even pick you up off the ground and correct your course if you've been knocked flat on your back by the trials of life.

Even if you've been knocked off your feet by your own actions, by the actions of others, or by some attack of the enemy, God's Word has the inherent ability to raise you up and make you stand again on more solid footing than you've ever had before. So regardless of any sin, hurt, or failure of the past, stand full of expectation concerning God's ability *and* His desire to "correct" you. As you yield to His working in you through the correction of His Word, He will stand you upright on your feet again and bring great blessing into your life.

Paul then went on to add, "For all scripture is given by inspiration of God, and is profitable for doctrine, for reproof, for correction, for instruction in righteousness." Let's look at the phrase "instruction in righteousness" to see how vital this particular role of God's Word will be for an erring last-days generation!

The word "instruction" is a form of the Greek word *paideia*, which means *to train, to educate,* or *to give a child everything necessary to prepare him for life.* It depicts *the laborious process of getting a child ready for life so he can later be sent out fully equipped to live successfully.* In the time of the New Testament, it became the word to describe *all types of instruction essential to the success of children or adults.*

By using this word *paideia*, Paul was saying that when the Bible is applied to a person's life, it has the supernatural ability to get that person ready to be a success in life. It doesn't matter how many failures this person has experienced or how many times he or she has faltered in life. If that person is willing to believe, embrace, and act on the Scriptures, he or she will release all the power needed to set that faltering life back on the road to success.

God's Word will work like the consummate parent in the lives of those who will submit to it — equipping them with teaching, understanding, and sufficient wisdom to help them make a course correction. And from that moment of decision onward, they will be headed toward their sure destination — leaving the place of failure to reach the pinnacle of victory!

Paul further stated that God's Word will give instruction or life training that will lead the recipient to a life of "righteousness." The word "righteousness" in this verse is the word *dikaiosune*, which is the word for *right living* and epitomizes *those who live by a righteous standard that results in upright living.*

More and more, this world we live in seems upside down, turned inside out, and put on its head by the destructive tendencies of the last days. In the midst of it all, God's Word has the inherent ability to take an unsuccessful, knocked-flat individual and set him upright on his feet again. And God doesn't stop there! Through the truth contained in His Word, God so thoroughly equips that person by His Spirit that he moves from wrong to right living.

That is the manifested power of God's Word when it is believed, embraced, and acted upon. That is how much power is resident within the Holy Scriptures. And that is why Satan is so determined to nullify the Word and remove it from society — because the eternal, unchangeable Word of the living God is the answer to *all* of society's dilemmas!

**God's Word has the inherent ability
to take an unsuccessful, knocked-flat individual
and set him upright on his feet again.
And God doesn't stop there!
Through the truth contained in His Word,
God so thoroughly equips that person by His Spirit
that he moves from wrong to right living.**

TOTALLY OUTFITTED AND EQUIPPED FOR LAST-DAYS SAILING!

Before we proceed into Second Timothy 3:17, I must remind you again how the Holy Spirit started in this chapter.

Let's once again return to the *RIV* of verse 1 in this prophetic portion of Scripture:

You emphatically and categorically need to know with unquestionable certainty that in the very end of days — when time has sailed to its last port and no more time remains for the journey — that last season will stand in the midst of uncontrollable, unpredictable, hurtful, treacherous, menacing times that will be emotionally difficult for people to bear.

In other words, the Holy Spirit began by telling us that the very end of this age will be filled with an unprecedented level of stormy weather.

But God has given us what we need to help us successfully sail through that tumultuous season! His Word — if believed, embraced, and acted upon — will release its supernatural ability to outfit any person with all the equipment needed to sail victoriously through the turbulence of the last-days storm.

Paul specifically stated that the Word of God will work to make "perfect." This particular word "perfect" is from the Greek word *artios*, which means *complete*, *mature*, or *fully functioning*. This emphatically means the Scriptures have the ability to bring us into a place of greater maturity than ever before and to so equip us that we'll be able to handle *any* challenge we ever encounter in life.

When God's Word is working in a person's life, that person is no longer a spiritual invalid. Instead, he becomes *the fully functioning believer* God knows he can be! Although the days ahead may be filled with unsettling events that shake the world, those who allow the Word of God to do its full work inside them will be completely prepared and fully functioning to successfully navigate the chaotic, stormy times that lie ahead.

Paul finally added, "All scripture is given by inspiration of God, and is profitable for doctrine, for reproof, for correction, for instruction in righteousness.

That the man of God may be perfect, *thoroughly furnished* unto all good works" (2 Timothy 3:16,17).

When God's Word is working in a person's life, that person is no longer a spiritual invalid. Instead, he becomes the *fully functioning believer* God knows he can be!

The phrase "thoroughly furnished" in this verse is translated from the Greek word *exartidzo*, which means *to completely deck out* or *to fully supply*. In one of its oldest senses, it was used frequently to describe *a boat*. But it didn't refer to just any kind of boat. It depicted a boat that was *completely outfitted* or *thoroughly furnished* for long-distance sailing, even through the roughest of waves.

This word *exartidzo* literally pictures a simple boat that was previously ill-equipped for long-distance sailing or rough waves — until its owner decked it out with new equipment and gear. Consequently, that simple boat was transformed and became *thoroughly furnished* to sail a long distance and through any type of bad weather. This was a boat that was *completely equipped* and *fully supplied*.

So let's use this example of a boat for a moment. There are many different kinds of boats. Some are made for rowing short distances. But let's face it — a simple boat won't get you very far off the shore, and it won't take you through rough waters. You can't depend on it in stormy, turbulent conditions because it is not equipped to handle large, tumultuous waves.

But what happens if you take that simple boat and *retrofit it* — *thoroughly furnishing* and *completely outfitting it* for long-distance sailing? Suddenly what was once a simple boat with few abilities is so transformed that it can travel great distances and outlast any storm. With a sturdy sail and all the other equipment needed, it can go a long distance and even navigate those tumultuous waves! This is exactly the picture that Paul presented in Second Timothy 3:17 when he said the Word of God can "thoroughly furnish" a simple believer "unto all good works."

As a believer consistently ingests the Word of God into his heart — and as he *keeps* it working in his heart, meditating on its truth and allowing those truths to renew his mind — the life and power in that Word *equips* him. That Christian is no longer a short-distance traveler with no ability to make it through rough waves. Rather, he becomes *thoroughly furnished* to go the whole distance, divinely equipped to make it through any storm that comes his way.

I must refer to my father for a moment. Dad loved to fish, so he purchased a boat many years ago. He started out with a basic boat, but then added a fish locator, a trolling motor, and all kinds of high-tech equipment. He even replaced the engine with a more high-powered engine. After a period of time, my dad's simple, basic boat was transformed into one that was *completely outfitted* and *thoroughly furnished* to take him anywhere he wanted to go on any lake and through almost any weather! Dad kept adding to that boat and improving it until, in the end, it was a totally different boat from the simple one he started with.

Similarly, before we came to Christ, we were broken, confused, and ignorant of spiritual things. Then we got saved and embarked on our spiritual journey — but we were just getting started. We were like a simple boat. But when the Word of God began to be implemented into our lives, we began to be steadily changed. The Word gave us new equipment that outfitted us for anything that we would ever encounter along the way.

Empowered by the ever-present help of the Holy Spirit, God's Word contains all that is needed to *thoroughly* furnish us. With that supernatural equipment, we are able to leave the shore and launch out into the deep of God's call on our lives and do whatever is necessary to successfully complete our journey in Him.

———◆———

As a believer consistently ingests the Word of God into his heart — and as he *keeps* it working in his heart, meditating on its truth and allowing those truths to renew his mind — the life and power in that Word *equips* him.

———◆———

WHAT WILL YOU DO WITH GOD'S WORD?

This is God's promise to us. When we allow His Word to do its work in us, the power in that Word enables us to excel at long-distance sailing and equips us so we can endure, survive, and even *thrive* in the worst of storms.

When you allow the Word of God to take its rightful, paramount place in your life, you position yourself to be *thoroughly furnished* — completely equipped and outfitted. You are ready to set your sails, take new territory, maintain an anchored position if needed, and fulfill with joy and victory any task or assignment that God gives you to do!

How I long to help you understand what a vast treasure is waiting for you within the pages of your Bible. The apostle Paul had that same passion — to help people know that God's Word was *full* of His supernatural presence and power! This is why it is so unfortunate that the very thing society is attempting to remove — the truth found in the Holy Scriptures — is the very ingredient that has the power to totally *recreate*, *redeem*, and *restore* society.

Friend, if you want your family to be protected in these last days — and if you want to make it all the way to the end of your own God-ordained journey — you must make a commitment to believe, embrace, and act upon the Word of God. The Holy Scriptures are filled with the power to "thoroughly furnish" you for the critical days ahead.

◆

**When you allow the Word of God to take its rightful,
paramount place in your life, you position yourself
to be *thoroughly furnished* — completely equipped and outfitted.
You are ready to set your sails, take new territory,
maintain an anchored position if needed,
and fulfill with joy and victory any task
or assignment that God gives you to do!**

◆

GOD'S WORD WILL EQUIP US
TO NAVIGATE ANY STORMY WEATHER

Years ago, I made a personal commitment to the Word of God. It was a fresh commitment to one I'd made much earlier in my Christian walk — that there would be no higher priority in my life than the Bible. From that time years ago until the present, I have lived by a self-imposed rule: *"No Bible — no food."*

In other words, I made a personal commitment that no food at all would go into my body until I'd read and meditated on God's Word to get it in my heart first thing every morning. I simply made a decision to put the Word of God first and make it my highest priority, even more than my necessary food (*see* Job 23:12).

This is *not* a biblical rule. It's my own rule based on my own personal conviction, because I needed to establish it for my own life.

Matthew 4:4 says, "…Man shall not live by bread alone, but by every word that proceedeth out of the mouth of God." I had to ask myself, *Why do we eat bread or natural food?* We eat it because that's what our body needs to maintain its strength and good health. Then I realized, *If our bodies need food every day, our spirits also need the Word of God every day for strength and spiritual vitality!*

It doesn't matter whether we're talking about a Christian who lived in the First Century or one who lives right now in the very last of the last days — God's people have always lived in a sin-darkened society. And the solution God gives His people to ensure that they are not hardened by the sinful environment that surrounds them has always been the same: "Thy word have I hid in mine heart, that I might not sin against thee" (Psalm 119:11).

We must continually saturate our hearts and our minds with the truths of God's Word, allowing that Word to release into our lives the very substance of God contained within its words. We have to open our Bible like we would open a treasure and allow *Who* is inside it to permeate every part of our being. As we do that, the Bible has the power to put us back on our feet again, secure our foundation, heal us, make us whole, protect us, and set our marriages and families on the right course.

◆

**We have to open our Bible like we would open a treasure
and allow *Who* is inside it
to permeate every part of our being.**

◆

So I encourage you today to renew your commitment to the Word of God like never before. Determine that in these last days, you will continually fill your heart and your mind with His creative, restorative substance — His very Person and nature — that provides you with healing, wholeness, deliverance, protection, and all the answers you need for life. Then the life resident within His Word will flow into and through you as a river of blessing to others. And as that river flows, it will release God's power, creativity, music, and fragrance of Heaven into your life and into any situation you face. God's Word will *thoroughly furnish* you for all good works.

The Bible has a sobering effect on God's people and helps them keep their head on straight while walking through the turmoil of the times. It helps them overcome in the challenges of life, bear fruit to the glory of God, and stay calm and stabilized in times of great *in*stability and *un*certainty.

Just as Paul told Timothy, you and I must *continue* in the things that we have learned (*see* 2 Timothy 3:14). If we do, we'll reap the reward of faith and stability as we victoriously sail through the last of the last days.

When all is said and done, the Word of God is the only thing that truly has the power to save us, heal us, deliver us, and transform our lives. I promise you that no matter how tumultuous the sea of your life may become — and we all encounter life's storms at one time or another — God's Word will never fail you. It will outfit you to sail victoriously to the other side of your test or trial every time, where the reward of faith awaits you!

GOD'S WORD AND HIS KINGDOM WILL RULE

Anytime I've been inwardly troubled about the "signs of the times" that are emerging at such a rapid speed all round us, I've laid hold of two verses that have always brought me comfort: Psalm 46:1 and Psalm 56:3. In Psalm 46:1, we read, "God is our refuge and strength, a very present help in trouble." And Psalm 56:3 tells us, "What time I am afraid, I will trust in thee."

In times of trouble, God is near to His people. Psalm 46:1 promises that He is a *very present help* in trouble. That is a promise I've claimed for myself through the years more times than I can count. And whenever I'm personally disturbed about something or tempted to be fearful, I always turn to David's words in Psalm 56:3 and pray them out loud: "What time I am afraid, I will trust in thee!"

I recommend that you put this same strategy into practice and make these verses a ready part of your own spiritual arsenal. You'll see how God's presence is released to shift the atmosphere as you speak those scriptures out loud. Those words of life will help bring peace to you when you feel tempted to be fearful during the perilous, troublesome times in which we live.

One thing is sure: We were not born at this time in God's prophetic timeline by accident. Rather than fret because the world seems to be going haywire, we need to embrace the anointing God has made available for each of us who are part of this last-days generation! Regardless of what we see, hear, or feel, these truths remain: Jesus *is* Lord, and God's Kingdom and His Word *will* prevail. *Nothing* will ever change that!

**Regardless of what we see, hear, or feel,
these truths remain: Jesus is Lord,
and God's Kingdom and His Word *will* prevail.
Nothing will ever change that!**

The Bible even says God sits in the Heavens and laughs (*see* Psalm 2:4)! Why? Because He knows that no matter how much the devil or wicked men try to dominate the world, He still sits on the throne. And He knows the end of the story! He isn't worried about or surprised by *anything* that happens around us.

All of the troublesome events we see today are clear signs that Jesus will soon return for His Church. So while we actively wait and seek to be busy about our Father's business, I encourage you to lay hold of those words in Psalm 56:3: "What time I am afraid, I will trust in thee." And boldly declare Psalm 46:1 on a daily basis as a continual reminder to yourself: "God is my refuge and strength, a very present help in trouble!"

WILL YOU SHINE YOUR LIGHT OR SHRINK BACK IN FEAR?

All the dark signs we have read about in Second Timothy 3 are *without a doubt* already occurring in these last days. But that doesn't mean these things have to happen to you and to me. We are not a part of this lost world system. And since the Holy Spirit warned us of these things in advance, we have the opportunity to take heed and take action to protect our families and our homes while we march forward with speed to preach the Gospel to those who are lost without Christ.

Even if it seems the conditions in the world around us "wax worse and worse" (2 Timothy 3:13), God wants this to be our greatest hour! We must never forget that people near us are looking for solutions to their deeply felt troubles. You and I have the answer they need — *so let's let our light shine*!

◆

All the dark signs we have read about in Second Timothy 3 are *without a doubt* already occurring in these last days. But that doesn't mean these things have to happen to you and to me. We are not a part of this lost world system.

◆

In Philippians 2:15 and 16, Paul said, "That ye may be blameless and harmless, the sons of God, without rebuke, in the midst of a crooked and perverse nation, among whom ye shine as lights in the world; holding forth the word of life...."

This is our hour to shine as lights in the world and to hold forth the word of life. As we await the glorious day of Jesus Christ when He returns for His Church, we must not allow negative events to cause us to draw back or to shrink back in fear. God has chosen us to live in these prophetic times, and He has anointed us to live in them victoriously!

As a Christian, you are anointed to help others who are struggling with what seems to be a sinking world all around them. You are called to be a part of a company of faithful, fearless believers in Jesus Christ who will act as His "hands and feet" and "His voice" in the earth. You can reach out to those who need strength and guidance in these perilous times. It's certain that you know people who need to see the light of Christ in you. You can be a source of deliverance and great comfort to them.

God wants us to recognize the season we are living in right now. In Second Timothy 3, the Holy Spirit has vividly shown us signs that will be evident all around us as we approach the close of this age. However, God doesn't want us to shrink back in discouragement or fear because of what we see happening around us. He wants us to stay awake spiritually and learn to live fully in Him. He is calling us to shake off the dust of despair and to rise to our fullest potential in Christ — the One who gives us light. *That's* how we will shine as lights to this lost world and help draw all men unto Him!

———◆———

God doesn't want us to shrink back in discouragement or fear because of what we see happening around us. He wants us to stay awake spiritually and learn to live fully in Him.

———◆———

THE END IS MUCH LIKE THE BEGINNING!

When Jesus came to earth as Savior, the world was very troubled, as it is today. The Romans had conquered the then-known world, and Israel was a captive nation. Subjugated to Roman rulers, Israel's citizens were treated atrociously. It was during this very tumultuous time — a truly catastrophic moment in history approximately 2,000 years ago — that Jesus was born to bring deliverance.

It seemed as if hope was lost and the darkness was getting darker. But then *suddenly* the Son of God was born into the earth and hope was born anew. What a miraculous moment that was in history!

Jesus was born into troubled times, and He is near to us in our troubled times today. Soon Jesus will come again — and when He comes, He will put down every evil force that has exalted itself against God's eternal plan. But until then, we must trust Jesus with our future as we lean upon the Word of God and the power of the Holy Spirit. We must not forget that God is a very present help in time of trouble to anyone who calls upon Him (*see* Psalm 46:1; Hebrews 4:16).

Remember that everything you see in the earthly realm is temporary and fleeting (*see* 2 Corinthians 4:18) — but God's Word and His Kingdom are unshakable and unchanging (*see* Hebrews 12:28). None of what you see happening in the world's system will last long anyway — so just keep drawing on His strength, and refuse to allow the outward circumstances you see and hear about to keep you in a state of inner turmoil.

Don't let the devil steal your joy. The Holy Spirit warned us in advance that all of this would happen, so focus on the fact that God has anointed you to live victoriously in this late hour. You can live as an overcomer, no matter what is going on in the world around you.

In recent times, events have occurred throughout the earth that have shaken the nations of the world and filled men's hearts with fear. I am convinced that part of this worldwide assault has been the devil's attempt to put believers in fear so they will retreat from this global advance of the Gospel.

But we are *never* to react in fear. Fear is *never* the answer, for it results in blurred thinking and bad decisions. And God's Word promises a "sound mind" — *if* we will claim it (*see* 2 Timothy 1:7).

The phrase "sound mind" is a translation of the Greek word *sophronismos*, which is a compound of the words *sodzo* and *phroneo*. The word *sodzo* is the Greek word for *salvation* and includes the ideas of *deliverance, protection,* and *soundness.* The word *phroneo* is the root for the word *mind.* When these two words are combined as in this verse, the new word is translated *sound mind.* The idea presented is *a mind that is saved and protected* or *a mind that is sound.* It is just the opposite of a mind given to fear, panic, or unfounded and unreasonable thinking. This word describes a mind that is thinking correctly!

◆

We are *never* to react in fear. Fear is *never* the answer, for it results in blurred thinking and bad decisions. And God's Word promises a "sound mind" — *if* we will claim it (*see* 2 Timothy 1:7).

◆

Because God has given us a "sound mind," we can think correctly about how to live in these last of the last days — a time that Second Timothy 3:1 predicted will be "perilous." As we have seen, the word "perilous" is the Greek word *chalepos,* and it literally means *something that is difficult, dangerous, or filled with risk.* This was given as a prophetic warning to let us know that those who live in the very end of the age will be confronted with a strange period of time such as mankind has never seen before. It will be a time filled with difficulty, danger, and risk.

The very fact that we are living in these end-time days should be a wakeup call to us all that we *must* develop an ever-greater sensitivity to the Spirit of God. Romans 8:14 declares that one of the privileges of being a son of God is that His Spirit desires to lead us. But we *must* allow the Holy Spirit to lead us. The Holy Spirit will assume the position of Leader and Guide in our lives only as we give Him this right.

**The very fact that we are living in these end-time days
should be a wakeup call to us all that we *must* develop
an ever-greater sensitivity to the Spirit of God.**

Just try to imagine how many times the Holy Spirit has wanted to be our Leader, but we went our own way and suffered the consequences as a result! He knew exactly how to lead us in order to circumvent every attack. He knew how to avoid each strategy of the devil!

Jesus also said that the Holy Spirit would "…shew you things to come" (John 16:13). The word "shew" is the Greek word *hodegeo*, which is the word for *a guide who shows a traveler the safest course through an unknown country.* This means the Holy Spirit *wants* to be our Guide through this end-time territory. He knows exactly the way we should go; He understands how to avoid every trap and obstacle along the way.

The Holy Spirit wants to show us how to take the safest route. *He knows exactly how to get us safely to our future point of destination.* He knows the future and wants to enlighten us with all the information we will need in every situation. *This is part of His ministry to you and me.*

As we obey the Word of God and listen to the Holy Spirit's leading, we will have wisdom to know every step we need to take in the days ahead. All we have to do is obey God's instructions, and He guarantees us blessing and provision even in difficult times. But if we try to take another approach, there is no guarantee for us to claim. *We must do what God says if we want to be assured of His divine blessing and protection.*

As a leader and friend, I want to encourage you to commit to the regular intake of the Word of God. I guarantee you that this one decision will immediately begin to increase the level of your faith. Especially in challenging times, we must stand on the Word of God, exercise faith, listen to the Holy Spirit, and obey what He tells us to do.

◆

All we have to do is obey God's instructions, and He guarantees us blessing and provision even in difficult times. But if we try to take another approach, there is no guarantee for us to claim. We must do what God says if we want to be assured of His divine blessing and protection.

◆

There is no doubt that we are living in some of the most challenging days the world has ever seen. But you and I can face these times victoriously. God has given us a sound mind; He has given us the promises of His Word; and He has given us the leadership of His Spirit. Never has there been a more crucial time for you to operate in faith, refuse to fear, and believe for a mighty move of God to take place on this earth!

If we'll listen to what the Holy Spirit speaks to our hearts and obey His leading, we won't see this last-days season only as days of peril on the earth. Instead, we'll see this time we're living in as days filled with greater opportunities than ever before to preach and teach the good news of the Gospel! We'll see fresh opportunities to win the lost, strengthen the weak, disciple believers in God's Word, and be used as instruments of God's power to demonstrate the miraculous where His delivering touch on people's lives is so desperately needed. We'll see hell move out of the way and the windows of Heaven opened to pour out God's blessings into our lives and the lives of others in unprecedented measures in the days ahead.

◆

**If we'll listen to what the Holy Spirit speaks to our hearts
and obey His leading, we won't see this last-days season
only as days of peril on the earth.
Instead, we'll see this time we're living in
as days filled with greater opportunities than ever before
to preach and teach the good news of the Gospel!**

◆

For those who listen to and obey the Lord, this day we're living in will be a season of great victory. Conversely, for those who don't know God or who *do not* heed His instruction, these days will be difficult. Without the foundation of the Word of God set beneath them to establish and stabilize them in these unsteady times, they will become easy prey for the enemy to terrorize them with reports of failing economies, political turmoil, new cases of potential pandemics, global unrest, insane violence, and a future filled with bewilderment and uncertainty.

As the children of God, we need to be alert to the dangerous days in which we live. But more importantly, we need to be ever mindful that when we're obedient to God and His Word, His power will enable us to live victoriously, even in perilous times, in ways that are far beyond what we could ever conceive or imagine!

CHAPTER 10

LAST-DAYS SURVIVAL GUIDE ACTION STEPS

IN RESPONSE TO THIS FINAL CHAPTER

In this book, we have dealt with the Holy Spirit's prophetic words regarding society at the end of the Church Age. As I have noted again and again, it was never the Spirit's purpose to scare anyone, but to prepare us — especially those of us living at the end of the last days who would see and experience the madness He said would erupt as the age came to a close.

This chapter contains the solution to sailing victoriously through this last season of the Church Age. In response to what you have read, I'd like you to ask yourself the following seven questions, which contain very important final action steps for you to act on in order to "land on your feet" as you turn the last page and move forward into the exciting and challenging days ahead.

1. "What person has been the greatest influence in my spiritual life?"

In this chapter, we saw the role that Timothy's mother and the apostle Paul played in contributing to his spiritual development. So ask yourself:

- *Looking back on my life, who has been the person who has contributed the most to my spiritual life?*

When I think of who influenced me, I cannot help but immediately think of the role my mother played in my life. But in addition to my mother, I was also influenced by other Sunday school teachers, by my childhood pastor, and by the pastor I served many years ago when I was a pastoral assistant. I cannot over-exaggerate the role that each of these individuals played in contributing to who I am today. Much of what God has done in my life can be attributed to the investments these people made into me at a young, impressionable age.

It would be good for you to take time to remember those who have made a spiritual contribution to your life. And then take a step beyond just recalling who they are. Take time to reach out to these individuals. Thank each of these significant people in your life for being such a positive influence and for helping to form a solid foundation for your life.

So many times people invest in others, but they later lose touch with the people they poured themselves into and never hear the good reports regarding the good fruit their spiritual contributions produced. It makes me think of the ten lepers that Jesus healed. Only one took time to come back and thank Jesus for what He did for him (*see* Luke 17:11-19).

So ask yourself:

- *Am I among the nine who walked away helped and changed, but never made the effort to return and say thank you?*

- *Or am I the one who took the time to come back and express my gratitude to the one who made a difference in my life?*

Consider this: If someone came back and thanked you for your influence in his or her life, wouldn't that mean a lot to you? Don't be guilty of robbing someone else of a blessing that you could easily give by saying thank you. Take time to act on this action step, and remember those who contributed to your spiritual formation. Reach out to them to say thank you for what they did for you to help prepare you to fulfill God's plan for your life.

2. "What exactly did I learn from that person who influenced me?"

Paul reminded Timothy that his mother taught him to respect and to revere the Holy Scriptures from the time he was young. He also reminded Timothy of his own personal example in the younger man's life, for he had taught Timothy that the Word of God has the power to sustain anyone in any situation that he will ever confront in life. It is clear that Paul believed Timothy needed to reflect on what he had learned from those who had spiritually influenced him.

Again, I think of my mother. I remember as a young child how she taught me (just as Timothy was taught by his mother) about repentance from sin, how to give my life to Jesus, and how to serve Him and His Church as my highest priority in life.

I also think of my childhood pastor — how he demonstrated spiritual authority to me and imparted to me a respect for the Word of God.

Finally, I can never overlook or forget how the pastor I served as a pastoral assistant took time to develop me, correct me, and help me learn how to mix anointing with scholarship and be consistent in my daily spiritual habits.

There are simply not enough words to express the powerful impact these individuals made on my spiritual growth.

When I think of all the ways they influenced me, it makes me think of my *own* influence in the lives of others around me.

Consider your role as an influence in other people's lives. Ask yourself:

- *How have I influenced others?*

- *What kind of difference have I made in someone else's spiritual growth?*

- *Am I making a difference in someone else's life right now?*

- *Have I been too self-focused to do this for others?*

- *Is there anyone who would say I have played a positive spiritual role in his or her life?*

These are very important questions. We saw clearly in this book that a last-days society will be tempted to be self-focused and self-absorbed. You do not want to become so self-absorbed that you live your life without helping others along their spiritual journey the way someone helped you.

Let your action step be to honestly evaluate what you have contributed to the lives of others. If you find that you have become too self-absorbed or distracted to give this kind of focused attention to help someone else, it's time for you to change that and to start thinking more about the welfare of others. And by the way, when you get your attention off yourself and focus on others around you, that very change of focus in itself will cause blessings and power to flow back into your life. It is the law of reciprocity, and it always works!

3. "What am I doing to 'continue' in what I learned?"

There are many temptations today to drift from those foundational truths that were placed in our lives. In my book *How To Keep Your Head on Straight in a World Gone Crazy*, I delve deeply into the activity of seducing spirits that will lead even many in the Church off track in these last of the last days. So ask yourself this:

- *Am I staying on track and continuing in the things I learned earlier in life?*

- *Or am I starting to drift from those foundational principles and truths that made me who I am today?*

What are those principles you were taught earlier in life that still have an impact on you today? For example, were you taught:

- That the Bible was to have primary authority in your life?

- To read, embrace, and act on the Scriptures?

- That you are to live your life in obedience to the Word of God?

- To read your Bible every day so it would strengthen you and renew your mind to godly thinking?

- To pray in the Spirit regularly to build up your faith?

- That you were to love your local church and to serve it regularly?

- To live a holy and upright life that pleases the Lord?

These questions may seem elementary — but can you say that you have continued to consistently follow these principles over the years? Or have you drifted from one or more of these essential practices as so many other Christians have done?

The pastor for whom I served as an assistant many years ago often told me, "Many people begin with a bang but end with a fizzle." If God were to tell you what He thinks, would He say you started with a bang but have become kind of a fizzle? Or would He say you've been pushing forward and diligently staying on track all of your spiritual life?

Let this action step be a time of evaluating the level of your consistency to do what you know to do in your spiritual walk. Ask yourself:

- *Have I stuck with the basics over the years since I was first born again, consistently practicing the basic principles that I know God has commanded me to do?*

- *Or have I allowed myself to get off track along the way?*

Most who get off track do it very gradually and ultimately feel like they are failing spiritually. However, that negative pattern can quickly be changed when a person asks for forgiveness, repents, and gets back on track with God again.

This is exactly why Jesus told the church of Ephesus, "Remember therefore from whence thou has fallen, repent, and do the first works…" (Revelation 2:5). This is a good time for you to remember and, if needed, to repent. Then be diligent from this point on to do the things you were taught to do when you first got started in your walk with God.

4. "What kind of commitment do I really have to sustaining a regular intake of the Bible?"

When we get busy, it is often the case that we begin to give the daily intake of the Bible a lower priority in our lives than we did in the beginning of our Christian walk. Then when our power and joy begin to wane, we wonder why. But the truth is, we have departed from the very Scriptures that are infused with God's divine presence, ready to fill us with His power and joy!

Even those in the ministry must make a firm commitment to make the daily intake of the Bible a priority. In my book *A Life Ablaze*, I vividly outline what happens to a believer who determines to put God's Word as the highest priority in his or her life. Suffice it to say here that the results of this decision are so far-reaching that it cannot be over-exaggerated.

If you want to walk in divine power, you must walk in the Word of God. And for that to happen, you have to set aside time to take in God's words through your eyes and ears. Your eyes and ears are the door to your heart. If you are not opening your eyes and ears to the Word of God, then that Word is not being firmly planted in the soil of your heart and throughout the recesses of your mind. Only as you continually hear the Word and put that Word before your eyes will it be able to release its divine power to transform you, energize you, empower you, and keep you on fire!

So ask yourself these questions:

- *How much time do I spend reading my Bible every day?*

- *How does the daily amount of time I spend in the Word compare to the amount of time I spend surfing the Internet or social media or watching television every day?*

- *How much does my life demonstrate that I believe the Bible is important?*

- *Would I like others to know how much I actually read my Bible?*

- *How much importance would God say I give to ingesting His Word into my life?*

Years ago when I got very busy doing lots of "good things" for the Lord, I inadvertently got so busy that I stopped making time for God's Word in my daily life. As time passed, it affected me so greatly that I became spiritually weak. As a result, the Holy Spirit spoke a strong word of correction to me, and I responded by repenting and self-correcting. I made a strict commitment to read my Bible every day as a first matter of priority before I do anything else. This one action has permanently changed my life.

Today I suggest your action step is to be honest with yourself — and with God — about the level of importance you have demonstrated in your life for the daily intake of the Bible. If you honestly conclude that you have slipped in this area, please don't condemn yourself for it. Self-condemnation is a waste of time that produces no change in anyone's life.

If you have slipped in this area, simply ask for forgiveness, repent, and make a firm decision to change. Give your time communing with God in His Word the highest priority in your daily schedule! If you need help in knowing how to get started, contact our ministry (**renner.org**), and we'll provide you with a daily Bible reading plan that will help you get started again!

5. "What demonstrations of God's power have I experienced as a result of God's Word working in my life?"

One of my favorite scriptures is Ecclesiastes 8:4. It says, "Where the word of a king is, there is power...." The Bible unquestionably teaches that the Scriptures are full of God's power!

In fact, in this chapter, we have seen very clearly that the Bible is not just a Book *about* God — it is actually a Book that *contains* God within its pages! When a person opens the Bible, ingests it, embraces what he reads in it, and acts upon it, the power that is locked inside the Bible is supernaturally released into that individual's life. That is a promise!

Take some time to reflect on your own personal walk with the Lord, asking yourself in what ways the Bible has been a source of God's power and inspiration for you. Then ask yourself:

- *Have I made a consistent choice to ingest and act on the truths I read in the Bible?*

- *Has that choice:*
  - *Changed the way I think?*
  - *Empowered me to walk free of sin?*
  - *Supplied me with supernatural direction?*
  - *Given me confidence and boldness?*
  - *Provided me with answers I needed?*

The promise in Ecclesiastes 8:4 is that "where the word of a king is, there is power." Therefore, it's clear that if the words of the King of kings are in us, those words *will* release power in our lives.

There is no higher authority in our lives than Jesus! Every time we declare "Jesus is Lord," we are acknowledging that He is the King in our lives. And according to Ecclesiastes 8:4, His Word is guaranteed to release divine power into our lives and into every situation we find ourselves in at any given moment.

As part of this action step, take time to remember how your life has been empowered in those times when you made God's Word a daily priority in your life.

Ask yourself:

- *Can I think of times in my life when I experienced God's power in amazing ways?*

- *Do I see a correlation between those special times in my walk with God and the daily intake of the Bible into my life or to times when I was consistently obeying what the Bible commanded me to do in some situation?*

Words are containers, and the words of the Holy Scriptures are *filled* with the life and power of God. It therefore makes sense that as you consistently take the words of the Bible into your heart, those words will release into your life the torrents of God's power that reside within them.

6. "What long-term 'correction' have the Scriptures produced in my life?"

We have seen in Second Timothy 3:16 that the Scriptures have the power to "correct" us when needed. We have also seen that the Greek word for "correction" in Second Timothy 3:16 actually depicts a person who has been knocked flat in life, but who has miraculously been set upright on his or her feet again. It is a picture of *total restoration*!

This means that even if people have been hurt or wounded in some way, they don't have to stay down. If they will believe, embrace, and act upon the Word of God, the power in the Bible will release its miraculous and supernatural ability to help these broken, disappointed individuals. They may feel knocked flat by some event or by several events in life — but they will *rise again*! That inherent, divine power will begin the process of picking those individuals back up and setting them upright on their feet once more!

This "stand-again" power can be seen throughout the Scriptures. It is available for any person who makes the decision to believe, embrace, and act upon God's Word (*see* Micah 7:8)!

This makes me think of Second Corinthians 4:9, where Paul wrote that he had been "cast down, but not destroyed." Paul was writing from personal experience. He knew how it felt to be knocked down and nearly knocked out, because it happened to him on several occasions. But the power in God's Word kept picking Paul back up and setting him upright on his feet again. That is why he could confidently write, "...We may be knocked down but we are never knocked out!" (2 Corinthians 4:9 *Phillips*).

So ask yourself these questions:

- *When I think on my own life, can I recall times when I have been knocked flat — and, naturally speaking, when I should have been permanently knocked out?*

- *In those times, what happened to me? Did I stay down, or did I eventually get back on my feet again?*

- *Did the Word of God cause me to get up and to get moving again?*

Maybe you feel knocked flat right now. If so, then it's time for you to believe, embrace, and act upon the Scriptures! The Bible has the power to pick you up, set you back on your feet, and get you moving again.

This is what Second Timothy 3:16 calls supernatural "correction"! So the last part of this action step is for you to answer this question:

- *Even if I do feel somewhat knocked flat right now, what am I going to do about it today — and every day hereafter! — to release the power of God's Word in me?*

It would also be good for you to take time to recall those amazing and wonderful moments in your past when you personally experienced the resurrection power of God's Word as it supernaturally put you back up on your feet. Never forget — the Scriptures are *full* of instances of God's "stand-again" power, which has the innate ability to pick you up, set you upright on your feet, and get you moving forward again!

7. "What is my personal response to all that I have read in this final chapter?"

Now we come to the final action step in this book. It is an action step that I myself must take, for I have been personally confronted with the truths in this chapter, even as I have been writing it.

Ask yourself these questions:

- *Do I believe the Bible truly represents God's Holy Scriptures? That is, do I believe that every letter, character, jot, and mark — even the smallest scribble in the Bible, and, in fact, all the ink on every page — is holy, sacred, and filled with the awesome and remarkable power of God?*

- *If my answer to the above is yes, how will this truth affect the way I personally manage the role of the Scriptures in my life going forward?*

According to Paul, every letter, jot, and tittle written on the pages of God's Word is filled with the awesome and remarkable power of God. It is not just a Book *about* God; it is a Book that actually contains God's presence and power. So what kind of role should this knowledge have in each of our lives as Christians?

We are living in the last of the last days, which is the stormiest season in the history of mankind. Those who embrace the Bible and allow it to play the central role in their lives will be "thoroughly furnished" to navigate the turbulent waves of these times until they make it all the way to the other side.

Unfortunately, there are many believers who will make it to the other side but will struggle along the way because they have not yet given God's Word its rightful place of priority and authority in their lives. Yet that one decision would equip them to sail through these end-time waters with everything needed for a journey filled with blessing and victory!

God has not appointed us to failure. In fact, Second Peter 1:3,4 clearly states that God has given us exceeding great and precious promises in the Scriptures. These divine promises are designed to empower us to escape the corruption in the world around us and to enable us to partake of His supernatural life. And the Scriptures pertain to *everything* in our lives! That means if we will believe, embrace, and act upon the Scriptures, we will supernaturally have every answer and all the power we need for living victoriously in life — even at the end of the age when it seems life is messed up all around us!

In this last action step, there is a quality decision to make about the Bible and its role in your life. Will you continue to give the Word of God the same level of importance that you have thus far in your spiritual life? Or if your self-assessment has found you lacking in this area, will you now give God's Word the highest and most important place of priority in your life from this day forward?

I cannot think of a more important action step for you to take than to carefully consider and prayerfully answer this question. I personally believe it is the most important question you can answer as a Christian. And it's not only your answer — it's how you follow through on that answer that will determine the nature of your journey going forward. Will you sail through these last of the last days with smooth and peaceful accuracy? Or will you struggle all along the way until you finally reach your ultimate destination? It all depends on how well outfitted you are for the trip.

So make the quality decision today that you're about to become one of the most thoroughly outfitted vessels on the face of these last-days waters. Then "anchors away!" — time to raise your sails! There is much territory to take for the Kingdom of God — right in the midst of the gathering storm!

A FINAL PRAYER

Lord, as an end-time believer, I need to be filled with faith and not with fear. Help me fill my heart with Your Word, stand on Your promises, follow the leading of the Holy Spirit, and exercise my faith more than ever before.

I know that fear has blurred my thinking in times past, but it will *not* have any place in my life from this day forward! Instead, I release my faith and confidently expect to be a partaker in the last and greatest harvest of souls ever to be reaped for the Kingdom of God! Holy Spirit, help me rise to the occasion as I become an instrument God can use in these last days.

I pray this prayer in Jesus' name!

A FINAL CONFESSION OF MY FAITH

I confess in Jesus' name that I am filled with faith and not fear and that I am called, anointed, appointed, *and excited* to live in these last remarkable days of the Church Age. God has chosen me to live in the most challenging days the world has ever seen, and He has provided everything I need to navigate these times victoriously.

God has not given me a spirit of fear, but He has given me a sound mind, the promises of His Word, and the supernatural leadership of His Spirit to guide me. Therefore, I will *not* retreat in fear or panic. Instead, I declare that I am chosen by God to be a source of healing and deliverance to others who need it in this last-days season. Even more, I declare that I will be a participant in the mightiest harvest of souls that history has ever seen!

I declare this by faith in Jesus' name!

PRAYER FOR OVERCOMING
THESE PERILOUS TIMES

I believe that by reading this book, it is clearer to you than ever before that we are living in the perilous times the Holy Spirit prophesied about so long ago. It is my prayer that this book has helped awaken you to take the action steps necessary to stay the course spiritually and to protect yourself and those you love from evil that lurks in society in the last of the last days.

We know that the Holy Spirit is not in the business of scaring anyone. He spoke all of these things in advance so those who actually live in the end of the age can safeguard themselves against these end-time developments.

First John 5:4 says, "For whatsoever is born of God overcometh the world: and this is the victory that overcometh the world, even our faith." If we know what the Bible teaches — and respond to it in faith — we are more than able to overcome anything that we face in the present or in the days to come. God doesn't want us to just *survive* — He wants us to *thrive*, even in the end times. *We can do it!*

This is the greatest hour for the Church of Jesus Christ! But the Scriptures show that events will occur at the end of the age that will shake the nations of the world and fill men's hearts with fear. Although we need to be wise and do what we can to protect ourselves in times such as these, we do *not* need to react in fear. Fear is *never* the answer, for it results in blurred thinking and bad decisions.

God's Word promises you a sound mind *if* you will claim it. Second Timothy 1:7 says, "For God hath not given us the spirit of fear; but of power, and of love, and of a sound mind."

The words "sound mind" come from the Greek word *sophronismos*. It is a compound of the words *sodzo* and *phroneo*. The word *sodzo* is the Greek word for *salvation*. It means *deliverance, protection,* and *soundness*. The word *phroneo* is a Greek word for *mind*. When these two words are put together, as in this verse, the new word is translated *sound mind*. The idea presented by the word *sophroneo* is *a mind that is saved and protected* or *a mind that is sound*. It is just the opposite of a mind given to fear, panic, or unfounded and unreasonable thinking. This word describes a mind that is thinking correctly!

Because God has given you a "sound mind," it means you can think correctly about how to live in these last days — the very time that Second Timothy 3:1 predicts will be "perilous." But because we live in the last of the last days, it is also important that we be led by the Holy Spirit. He knows exactly how to lead us past every attack and how to avoid each strategy of the devil plotted against us. Jesus promised that the Holy Spirit would show us things to come (*see* John 16:13).

The word "shew" is the Greek word *hodegeo* and is the word for *a guide who shows a traveler the safest course through an unknown country*. This means the Holy Spirit is your Guide. He knows the way you should go. He understands how to avoid every trap and obstacle along the way. The Holy Spirit wants to show you how to take the safest route. *He knows exactly how to get you safely to your future point of destination.* The Holy Spirit knows the future and wants to enlighten you with all the information you need in every situation. *This is part of His ministry to you and me.*

As you obey the Word of God and listen to the Holy Spirit's leading, you will have wisdom to know every step you need to take in the days ahead. All you have to do is obey God's instructions, and He guarantees you blessing and provision even in difficult times. But if you try to take another approach, there is no guarantee for you to claim. *You must do what God says if you want to be assured of His divine blessing and protection.*

As a spiritual leader and friend, I want to encourage you to increase your level of faith, especially if you are facing challenging times. Stand on the Word of God; exercise your faith; listen to the Holy Spirit; and obey what He tells you to do. As you do these things, God's supernatural blessings will kick into action, and you will soon find a river of supernatural power, protection, and divine provision flowing to you.

We are living in some of the most challenging days the world has ever seen. But you can face these times victoriously because God has given you a sound mind; He has given you the promises of His Word; and He has given you the leadership of His Spirit. *And* you have faith to overcome the world! Never has there been a more crucial time for you to operate in faith and not fear and to believe for a mighty move of God to take place on this earth!

As you conclude this book, I urge you right now to pray this prayer with me:

Lord, as an end-time believer, I need to be filled with faith and not with fear. Help me fill my heart with Your Word, stand on Your promises, follow the leading of the Holy Spirit, and exercise my faith more than ever before! I know that fear has blurred my thinking in times past, but it will *not* have any place in my life from this day forward! Instead, I release my faith and confidently expect to be a partaker in the last and greatest harvest of souls ever to be reaped for the Kingdom of God! Holy Spirit, help me rise to the occasion as I become an instrument You can use in these last days. I pray this prayer in Jesus' name.

PRAYER TO RECEIVE SALVATION

When Jesus Christ comes into your life, you are immediately set free from slavery to sin! If you have never received Jesus as your personal Savior, it is time to experience this new life for yourself. The first step to freedom is simple. Just pray this prayer out loud from your heart:

Lord, I can never adequately thank You for all You did for me on the Cross. I am so undeserving, Jesus, but You came and gave Your life for me anyway. I repent for rejecting You, and I turn away from my life of rebellion and sin right now. I turn to You and receive You as my Savior, and I ask You to wash away my sin and make me completely new in You by Your precious blood.

I thank You from the depths of my heart for doing what no one else could do for me. Had it not been for Your willingness to lay down Your life for me, I would be eternally lost. Thank You, Jesus, that I am now redeemed by Your blood. On the Cross, You bore my sin, my sickness, my pain, my lack of peace, and my suffering. Your blood has removed my sin, washed me whiter than snow, and given me rightstanding with the Father. I have no need to be ashamed of my past sins because I am now a new creature in You. Old things have passed away, and all things have become new because I am in Jesus Christ (*see* 2 Corinthians 5:17).

Because of You, Jesus, today I am forgiven; I am filled with peace; and I am a joint-heir with You! Satan no longer has a right to lay any claim on me. From a grateful heart, I will faithfully serve You the rest of my days! I pray this in Jesus' name!

If you prayed this prayer from your heart, something marvelous just happened to you. No longer a servant to sin, you are now a servant of Almighty God. The evil spirits that once exacted every ounce of your being and required your all-inclusive servitude no longer possess the authorization to control you or dictate your destiny!

As a result of your decision to turn your life over to Jesus Christ, your eternal home has been decided forever. Heaven will now be your permanent address for all eternity.

God's Spirit has moved into your own human spirit, and you have become the "temple of God" (*see* 1 Corinthians 6:19). What a miracle! To think that God, by His Spirit, now lives inside you!

Now you have a new Lord and Master, and His name is Jesus. From this moment on, the Spirit of God will work in you and supernaturally energize you to fulfill God's will for your life. Everything will change for you as you yield to His leadership in your life — and it's all going to change for the best!

PRAYER TO RECEIVE THE BAPTISM IN THE HOLY SPIRIT

The baptism in the Holy Spirit is a free gift to *everyone* who has made Jesus Savior and Lord of his or her life (*see* Acts 2:39).

After you made Jesus your Lord at the time of the new birth, the Holy Spirit came to live inside you, and your old, unregenerate spirit was made completely new. This subsequent gift is the "baptism into," or *an immersion in*, the Holy Spirit.

The baptism in the Holy Spirit supplies the supernatural power of God for witnessing about Christ, for enjoying a deeper, more intimate relationship with the Holy Spirit, and for victorious Christian living.

Receiving this precious gift is easy. Before you pray to receive the infilling of the Holy Spirit, you might want to read and meditate on the Scripture references I provide at the end of this prayer. Then expect to receive what you ask for *the moment* you pray!

If you would like to be baptized in the Holy Spirit and speak with new tongues (*see* Acts 2:4), simply pray the following prayer and then act on it!

Lord, You gave the Holy Spirit to Your Church to help us fulfill the Great Commission. I ask You in faith for this free gift, and I receive right now the baptism in the Holy Spirit. I believe that You hear me as I pray, and I thank You for baptizing me in the Holy Spirit with the evidence of speaking with a new, supernatural prayer language. Amen.

As a result of praying this prayer, *your life will never be the same*. You will grow in operating in the gifts of the Holy Spirit. You will learn to experience Jesus' victory as a living reality every day.

Scripture References for Study and Review: Mark 16:17; Luke 24:49; Acts 1:4,5,8; 2:4,39; 10:45,46

ABOUT THE AUTHOR

RICK RENNER is a highly respected Bible teacher and leader in the international Christian community. Rick is the author of a long list of books, including the bestsellers *Dressed To Kill* and *Sparkling Gems From the Greek 1* and *2*, which have sold millions of copies in multiple languages worldwide. Rick's understanding of the Greek language and biblical history opens up the Scriptures in a unique way that enables readers to gain wisdom and insight while learning something brand new from the Word of God.

Rick is the founding pastor of the Moscow Good News Church. He also founded Media Mir, the first Christian television network in the former USSR that broadcasts the Gospel to countless Russian-speaking viewers around the world via multiple satellites and the Internet. He is the founder and president of RENNER Ministries, based in Tulsa, Oklahoma, and host to his TV program that is seen around the world in multiple languages. Rick leads this amazing work with his wife and lifelong ministry partner, Denise, along with the help of their sons and committed leadership team.

CONTACT RENNER MINISTRIES

For further information
about RENNER Ministries, please contact
the RENNER Ministries office nearest you,
or visit the ministry website at:
www.renner.org

**ALL USA
CORRESPONDENCE:**
RENNER Ministries
P. O. Box 702040
Tulsa, OK 74170-2040
(918) 496-3213
Or 1-800-RICK-593
Email: renner@renner.org
Website: www.renner.org

MOSCOW OFFICE:
RENNER Ministries
P. O. Box 789
101000, Moscow, Russia
+7 (495) 727-14-67
Email: blagayavestonline@ignc.org
Website: www.ignc.org

RIGA OFFICE:
RENNER Ministries
Unijas 99
Riga LV-1084, Latvia
+371 67802150
Email: info@goodnews.lv

KIEV OFFICE:
RENNER Ministries
P. O. Box 300
01001, Kiev, Ukraine
+38 (044) 451-8315
Email: blagayavestonline@ignc.org

OXFORD OFFICE:
RENNER Ministries
Box 7, 266 Banbury Road
Oxford OX2 7DL, England
+44 1865 521024
Email: europe@renner.org

BOOKS BY RICK RENNER

Chosen by God*

Dream Thieves*

Dressed To Kill*

The Holy Spirit and You*

How To Keep Your Head on Straight in a World Gone Crazy*

How To Receive Answers From Heaven!*

Insights to Successful Leadership

Last-Days Survival Guide

Life in the Combat Zone*

A Life Ablaze*

A Light in Darkness, Volume One,
   Seven Messages to the Seven Churches series

The Love Test*

No Room for Compromise, Volume Two,
   Seven Messages to the Seven Churches series

Paid in Full*

The Point of No Return*

Repentance*

Signs You'll See Just Before Jesus Comes*

Sparkling Gems From the Greek Daily Devotional 1*

Sparkling Gems From the Greek Daily Devotional 2*

Spiritual Weapons To Defeat the Enemy*

Ten Guidelines To Help You Achieve
   Your Long-Awaited Promotion!*

Turn Your God-Given Dreams Into Reality*

Why We Need the Gifts of the Spirit*

The Will of God — The Key to Your Success*

You Can Get Over It*

*Digital version available for Kindle, Nook, and iBook.

Note: Books by Rick Renner are available for purchase at:

www.renner.org

SPARKLING GEMS FROM THE GREEK 1

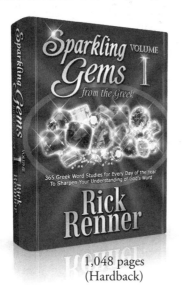

1,048 pages
(Hardback)

In 2003, Rick Renner's *Sparkling Gems From the Greek 1* quickly gained widespread recognition for its unique illumination of the New Testament through more than 1,000 Greek word studies in a 365-day devotional format. Today *Sparkling Gems 1* remains a beloved resource that has spiritually strengthened believers worldwide. As many have testified, the wealth of truths within its pages never grows old. Year after year, *Sparkling Gems 1* continues to deepen readers' understanding of the Bible.

To order, visit us online at: **www.renner.org**

SPARKLING GEMS FROM THE GREEK 2

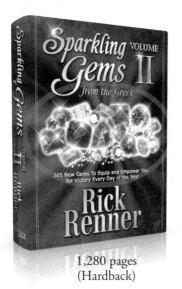

1,280 pages
(Hardback)

Rick infuses into *Sparkling Gems From the Greek 2* the added strength and richness of many more years of his own personal study and growth in God — expanding this devotional series to impact the reader's heart on a deeper level than ever before. This remarkable study tool helps unlock new hidden treasures from God's Word that will draw readers into an ever more passionate pursuit of Him.

To order, visit us online at: **www.renner.org**

A LIGHT IN DARKNESS
VOLUME ONE

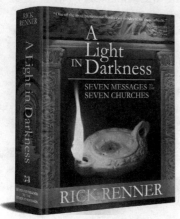

840 pages
(Hardback)

Step into the world of the First Century Church as Rick Renner creates a panoramic experience of unsurpassed detail to transport you into the ancient lands of the seven churches of Asia. Within the context of this fascinating — and, at times, shocking — historical backdrop, Rick outlines the challenges that early believers faced in taking the Gospel to a pagan world. After presenting a riveting account of the apostle John's vision of the exalted Christ, Rick leads you through an in-depth study of Jesus' messages to the churches of Ephesus and Smyrna — profoundly relevant messages that still resonate for His Church today.

Rick's richly detailed historical narrative, enhanced by classic artwork and superb photographs, will make the lands and the message of the Bible come alive to you as never before. Parallels between Roman society of the First Century and the modern world prove the current relevance of Christ's warning and instructions.

In this first volume of the *Seven Messages to the Seven Churches* series, you will discover:

- In-depth scriptural teaching that makes the New Testament come alive.

- A more than 800-page beautifully designed full-color hardback book — filled with photos shot on location, plus photos of classic artwork, artifacts, illustrations, maps, *and much more*.

- A comprehensive, completely indexed reference book.

A Light in Darkness, Volume One, is an extraordinary book that will endure and speak to generations to come. This authoritative first volume is a virtual encyclopedia of knowledge — a definitive go-to resource for any student of the Bible and a classic must-have for Christian families everywhere.

Faced with daunting challenges, the modern Church must give urgent heed to what the Holy Spirit is saying in order to be equipped for the end of this age.

To order, visit us online at: **www.renner.org**

Book Resellers: Contact Harrison House at 800-722-6774
or visit **www.HarrisonHouse.com** for quantity discounts.

NO ROOM FOR COMPROMISE
VOLUME TWO

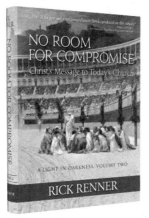

448 pages
(Hardback)

No Room for Compromise: Jesus' Message to Today's Church is *Volume Two* of the *Seven Messages to the Seven Churches* series. It presents an engaging exploration of the pagan culture of the First Century Church, with an emphasis on the city of Pergamum. Against this historical backdrop, Rick Renner highlights Jesus' message to the church of Pergamum when He appeared in a vision during the apostle John's imprisonment on the island of Patmos.

With superb photographs, many of which were shot on location in Turkey, Rick guides readers through a fascinating, detailed explanation of Jesus' message to the Pergamene church as he prophetically declares the critical significance of this message to the Church in these last days before Jesus returns. Rick also gives the reader a larger context within which to frame the pivotal moment when Jesus appeared to John on that isolated island. Rick takes the reader through a revealing overview of the first three centuries AD in which the infant Church grew amidst much opposition within a pagan world, demonstrating that darkness can never overcome the light, life, and power that the truth of Jesus Christ offers all those who believe.

Volume Two is a comprehensive, completely indexed reference book and provides:

- In-depth scriptural teaching that makes the New Testament come alive.

- Over 400 pages, including 330 beautifully designed, full-color pages.

- Nearly 400 images — including over 100 shot on location — classic artwork, artifacts, illustrations, and maps.

To order, visit us online at: **www.renner.org**

Book Resellers: Contact Harrison House at 800-722-6774 or visit **www.HarrisonHouse.com** for quantity discounts.

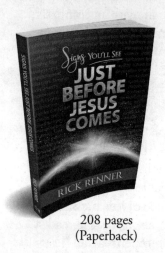

HOW TO KEEP YOUR HEAD ON STRAIGHT IN A WORLD GONE CRAZY

400 pages
(Paperback)

The world is changing. In fact, it's more than changing — it has *gone crazy*.

We are living in a world where faith is questioned and sin is welcomed — where people seem to have lost their minds about what is right and wrong. It seems truth has been turned *upside down*.

In Rick Renner's book ***How To Keep Your Head on Straight in a World Gone Crazy***, he reveals the disastrous consequences of a society in spiritual and moral collapse. In this book, you'll discover what Christians need to be doing to stay out of the chaos and remain anchored to truth. You'll learn how to stay sensitive to the Holy Spirit, how to discern right and wrong teaching, how to be grounded in prayer, and how to be spiritually prepared for living in victory in these last days.

Leading ministers from around the world are calling this book essential for every believer. Topics include:

- Contending for the Faith in the Last Days
- How To Pray for Leaders Who Are in Error
- How To Judge if a Teaching Is Good or Bad
- Seducing Spirits and Doctrines of Demons
- How To Be a Good Minister of Jesus Christ

DRESSED TO KILL
A BIBLICAL APPROACH
TO SPIRITUAL WARFARE AND ARMOR

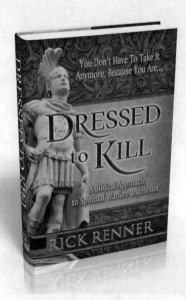

Rick Renner's book ***Dressed To Kill*** is considered by many to be a true classic on the subject of spiritual warfare. The original version, which sold more than 400,000 copies, is a curriculum staple in Bible schools worldwide. In this beautiful volume, you will find:

- 504 pages of reedited text

- 16 pages of full-color illustrations

- Questions at the end of each chapter to guide you into deeper study

In ***Dressed To Kill***, Rick explains with exacting detail the purpose and function of each piece of Roman armor. In the process, he describes the significance of our *spiritual* armor not only to withstand the onslaughts of the enemy, but also to overturn the tendencies of the carnal mind. Furthermore, Rick delivers a clear, scriptural presentation on the biblical definition of spiritual warfare — what it is and what it is not.

When you walk with God in deliberate, continual fellowship, He will enrobe you with Himself. Armed with the knowledge of who you are in Him, you will be dressed and dangerous to the works of darkness, unflinching in the face of conflict, and fully equipped to take the offensive and gain mastery over any opposition from your spiritual foe. You don't have to accept defeat anymore once you are *dressed to kill*!

A LIFE ABLAZE

Ten Simple Keys to Living on Fire for God

448 pages
(Paperback)

Do you struggle to keep the fire of the Holy Spirit burning in your heart as it may have burned earlier in your life? Do you sometimes feel like all that's left are a few small glowing embers — and that perhaps even those embers are starting to die out and become cold?

How do you stoke the embers of the fire within you so that those flames begin to burn red-hot in your heart again? Once you have that fire burning hot and bright, how do you sustain and grow the intensity of that inner fire for the rest of your time on this earth?

In *A Life Ablaze,* Rick teaches you about the ten different kinds of fuel you need to stay spiritually ablaze for years to come. As you learn about these fuels, you will discover how to throw them into the fire in your heart so you can keep burning spiritually.

Topics include:

- What is the real condition of your spiritual fire right now?

- What to do if your spiritual embers are about to go out.

- What to do to help others whose flames are burning low.

THE WILL OF GOD — THE KEY TO YOUR SUCCESS

Positioning Yourself To Live in God's Supernatural Power, Provision, and Protection

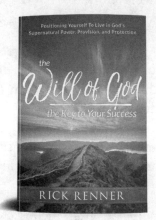

264 page
(Paperback)

A faith-filled adventure awaits you as you step out to do what God is beckoning you to do. It may seem daunting at first, but once the journey begins, you'll never regret that you left your comfort zone to follow His leading! But as you step out in faith, it's essential that you stay on track with God's plan if you want to experience His power, protection, and supernatural provision.

Author Rick Renner writes: "If you are seeking to know the will of God for your life, I believe this is a book that you will find very helpful in your journey of faith. It is important for you to understand that *knowing* the will of God and actually being *in* it are two very different things. Many know God's will, but they struggle to comply with what He has revealed about the path He has ordained for them to walk in."

So get ready for an eye-opening undertaking as Rick delves into the journey of the apostle Paul and other key Bible characters as they sought to walk out God's will for their lives. Along the way in this fascinating process, Rick will reveal vital lessons to help you in your own pursuit to fully align with God's will for your life — which is the key to your lasting success!

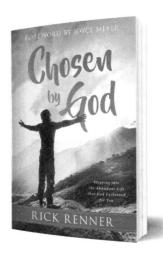

Connect with us on

Facebook @ HarrisonHousePublishers

and Instagram @ HarrisonHousePublishing

so you can stay up to date with news

about our books and our authors.

Visit us at **www.harrisonhouse.com**

for a complete product listing as well as

monthly specials for wholesale distribution.

The Harrison House Vision

Proclaiming the truth and the power

of the Gospel of Jesus Christ with excellence.

Challenging Christians

to live victoriously,

grow spiritually,

know God intimately.